COUNTRY COOKING
MADE EASY

COUNTRY COOKING
MADE EASY

OVER 1000 DELICIOUS RECIPES FOR PERFECT HOME-COOKED MEALS

Firefly Books

A FIREFLY BOOK

Published by Firefly Books Ltd. 2013
Copyright © 2013 Firefly Books Ltd.
Text copyright © 2013

First Printing

Publisher Cataloging-in-Publication Data (U.S.)
Country cooking made easy : Over 1000 delicious recipes for perfect
home-cooked meals / the editors of Firefly Books.
[528] p. : col. photos. ; cm.
Summary: Tried-and-true classic recipes with easy-to-follow
direction for any breakfast, lunch, dinner and snacks.
ISBN-13: 978-1-77085-095-8 (pbk.)
1. Cooking. I. Title.
641.5 dc23   TX714.C675 2013

Library and Archives Canada Cataloguing in Publication
Country cooking made easy : Over 1000 delicious recipes for
perfect home-cooked meals / the editors of Firefly Books.
Includes index.
ISBN 978-1-77085-095-8
1. Cooking. 2. Cookbooks. I. Firefly Books
TX714.C679 2013   641.5   C2012-906736-9

Published in the United States by   Published in Canada by
Firefly Books (U.S.) Inc.   Firefly Books Ltd.
P.O. Box 1338, Ellicott Station   50 Staples Ave., Unit 1
Buffalo, New York 14205   Richmond Hill, Ontario L4B 0A7

Cover design: Interrobang Graphic Design Inc.

Cover photo: Paul Webster/Getty Images

Printed in Canada

The publisher gratefully acknowledges the financial support for our publishing program by the Government of Canada through the Canada Book Fund as administered by the Department of Canadian Heritage.

Photo Credits
See insert section at middle. Listed in
sequential order.

© M. Sheldrake/Shutterstock.com
© Zaneta Baranowska/Shutterstock.com
© Kate (45671)/Shutterstock.com
© Vania Georgieva/Shutterstock.com
© Robyn Mackenzie/Shutterstock.com
© Sarsmis/Shutterstock.com
© Marco Mayer/Shutterstock.com
© Elena Gaak/Shutterstock.com

© Barbara Dudzinska/Shutterstock.com
© Ildi Papp/Shutterstock.com
© HLPhoto/Shutterstock.com
© Lilyana Vynogradova/Shutterstock.com
© Llaszlo/Shutterstock.com
© Sarsmis/Shutterstock.com
© Avesun/Shutterstock.com
© Stanjoman/Shutterstock.com
© Josh Resnick/Shutterstock.com
© Joe Gough/Shutterstock.com
© Elena Gaak/Shutterstock.com
© Giuseppe Parisi/Shutterstock.com

© Monkey Business Images/Shutterstock.com
© Lilyana Vynogradova/Shutterstock.com
© ARENA Creative/Shutterstock.com
© Giuseppe Parisi/Shutterstock.com
© Vezzani Photography/Shutterstock.com
© Grintan/Shutterstock.com
© Bonchan/Shutterstock.com
© Sarsmis/Shutterstock.com
© David P. Smith/Shutterstock.com
© Christian Jung/Shutterstock.com
© Elena Elisseeva/Shutterstock.com
© Anna Hoychuk/Shutterstock.com

CONTENTS

Breakfast & Snacks

Blueberry-Bran-Wheat Germ Muffins

"These muffins passed my daughter's test — and she does not care for bran or wheat germ." We thought they were great — really moist and flavorful.

Ingredients

3 eggs
1 cup brown sugar
½ cup oil
2 cups buttermilk
1 tsp. vanilla
1 cup wheat germ
1 cup bran
2 cups flour
2 tsp. baking powder
2 tsp. baking soda
½ tsp. salt
1½ cups blueberries

Directions

Beat eggs well, add sugar and beat, then add oil, buttermilk and vanilla and mix well. Stir in wheat germ and bran.

In smaller bowl, combine flour, baking powder, baking soda and salt, then stir in blueberries. Pour into liquid ingredients and stir until just mixed. Spoon into greased muffin cups and bake at 400°F for 20 to 25 minutes.

Makes 24 muffins.

—Sandy MacLennan

Aunt Nell's Hush Puppies

Light and flavorful, crispy outside and moist inside, these hush puppies are quick and easy to make.

Ingredients

1 cup cornmeal
1 tsp. baking soda
1 cup flour
2 Tbsp. sugar
1 clove garlic, crushed
1 egg
1 large onion, chopped
1 cup buttermilk
fat for frying

Directions

Combine all ingredients. Let rise for 30 minutes. Drop by tablespoonsful into deep hot fat and fry until golden brown.

Makes approximately 18 hush puppies.

—Carolee Gosda

Virginia Corn Muffins

"My grandmother from Tennessee taught me this recipe — why she called it 'Virginia' Corn Muffins, I don't know."

Ingredients

1 cup white cornmeal
½ cup flour
¼ cup sugar
5 tsp. baking powder
¾ tsp. salt
1 egg
½ cup milk
2 tsp. oil

Directions

Mix together cornmeal, flour, sugar, baking powder and salt. Beat together egg, milk and oil. Quickly stir liquid into dry ingredients. Place in 12 greased muffin cups and bake at 375°F for 25 minutes.

Makes 12 muffins.

—Ruth Ellis Haworth

Banana Muffins

Ingredients

1 cup white sugar
½ cup butter
1 egg, beaten
1 cup mashed bananas
1½ cups flour
1 tsp. baking soda
½ tsp. nutmeg
½ tsp. vanilla
salt

Directions

Cream sugar and butter, then add egg and mix well. Add bananas and flour. Dissolve baking soda in 1 Tbsp. hot water, then add to creamed mixture along with nutmeg, vanilla and salt. Spoon into greased muffin cups and bake at 350°F for 20 minutes.

Makes 12 muffins.

—Ann Coyle

Oat Muffins

"I first made these when I was 10, and I make and enjoy them to this day." They are light muffins with an even, spongy texture.

Ingredients

1 cup rolled oats
1 cup buttermilk
1 cup flour
1 tsp. baking powder
½ tsp. baking soda
1½ tsp. salt
½ cup brown sugar
1 egg, beaten
¼ cup oil or melted butter

Directions

Soak oats in buttermilk for 1 hour. Combine flour, baking powder, baking soda, salt and sugar and mix well. Stir egg and oil into oat mixture. Make a well in dry ingredients, pour in liquid and stir quickly until just mixed. Pour into greased muffin cups and bake at 400°F for 20 minutes.

Makes 12 muffins.

—Faye Cassia

Grandma's Scottish Potato Scones

"On all of her visits, Grandma would take leftover potatoes from the day before and make us potato scones to have hot, slathered with butter, as a bedtime snack." Our tasters thought these scones were good enough to warrant purposely cooking extra potatoes.

Directions

Mash cold potatoes well on well-floured surface. Knead in as much flour as potatoes will absorb. Add salt to taste. Roll out to ¼-inch thickness and cut into large circles. Quarter circles and cook on slow griddle, turning when lightly flecked with brown.

Eat hot with butter or honey.

—Lesley-Anne Paveling

Upside-Down Rhubarb Muffins

Our Vermont tester says, "These muffins are ter-
rific — not too sweet, with a good combination
of tastes and textures."

Ingredients

1 cup finely chopped rhubarb
¼ cup melted butter
½ cup packed brown sugar
⅓ cup soft butter
⅓ cup sugar
1 egg
1½ cups flour
2 tsp. baking powder
½ tsp. salt
½ tsp. nutmeg
½ cup milk

Directions

Beat eggs well, add sugar and beat, then add oil,
buttermilk and vanilla and mix well. Stir in wheat
germ and bran.

Combine rhubarb, melted butter and brown
sugar in small bowl and mix well. Place in
12 greased muffin cups.

Beat together butter, sugar and egg until
fluffy. Combine flour, baking powder, salt and
nutmeg and add to creamed mixture alternately
with milk. Stir just to moisten, then spoon on top
of rhubarb mixture.

Bake at 350°F for 20 to 25 minutes. Invert
on cooling rack and leave pan over muffins for
a few minutes so all rhubarb moisture runs out.
Serve warm.

Makes 12 muffins.

—Joan Airey

Orange Pecan Muffins

Ingredients

1 cup buttermilk
¼ cup melted butter
1 egg
½ tsp. vanilla
juice & grated rind of 1 orange
1 cup rolled oats
1⅓ cups flour
⅓ cup demerara sugar
1½ tsp. baking powder
½ tsp. baking soda
½ tsp. salt
⅔ cup coarsely chopped pecans

Directions

Combine buttermilk, butter, egg, vanilla, orange
juice, orange rind and rolled oats and let stand for
15 minutes. Combine remaining ingredients and
add to liquid mixture. Mix lightly. Fill greased
muffin cups ⅔ full. Bake at 375°F for 15 to
20 minutes.

Makes 12 muffins.

—Beth Caldwell

German Bread Griddle Cakes

Our tester declared these to be "Delicious! Especially light. Just excellent." We agreed and thought they made a tasty, light alternative to pancakes.

Ingredients

1½ cups milk
2 Tbsp. butter
1½ cups stale bread crumbs
2 eggs, well beaten
½ cup flour
4 tsp. baking powder
½ tsp. salt
oil for cooking

Directions

Scald milk, then add butter and stir until butter has melted. Pour over bread crumbs and let soak for 30 minutes. Beat in remaining ingredients. Cook in hot oil over medium heat until golden brown.

Serves 2 to 3.

—Jean Perkins

Puff Ball Doughnuts

Also known as Beaver Tails and Elephant Ears in Canada, these are a real treat. Roll in sugar, roll up with grated cheese as a filling, or brush with garlic butter.

Ingredients

3 eggs
1 cup sugar
2 cups milk
lemon extract
3 cups flour
3 tsp. baking powder
½ tsp. salt
oil for deep-frying

Directions

Beat eggs, add sugar and beat well. Add milk and lemon extract. Sift together flour, baking powder and salt and fold into egg mixture. Using two spoons, drop into oil heated to 375°F. Fry until golden brown. Dough should turn by itself. If not, turn with a fork making certain not to pierce dough.

Serves 4 to 6.

—Myrna Smith

Thistle-Down Place Scones

Ingredients

½ cup raisins
2 cups flour
3 Tbsp. sugar
2 tsp. baking powder
½ tsp. salt
½ tsp. baking soda
5 Tbsp. butter
1 cup sour cream
1 egg, separated
1 tsp. sugar
½ tsp. cinnamon

Directions

Cover raisins with warm water and let stand for 5 minutes. Drain well and set aside.

Combine flour, sugar, baking powder, salt and baking soda. Cut in butter to make a coarse crumb texture. Stir in raisins.

In another bowl, combine sour cream and egg yolk. Make well in center of dry ingredients and pour in egg-cream mixture. Stir just until dough clings together.

Turn out onto floured surface and knead gently 10 or 12 times. Pat into ½-inch-thick circle and cut into 4-inch rounds. Place on ungreased baking sheet, brush with egg white and sprinkle with sugar and cinnamon. Cut each round into quarters but do not separate. Bake at 425°F for 15 minutes, or until golden.

Makes 16 scones.

—Irene Louden

Finnish Oven Pancake

"This pancake puffs up, then collapses. It is good hot or cold. I serve it with syrup and sliced fresh fruit."

Ingredients

3 eggs
1 cup milk
½ cup flour
2 Tbsp. sugar
¼ tsp. salt
1 tsp. vanilla (optional)
¼ cup butter

Directions

Beat eggs until fluffy. Add remaining ingredients, except for butter, beating continuously. Melt butter in ovenproof skillet, then pour in batter. Bake at 400°F for 20 to 25 minutes, or until knife inserted in middle comes out clean.

Serves 2.

—Jeanne Reitz

Gingerbread Waffles

A flavorful winter breakfast, these waffles are also cakey enough to be served (perhaps dusted with confectioners' sugar) as part of an afternoon tea.

Ingredients

2 cups flour
½ tsp. salt
1 tsp. baking powder
2 tsp. ginger
1 tsp. cinnamon
¼ tsp. cloves
1 cup molasses
¾ cup milk (approximately)
1 egg, beaten
½ cup oil

Directions

Combine flour, salt, baking powder, ginger, cinnamon and cloves. Mix together molasses, milk, egg and oil and stir into dry ingredients, adding additional milk if necessary. Bake in hot waffle iron until golden brown. Serve with sweetened whipped cream.

Serves 4.

—Sybil D. Hendricks

Orange Waffles

Use unpeeled oranges for this recipe — but wash them well and remove seeds first. If your oranges are not very juicy, you may need to add a bit more liquid.

Ingredients

1½ cups flour
½ tsp. salt
1½ tsp. baking powder
2 eggs, separated
1 cup milk
¼ cup oil
2 oranges, quartered

Directions

Sift dry ingredients together. Blend egg yolks, milk and oil well in blender or food processor. Add orange quarters one at a time and blend well. Beat egg whites until stiff. Add orange mixture to dry ingredients and stir well. Gently fold in egg whites. Bake in waffle iron until golden brown.

Serves 4.

—George Driscoll

Apple Pancakes

"These pancakes freeze well. The recipe is of Polish origin and has been handed down through my family for three generations."

Ingredients

2 Tbsp. yeast
2 cups warm water
½ cup honey
2 cups milk
¼ cup butter
4 eggs, beaten
6 cups flour
½ tsp. salt
6 apples, peeled & thinly sliced
oil for cooking

Directions

Proof yeast in water and honey for 10 minutes. Add remaining ingredients and mix well. Knead briefly, then let rise for at least 1 hour. Fry in hot oil over medium heat until golden brown.

Makes 2 dozen large pancakes.

—*Karen Havelock*

Banana Bran Bread

Vary this recipe by substituting dark rum for the orange juice or walnuts for the raisins. This is a delicious bread with a wonderful texture.

Ingredients

¾ cup butter
1½ cups brown sugar
3 eggs
2 cups bran
3 cups mashed banana
¼ cup orange juice
3 cups flour
4 tsp. baking powder
1 tsp. salt
1 tsp. baking soda
1½ cups raisins

Directions

Cream butter and sugar, then add eggs and beat until light. Stir in bran. Mix bananas with orange juice. Sift together dry ingredients. Add dry ingredients alternately with bananas to creamed mixture, beating after each addition. Fold in raisins. Pour into greased and floured loaf pans and bake at 350°F for 1 hour.

Makes 2 loaves.

—*Donna Jubb*

Fruit Pancake

"This is our favorite leisurely morning breakfast. I use apples, plums or peaches — fresh or frozen." Add a brandy sauce, and this pancake becomes a tasty dessert.

Ingredients

¼ cup butter
¼ cup brown sugar
1 tsp. cinnamon
4 apples, plums or peaches
4 eggs, separated
⅓ cup sugar
⅓ cup flour
½ tsp. baking powder
⅓ cup milk

Directions

Heat oven to 400°F and melt butter in 10"-round baking dish. Remove from oven and sprinkle with brown sugar and cinnamon. Slice fruit and arrange in dish, then return to oven for 8 to 10 minutes.

Meanwhile, beat egg whites until foamy and gradually beat in sugar until stiff. In another bowl, combine flour and baking powder, beat in milk and yolks, then fold in egg white mixture. Spread evenly over fruit.

Bake for 20 minutes. Loosen edges and invert onto serving plate.

Serves 2 to 3.

—Adele Dueck

Lemon Bread

This is a sweet cakelike bread, rich with lemon flavor.

Bread Ingredients

1 cup butter
2 cups sugar
4 eggs
½ tsp. salt
½ tsp. baking soda
3 cups flour
1 cup buttermilk
grated rind of 1 lemon
1 cup chopped pecans

Glaze Ingredients
1 cup sugar
juice of 3 lemons

Directions

Cream butter and sugar, then add eggs one at a time and mix well. Sift together salt, baking soda and flour and add to creamed mixture alternately with buttermilk. Add lemon rind and nuts and pour into 2 large greased and floured loaf pans. Bake at 350°F for 1 hour.

Meanwhile, prepare glaze. Heat sugar and lemon juice slowly to dissolve sugar. Pour over loaves while cooling in pans.

Makes 2 loaves.

—Susan Robinson

French Honey Bread

Ingredients

1 cup honey
1 cup milk
½ cup sugar
2 egg yolks, beaten
2½ cups flour
1 tsp. baking soda
½ tsp. salt
¾ cup currants or chopped nuts

Directions

Combine honey, milk and sugar in heavy pot and heat slowly until well blended. Cool slightly, then add egg yolks. Combine flour, baking soda and salt, then stir slowly into honey mixture. Stir in currants or nuts. Pour into greased loaf pan and bake at 325°F for 1 to 1½ hours.

Makes 1 loaf.

—*Giedre Abromaitis*

Banana-Oatmeal Coffeecake

Cake Ingredients

¾ cup flour
¾ cup whole wheat flour
¾ cup oats
1 tsp. baking powder
¾ tsp. baking soda
½ tsp. salt
½ cup butter, softened
½ cup brown sugar
½ cup white sugar
2 eggs
1 tsp. vanilla
2 ripe bananas, mashed
⅓ cup sour milk

Topping Ingredients

⅓ cup brown sugar
¼ cup chopped pecans
3 Tbsp. flour
2 Tbsp. butter

Directions

Combine flours, oats, baking powder, baking soda and salt and mix well. Cream together butter and sugars, then add eggs and vanilla. Beat in bananas, then milk. Fold wet ingredients into dry.

Make topping by combining ingredients and mixing until crumbly. Pour batter into greased and floured 9" x 13" pan, sprinkle with topping and bake at 375°F for 20 to 25 minutes.

—*Ann Lutz*

Honey Sour Cream Coffeecake

"I found this coffeecake and the recipe for it on my doorstep shortly after my daughter's birth. What a treat!" The recipe is very versatile — add fruit or cocoa for a different taste.

Cake Ingredients

¼ cup butter
½ cup honey
2 eggs, lightly beaten
1 tsp. baking soda
1 cup sour cream or yogurt
1½ cups flour
1½ tsp. baking powder
1 Tbsp. vanilla

Topping Ingredients

¼ cup chopped nuts
½ tsp. cinnamon
2 Tbsp. butter
1 Tbsp. honey

Directions

Cream together butter, honey and eggs. Stir baking soda into sour cream, then add to butter mixture. Combine flour and baking powder, then stir into liquid ingredients. Add vanilla. Pour into greased and floured tube pan.

Combine topping ingredients and sprinkle over cake. Bake at 350°F for 45 minutes, open oven door and let cool in oven.

—Leslie Pierpont

Cheddar Dill Loaf

"We serve this loaf, a family favorite, very thinly sliced and lightly buttered with smoked turkey and ham as a pre-dinner snack."

Ingredients

2 cups flour
2 Tbsp. sugar
3 tsp. baking powder
1½ Tbsp. dill seed
2 Tbsp. minced onion
1 cup grated sharp Cheddar cheese
1 cup milk
1 egg
3 Tbsp. melted butter

Directions

Combine flour, sugar, baking powder and dill in large bowl. Add onion and cheese and mix well.

Combine milk, egg and butter in small bowl. Add all at once to dry ingredients and stir to moisten. Bake in greased loaf pan at 350°F for 50 to 55 minutes.

Makes 1 loaf.

—Jim & Penny Wright

Christine's Cornbread

Ingredients

¾ cup sugar
½ cup butter
2 eggs, beaten
½ tsp. salt
2 tsp. baking powder
1½ cups flour
1 cup cornmeal
1½ cups milk

Directions

Cream together sugar, butter and eggs. Sift together salt, baking powder, flour and cornmeal, then add to creamed mixture alternately with milk. Bake in greased 9" x 13" pan at 375°F for 25 to 30 minutes.

—Laine Roddick

German Fruit Crumb Coffeecake

"I grew up with this recipe. Whenever we would go to visit my grandmother, she had one of these coffeecakes in her pantry waiting to be sliced and enjoyed by her children and grandchildren. More recently, I have made this for our local natural-food market, where it was extremely popular." Use plain water if you do not have just-boiled potatoes.

Cake Ingredients
2 cups hot potato water
¼ cup honey
1 tsp. salt
2 pkgs yeast
1 egg, beaten
½ cup melted unsalted butter
7 cups flour

Topping Ingredients
4 cups flour
2 cups sugar
¼ tsp. salt
1 tsp. cinnamon
1 cup melted unsalted butter
milk
6-8 cups sliced fruit

Directions

Combine water, honey and salt and stir until honey is dissolved. When lukewarm, add yeast and let dissolve. Stir in egg, then add butter and 3½ cups flour. Beat well, then gradually add remaining flour.

Turn out on lightly floured surface and let rest for 10 minutes. Knead until smooth and elastic. Place in greased bowl, turning once to grease all sides of dough. Let rise until doubled in size — about 1 hour.

While dough is rising, make topping. Combine flour, sugar, salt and cinnamon, then stir in butter until mixture forms crumbs.

Punch down dough. (It can be covered with a damp cloth and kept refrigerated for up to 5 days, if desired, at this point.) Divide in half and pat each half out onto a greased cookie sheet. Prick with fork and brush with milk. Spread fruit out evenly over dough, then cover with crumb mixture. Let rise for 30 minutes more, then bake at 350°F until lightly brown — 30 to 45 minutes.

Makes 2 cakes.

—Nancy Wellborn

Honey-Pecan Rolls

"We keep bees, so this recipe helps us use up our plentiful supply of honey."

Roll Ingredients

1 Tbsp. yeast
2 tsp. honey
½ cup warm water
1 tsp. salt
¼ cup honey
2 eggs, lightly beaten
½ cup butter, melted
3–3½ cups flour
1 cup coarsely chopped pecans

Glaze Ingredients

¾ cup honey
¾ cup brown sugar
6 Tbsp. butter

Filling Ingredients

melted butter
½ cup brown sugar
2 tsp. cinnamon

Directions

Combine yeast, 2 tsp. honey and water and let sit for 10 minutes. Add salt, ¼ cup honey, eggs and ½ cup melted butter and mix well. Add flour to make thick dough.

Turn out onto floured board and knead for 5 minutes. Place in greased bowl, turning once. Cover and let rise until double — 1 hour.

Place pecans in bottom of 9" x 13" pan. For glaze, combine honey, ¾ cup sugar and butter in heavy saucepan. Bring to a boil, remove from heat and cool slightly.

Roll dough into 15-by-13-inch rectangle. Brush with melted butter and sprinkle with ½ cup brown sugar and cinnamon. Roll up and cut into 1-inch slices. Place over pecans, pour glaze over and let rise for 1 hour. Bake at 350°F for 30 minutes.

Makes 15 rolls.

—Mary Ellen Hoar

Honey-Pecan Butterballs

Ingredients

1 cup butter
¼ cup honey
2 cups flour
½ tsp. salt
2 tsp. vanilla
2 cups finely chopped pecans

Directions

Cream butter and honey, then stir in flour, salt and vanilla. Fold in nuts. Form into small balls and place on greased cookie sheets. Bake at 300°F for 40 to 45 minutes or until lightly browned.

Makes 3 to 4 dozen cookies.

—Teresa Caret

Cranberry Coffeecake

"My husband and I run a small seasonal marina and waterfront café. This coffeecake is a favorite among our clientele."

Ingredients

8 oz. cream cheese, softened
1 cup butter
1½ cups sugar
1½ tsp. vanilla
4 eggs
2¼ cups flour
1½ tsp. baking powder
2 cups fresh cranberries
½ cup chopped nuts
confectioners' sugar

Directions

Thoroughly cream together cream cheese, butter, sugar and vanilla. Add eggs one at a time, mixing well after each addition.

Gradually add 2 cups flour and baking powder. Combine remaining ¼ cup flour with cranberries and nuts and fold into batter.

Pour into greased and floured tube pan and bake at 350°F for 1 hour and 15 minutes. Let stand for 5 minutes before removing from pan. Dust with confectioners' sugar.

—Mrs. Robert Uttech

Cinnamon Buns

Make up the dough the night before and let the buns rise for the final time in the refrigerator overnight. This then becomes a quick but very special breakfast.

Ingredients

½ cup warm water
½ tsp. white sugar
1 pkg. yeast
2 cups milk
½ cup butter, softened
1 cup white sugar
1 tsp. salt
1 tsp. vanilla
5 cups flour
melted butter
¼ cup brown sugar
1 Tbsp. cinnamon

Directions

Combine water and ½ tsp. white sugar, then add yeast. Let sit for 10 minutes, then add milk, butter, 1 cup white sugar, salt, vanilla and flour (only enough so dough can still be mixed with a wooden spoon). Mix well, then let rise for 2 to 3 hours.

Turn out onto well-floured work surface. Punch down, then flatten into rectangular shape. Brush with melted butter, then sprinkle with brown sugar and cinnamon. Roll up and cut into 1¼-inch slices. Place in greased muffin tins and let rise until doubled in size. Bake at 375°F for 30 minutes.

Makes approximately 24 buns.

—Rose Strocen

Cinnamon-Sour Cream Twists

There are few people who will turn down this breakfast delicacy. Served hot from the oven and dripping with butter, they are irresistible. Make this dough the day before and then bake up the twists for a special breakfast.

Ingredients

1 pkg. yeast
¼ cup warm water
4 cups flour
1 cup butter, melted
1 cup sour cream
2 eggs, beaten
1 tsp. salt
1 tsp. vanilla
1 cup sugar
1 tsp. cinnamon

Directions

Sprinkle yeast into water and stir until dissolved. Combine flour, butter, sour cream, eggs, salt and vanilla. Stir in yeast and work until smooth. Cover with damp cloth and refrigerate for at least 2 hours or up to 2 days.

Combine sugar and cinnamon. Roll dough into 15-by-18-inch rectangle, then coat both sides with sugar-cinnamon mixture. Fold over in thirds, then roll into ¼-inch-thick rectangle. Cut into 1-inch-wide strips, twist and place on greased baking sheet. Bake at 375°F for 15 minutes.

Makes approximately 18 twists.

—Marklyn A. Hallett

Caramel Rolls

There can be few things better at tempting people out of bed in the morning than the smell of sticky buns baking and coffee brewing. These are attractive, delicious and easy to make. Eat them right away, though, as they do not keep well.

Ingredients

2 cups flour
4 tsp. baking powder
½ tsp. salt
½ cup butter
¾ cup milk
2 Tbsp. soft butter
1 cup brown sugar
1 Tbsp. cinnamon

Directions

Combine flour, baking powder and salt. Cut in ¼ cup butter until butter is size of peas, then stir in milk. Mix this to a soft dough.

Turn onto floured board and pat into a ⅜-inch-thick rectangle. Spread dough with 2 Tbsp. soft butter and sprinkle with ½ cup brown sugar mixed with cinnamon. Roll up and cut into 1-inch slices.

Place remaining ¼ cup butter in two 9"-round pans and melt. Sprinkle with remaining ½ cup sugar. Arrange rolls on this, and bake at 450°F for 15 to 20 minutes, moving to top oven shelf after 12 minutes. Turn out onto serving dish at once, scraping out any caramel that remains in pan.

Makes 12 rolls.

—Janeen Clynick

Sticky Buns

As with the other yeast recipes in this section, work on these buns can be started the evening before they are to be eaten. Breakfast-eaters will be most appreciative and will think you rose before the sun to make them.

Ingredients

1 Tbsp. yeast
¼ cup lukewarm water
1 cup scalded milk
¾ cup sugar
2 Tbsp. shortening
1 tsp. salt
4 cups flour
1 egg
¼ cup melted butter
2 tsp. cinnamon
¼ cup raisins
light corn syrup
½ cup chopped pecans

Directions

Soften yeast in water and let stand for 10 minutes. Combine scalded milk, ¼ cup sugar, shortening and salt and cool to lukewarm. Stir in 1½ cups flour and egg. Stir in the yeast then add remaining flour. Mix well, let rest for 10 minutes, then knead until smooth.

Let rise until doubled — 1 hour. Punch down and roll out to ¼-inch-thick rectangle. Brush on melted butter, then sprinkle with remaining ½ cup sugar, cinnamon and raisins. Roll dough up.

Butter a 9" x 13" baking pan. Drizzle thin layer of corn syrup in bottom of pan, and sprinkle with nuts. Cut dough into 12 slices, and place in pan. Bake at 350°F for 20 to 30 minutes.

Makes 12 buns.

—Anne Morrell

Tante Vivien's Butterscotch Brownies

Not too sweet, these brownies are very quick and easy to make.

Ingredients

½ cup melted butter
1 cup brown sugar
1 egg, beaten
1 tsp. vanilla
¾ cup flour
1 tsp. baking powder
½ cup walnuts
½ cup coconut
½ cup currants

Directions

Combine all ingredients and mix well. Bake in greased 9" x 9" pan at 350°F for 30 minutes. Cut into squares while still warm.

Makes 12 to 16 squares.

—Olga Zuyderhoff

White Chocolate Mocha Java Bars

Cut these bars before the white chocolate hardens completely. They are a deliciously decadent variation of Nanaimo Bars.

Ingredients

¾ cup butter
½ cup sugar
1 tsp. vanilla
1 egg
2 cups graham cracker crumbs
1 cup desiccated coconut
½ cup finely chopped toasted hazelnuts
2 tsp. instant coffee crystals
2 Tbsp. hot coffee
2½ cups icing sugar
¼ cup cocoa
2 Tbsp. milk
6 oz. white chocolate

Directions

Combine ½ cup butter, sugar, vanilla and egg in top of double boiler. Cook, stirring, over boiling water until slightly thickened. Blend in cracker crumbs, coconut and hazelnuts and spread evenly in greased 9" x 9" baking pan. Let stand 15 minutes.

Meanwhile, dissolve instant coffee crystals in hot coffee. Blend well with icing sugar, cocoa, remaining ¼ cup butter and milk. Spread over crust and chill for 10 minutes. Melt chocolate and spread over filling. Chill well.

Makes 16 to 18 squares.

—Denise Atkinson

Carrot-Zucchini Squares

Moist and tasty, these squares are a good way to get children to eat the often unpopular zucchini.

Ingredients

⅔ cup firmly packed light brown sugar
½ cup butter
1 egg
1 tsp. vanilla
1½ cups flour
1 tsp. baking powder
salt
⅔ cup coarsely grated carrot
⅔ cup coarsely grated zucchini, drained
½ cup raisins

Directions

Beat sugar and butter together. Add egg and vanilla and beat thoroughly. Add remaining ingredients and stir together. Spoon into greased 9" x 9" pan. Bake at 350°F for 30 minutes, or until a toothpick inserted in the center comes out clean.

Makes 12 to 16 squares.

—Rosalind Mechefske

Poppy Seed Squares

Poppy seeds, coconut and honey are a winning combination. The squares are chewy and delicious.

Ingredients

1¾ cups flour
1 tsp. baking powder
¼ tsp. baking soda
1¼ cups sugar
½ tsp. salt
½ cup butter, melted
⅓ cup honey
2 eggs
2 Tbsp. milk
1 tsp. vanilla
1 cup coconut
½ cup poppy seeds
icing sugar

Directions

Sift flour, baking powder, baking soda, sugar and salt into mixing bowl. Add butter, honey, eggs, milk and vanilla. Beat with electric mixer until well blended, then stir in coconut and poppy seeds. Spread evenly in greased 9" x 13" pan. Bake at 350°F for 25 to 30 minutes. Remove to wire rack and cool, then sprinkle top with icing sugar.

Makes approximately 24 squares.

—Tracy Willemsen

Welsh Currant Cakes

"These cookies take some practice to make perfectly. They should look like English muffins and be as light and flaky as biscuits." Well-cleaned empty tuna cans can be kept and used as cutters for these and similar biscuits.

Ingredients

3 cups flour
1 cup sugar
1½ tsp. baking powder
1¼ tsp. salt
½ tsp. baking soda
2 tsp. nutmeg
1 cup shortening
1 cup currants
2 eggs
6 Tbsp. milk

Directions

Sift together flour, sugar, baking powder, salt, baking soda and nutmeg. Cut in shortening, then add currants. Beat eggs and milk together. Add to flour mixture and mix to make a stiff dough. Chill for 1 to 2 hours.

Divide dough into thirds, then roll out to ¼-inch thickness on lightly floured board. Cut into round biscuits.

Heat griddle until water drops bounce off it. Lightly grease, then cook biscuits until tops puff and turn shiny. Flip and bake until golden.

Makes 24 biscuits.

—Mary Bacon

Lace Cookies

"Thin, crisp and almost transparent, these splendid cookies are easy to make." Bake the cookies on parchment paper — it is available in cooking supply stores, can be used over and over, and the cookies will lift off easily, thus eliminating the frustration of having a perfect cookie glued forever to the cookie sheet.

Ingredients

1½ cups oatmeal
1½ cups light brown sugar
2 Tbsp. flour
½ tsp. salt
⅔ cup melted butter
1 egg, lightly beaten
½ tsp. vanilla

Directions

Combine oatmeal, sugar, flour and salt and mix well. Stir in melted butter, then egg and vanilla. Line cookie sheets with parchment paper. Drop batter by half-teaspoonsful, 2 inches apart.
Flatten cookies with fork dipped in water.

Bake at 350°F until lightly browned — approximately 5 minutes. Cool cookies on parchment paper, just slide off cookie sheet, then lift off with spatula.

Makes approximately 40 cookies.

—Sharon McKay

Grandma Marion's Coconut-Oatmeal Cookies

"The taste and texture of these cookies vary depending on their thickness. If pressed very thin, they are crisp, caramel-like and quick-cooking. If thicker, they are a softer, heartier cookie."

Ingredients

¾ cup brown sugar
¼ cup white sugar
1 cup butter
1 egg
1½ cups flour
1 tsp. baking powder
1 tsp. baking soda
1½ cups rolled oats
¾ cup coconut
¼ tsp. vanilla

Directions

Cream sugars and butter, then add egg. Sift in flour, baking powder and baking soda, then mix in rolled oats and coconut. Stir in vanilla. Shape into balls, place on greased cookie sheet and flatten with fork dipped in cold water. Bake at 375°F for 5 to 10 minutes.

Makes 3 dozen cookies.

—Isabel Bradley

Oatmeal Cookies

Ingredients

1 cup raisins
2½ tsp. baking soda
3 eggs
1 tsp. vanilla
1 cup butter
1 cup brown sugar
1 cup white sugar
2½ cups flour
1 tsp. salt
1 tsp. cinnamon
2 cups oatmeal

Directions

Place raisins and 2 cups water in saucepan and boil for 5 minutes. Add 1 tsp. baking soda, stir, then remove raisins and drain, discarding water and baking soda. Beat eggs well, add raisins and vanilla and let stand, covered, for at least 1 hour.

Cream butter and sugars. Add flour, salt, cinnamon and remaining 1½ tsp. baking soda. Mix well, then blend in egg-raisin mixture and oatmeal. Drop by large teaspoonful on ungreased cookie sheet and bake at 350°F for 10 to 12 minutes.

Makes 5 to 6 dozen cookies.

—*Laurabel Miller*

Linzer Cookies

"This recipe has been passed through five generations of my family. The book containing it is close to disintegration from so many years of use."

Ingredients

¾ cup lard
¾ cup butter
¾ cup sugar
2 eggs
rind & juice of 1 lemon
4 cups flour
jam
icing sugar

Directions

Cream lard and butter, then add sugar, eggs and lemon rind and juice. Mix in flour. Roll out to ¼-inch thickness and cut into 2-inch rounds. Bake at 350°F for 20 minutes, or until golden. Cool on rack. Spread half the rounds with jam, then cover with remaining cookies. Dust with icing sugar.

Makes 2 dozen sandwich cookies

—*Margaret Smit*

Perfect Peanut Butter Cookies

A lofty claim, perhaps, but one that our testers assure us is valid. Use either smooth or crunchy peanut butter.

Ingredients

½ cup butter
½ cup peanut butter
½ cup white sugar
½ cup packed brown sugar
1 egg
¾ tsp. vanilla
1¼ cups flour
¾ tsp. baking soda
¼ tsp. salt

Directions

Beat butter, peanut butter, white sugar and ¼ cup brown sugar until light and fluffy. Beat in egg and vanilla. Combine flour, baking soda and salt, then beat into butter mixture until blended. Sprinkle remaining ¼ cup brown sugar on top of dough and gently fold so sugar granules are still visible.

Roll dough into teaspoonful-sized balls and place 2 inches apart on ungreased cookie sheets. Press into ¼-inch-thick circles. Bake at 375°F for 8 to 10 minutes.

Makes 3 dozen cookies.

—Carlene T. Blankenship

Cookie Jar Gingersnaps

These are light and gingery — they won't last long in your cookie jar.

Ingredients

¾ cup shortening
1 cup sugar
1 egg
¼ cup molasses
2 cups flour
1 Tbsp. ginger
2 tsp. baking soda
1 tsp. cinnamon
½ tsp. salt
granulated sugar

Directions

Cream shortening, then add sugar, egg and molasses. Mix in flour, ginger, baking soda, cinnamon and salt. Form teaspoonsful of dough into round balls, roll in granulated sugar and place 2 inches apart on ungreased cookie sheets. Bake at 350°F for 10 to 15 minutes.

Makes 3 dozen cookies.

—Hazel Schwartz

Molasses Sugar Cookies

Increase the baking time if you prefer a crisp cookie. The time given here will result in a soft, chewy cookie.

Ingredients

¾ cup shortening
1 cup sugar
¼ cup molasses
1 egg
2 cups flour
2 tsp. baking soda
½ tsp. cloves
½ tsp. ginger
1 tsp. cinnamon
½ tsp. salt

Directions

Melt shortening in heavy pan, remove from heat and let cool. Combine sugar, molasses and egg, beat well, then add shortening. Sift together flour, baking soda, cloves, ginger, cinnamon and salt. Add to sugar mixture and mix well. Chill, then form into 1-inch balls. Roll in granulated sugar and place on greased cookie sheets 2 inches apart. Bake at 375°F for 8 minutes.

Makes 3 dozen cookies.

—Mrs. John Schobelock

Crunchy Maple Cookies

"This is my husband's favorite cookie to take on fishing or hunting trips."

Ingredients

1 cup shortening
1 cup brown sugar
1 egg
1 cup maple syrup
1 tsp. vanilla
4 cups flour
½ tsp. salt
2 tsp. baking soda
granulated sugar

Directions

Cream shortening and brown sugar, then blend in egg, syrup and vanilla. Add flour, salt and soda, and beat until blended. Shape into 1-inch balls, and coat with granulated sugar. Bake on greased cookie sheets at 350°F for about 10 minutes.

Makes about 5 dozen cookies.

—Helen Potts

Eggs & Cheese

Quiche Lorraine

This quiche can also be made into individual pies in muffin tins and served as hors d'oeuvres. Variations are almost endless — asparagus, shrimp, leeks, ham and mushrooms all make delicious additions.

Ingredients

Pastry for 9-inch pie shell
8 slices bacon
1 cup grated Swiss cheese
4 eggs
1½ cups milk or light cream
½ tsp. salt
⅛ tsp. pepper
⅛ tsp. nutmeg

Directions

Bake pie shell at 400°F for 10 minutes. Remove from oven and reduce temperature to 350°F.

Chop bacon and fry until crisp. Drain and place in pie shell. Top with grated cheese. Beat eggs, milk and seasonings together. Pour into shell and bake 25 to 35 minutes or until firm and lightly browned.

—Mary Lou Ross

Cheese and Onion Pie

This egg pie is very dense, and with only a green salad is a meal in itself. Chopped cooked bacon or ham may be added for variety.

Ingredients

Pastry for 9-inch pie shell
3 medium onions
1 cup water
4 eggs
½ cup milk
1–1½ cups grated Cheddar cheese

Directions

Line pie plate with pastry, prick with a fork and bake at 350°F for 10 minutes.

Peel and slice onions, place in saucepan and cover with 1 cup boiling water and boil, covered, for 5 to 10 minutes. Cool. Beat together eggs and milk. Alternate layers of onions and grated cheese in the pastry shell. Pour custard over all. Bake at 350°F for 20 minutes or until set.

—Rae Anne Huth

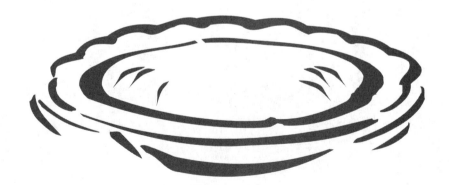

Tomato & Basil Tart

This fragrant tart can be served hot or cold, for breakfast, lunch or as an opening course with dinner.

Ingredients

Pastry for 9-inch pie shell
3 Tbsp. sweet butter
2 medium onions, finely chopped
2 lbs. tomatoes, peeled, seeded & chopped
1 cup whipping cream
3 large eggs
1½ tsp. salt
½ tsp. pepper
2 tsp. dried basil
1½ tsp. finely sliced green peppers

Directions

Melt the butter in a frying pan. Add onions and cook until transparent. Strain the tomatoes and add to the onions. Cook over low heat until the tomatoes are reduced to a pulp. Remove from the heat and cool.

Beat together cream and eggs. Add cooled tomato mixture and season with salt, pepper, basil and green onions.

Line tart pan with pastry and bake at 350°F for 5 minutes. Add filling and bake 30 to 35 minutes longer.

—Auberge du Petit Prince

Spinach Quiche

Spinach, Swiss chard or beet greens—whatever your garden provides—are good in this quiche.

Ingredients

1 cup flour
½ tsp. salt
¼ cup oil
2 Tbsp. milk
1 lb. fresh spinach
1 small onion, chopped
2 Tbsp. oil
2 eggs
1 cup yogurt
½ cup dried milk
½ tsp. salt
⅓ cup grated Parmesan cheese

Directions

To prepare crust, combine flour and salt. Add oil and milk and mix with a fork. Roll out to fit a 9-inch pie plate, or simply spread dough in plate with your fingers.

Wash and cook spinach until just limp. Drain and chop well. Heat oil in a frying pan and add onion and spinach, cooking a few minutes until liquid has evaporated.

In a bowl, beat eggs and stir in yogurt, milk and salt. Add spinach and onions. Stir together and pour into the unbaked pie crust. Sprinkle with cheese and bake at 375°F for 25 minutes or until firm and starting to brown.

—Mikell Billoki

Overnight Soufflé

Ingredients

12 slices bread, trimmed & cubed
½ lb. sharp Cheddar cheese, grated
3¼ cups milk
7 eggs, beaten
¾ tsp. salt
1 tsp. Worcestershire sauce
¼ cup grated Parmesan cheese

Directions

In a buttered 9" x 13" casserole dish, layer the bread and cheese: first spread out half the bread, cover with half the cheese, then the rest of the bread and the rest of the cheese.

Mix milk, eggs and seasonings, and pour over bread and cheese. Cover and refrigerate overnight.

Sprinkle with Parmesan cheese and bake uncovered at 325°F for 45 to 55 minutes, or until set. Serve immediately.

Serves 6.

—Joan Panaro

Broccoli Cheese Soufflé

An interesting and attractive dish, this soufflé is good served with rolls and a green salad.

Ingredients

1 tsp. butter
1 Tbsp. Parmesan cheese
3 Tbsp. butter
3 Tbsp. flour
⅓ cup powdered milk
¾ cup boiling water
½ tsp. salt
⅛ tsp. pepper
Cayenne & nutmeg
4 egg yolks
⅔ cup grated Swiss, Parmesan or Cheddar cheese
⅔ cup cooked chopped broccoli
1 egg white
Salt

Directions

Preheat oven to 400°F. Butter a 6-cup soufflé dish with 1 tsp. butter and sprinkle with 1 Tbsp. Parmesan cheese.

Melt the 3 Tbsp. of butter in a saucepan and stir in the flour. Cook for about 2 minutes without letting it brown. Remove from heat and add powdered milk mixed with boiling water. Beat with a wire whisk until well blended. Add seasonings and return to moderate heat. Remove from heat after 1 minute.

Add egg yolks to mixture, one at a time, beating well after each one. Correct the seasoning. Add cheese and broccoli.

Beat egg white with a pinch of salt until stiff. Blend one-quarter of the egg white into the cheese mixture, then carefully fold in the remaining egg whites.

Turn the mixture into the soufflé dish and smooth the top. Place on middle rack of oven and reduce heat to 375°F. Do not open the oven door for at least 20 minutes. Bake 25–30 minutes (4–5 minutes longer if you like it quite firm). Serve immediately.

Serves 4 to 6.

—Olga Harrison

Spinach Pie

Spinach, eggs and feta cheese combined in layers with filo pastry give this dish a delectably rich flavor.

Ingredients

¼ cup olive oil
½ cup finely chopped onions
¼ cup finely chopped scallions
2 lbs. fresh spinach, washed, drained & finely chopped
¼ cup finely cut fresh dill leaves (2 Tbsp. dried)
¼ cup finely chopped parsley
½ tsp. salt
Freshly ground black pepper
⅓ cup milk
½ lb. feta cheese, finely crumbled
4 eggs, lightly beaten
½ lb. butter, melted
16 sheets filo pastry

Directions

Heat olive oil in a heavy skillet. Add onions and scallions and cook, stirring frequently, until soft but not brown. Stir in spinach, cover tightly and cook for 5 minutes. Add dill, parsley, salt and a few grindings of pepper while stirring and shaking pan. Cook uncovered for about 10 minutes — until most of the liquid has evaporated and spinach sticks slightly to the pan.

Transfer to a bowl, add milk and cool to room temperature. Add cheese and slowly beat in eggs. Taste for seasoning.

With a pastry brush, coat the bottom and sides of a 7″ x 12″ dish with melted butter. Line the dish with a sheet of filo, pressing the edges into the corners of the dish. Brush the surface of the pastry with 2 or 3 tsp. of butter. Lay another sheet on top. Again, spread with 2 or 3 tsp. of butter. Continue until there are 8 layers of filo in the pan.

Spread the spinach mixture on top of the filo. Place another layer of filo on top, coat with butter, and repeat, as before, until there are 8 layers. With scissors, trim the excess filo from around the edges of the dish. Brush top with remaining butter.

Bake at 300°F for 1 hour or until pastry is golden brown. Cut into squares and serve hot or at room temperature.

—Carol Gasken

Spinach Cream Cheese Pie

Although this pie has no crust, the wheat germ bakes to a crispy texture, resulting in a quiche-like dish.

Ingredients

10 oz. spinach
8 oz. cream cheese
1 Tbsp. minced onion
Dash nutmeg
6 eggs
Wheat germ
¼ lb. Cheddar cheese, sliced
Paprika
1 Tbsp. flour
1 tsp. water

Directions

Cook spinach, drain and press out excess water. Soften cream cheese and add spinach, onion and nutmeg. Beat 5 of the eggs and stir into the spinach mixture. Grease sides and bottom of a pie plate, sprinkle it with wheat germ and pour in spinach mixture. Cover with cheese slices and sprinkle with paprika. Beat remaining egg with flour and water and pour over the cheese. Bake at 350°F for 35 to 45 minutes, until top is lightly browned.

Serves 4.

—Laura Poitras

Summer Omelette

An omelette can contain almost any filling, including cooked meats and seafood. The two presented here make use of summer vegetables. Variations could include tomatoes, green pepper or other vegetables.

Ingredients

6 eggs
⅓ cup milk
Salt & pepper
¼–½ cup chopped celery
2–3 Tbsp. chopped onion
¼ cup sliced mushrooms
¼–½ cup grated Cheddar or Swiss cheese

Directions

Beat together eggs, milk, salt and pepper. Lightly sauté celery, onion and mushrooms. Add to egg mixture along with the cheese. Mix well and pour into greased 8-inch square cake pan. Bake at 350°F for approximately 30 minutes or until knife comes out clean.

Serves 4.

Zucchini Omelette

Zucchini recipes are always welcome. This one, an Italian standard, is a boon for those overburdened with both zucchini and eggs.

Ingredients

2 small zucchini
2 Tbsp. cooking oil
2 eggs
Salt & pepper
½ tsp. dried oregano
½ cup grated Romano or Parmesan cheese

Directions

Cut zucchini into ⅛-inch slices. Sauté in hot oil in a small cast-iron frying pan, stirring constantly, until golden brown. Reduce heat to medium low. Beat eggs with wire whisk until well blended but not frothy, and add to zucchini in pan. Sprinkle with remaining ingredients.

Cook, covered, until egg is set. Fold omelette in half, allow to cook a few seconds longer, then remove to warmed plate and cut into wedges.

Serves 2.

—Dorothy Farniloe

Crêpes

The variety of fillings for crêpes is almost unlimited, though the most common is cottage cheese. Crêpes may be served hot or cold, as a main course or as a dessert.

Ingredients
¾ cup flour
Salt
1 egg yolk
1 egg
1¼ cups milk
1 Tbsp. melted butter or light oil

Directions
Sift the flour into blender or mixing bowl. Add salt, egg yolk, whole egg and half the milk. Blend for 1 minute or stir with a wire whisk until smooth. Add the rest of the milk and the melted butter or oil.

Let rest, refrigerated, for 1 hour.

To cook, heat 1 Tbsp. butter in small, heavy frying pan. When bubbling, pour in a very small amount of batter and immediately swirl pan to coat. The thinner the crêpe the better.

Cook over high heat for approximately 1 minute, or until crêpe is lightly browned and firm enough to flip with a spatula. Brown other side and remove to a warmed plate. Continue cooking and stacking crêpes until batter is used up. No additional greasing should be necessary. The crêpes will not stick together when stacked. If the first few crêpes do not turn out, do not become discouraged — it often takes a little time to season the pan and to refine the swirling technique. Spread filling as a thin layer overtop, then roll from one side to the other.

Makes 12 crêpes.

Cooked crêpes may be kept refrigerated for several days or frozen for several months. Crêpe batter may be refrigerated overnight, but it may need to be thinned with 1–2 Tbsp. milk when used.

—Jeanne Nugent

Pancake Mix

This homemade pancake mix, as well as being convenient, has the additional charm of flexibility — it can be tailor-made to suit individual tastes by using, for example, whole wheat flour, wheat germ or buttermilk flour.

Ingredients
12 cups flour
4 cups milk powder
¾ cup baking powder
¾ cup sugar
2 Tbsp. salt

Directions
Mix well and store in airtight containers.

Makes 16 cups mix.

To use: Combine 1½ cups mix, 1 cup water, 1 egg and 2 Tbsp. oil.

Makes 8 pancakes.

—Dawn Livingstone

Bran Pancakes

Ingredients

1 cup bran
1 cup whole wheat flour
1 cup unbleached white flour
½ cup raisins (optional)
¼ cup brown sugar
1 Tbsp. baking powder
½ tsp. salt
2½ cups milk
2 eggs
¼ cup oil

Directions

Proof yeast in water and honey for 10 minutes. In a large mixing bowl, combine flour, bran, raisins, sugar, baking powder and salt, and mix well.

In a small bowl, beat milk, eggs and oil until blended. Add to flour mixture and mix well.

Pour batter, using about ⅓ cup for each pancake, into a hot, greased frying pan. Cook, turning once, until both sides are golden brown. Serves 5 to 6.

—*Marnie Horton*

A Quick Pancake

A cross between a pancake and an omelette, this has a light texture and a pleasant, nutty flavor. Fresh fruit, chopped, sautéed in butter and brown sugar and placed in the bottom of the pan, can provide a delicious variation.

Ingredients

2 eggs, separated
1 cup yogurt
1 cup quick cooking oats
1 Tbsp. sugar
¼ tsp. baking soda
¼ tsp. baking powder
¼ tsp. salt
1 Tbsp. butter

Directions

Beat egg yolks well and stir in yogurt. Add dry ingredients and mix well. Beat egg whites until stiff, then gently fold into batter.

Melt butter in a large frying pan which can be used in the oven. Spoon batter into pan and bake for 20 minutes at 350°F.

Serve with honey or jam.

—*Carol Frost*

Egg Casserole

A hearty, substantial casserole of particular interest to garlic lovers, this dish makes a good brunch when you have a lot of visitors.

Ingredients

12 eggs
½ lb. bacon
¼ cup butter
¼ cup flour
1 cup light cream
1 cup milk
1 lb. sharp Cheddar cheese, grated
2 small cloves garlic, crushed
¼ tsp. thyme
¼ tsp. marjoram
¼ tsp. basil
¼ tsp. chopped parsley
¾ cup bread crumbs

Directions

Hard boil the eggs, peel and slice them. Broil the bacon until crisp, drain and crumble. Melt butter, stir in flour and gradually mix in cream and milk. Heat, stirring constantly, until sauce thickens. Add cheese and seasonings. Pour half the sauce into a well-greased casserole dish. Add the eggs as the next layer, then the bacon. Top with the rest of the sauce and sprinkle bread crumbs over it. Bake at 350°F for 30 minutes.

Serves 8 to 10.

—Jody Schwindt

Potato Pancakes

Ingredients

4 medium raw potatoes, shredded
Salt & pepper
3 Tbsp. flour
1 egg, beaten
¼ cup grated onion
½ cup grated Cheddar cheese
Heavy cream
Butter

Directions

Mix shredded potatoes with flour, egg, onion, cheese, salt and pepper. Add enough cream to make a moist but not wet batter.

Heat butter in a heavy skillet and drop batter by spoonfuls into the hot fat. Fry until both sides of pancakes are golden brown, then slide onto a cookie sheet. Bake at 400°F for 4 minutes.

Serve hot with butter and maple syrup.

Serves 4 to 6.

—Pearl Lentz

Eggs Kariel

Tasty, nutritious and quick to prepare, this serve-it-anytime dish can be easily adjusted to suit the number of hungry people present.

Ingredients

1 lb. fresh spinach
8 eggs
1 cup Cheddar cheese

Directions

Clean and rinse spinach. Place in a wide saucepan containing enough water to cover bottom of the pan, cover and steam briefly — until spinach is wilted.

Make hollows in spinach and break eggs into them. Replace cover and continue to steam until eggs are poached. Sprinkle cheese over top, recover, and cook until cheese is melted.

Serves 4 for lunch, 8 for breakfast.

—N. Kariel

Egg McRivers

Ingredients

2 English muffins split, toasted & buttered
4 slices cooked ham
4 poached eggs
½ cup Cheddar cheese, grated

Directions

Place English muffins on a cookie sheet. On each, place a slice of ham and a poached egg, and sprinkle Cheddar cheese on top. Broil until cheese is bubbly.

Serves 4.

—Deborah Rivers

Baked Eggs

A hearty, tasty breakfast or brunch dish, this can be prepared the night before, ready to pop into the oven in the morning.

Ingredients

1 lb. ground sausage meat or ham
6 eggs
2 cups milk
2 slices bread, trimmed & cubed
1 tsp. dry mustard
1 cup grated mild cheese

Directions

Brown sausage meat or ham and drain on towels. Beat eggs and combine all ingredients in a 9" x 13" baking dish. Bake at 350°F for 45 minutes or until lightly browned.

Serves 6.

—Mrs. J. Hall-Armstrong

Scotch Eggs

Hot or cold, these eggs are delicious as hors d'oeuvres, snacks or accompaniments to salads.

Ingredients

12 hard-boiled eggs, peeled
½ cup flour
2 lbs. skinless sausage meat
1 egg
1 Tbsp. water
Fine bread crumbs or quick-cooking rolled oats

Directions

Roll cooked eggs in flour. With floured hands, coat each egg with sausage meat.

Combine raw egg and water and beat together. Dip sausage-covered eggs into egg mixture, then roll in bread crumbs.

Fry in deep fat until golden brown. If preferred, eggs can be cooked in shallow fat or baked at 350°F until the bread crumbs are crisp and the meat is thoroughly cooked.

—Sherri McMillan

Eggs Florentine

Another brunch, lunch or dinner favorite, this is a delicious and attractive dish.

Ingredients

2 Tbsp. butter
1 Tbsp. minced onion
1½ tsp. flour
¼ tsp. salt
Pepper & nutmeg
1 cup milk
¼ cup Parmesan cheese
1 pkg. spinach
4 eggs
Parmesan cheese

Directions

Sauté onion in melted butter. Add flour, salt, pepper and nutmeg and stir until smooth. Blend in milk, bring to a boil, then reduce heat and simmer, stirring constantly, for 3 minutes. Add ¼ cup Parmesan cheese.

Cook and drain spinach and combine with milk mixture. Turn into a shallow baking dish.

Poach the eggs and arrange them on top of the spinach mixture. Sprinkle with Parmesan cheese and place under the broiler just long enough to melt the cheese.

Serves 4.

—Brenda Eckstein

Egg Salad

This cool, refreshing spread is good served on whole wheat bread, pita bread, sesame crackers, or wrapped in spinach or lettuce leaves.

Ingredients

5 hard-boiled eggs
⅓ cup finely chopped carrot
⅓ cup finely chopped celery
⅓ cup finely chopped onion
½ cup toasted sunflower seeds
½ cup toasted sesame seeds, ground
½ cup ricotta cheese
¼ cup yogurt
¼ cup mayonnaise
Salt
Paprika

Directions

Mash the eggs in a bowl. Add other ingredients and mix well. Refrigerate for several hours before serving.

Serves 4 to 6.

—*N. Burk*

Eggs Molière

Ingredients

4 eggs
4 tomatoes
2 Tbsp. oil
½ lb. mushrooms, thinly sliced
2 scallions, chopped
2 Tbsp. flour
1½ cups hot chicken stock
Salt & pepper

Directions

Boil eggs until they can be peeled but are not hard cooked, about 5 minutes. Peel and set aside.

Cut off the tops of the tomatoes and hollow them out with a spoon. Season with salt and pepper and place in an ovenproof baking dish. Bake for 10 minutes at 375°F and set aside.

Heat the oil in a saucepan. Add the mushrooms and the scallions, season to taste and cook over medium heat for 3 to 4 minutes. Stir in the flour and continue to cook for 2 to 3 minutes. Add the hot chicken stock and correct seasoning. Cook over low heat for another 15 minutes.

Place 1 peeled egg inside each cooked tomato shell. Cover with the sauce and bake for 7 to 8 minutes. Garnish with parsley.

Serves 4.

—*Brenda Eckstein*

Rarebit Fondue on Toast

An adaptation of a traditional fondue recipe, this rarebit has a very satisfying and pleasantly garlicky flavor.

Ingredients

8 thick slices whole wheat bread
Butter
½ lb. mushrooms, sliced
½ cup finely chopped onion
2 cups dry white wine
½ clove garlic, chopped
½ lb. Gruyère cheese, grated
2 Tbsp. or more whole wheat flour
Freshly ground pepper

Directions

Butter bread on both sides and bake at 400°F for 5 to 8 minutes — until golden brown on both sides.

Sauté mushrooms and onion in butter until the onion is soft. Add garlic and wine. Mix flour and cheese and add to the hot wine mixture, 1 handful at a time, stirring until each addition of cheese melts. Cook, stirring, over low heat until the sauce bubbles and thickens. Season with pepper.

Place the toast on individual serving plates and top with sauce.

Serves 4.

—Janet Flewelling

Kafkades

These traditional Greek patties are delicious as well as wholesome.

Ingredients

2 cups cottage cheese
2 egg yolks
1 cup flour
2 cups loosely packed bite-sized spinach
Olive oil
Salt & pepper

Directions

Combine cottage cheese, egg yolks and flour. Mix well, if necessary, adding more flour, until mixture becomes a thick paste. Add spinach.

In a large skillet, heat oil to cover the bottom of the pan to a medium high temperature. For each patty, drop batter from a large spoon onto the pan. Cook until golden brown on one side, then turn carefully and cook until the other side is done. Season with salt and pepper.

Makes 10 to 12 patties.

—Susan Gammon

Cheese Snacks

These tasty instant canapes can be prepared ahead of time, frozen, brought out and baked as the need or the inclination arises.

Ingredients

1 loaf unsliced whole wheat bread
¾ cup butter, softened
2 egg whites
½ lb. old Cheddar cheese, grated
Salt
½ tsp. dry mustard

Directions

Cut bread into bite-sized pieces.

Beat butter, egg whites, cheese, salt and mustard together until creamy and smooth — about 5 minutes. Spread cheese mixture on bread.

Freeze on a cookie sheet, then pack into plastic bags to store.

To serve, bake at 350°F for 8 to 10 minutes, until bubbly.

Serve warm.

—Marie Blundell

Onion Cheese Squares

Delicious as a main course for lunch or dinner, these squares are inexpensive and simple to make.

Ingredients

¾ cup chopped onion
2 Tbsp. butter
¾ cup scalded milk
2 eggs, beaten
1 cup grated Cheddar cheese
Salt & pepper
¼ cup pimento, diced or 1 tomato, chopped
2 Tbsp. chopped fresh parsley
2 Tbsp. wheat germ
2 Tbsp. (or more) bread crumbs
Sesame seeds

Directions

Sauté onion in butter until soft and golden. Remove from heat. Combine milk and eggs and add to onion. Add all remaining ingredients except sesame seeds. If mixture seems very runny, add extra bread crumbs. Pour into greased 8-inch pie plate. Sprinkle with sesame seeds. Bake at 325°F for 45 minutes, or until knife inserted into center comes out clean.

—Pam Collacott

Cheese & Tomato Bake

Ingredients

5 slices bacon
4 Tbsp. flour
3 cups tomato juice
1 tsp. salt
½ small onion, minced
1 cup grated Cheddar cheese
3 cups cooked whole wheat
¼ cup buttered bread crumbs

Directions

Fry bacon until lightly browned. Cut into ½-inch pieces and set aside. Reserve 1 Tbsp. of the fat.

Stir flour into reserved bacon fat. Add tomato juice, salt and onion and cook, stirring, until thickened. Remove from heat and add the bacon and three-quarters of the cheese.

Place wheat in a greased baking dish and pour the tomato mixture over it. Sprinkle with bread crumbs and remaining cheese. Bake at 350°F for 45 minutes.

Serves 4 to 6.

—Joanne Ramsy

Potato Cheese Casserole

Ingredients

½ cup milk
2 large eggs, beaten
2 cups mashed potatoes
1-2 onions, chopped
½–¾ cup grated Parmesan cheese
4 Tbsp. wheat germ

Directions

Combine milk, eggs, potatoes and onions. Pour into a 9-inch square buttered pan and sprinkle with Parmesan cheese and wheat germ. Bake at 350°F for 30 minutes, until top is golden brown.

Serves 4 to 6.

—Richard & Elaine Domsy

Gouda Sesame Log

Ingredients

3 cups coarsely grated Gouda cheese
1 cup coarsely grated ice-cold butter
1 tsp. hot mustard
2 Tbsp. whiskey
¾ cup toasted sesame seeds

Directions

Cream cheese and butter together until well blended. Mix in mustard and whiskey. Shape into log and roll in sesame seeds. Refrigerate for 24 hours before serving.

Makes 3 to 4 cups.

—Kumari Campbell

Hot Cheese Dip

Ingredients

2 cups light cream
2 tsp. dry mustard
1 Tbsp. Worcestershire sauce
1 clove garlic, cut in half
3 Tbsp. flour
6 cups coarsely grated sharp Cheddar cheese
¼ tsp. salt
2 Tbsp. sherry

Directions

In a glass or enamel saucepan, heat cream, mustard, Worcestershire sauce and garlic. Mix cheese with flour, and drop, a handful at a time, into the hot cream. Cook over low heat, stirring with a wooden spoon, until cheese is melted and mixture is smooth. Add salt and sherry. If only a mild hint of garlic is desired, remove it now from the dip.

Pour dip into a chafing dish or heavy fondue pot and serve with such dunking delights as raw vegetables, chunks of quality fresh bread or cooked shrimp.

Makes 4 to 6 cups.

—Dorothy Hurst

Boursin

A homemade recipe for this delicate cheese spread is a boon to addicts, since it is easy to make and considerably less expensive than the commercially produced versions.

Ingredients

16 oz. cream cheese
¼ cup mayonnaise
2 tsp. Dijon mustard
2 Tbsp. finely chopped chives
2 Tbsp. finely chopped dill
1 clove garlic, minced

Directions

Soften cheese, then, using an electric mixer, thoroughly blend in mayonnaise, mustard, chives, dill and garlic. Spoon into a small serving bowl, cover and refrigerate for 24 hours.

Serve with bagels, crackers, Melba toast, rye bread, pumpernickel bread, celery, mushrooms or other raw vegetables.

Makes 2½ cups.

—Shirley Hill

Val's Onion Cheese Pie

Crust Ingredients
¾ cup flour
½ tsp. salt
½ tsp. dry mustard
1 cup grated sharp Cheddar cheese
½–1 cup melted butter

Filling Ingredients
2 cups thinly sliced onions
2 Tbsp. butter
1 cup cooked thin egg noodles
2 eggs
1 cup hot milk
1 cup grated Cheddar cheese
Salt & pepper

Directions

To make crust, mix together flour, salt, mustard and cheese. Slowly pour in melted butter until a workable dough results. Press into a deep 9-inch pie plate.

For filling, sauté onions in butter and add noodles. Place in pie shell. Beat eggs, then add hot milk and cheese while continuing to beat. Add salt and pepper to taste. Pour over onion and noodle mixture. Bake at 350°F for 40 minutes.

Serves 6 to 8.

—Kirsten McDougall

Tomato Cheese Pie

Filling Ingredients
2 Tbsp. butter
¼ cup chopped green onions
1 cup bread crumbs
¼ cup chopped parsley
1 tsp. basil
⅛ tsp. salt
Pepper
10 firm red tomatoes, peeled

Topping Ingredients
1 cup flour
1½ tsp. baking powder
½ tsp. salt
2 Tbsp. butter
¼ cup milk
½ cup grated Cheddar cheese

Directions

Melt butter in skillet. Add onions and cook for 3 or 4 minutes. Stir in bread crumbs and cook until golden. Remove from heat; stir in parsley, basil, salt and pepper.

Cut tomatoes into slices ½-inch thick. Place half the slices in greased pie plate. Sprinkle with half the bread crumb mixture. Repeat.

To make the topping, sift together flour, baking powder and salt. Cut in butter to make fine crumbs. Add milk to make a soft dough, then work in cheese. Knead until smooth, wrap and refrigerate for 1 hour. On lightly floured surface, roll dough to a 9-by-12-inch rectangle, ½-inch thick. Cut into 12 strips ½-inch wide. Make lattice top for pie, crimping edges to pan. Bake at 350°F for 30 to 35 minutes, or until crust is golden.

Serves 6 to 8.

—Jill Leary

Cauliflower Cheese Pie

Ingredients

2 cups packed, grated potatoes
1 tsp. salt
3 eggs
¼ cup grated onion
1 cup chopped onion
1 clove garlic, minced
3 Tbsp. butter
Thyme
Pepper
Paprika
½ tsp. basil
1 cauliflower, broken into florets
1 heaping cup grated Cheddar cheese
¼ cup milk

Directions

Salt the grated potatoes with ½ tsp. salt. Let stand for 10 minutes, then squeeze out excess water. Beat 1 egg and add along with grated onion. Pat into well-oiled pie plate and bake at 375°F for 30 minutes or until golden brown.

Sauté chopped onion and garlic in butter. Add herbs (including ½ tsp. salt) and cauliflower and cook for 10 minutes. Spread half the cheese in pie plate, then cauliflower mixture, then remaining cheese. Beat together 2 remaining eggs and milk and pour over all.

Bake at 375°F for 30 to 40 minutes, or until set.

Serves 4.

—Nancy Beltgens

Spinach Feta Cheese Quiche

Ingredients

Pastry for 9-inch pie shell
2 Tbsp. olive oil
½ cup finely chopped mushrooms
1 shallot, chopped
¼ cup pine nuts
2 cups finely chopped spinach
2 eggs, beaten
¼ lb. feta cheese, crumbled
¼ cup milk
Parmesan cheese
Nutmeg

Directions

Heat oil and sauté mushrooms, shallot and pine nuts. Steam spinach until limp but still bright green. Beat together eggs, feta cheese and milk. Add vegetables and spoon into pastry-lined pie plate. Top with Parmesan cheese and nutmeg. Bake at 350°F for 40 to 45 minutes.

Serves 4 to 6.

—P.S. Reynolds

Cheese Pie

Ingredients

1 egg
Salt & pepper
1 cup grated cheese
1 cup milk
¾ cup flour

Directions

Butter a 9-inch pie plate. Blend milk, flour, egg, salt and pepper. Stir in half of cheese. Pour into pie plate and bake at 350°F until puffed and golden, about 25 minutes. Sprinkle remaining cheese over top. Continue baking until cheese melts — 3 to 4 minutes. Serve immediately.

Serves 2.

—Barb Alguire

Spinach Quiche

Ingredients

Pastry for 9-inch pie shell
2 Tbsp. finely chopped onion
1 cup grated cheese
2 eggs
1 cup yogurt
1 Tbsp. flour
½ tsp. salt
¼ tsp. pepper
Dash nutmeg
1 cup chopped cooked spinach

Directions

Bake crust at 450°F for 10 minutes. Let cool and sprinkle onion and cheese over crust.

Beat eggs, then add yogurt, flour and seasonings. Stir well. Add and stir in spinach. Pour this mixture into the baked pie shell.

Bake at 450°F for 15 minutes. Reduce heat to 350°F and bake for 30 minutes longer.

Serves 4 to 6.

—Susan Lord

Potato Pie

Ingredients

Pastry for 10-inch pie shell
1 lb. cottage cheese
2 cups mashed potatoes
½ cup sour cream
2 eggs
2 tsp. salt
⅛ tsp. cayenne
½ cup scallions, sliced
3 Tbsp. grated Parmesan cheese

Directions

Line pie plate with pastry. Process cottage cheese in blender until smooth, then beat in mashed potatoes. Beat in sour cream, eggs, salt and cayenne. Stir in scallions. Spoon into pastry shell and sprinkle with cheese.

Bake at 450°F for 50 minutes or until golden brown.

Serves 4 to 6.

—Marsha Plewes

Eggplant Tomato Quiche

Ingredients

Pastry for 9-inch pie shell
1 cup chopped tomatoes
1 Tbsp. chopped parsley
½ tsp. oregano
½ tsp. basil
1 Tbsp. butter
½ cup chopped mushrooms
1 clove garlic, minced
1 shallot, chopped
1 small eggplant, unpeeled
3 eggs
1 cup grated Cheddar cheese
Bread crumbs

Directions

Simmer tomatoes, parsley, oregano and basil for 20 minutes. Heat butter and sauté mushrooms, garlic and shallot. Add to tomato mixture and let cool.

Thinly slice unpeeled eggplant and bake at 350°F for 10 minutes. Line pie plate with pastry and cover with eggplant slices.

Beat eggs and mix with tomatoes. Spoon half of this over eggplant, then add ½ cup cheese. Repeat layers and top with bread crumbs. Bake at 375°F for 40 to 45 minutes.

Serves 6 to 8.

—P.S. Reynolds

Chicken Quiche

Ingredients

Pastry for 9-inch pie shell
3 eggs
3 Tbsp. cornstarch
½ tsp. salt
⅛ tsp. pepper
½ tsp. thyme
¼ tsp. sage
1½ cups chicken stock
1 cup grated Cheddar cheese
½ cup chopped green pepper
1–2 cups minced cooked chicken

Directions

In large bowl, beat eggs until creamy. Mix cornstarch, salt, pepper, thyme and sage and slowly stir in chicken stock until smooth. Slowly beat into eggs. Add remaining ingredients and mix. Pour into pastry shell.

Bake at 425°F for 15 minutes; lower temperature to 325°F and bake 30 to 45 minutes longer or until filling is set. Cool for 5 to 10 minutes before serving.

Serves 4 to 6.

—Janice Chammartin

Leek Soufflé

This soufflé can be made using leeks that have been sliced and frozen for a pleasant midwinter taste of spring.

Ingredients

½ cup & 2 Tbsp. Parmesan cheese
2 leeks, sliced
6 Tbsp. butter
3 Tbsp. water
½ tsp. salt
¼ tsp. pepper
3 Tbsp. flour
1 cup milk
4 egg yolks, slightly beaten
Salt & pepper
6 egg whites

Directions

Coat inside of greased, 2-quart soufflé dish with 2 Tbsp. Parmesan cheese. Simmer leeks in 3 Tbsp. butter and water with salt and pepper, covered, until water evaporates — about 5 minutes.

Melt remaining 3 Tbsp. butter, then stir in flour. Cook over low heat, stirring constantly, for 2 minutes. Gradually stir in milk. Heat to boiling, stirring. Add leeks and ½ cup Parmesan cheese. Cook over medium heat, stirring constantly, until mixture boils. Remove from heat.

Stir ¼ cup of leek mixture into egg yolks, then gradually stir this back into leek mixture. Season with salt and pepper and cool to lukewarm.

Beat egg whites until stiff but not dry and fold into leek mixture. Pour into prepared soufflé dish. Bake at 400°F for 35 minutes, or until golden and firm.

Serves 6.

—Pam Collacott

German Omelette

Ingredients

1 lb. sausage meat
1 medium onion, chopped
Salt & pepper
1 tsp. dry mustard
2 Tbsp. parsley
6 eggs
2 cups milk
3 slices bread, cubed
1 cup grated Cheddar cheese
1 cup grated mozzarella cheese

Directions

Brown sausage meat and drain off excess fat. Add onion, salt, pepper, mustard and parsley and cook until onion is tender.

Mix together eggs, milk, bread and cheeses. Add meat mixture and stir. Pour into a 9" x 13" baking dish and chill overnight. Bake at 350°F for 45 minutes, or until knife inserted in center comes out clean.

Serves 6 to 8.

—Lynda Watson

Potato Omelette

Ingredients

1 medium potato
Butter
2 eggs
Milk
Salt & pepper
Sliced mushrooms

Directions

Slice the potato ⅛- to ¼-inch thick and lay on a lightly oiled cookie sheet. Dot with butter and bake at 350°F until golden brown, turning once. Meanwhile, beat eggs with a little milk and season with salt and pepper. Sauté mushrooms.

Layer potato slices in an oiled frying pan. Add mushroom-egg mixture. Cover and cook slowly on both sides.

Serves 1.

—Veronica Clarke-Hanik

Buckwheat Crêpes with Maple Orange Sauce

Crêpes Ingredients

1½ cups buckwheat flour
½ tsp. salt
3 eggs & milk to make 4 cups
Oil

Sauce Ingredients

1 cup maple syrup
½ cup butter
¼ cup grated orange peel
Cottage cheese

Directions

Combine flour and salt in large bowl. Add 1 cup of egg-milk mixture at a time, whisking well. Continue adding liquid until mixture is consistency of heavy cream. Reserve extra liquid.

Pour ⅓ cup batter into hot pan and roll around to coat bottom evenly. Cook on medium-high until crêpe is golden brown on bottom and sturdy enough to flip — 30 to 45 seconds per side. If batter thickens as cooking continues, add some of reserved liquid.

To make sauce, place maple syrup, butter and orange peel in saucepan. Bring to a boil, lower heat and simmer for 5 minutes.

To serve, fill crêpes with cottage cheese and pour sauce over top.

Makes approximately 15 crêpes.

—Marilyn Rootham

Poppy Seed Pancakes

The most flavorful poppy seeds are grown in Holland. The seed is best when steamed or roasted, then crushed to release its full flavor. For those who really enjoy poppy seeds, it is possible to buy a hand mill to grind the seeds at home.

Ingredients

1 cup whole wheat flour
1 Tbsp. sugar
½ tsp. salt
1 Tbsp. baking powder
1 egg, beaten
1 cup milk
2 Tbsp. oil
2 Tbsp. poppy seeds

Directions

Mix together flour, sugar, salt and baking powder. Beat egg and add milk, then oil. Add to dry ingredients. Add poppy seeds and stir until seeds are just moistened.

Pour batter by scant quarter cupfuls onto hot greased griddle. Cook until bubbly. Turn with pancake turner and cook until underside is golden. Place on platter and keep warm.

Makes about 15 three-inch pancakes.

—Suzanne Moore

Buckwheat Pancakes

Ingredients

2 eggs
1¼ cups buttermilk
2 Tbsp. oil
½ cup buckwheat flour
½ cup whole wheat flour
¼ cup wheat germ
½ tsp. baking soda
1 tsp. baking powder
½ tsp. salt
1 cup diced fruit (optional)

Directions

Beat together eggs, buttermilk and oil. Gradually mix in flours, wheat germ, baking soda, baking powder, salt and diced fruit. Fry on hot greased griddle.

Makes approximately 16 pancakes.

—Marjorie Moore

Corn Meal Pancakes

Ingredients

¼ cup flour
1 tsp. sugar
2 tsp. baking powder
¾ tsp. salt
½ tsp. baking soda
1 cup corn meal
3 eggs, beaten
1½ cups buttermilk
2 Tbsp. melted butter

Directions

Combine and mix flour, sugar, baking powder, salt and baking soda. Stir in corn meal. Add eggs, buttermilk and butter and stir until dry mixture is moistened. Pour ¼ cup batter onto hot griddle. Brown one side, turn and brown on other. Repeat with remaining batter.

Makes 12 pancakes.

—Judy Cushman

Oatmeal Pancakes

Ingredients

1½ cups oatmeal
2½ cups milk
1 cup flour
1 Tbsp. brown sugar
½ tsp. salt
1 tsp. cinnamon
1 Tbsp. baking powder
1 egg, beaten
¼ cup oil

Directions

Pour milk over oatmeal and let sit for 10 minutes. Sift flour, sugar, salt, cinnamon and baking powder together, then add to oatmeal mixture. Add egg and oil and mix well. Cook on hot griddle.

Makes 10 to 12 pancakes.

—Judy Wuest

Cheese Corn Pancakes

Ingredients

2 cups flour
3 tsp. baking powder
1 tsp. salt
2 Tbsp. brown sugar
2 cups milk
2 eggs, slightly beaten
¼ cup oil or melted butter
2 cups corn
Small cubes Cheddar cheese

Directions

Combine flour, baking powder, salt and sugar. In another bowl, combine milk, eggs, oil and corn. Pour liquid ingredients over flour mixture and combine with a few strokes — batter should be lumpy.

Pour ¼ cup of batter onto greased griddle. While first side is cooking, top with 5 or 6 cheese cubes. Flip to cheese side and cook until golden brown.

Makes 8 to 10 pancakes.

—Rae Anne Huth

Banana Pancakes

Ingredients

2 eggs
2 cups buttermilk
1 Tbsp. baking soda
1 Tbsp. baking powder
2 cups flour
5 Tbsp. oil
1 cup mashed ripe bananas

Directions

Mix together eggs, buttermilk, baking soda and baking powder. Add flour and then oil, stirring only until blended. Fold in bananas. Spoon onto hot griddle or frying pan.

Makes approximately 12 pancakes.

—Marilynn Janzen

Parmesan Cheese Ball

Every cook has his or her own favorite cheese ball recipes. They are good as an accompaniment to raw vegetables, crackers or potato chips, and make ideal potluck fare. They can also be made well ahead of time, wrapped carefully, and kept refrigerated until needed. The following recipe makes a very mild cheese ball that is well complemented by raw vegetables.

Ingredients

8 oz. cream cheese, softened
⅓ cup Parmesan cheese
1 small onion, finely chopped
1 clove garlic, crushed
2 tsp. soy sauce
1 Tbsp. finely chopped parsley
¼ tsp. white pepper
½ cup finely chopped dill or parsley

Directions

Combine cream cheese, Parmesan cheese, onion, garlic, soy sauce, 1 Tbsp. parsley and white pepper. Blend well and form into ball. Roll in chopped dill or parsley. Chill.

Makes approximately 2 cups.

—Trudi Keillor

Herbed Cheese

The contributor of this recipe uses fresh goat's milk cream cheese, which adds flavor. This, of course, is not imperative, but fresh herbs must be used.

Ingredients

1½ lbs. creamed cottage
cheese, drained
1 lb. cream cheese
3 tsp. sour cream
3 cloves garlic, finely minced
½ tsp. salt
½ tsp. white pepper
1 tsp. minced basil
1 tsp. minced tarragon
½ tsp. minced thyme
½ tsp. minced sage
2 Tbsp. minced chives
2 Tbsp. minced parsley

Directions

Beat cheeses and sour cream until smooth, then beat in herbs. Cover and refrigerate for 24 hours to cure.

Place in a 3-cup mold lined with plastic wrap, refrigerate until set and remove from mold. Garnish with fresh herbs.

Makes 3 cups.

—Janet Ueberschlag

Knedlyky

This recipe for cottage cheese dumplings is a simplified version of a traditional Czechoslovakian dish prepared the way they used to be made during the harvest, when there was not much time to fuss in the kitchen. It is usually served as a side dish in place of noodles or potatoes.

Ingredients

1 cup cottage or ricotta cheese
1 egg
2 cups fine semolina

Directions

Mix cheese well with egg. If cheese curds are very large, break first with a pastry cutter or fork. Add semolina to make a workable dough — the exact amount will depend upon how moist the cheese is.

Form dough into walnut-sized balls, moistening hands with water to prevent sticking. Drop into a large pot of boiling salted water and cook for 7 minutes. Drain and serve.

Serves 6.

—Moira Abboud

Baked Vegetable Frittata

A frittata is little more than an omelette, the difference being that the filling is usually mixed into the eggs before they are cooked. Frittatas may be baked or cooked, covered, on top of the stove.

Ingredients

2 Tbsp. butter
1 onion, finely chopped
1 clove garlic, minced
1 green pepper, diced
¼ cup chopped parsley
19-oz. can tomatoes, drained & chopped
4–5 eggs
½ cup bread crumbs
1 tsp. salt
¼ tsp. pepper
1 tsp. Worcestershire sauce
2 cups grated Swiss cheese
1 green pepper, cut in rings

Directions

In skillet, melt butter over medium heat and cook onion and garlic until tender. Add green pepper and parsley and cook for 1 minute longer. Remove from heat and add tomatoes.

In large bowl, beat eggs well. Stir in bread crumbs, salt, pepper, Worcestershire sauce and cheese. Gently stir in vegetables. Pour mixture into buttered 9"-round baking dish. Bake, uncovered, at 350°F for 30 to 35 minutes, or until top is golden brown. Let stand for 5 minutes before serving. Garnish with green pepper rings.

Serves 4.

—Grace Neumann

Simple Potato Omelette

Omelettes require delicate handling, but with a little practice can be mastered by anyone. They come in 2 basic varieties — plain, in which the eggs are beaten whole, and soufflé, in which the yolks and whites are beaten separately. Plain omelettes are generally savory (like those here) while soufflé omelettes are commonly sweet and served as dessert. This is a simple, tasty omelette. Serve with spicy tomato salsa for added color and flavor.

Ingredients

4 potatoes, diced
2 onions, finely chopped
¼ cup oil
salt & pepper
6 eggs
2 Tbsp. milk

Directions

Sauté potatoes and onions in oil until tender. Add salt and pepper to taste. Beat eggs and milk together. Pour over potatoes and mix evenly. Cover and cook gently until mixture is set. Cut in wedges and serve hot or cold.

Serves 4 to 6.

—Dorothy Cage

Vegetable Omelette

Ingredients

10 eggs
4 mushrooms, sliced
2 green onions, sliced
1 Tbsp. finely chopped green pepper
1 Tbsp. cooked squash
1 Tbsp. finely chopped sweet red pepper
1 Tbsp. finely chopped celery
⅔ cup grated Cheddar cheese
salt & pepper

Directions

Beat eggs until frothy. Add remaining ingredients and mix well. Pour into ungreased casserole dish and bake, uncovered, at 350°F for 25 to 30 minutes.

Serves 4 to 6.

—Kelvin Mayes

Spinach Squares

Ingredients

2-3 eggs
6 Tbsp. whole wheat flour
1 lb. fresh spinach
1 lb. cottage cheese
½ lb. grated Cheddar cheese
½ tsp. salt
3 Tbsp. wheat germ

Directions

Beat eggs and flour in large bowl. Tear up spinach and add. Mix in cottage cheese, Cheddar cheese and salt. Combine well. Pour into a well-greased 9" x 13" baking pan and sprinkle with wheat germ. Bake, uncovered, at 350°F for approximately 45 minutes. Cut into squares for serving.

Serves 6 to 8.

—Barbara Zikman

Indian Eggs

This makes a great brunch for corn lovers.

Ingredients

8 slices bacon
1 onion, chopped
1½ cups corn
1 Tbsp. Worcestershire sauce
salt & pepper
8 eggs, lightly beaten

Directions

Fry bacon, drain, then crumble and set aside. Pour off half the bacon fat and add onion. Sauté until onion is soft. Add corn and seasonings. Heat through, then add eggs. Cook, stirring, until set. Serve with bacon sprinkled over the top.

Serves 3 to 4.

—Ann Kostendt

New Zealand-Style Eggs

This is a quick and easy egg dish for a late break-fast or a lunch. Served with a salad it makes a satisfying light meal.

Ingredients

4 Tbsp. butter
¼ cup minced onion
1 cup cold diced cooked potatoes
5 eggs
½ cup milk
salt & pepper
2 Tbsp. snipped parsley
4 tomatoes, quartered

Directions

In 3 Tbsp. butter, sauté onion and potatoes until golden. Beat eggs with milk, ¾ tsp. salt, pepper and parsley, until just blended, then pour over potatoes. Cook over medium heat, gently scraping the mixture from the bottom as it cooks, until it is set but still moist.

Meanwhile, sprinkle tomatoes with salt and pepper. Sauté until tender in 1 Tbsp. butter in another skillet. Arrange tomatoes around potatoes.

Serves 4.

—Alyson Service

Golden Eggs Mayonnaise

Ingredients

4 Tbsp. butter
1 Tbsp. oil
2 Tbsp. curry powder
8 eggs, hard-cooked & peeled
1 cup mayonnaise
3 Tbsp. chopped chutney
1 head lettuce
½ cup chopped olive

Directions

Heat butter and oil in saucepan over medium heat. Stir in curry powder until well blended. Add eggs and cook, turning constantly, over low heat for 10 minutes. Remove to plate with slotted spoon, cover and cool, but do not refrigerate.

To serve, mix mayonnaise with chutney. Cut eggs in half. Make a nest of lettuce in salad bowl, add eggs, then pour mayonnaise over them. Sprinkle chopped olives around the mayonnaise.

Serves 4 to 6.

—Donna Jubb

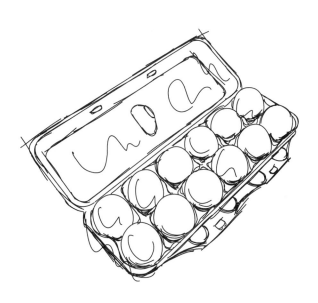

Summer Cheese Soufflé

This soufflé can be assembled up to two days before cooking and serving. It puffs up beautifully while baking and is a very attractive dish, equally delicious for brunch or lunch, or served with ham for dinner.

Ingredients

5 slices crusty Italian bread
butter, softened
¾ lb. sharp Cheddar cheese, grated
4 eggs, beaten
2 cups milk
1 tsp. dry mustard
1 tsp. Worcestershire sauce
½ tsp. curry powder
½ tsp. salt

Directions

Butter each slice of bread lightly on both sides and cut into cubes. Layer bread and cheese in ungreased 1-quart casserole dish. Combine remaining ingredients and pour over bread and cheese. Cover and refrigerate for up to 2 days.

Bake, uncovered, at 350°F for 50 minutes.

Serves 6.

—*Donna Jubb*

Egg & Cheese Puffs

Less tricky to make than a soufflé, these individual egg puffs still rise beautifully.

Ingredients

6 eggs
½ cup light cream
3 Tbsp. flour
1½ tsp. dry mustard
¼ tsp. salt
⅛ tsp. white pepper
1½ cups grated Cheddar cheese

Directions

Combine all ingredients but cheese and beat well. Grease 4 10-oz. soufflé dishes or custard cups well, then sprinkle cheese in them. Pour in egg mixture.

Bake at 350°F for 30 to 35 minutes, or until puffy and golden.

Serves 4.

—*Elaine Darbyshire*

Italian Cheese Loaf

This loaf can be served hot or cold, or it can be cut into 2-inch squares, fried in butter and served with bacon. We served this with Tomato Curry (see page 150) with delicious results.

Ingredients

1 cup dry rice
4 eggs
6 Tbsp. oil
½ tsp. basil
¼ cup minced parsley
1 cup grated sharp Cheddar cheese
salt & pepper

Directions

Cook rice. Beat 3 eggs, add oil and beat well. Add remaining ingredients (except last egg) and cooked rice.

Grease loaf pan. Pour in mixture, spreading it evenly and spread with remaining egg, well beaten. Bake at 350°F for 1 hour.

Serves 6.

—*Donna Jubb*

Egg Casserole

Ingredients

3 cups cubed, cooked ham
½ lb. sharp Cheddar cheese, grated
3 cups cubed rye bread
3 Tbsp. melted butter
3 Tbsp. flour
1 tsp. dry mustard
4 eggs
3 cups milk

Directions

Layer ham, cheese and bread in greased 9" x 13" pan. Drizzle with butter. Combine flour and mustard and sprinkle over mixture in pan. Beat eggs, add milk and mix well. Pour over pan mixture. Refrigerate for 4 to 24 hours.

Bake, uncovered, at 350°F for 1 hour.

Serves 8 to 10.

—Jackie Dysart

Eggs in Nests

Simpler to make than its appearance would lead you to believe, this is a delicious brunch dish.

Ingredients

2 Tbsp. butter
2 Tbsp. flour
½ tsp. salt
pepper
1 cup milk
½ cup grated sharp Cheddar cheese
4 slices toast
4 eggs
cream of tartar
16–20 asparagus spears, steamed

Directions

Melt butter, then stir in flour and cook over low heat for 1 minute. Stir in salt, pepper and milk. Bring to a boil, stirring, and cook until thickened. Stir in cheese. Set aside, keeping warm.

Place toast on cookie sheet. Separate eggs, keeping yolks whole and separate from one another. Beat whites with a pinch of cream of tartar until stiff.

Place 4 or 5 asparagus spears on each slice of toast. Pile egg whites over asparagus, then make a dent in each pile. Drop 1 yolk into each dent.

Bake at 350°F for 8 to 10 minutes, or until meringue edges are golden and yolks are still runny. Serve with cheese sauce.

Serves 4.

—Cary Elizabeth Marshall

Broccoli & Cheese Pie

Crust Ingredients

1 cup grated Cheddar cheese
¾ cup flour
¼ tsp. salt
¼ tsp. dry mustard
¼ cup butter, softened

Filling Ingredients

1½ cups broccoli florets, steamed
1 cup evaporated milk
1 cup chopped onion
1 cup sliced mushrooms
½ tsp. salt
¼ tsp. nutmeg
pepper
3 eggs, lightly beaten

Directions

Combine crust ingredients and press into 9-inch pie plate. Place broccoli in pie plate. Combine milk, onion, mushrooms, salt, nutmeg and pepper in saucepan and simmer for a few minutes. Stir a bit of this into the eggs, then stir eggs into remaining hot mixture. Pour over broccoli.

Bake at 400°F for 15 minutes, reduce heat to 375°F and bake for another 30 to 35 minutes, or until firm. Let stand for 5 minutes before serving.

Serves 4 to 6.

—*Ingrid Magnuson*

French Canadian Onion Cheese Quiche

Crust Ingredients

¾ cup flour
½ tsp. salt
¼ tsp. dry mustard
1 cup grated Cheddar cheese
¼ cup melted butter

Filling Ingredients

2 cups finely chopped onion
2 Tbsp. butter
1 cup cooked noodles
2 eggs
1 cup hot milk
½ tsp. salt
pepper
1 cup grated Cheddar cheese

Directions

For crust: Combine flour, salt, mustard and cheese. Add melted butter and mix well. Pat into bottom and sides of 9-inch pie plate.

For filling: Cook onions in butter until transparent, then add noodles. Mix, then pour into pie plate. Beat together eggs, hot milk, salt, pepper and cheese. Pour over noodles.

Bake at 325°F for 35 to 40 minutes.

Serves 6.

—*Jeannine Bélanger*

Bacon & Egg Pie

Ingredients

Pastry for single 9-inch pie shell
½ lb. bacon
1 tomato
6 eggs
6 Tbsp. milk
salt & pepper
1 cup grated Cheddar cheese

Directions

Line pie plate with pastry. Fry bacon, drain well and place on pastry. Slice tomato over bacon. Beat eggs and milk together. Pour over tomato and bacon. Season with salt and pepper to taste. Top with grated cheese. Bake at 450°F for 45 minutes.

Serves 4.

—*Sheelagh Stone*

Crab & Asparagus Tart

A delicious appetizer, this tart is also suitable for a lunch or supper main dish and can be frozen successfully.

Ingredients

Pastry for single 9-inch pie shell
1 Tbsp. butter
1 Tbsp. flour
½ cup milk
nutmeg
½ cup whipping cream
2 Tbsp. sherry
12 oz. crabmeat
salt & pepper
2 egg yolks
12 stalks asparagus, lightly steamed
¼ cup grated Gruyère cheese

Directions

Line pie plate with pastry and bake at 350°F for 10 minutes.

Melt butter, stir in flour until smooth, then stir in milk and cook until thickened. Add a grating of nutmeg. Remove from heat, stir in cream and sherry. Add crab and salt and pepper. Lightly beat egg yolks, then add to crab mixture and stir gently. Pour into pastry shell. Lay asparagus decoratively on top, then sprinkle with cheese.

Bake at 350°F for 20 minutes.

—*Sandy Campisano*

Soups &
Chowders

Beef Stock

Ingredients

2–3 lbs. beef bones
8 cups water
1 onion, unpeeled
1 carrot, scrubbed & sliced
Celery leaves
2–3 sprigs parsley
5–6 whole peppercorns
3 whole cloves
Several basil leaves (1 tsp. crushed)
1 clove garlic
2 Tbsp. vinegar
2 tsp. salt

Directions

Brown bones slowly in a heavy pot. Add remaining ingredients and simmer, covered, for several hours. Strain broth and cool. Skim fat from top of stock.

—Jan Gilbert

Turkey Stock

Ingredients

1 turkey carcass
1 onion, halved
1 carrot, halved
1–2 celery stalks
2–3 sprigs parsley
5–6 peppercorns
1–2 bay leaves
1 tsp. savory
1 tsp. basil
4 whole cloves
2 tsp. salt
1 Tbsp. vinegar

Directions

Place all ingredients in a large pot and cover with cold water. Cover and simmer for several hours. Strain and chill. Skim fat from top of stock.

—Jan Gilbert

Chicken & Mushroom Soup

Ingredients

¼ cup minced shallots
¼ cup diced celery
¼ cup sliced mushrooms
1½ tsp. butter
6 cups chicken stock
¼ tsp. salt
Pepper
½ cup fine egg noodles
⅓ cup diced chicken
½ tsp. fresh parsley

Directions

Sauté vegetables in butter. Add chicken stock, salt and pepper and cook for 20 minutes.

Cook egg noodles separately in salted water. Drain and rinse well under cold water. Add to soup. Add chicken and parsley.

Serves 6.

—Nicole Chartrand

Chicken Velvet Soup

The cream and milk impart a rich, smooth, velvety texture to this soup.

Ingredients

6 Tbsp. butter
⅓ cup flour
½ cup milk
½ cup light cream
3 cups chicken broth
1 cup finely chopped cooked chicken
Pepper to taste
Parsley & pimento to garnish

Directions

Melt butter in saucepan and blend in flour. Add milk, cream and broth and cook, stirring, until mixture thickens and comes to a boil. Reduce heat.

Stir in chicken and pepper. Heat again to boiling. Serve at once, garnished with parsley and pimento.

Serves 4.

—Pam Collacott

Turkey Noodle Soup

Ingredients

1 turkey carcass
1 onion, finely chopped
Small handful celery leaves, finely chopped
¼ tsp. each of savory, marjoram, thyme, sage
  & curry powder
Salt & pepper
2 tsp. soy sauce
2 cups fine egg noodles
Chopped parsley

Directions

Cover turkey carcass with cold water. Bring to a boil and simmer for several hours. Remove bones and meat from broth and chop meat. Return meat to the broth and chill. Skim off fat.

Reheat broth to boiling, add onion, celery leaves, seasonings and soy sauce. Simmer gently for 3 hours. Add egg noodles half an hour before serving. Top with chopped parsley.

Serves 6 to 8.

—*Ruth Anne Laverty*

Beef Lentil Soup

Ingredients

½ cups raw lentils
2-3 lbs. beef soup bones
2 onions, chopped
3 stalks celery, chopped
¼ lb. spinach, torn into bite¬-sized pieces
3 large tomatoes, chopped
Salt & pepper
Oregano & basil
2 cloves garlic, minced
2-3 bratwurst sausages, chopped

Directions

Soak lentils in water for 2 hours. Brown soup bones, then cover with water and pressure cook for 1 hour. Remove bones and skim fat. Sauté onions, celery, spinach and tomatoes and add to beef and stock. Add lentils, seasoning, garlic and sausages. Simmer for several hours, adding water if necessary.

Serves 6 to 8.

—*D. Parsons*

Hearty Winter Soup

Ingredients

3 lbs. meaty soup bones
10 cups water
2 tsp. salt
3 slices onion
3 peppercorns
¾ lb. ground beef
1 egg
½ cup dry bread crumbs
¼ cup tomato juice
¾ tsp. salt
¼ cup chopped onion
¼ tsp. garlic powder
1 cup egg noodles
15-oz. can tomatoes
2 cups mixed chopped vegetables

Directions

Cover bones with water and add salt, onion and peppercorns. Simmer, covered, for 3 hours. Remove bones and boil to reduce stock to 6 cups.

Meanwhile, combine ground beef, egg, bread crumbs, tomato juice, salt, onion and garlic powder. Shape into small balls and fry until a rich brown color. Drain and set aside.

Cook noodles in salted water and drain.

Add vegetables and tomatoes to stock and cook until just tender. Add noodles and meatballs and boil gently for 15 minutes.

Serves 8.

—Shirley Hill

Habitant Pea Soup

Considered a national dish in Canada, this soup originated in Quebec and is simple, substantial and delicious.

Ingredients

1 lb. split yellow peas
2 qts. water
1 small carrot, grated
1 medium onion, diced
2 tsp. salt
2 sprigs parsley, minced
1 bay leaf
2 thick slices heavily smoked bacon
Pepper

Directions

Soak the peas in water overnight. In the morning, bring to a boil in a large saucepan and add carrot, onion and salt. Reduce heat to simmer.

Add parsley, bay leaf and chopped bacon to the soup and simmer for 3 to 4 hours, until thick, adding additional water as needed.

Remove bay leaf, adjust seasonings and serve.

Serves 6 to 8.

—Cary Elizabeth Marshall

Vegetable Beef Soup

This soup can be stored in the refrigerator and reheated, with additional leftover vegetables, for several days running.

Ingredients

Beef bones
2 cups canned tomatoes or tomato juice
2 onions, chopped
Small handful celery leaves, chopped
3 large potatoes, peeled & diced
6 carrots, diced
2 cups leftover cooked vegetables & gravy
½ cup rice or barley
¼ tsp. each of savory, marjoram, thyme & cumin
1 bay leaf
Salt & pepper
1 tsp. Worcestershire sauce or soy sauce

Directions

Cover bones with cold water and bring to a boil. Simmer for several hours. Remove bones, cut off meat and return meat to stock. Chill and skim off fat. Reheat stock to boiling and add vegetables and seasonings. Simmer until vegetables are tender.

Serves 6 to 8.

—*Ruth Anne Laverty*

Minestrone

Ingredients

1 clove garlic, minced
1 medium onion, chopped
½ cup chopped celery
1 Tbsp. oil
1 cup diced carrots
1 cup shredded cabbage
19-oz. can tomatoes
5 cups beef stock
½ cup chopped parsley
½ tsp. pepper
Salt
1 cup broken spaghetti noodles
1 cup thinly sliced zucchini
2–3 cups cooked kidney beans, undrained
2 cups cooked beef, finely chopped
Grated Parmesan cheese to garnish

Directions

In a heavy pot, sauté garlic, onion and celery in oil. Add carrots, cabbage, tomatoes, stock, parsley, pepper and salt. Cover and simmer for 20 minutes.

Add noodles, zucchini, beans and meat. Simmer 10 minutes longer or until spaghetti and vegetables are cooked. Add more salt if necessary.

Serve topped with freshly grated Parmesan cheese and accompanied by hot crusty bread.

Serves 6.

—*Jan Gilbert*

Bean & Ham Soup

Ingredients

1½ cups dried lima beans
2 lbs. ham, with bone
1 large onion, quartered
1 large clove garlic, crushed
8¾ cups water
1 bouquet garni, consisting of 4 parsley sprigs,
1 spray thyme & 1 bay leaf
½ tsp. white pepper
20 large black olives, cut in half
3 Tbsp. chopped parsley to garnish

Directions

Put the beans in a bowl, cover with water and let soak overnight. Drain and place in a large saucepan with the ham, onion and garlic. Add water, place the pot on high heat and bring to a boil.

Add the bouquet garni and pepper to the pot and stir well. Lower the heat and simmer the soup for 1½ to 2 hours, or until the beans are cooked.

Remove the meat and cut into pieces. Remove the bouquet garni and discard. Purée some of the beans and return to soup to thicken. Stir in the ham pieces and the olives. Taste and add more salt and pepper if necessary. Pour the soup into bowls and garnish with parsley.

Serves 6 to 8.

—Dolores de Rosario

Pea Soup

Ingredients

1 ham bone
1 large onion, chopped
1 rib celery, chopped
1 cup chopped celery leaves
1 carrot, finely diced
1 bay leaf
1 lb. split peas
Salt & pepper
2 sprigs fresh parsley
1 cup sour cream

Directions

Place all ingredients except sour cream in large, heavy pot and cover with cold water. Bring to a boil, lower heat and simmer for several hours, until peas are very soft.

Remove bone and chop meat. Put soup through blender, 2 cups at a time, and return to pot with chopped ham. Add sour cream, stir and heat through.

Serves 12.

—Virginia Mitchell

Navy Bean Soup

Ingredients

2 cups navy beans
6 cups water
1 large onion
1 large stalk celery
2 carrots
Bay leaf
Salt

Directions

Cook beans in water until tender — 45 minutes to 1 hour. Add remaining ingredients and cook until vegetables are tender — 1 to 2 hours.

Serves 6.

—Nel vanGeest

Borscht

Ingredients

6 medium beets
1 medium onion
1 medium potato
1 medium apple
2 carrots
½–1 lb. beef, tenderized & thinly sliced
2 Tbsp. butter
6–8 cups boiling water
½ small cabbage
Salt & pepper
1 tsp. dill weed
½ cup lemon juice
Sour cream to garnish

Directions

Peel vegetables and apple and grate coarsely. Brown meat in oil in large soup pot.

Melt butter, add vegetables except cabbage, and cook, covered, for 1 hour, stirring occasionally.

Add boiling water, cabbage, salt, pepper, dill weed and lemon juice. Cook 15 minutes longer. Adjust seasonings if necessary. Serve with sour cream.

Serves 8.

—Lois Pope

Fresh Tomato Soup

Ingredients

½ cup chopped onion
¼ cup butter
¼ cup flour
1 cup water
6 medium tomatoes, peeled, seeded & diced
1 Tbsp. minced parsley
1¼ tsp. salt
½ tsp. thyme leaves
¼ tsp. pepper
1 bay leaf
Lemon slices to garnish

Directions

In a 3-quart saucepan over medium heat cook onion in butter until tender. Stir in flour until blended. Gradually stir in water.

Add tomatoes and remaining ingredients, except lemon slices, and heat mixture until boiling. Reduce heat to low, cover and simmer for 30 minutes, stirring frequently. Add more water if needed. Discard bay leaf. Serve with lemon slices.

Serves 3 to 4.

—Margaret Godbeer Houle

Tomato & Cheddar Cheese Soup

Ingredients

4 cups finely chopped onions
½ lb. butter
12 cups crushed tomatoes
12 cups water
18 cups grated Cheddar cheese
12 cups sour cream

Directions

Sauté onions in butter until soft. Add tomatoes, water and cheese and cook, stirring, until cheese is mostly melted.

Stir in sour cream.

Serves 50 to 70.

—Terry Shoffner

Spinach Soup

Ingredients

4 cups chicken stock
¾ lb. spinach
Hard-boiled eggs & sour cream to garnish

Directions

Bring stock to a boil. Wash spinach and tear into bite-sized pieces. Add to boiling stock and simmer briefly.

Place in individual bowls and garnish with sour cream and hard-boiled eggs.

Serves 4.

—Carole Peterson

Mushroom Barley Soup

Ingredients

½ cup raw barley
4 cups vegetable or chicken stock
½ cup chopped celery
½ cup diced carrots
3 Tbsp. butter
1 clove garlic
1 cup chopped mushrooms
½ cup chopped onion
Salt

Directions

Cook barley in stock over low heat for 45 minutes or until barley is tender.

Meanwhile, sauté celery and carrots in butter with garlic. After 10 minutes add mushrooms and onion. Cook until onion is soft. Remove garlic.

Add vegetables to barley and stock and cook for 5 minutes.

Serves 4.

—Debbi Walsh

Sherried Wild Rice Soup

Ingredients

2 Tbsp. butter
1 Tbsp.–½ cup minced onion
¼ cup flour
4–5 cups chicken stock
1–2 cups cooked wild rice
½ tsp. salt
1 cup light cream
¼ cup dry sherry
Parsley or chives, minced

Directions

Melt butter in saucepan, add onion and cook until onion is golden. Blend in flour and stock, stirring constantly until thickened. Stir in rice and salt and simmer 5 minutes.

Blend in cream and sherry and simmer until well heated. Garnish with minced parsley or chives.

Makes 6 cups.

—Anne Ulmer

Miso Soup

Ingredients

2 carrots
2 onions
Oil for frying
4 cups water
1 strip kombu (seaweed), chopped & soaked until soft
4 Tbsp. miso

Directions

Chop carrots and onions and fry in oil. Bring water to a boil, add vegetables and seaweed and simmer for 20 to 30 minutes.

Remove from heat and add miso. Stir.

Serves 4.

—Terry Bethune

Manhattan Clam Chowder

Ingredients

¼ cup chopped onion
2 Tbsp. butter
1 cup diced potato
¼ cup chopped celery
2 cups boiling water
1 cup canned tomatoes
1 tsp. salt
Pepper
¼ tsp. thyme
1 cup chopped clams
1 cup clam liquor

Directions

Brown onion in butter. Add potato, celery and boiling water and cook for 10 minutes or until potato is tender.

Add remaining ingredients and simmer for 20 minutes.

Serves 4 to 6.

—Delia Schlesinger

Fish Chowder

Ingredients

2 slices bacon
1 medium onion, chopped
¼ green pepper, chopped
1 medium potato, peeled & sliced
½ pkg. frozen cod fillets, thawed
1 cup water
1 tsp. salt
1 bay leaf
⅛ tsp. basil, thyme or fennel
3 Tbsp. flour
1 cup milk
1 cup table cream

Directions

Fry bacon in large heavy saucepan until crisp. Lift out and crumble. Turn heat to low and fry onion and green pepper for 2 minutes. Drain and reserve bacon fat. Put potato, fish, water and seasonings in pot, bring to a boil and simmer gently, covered, for 10 minutes.

Remove fish, separate into large chunks and return to the pot. Blend together 3 Tbsp. reserved bacon fat, flour and milk. Add to pot, discarding bay leaf. Add cream and bacon bits. Reheat, without boiling, and stir gently as it thickens.

Serves 4 to 6.

—Joan Graham

Cream of Cauliflower Soup

Ingredients

½ cup butter
1 onion, finely chopped
2 stalks celery, finely chopped
1 apple, peeled & finely chopped
1 tsp. curry powder
¼ cup flour
4 cups chicken stock
1 small head cauliflower, cut into
    small flowerettes
1 egg yolk, lightly beaten
1 cup light cream
Salt & pepper
2 Tbsp. parsley, to garnish

Directions

Melt butter and sauté onions, celery and apple. Sprinkle with curry powder and flour. Cook, stirring, for 2 more minutes.

Gradually stir in stock. Bring to a boil and add the cauliflower. Cook, covered, for 10 minutes. Combine egg yolk and cream and gradually stir into mixture. Heat but do not boil.

Sprinkle each serving with parsley.

Serves 4.

—Olga Harrison

Leek & Potato Soup

This is a hearty variation of the cold soup, vichyssoise. It can be blended immediately before serving for a smoother texture.

Ingredients

1 slice bacon
1 oz. butter
1 lb. potatoes
2 large leeks
1½ cups chicken stock
Salt & pepper
½ cup milk
½ cup grated cheese
Parsley

Directions

Cut up the bacon and fry in butter. Peel and cut potatoes, and clean and cut up leeks. Add to the saucepan and fry for 5 minutes. Stir in stock, add salt and pepper to taste. Cover and simmer for 30 minutes until the vegetables are tender. Add milk and reheat but do not boil. If desired, blend for a few seconds. Serve with grated cheese and parsley.

Serves 4.

—Mary Rogers

Potato Soup

Ingredients

5 medium potatoes
Garlic salt
½ small onion, chopped
Celery salt
2 Tbsp. butter
¼ cup flour
3 cups milk

Directions

Peel and wash potatoes and cut into 1-inch pieces. Cover with water and bring to a boil. Add garlic salt, onion and celery salt and cook until potatoes are tender.

Remove from heat; do not drain. Mash well. Cover with a lid and set aside.

Melt butter in a small saucepan and slowly add flour to make a fine paste. Remove from heat.

Return potatoes to heat and add flour paste a little at a time. Bring to a boil, stirring constantly. Add milk slowly, stirring to avoid scorching, and cook until thoroughly heated.

Serves 4.

—Deborah Exner

Cheesy Onion & Potato Soup

Ingredients

3 medium onions, chopped
2 Tbsp. butter
4 medium potatoes, peeled & cubed
2 cups chicken stock
¼ tsp. salt
Pepper
3 cups milk
1 cup shredded Cheddar cheese

Directions

Cook onions in butter until soft but not brown. Add potatoes, stock, salt and pepper. Cover, bring to a boil, then simmer until potatoes are tender, about 15 minutes.

Remove from heat and blend in parts in blender or food processor. Return to saucepan, add milk and cheese and reheat slowly until cheese melts. Do not boil.

Makes 6 servings.

—Christine Steele

Springtime Soup

This soup is a wonderful way to serve fresh, young vegetables —their delicate flavors are preserved by the short cooking time. Vegetables may be varied according to season.

Ingredients

1 cup chopped green onions
1 cup chopped baby beets & tops
1 cup chopped new carrots & tops
1 cup chopped new potatoes
1 cup edible podded peas
1 cup sliced green beans
6 cups goat's milk (light cream may be substituted)
Salt

Directions

Cook vegetables until tender in just enough water to prevent scorching. Add milk or cream and salt to taste. Heat to serving temperature, but do not boil.

—Harvey Lyons

Won Ton Soup

Ingredients

2 water chestnuts, finely chopped
½ lb. ground pork
1 lb. won ton wrappers
6 cups chicken stock
1 small head chard or spinach, chopped
Chopped green onion to garnish

Directions

Mix water chestnuts with ground pork.

Place a small amount of the meat on one corner of each won ton wrapper. Fold up meat and roll toward the center. Shape into a crescent. Boil the won ton in batches in boiling water and drain. Combine chicken stock and chard or spinach. Add won ton and heat thoroughly.

Serve sprinkled with green onion.

Serves 6.

—Bryanna Clark

Mushroom Soup

Ingredients

½ cup butter
¼ cup chopped onion
½ lb. mushrooms, chopped
¼ cup flour
1 tsp. salt
Pepper
1 cup chicken broth
3 cups milk
1 Tbsp. lemon juice
Parsley

Directions

Sauté onions in butter until tender. Remove and set aside. Sauté mushrooms until soft — about 10 minutes. Blend in flour, salt and pepper and gradually stir in broth and milk. Cook until mixture thickens and comes to a boil.

Add onions, lemon juice, salt and pepper and simmer 10 minutes. Serve with sprinkle of parsley.

Serves 6.

—Mary VanderSchaaf

Squash Blossom Soup

This soup provides a tasty way to thin out the garden in late July when the squash looks as though it is going to overrun everything else.

Ingredients

3 Tbsp. butter
⅔ cup minced onion
36 squash blossoms, stems discarded & coarsely chopped
3 cups chicken stock
1 cup light cream
1 egg yolk
Salt, pepper & nutmeg

Directions

Melt butter in heavy saucepan over medium heat. Add onion and sauté until soft. Stir in blossoms and soften.

Add stock and bring to a boil, reduce heat, cover and simmer for 10 minutes.

Beat cream with egg yolk, then stir in a small amount of hot stock. Slowly add this mixture to the rest of the soup, stirring constantly. Heat through and season to taste.

Serves 3 to 4.

—Ingrid Birker

Avoglimono

This Greek lemon soup has a smooth texture and is simple to assemble.

Ingredients

2 eggs
1 lemon
6 cups chicken stock
Salt
4 slices lemon to garnish

Directions

Beat eggs until frothy. Squeeze juice from lemon into the eggs, drop by drop, beating the whole time.

Heat chicken stock and stir in the lemon and eggs, adding salt to taste. Beat while heating for 1 minute.

Serve each bowl with a thin slice of lemon floating on top.

Serves 4.

—Cary Elizabeth Marshall

Hungarian Soup

Ingredients

3-4 medium potatoes
3 Tbsp. butter
2 Tbsp. flour
1 large tsp. Hungarian paprika
1-2 carrots, chopped
½ onion, chopped
1 small tomato, minced
1½ cups cubed turnip
Salt
8 cups water
1 cup spaghetti, broken into 1-inch lengths

Directions

Peel potatoes, cut into small cubes and reserve in cold water. Melt butter in large pot and add flour, stirring until golden brown. Add paprika, potatoes, carrots, onion, tomato, turnip and salt. Add water.

Simmer, covered, until vegetables are partially done. Add spaghetti and cook until tender.

Serves 6.

—Darlene Abraham

Cold Yogurt Cucumber Soup

Ingredients

2 medium-sized cucumbers
Olive oil
½ tsp. salt
1 tsp. minced garlic
2 Tbsp. chopped fresh dill
Pepper
2 cups yogurt
1 cup iced water
⅓ cup chopped walnuts or almonds

Directions

Peel cucumbers if necessary. Cut in quarters lengthwise, then slice. Toss with a little olive oil to glaze them lightly. Add salt, garlic, dill and pepper to taste.

Chill for 1 to 3 hours. Drain and combine with yogurt, iced water and nuts. Check seasoning and serve very cold.

Serves 4.

—N. Burk

Cold Cucumber Soup

Ingredients

2 Tbsp. butter
¼ cup chopped onion
2 cups diced, peeled cucumber
½ cup chopped celery leaves
1½ cups basic white sauce, page 129
1 large potato, cooked, peeled & finely diced
Salt & pepper
¼ tsp. dry mustard
¾ cup water
Parsley to garnish

Directions

Melt butter, add onion and cook until transparent. Add cucumber, celery leaves, white sauce, potato, salt, pepper, mustard and water. Bring to a boil, reduce heat and cook for 10 minutes.

Blend in a blender for 40 seconds. Chill for several hours. Serve garnished with parsley.

Serves 4 to 6.

—Shirley Hill

Fruit Moos

Frozen or dried fruits are as good in this soup as fresh ones. If you are using dried fruit, soften it first in water or juice.

Ingredients

1 cup plums
1 cup peaches
1 cup rhubarb
1 cup cherries, pitted
Water
1 cup sugar
3 Tbsp. flour

Directions

Slice plums and peaches and chop rhubarb into 1-inch pieces. Place in saucepan with cherries and water to cover. Cook until tender. Remove fruit.

Combine sugar and flour and blend with enough water to make a thick paste. Stir into the water in saucepan and cook, stirring, over low heat until the mixture resembles a white sauce.

Add fruit and heat through. Taste and add sugar if a sweeter soup is desired.

Serve with heavy sweet cream.

Serves 4 to 6.

—Valerie Lanctôt

Mushroom Potato Soup

Ingredients

½ lb. mushrooms, chopped
1 medium onion, minced
1 Tbsp. butter
5 cups water
2 potatoes, peeled & cubed
2 tsp. soy sauce
Worcestershire sauce
1 Tbsp. lemon juice
1 tsp. salt
Pepper
½ Tbsp. cornstarch
⅛ tsp. nutmeg
Chopped chives

Directions

In a Dutch oven, cook mushrooms and onion in butter for about 5 minutes. Stir in water and bring to a boil. Add potatoes, soy sauce, Worcestershire sauce, lemon juice, salt and pepper. Cover and simmer for about 45 minutes. Add cornstarch (in a paste made by adding a small amount of cold water) and stir until mixture thickens slightly. Top with nutmeg and chopped chives.

Serves 8.

—Anne Ulmer

Mushroom Leek Soup

Ingredients

2 bunches leeks
½ cup butter
½ lb. mushrooms, chopped or sliced
¼ cup flour
1 tsp. salt
Cayenne
1 cup chicken stock
3 cups milk
1 Tbsp. dry sherry
Salt & pepper

Directions

Wash leeks well; slice and use white part only. In ¼ cup butter, sauté leeks until tender but not browned. Remove and set aside. In remaining butter, sauté mushrooms until soft — about 10 minutes. Blend in flour, salt and cayenne. Gradually stir in stock and milk. Cook, stirring, until mixture thickens and comes to a boil. Add leeks, sherry and salt and pepper to taste. Simmer for 10 minutes.

Serves 4.

—Vanessa Lewington

Onion Soup

Ingredients

4-6 large onions
3-4 Tbsp. butter
4-5 cups chicken stock
¼ tsp. thyme
2 egg yolks, beaten with a little water

Directions

Halve onions and slice thinly. Sauté in butter until golden. Add stock and thyme, bring to a boil and cook for 15 minutes.

Blend about three-quarters of the soup in blender and return it to soup pot. Bring back to a boil and stir in egg yolks. Serve.

Serves 4.

—Gabriele Klein

Noel's Soup

Ingredients

1 cup finely chopped zucchini
1 cup finely chopped celery
¼ cup finely chopped green pepper
48-oz. can tomato juice
2 cups chicken or beef stock
1 small onion, chopped
Oregano
Salt & pepper

Directions

In a large pot, lightly sauté the zucchini, celery and green pepper. Add juice, stock and onion. Season with oregano, salt and pepper and simmer for 20 minutes.

Serves 4 to 6.

—Patricia Daine

Parsley Soup

Ingredients

4 cups chicken stock
2 cups firmly packed, chopped parsley
½ cup chopped onion
½ tsp. salt
Pepper
1 cup milk
2 cups peeled & diced potatoes
2 Tbsp. butter
¼ cup flour
1 Tbsp. dry sherry
Parsley

Directions

Place chicken stock, parsley, onion, salt and pepper in heavy saucepan. Bring to a boil, reduce heat and simmer, covered, for 30 minutes. Strain and reserve stock.

Place milk and potatoes in small saucepan, cover and cook over medium heat until potatoes are tender — about 15 minutes. Set aside.

Melt butter, stir in flour and cook over low heat, stirring constantly, until smooth and bubbly. Slowly stir in stock, heat to boiling and cook, continuing to stir, until slightly thickened — about 2 minutes. Reduce heat. Add potato mixture and sherry and heat through. Garnish with parsley.

Serves 4.

—Pam Collacott

Zucchini Soup

There can never be too many zucchini recipes for those who garden. This soup can be made from either freshly harvested or frozen zucchini. The addition of cream cheese makes the flavor irresistible.

Ingredients

1 large onion, sliced
1 clove garlic, crushed
4 Tbsp. butter
4 medium zucchini, chopped
1 tsp. basil
½ tsp. oregano
4 cups chicken stock
4 oz. cream cheese
Salt & pepper

Directions

Sauté onion and garlic in butter for 5 minutes. Add zucchini and herbs and cook over low heat for 5 minutes. Stir in chicken stock and heat through. Blend with cream cheese until smooth. Return to pot, add salt and pepper and heat.

Serves 4.

—Sharon Sims

Strawberry Soup

Ingredients

2 pints strawberries
2 cups yogurt
½ cup orange juice
½ cup sugar
½ cup water
⅛ tsp. cardamom

Directions

Combine all ingredients and mix well in blender. Chill and serve.

Serves 4 to 6.

—M. Cummings

Rhubarb Soup

In Finland, as in other Scandinavian countries, fruit soup is popular and may be served either as a dessert or at the beginning of a meal.

Ingredients

2 lbs. red rhubarb
8 cups water
1 stick cinnamon
2 slices lemon
½ cup sugar
2 Tbsp. cornstarch
⅓ cup cold water
1 egg yolk, beaten
½ cup heavy cream, whipped

Directions

Cut rhubarb into 1-inch pieces and cook in 8 cups water until tender. Drain liquid through sieve, discarding pulp. Return juice to saucepan and cook with cinnamon and lemon for 5 minutes. Add sugar.

Mix cornstarch with ⅓ cup water and stir into hot juice. Cook, stirring constantly, for 5 minutes. Remove cinnamon and lemon.

Just before serving, combine beaten egg yolk with whipped cream and stir into hot soup.

Serves 8 to 10.

—*Ingrid Birker*

Chicken Curry Soup

Ingredients

3 lbs. chicken
10 cups water
½ cup butter
1 onion, chopped
1 Tbsp. flour
1 Tbsp. curry powder
26-oz. can tomatoes
1 green pepper, diced
1 lb. carrots, diced
2 apples, diced
2 stalks celery, diced
1 tsp. mace
½ tsp. pepper
¼ cup rice

Directions

Cook chicken in water until tender — about 2 hours. Remove chicken from stock and set stock aside. Debone chicken, fry in butter and return to stock. Brown onion in remaining butter.

Combine flour and curry powder, adding a little water to form a paste. Add to onion and mix well.

Stir remaining ingredients into onion mixture, then add stock and chicken. Bring to a boil, reduce heat and simmer until vegetables are tender and rice is cooked.

Serves 8.

—*Kathryn MacDonald*

Hearty Meatball Soup

Ingredients

2 Tbsp. oil
1 medium onion, chopped
1 stalk celery with top, chopped
28-oz. can tomatoes
2 cups beef stock
1 lb. ground beef
1 egg
Grated Parmesan cheese
Salt & pepper
½ cup elbow macaroni
Chopped fresh parsley

Directions

Heat oil in large saucepan and sauté onion and celery for 5 minutes, or until tender. Add tomatoes and stock and cook over medium heat until mixture comes to a boil. Reduce heat and simmer.

Meanwhile, combine beef, egg, 1 Tbsp. Parmesan cheese, 1 tsp. salt, and pepper to taste. Shape into small (about 1-inch) meatballs and fry until browned. Drain off fat and drop into soup. Cover and simmer for about half an hour. Add macaroni, cover and simmer for 20 minutes longer, or until macaroni is tender.

To serve, sprinkle with Parmesan cheese and chopped parsley.

Serves 6.

—*Judith Asbil*

Meal in a Soup

Ingredients

1 lb. ground beef
2 medium onions, sliced
3 stalks celery, sliced
2 large carrots, sliced
1 medium potato, diced
1 parsnip, diced
1½ cups cauliflower florets
9-oz. can tomatoes
½ tsp. salt
⅛ tsp. pepper
½ tsp. basil
¼ tsp. rosemary
½ tsp. thyme
½ tsp. sage
6 cups water
1 cup macaroni

Directions

Brown ground beef and drain well. Add remaining ingredients except macaroni. Cover and bring to a boil. Reduce heat and simmer for 30 minutes.

Add macaroni about 7 to 10 minutes before end of cooking time.

Serves 4 to 6.

—*Susan Ching*

Beef Lentil Soup

Ingredients

1 lb. ground beef
1 medium onion, chopped
1 clove garlic, finely chopped
1 cup chopped mushrooms
28-oz. can tomatoes
1 medium stalk celery, sliced
1 large carrot, sliced
1 cup dried green lentils
3 cups beef stock
¼ cup red wine
1 bay leaf
2 Tbsp. snipped parsley
2 tsp. sea salt
¼ tsp. pepper

Directions

Cook and stir ground beef, onion and garlic in large pot until beef is light brown; drain. Stir in remaining ingredients. Heat to boiling, then reduce heat. Cover and simmer, stirring occasionally until lentils are tender — about 40 minutes.

Serves 4 to 6.

—Lois Verfaillie

Lamb & Lentil Soup

Ingredients

1 cup dried lentils
1½ lbs. lamb shoulder, trimmed of fat & diced
2 Tbsp. vegetable oil
1 large onion, chopped
1 small turnip, peeled & diced
2 carrots, peeled & diced
6 cups beef broth
Salt & pepper

Directions

Rinse lentils in cold water, place in bowl and cover with fresh, cold water. Soak for 2 hours, then drain.

In a pot, cook the lamb in oil over medium heat until evenly browned. Add the onion and cook until soft. Stir in the drained lentils, turnip, carrots, broth and salt and pepper.

Simmer, stirring frequently, for 3 hours, or until the lamb is fork-tender. Adjust seasonings.

Serves 6.

—Janet Ueberschlag

Beef & Barley Soup

Ingredients

2 cups stewing beef, browned
9 cups cold water
1 cup tomato juice
1 cup raw barley
½ cup finely chopped onion
½ cup carrots, cut in very thin strips
3 beef bouillon cubes (optional)
1 tsp. salt
⅓ cup finely chopped celery

Directions

Combine all ingredients in large pot and simmer, covered, for 3 hours or until barley is tender. Taste for salt and adjust if necessary.

—Wendy Neelin

Leek & Lentil Soup

Ingredients

2 Tbsp. butter
2 Tbsp. oil
2 large leeks, chopped
1 medium onion, chopped
1 clove garlic, minced
1 cup lentils, washed
¼ cup pot barley
6 cups chicken stock
1 large carrot, sliced
1 large potato, chopped
1 stalk celery, chopped
2 cups canned tomatoes, chopped
Thyme
1 bay leaf, crumbled
Salt & pepper
Chopped parsley

Directions

In a big, heavy soup pot, melt the butter and oil. Add leeks, onion and garlic. Cook for a few minutes to soften.

Add lentils, barley and stock. Bring to a boil, then cover and simmer for about half an hour.

Add vegetables and seasonings. Cover and simmer about an hour longer, or until the vegetables are tender. Add parsley during last few minutes. Season to taste.

Serves 12.

—Sylvia Petz

Indian Lentil Soup

This soup makes an excellent accompaniment to a curry, and is delicious topped with a spoonful of yogurt. For a hearty lunch, serve this soup with warmed pita bread.

Ingredients

2 cups lentils
8 cups chicken or vegetable stock
1 onion, chopped
1 stalk celery, chopped
1 carrot, shredded
1 tsp. salt
¼ tsp. pepper
1 tsp. curry
½ tsp. cumin
½ tsp. coriander
¼ tsp. turmeric
¼ tsp. garlic powder

Directions

Put lentils in soup pot, cover with stock and bring to a boil. Add vegetables. Lower heat to simmer and add all spices. Simmer until lentils are soft, and soup is thickened with dissolved lentils — about 1 hour.

Serves 8.

—Marcy Goldman-Posluns

Bean Soup

Ingredients

3 cups dry white pea beans
10 slices bacon
3 cups chopped onion
1½ cups diced celery
10 cups liquid (use bean stock, adding water if necessary)
1 Tbsp. salt
1 tsp. pepper
2½ quarts milk
¼ cup chopped parsley
1½ cups grated carrot or other vegetable

Directions

Soak beans. For each cup of beans, add 2½ to 3 cups of water. Let stand for 12 hours, or overnight. Or, for a quick soak, slowly bring to a boil and cook gently for 2 minutes. Remove from heat and let stand 1 hour. Drain beans, reserving liquid.

Fry bacon until crisp, then drain. Sauté onion and celery in bacon fat until onion is transparent. Add bean liquid, beans and seasonings. Cover and cook until beans are tender and water is almost absorbed, about 2 hours. Add milk, parsley and carrot and bring to a boil. Sprinkle with crumbled bacon and serve.

Serves 16.

—Nancy Willard

Austrian Cream Cheese Soup

Ingredients

6 Tbsp. butter
6 medium leeks, finely chopped
4 celery stalks, finely chopped
6 Tbsp. flour
8 cups chicken stock
1 tsp. salt
1 lb. cream cheese, at room temperature
2 cups yogurt, at room temperature
4 egg yolks, beaten
White pepper
Parsley, chopped

Directions

Melt butter in heavy soup pot and sauté leeks and celery until limp. Stir in flour and cook, stirring, for 2 to 3 minutes. Add stock and salt, bring to a boil and simmer for 15 minutes.

Whisk cream cheese, yogurt and egg yolks until smooth. Add 2 cups of soup to cheese mixture, blend thoroughly and return to the pot. Stir until smooth and heat through, but do not boil. Sprinkle with pepper and parsley.

Serves 10.

—Charlene Skidmore

Souppa Fakki

This thick Greek bean soup served with fresh baked rolls and a salad can take the chill out of a cold winter's day.

Ingredients

1 lb. brown lentils
1 medium onion, coarsely chopped
2 stalks celery with tops, chopped
2 cloves garlic, minced
½ cup olive oil
3 Tbsp. tomato paste
1 Tbsp. wine vinegar
Salt & pepper

Directions

Put lentils in a 2-quart saucepan and cover with water 2 inches above lentils. Add onion, celery, garlic, olive oil, tomato paste and pepper. Cover, bring to a boil, reduce heat and cook slowly over medium heat for 30 minutes.

Check occasionally and add more water if needed. Soup should be thick. Just before serving, add vinegar and salt to taste.

Serves 4.

—Jan Post

Broccoli Garbanzo Soup

Ingredients

¼ cup butter
¼ cup flour
1 tsp. salt
⅛ tsp. pepper
2 tsp. turmeric
4 cups milk
1 cup cream
2 cups broccoli, steamed & cut into ½-inch pieces
1½ cups cooked garbanzo beans, drained

Directions

Melt butter in 3-quart saucepan. Stir in flour, salt, pepper and turmeric. Cook slowly until mixture is smooth and bubbly. Using a wire whisk, gradually stir in the milk. Bring to a boil, stirring constantly, and cook for 1 minute. Add the cream, broccoli and garbanzo beans and heat through gently.

Serves 4.

—Kristine Reid

Pork Hock & Lima Bean Soup

Ingredients

1 lb. dry baby lima beans
2 pig's feet or pork hocks
2 bay leaves
1 Tbsp. salt
4 onions, coarsely chopped
Several stalks celery, chopped

Directions

Soak beans overnight in water to cover. Drain and combine with remaining ingredients, add water and cook until the beans are tender and meat falls away from the bones.

Serves 6.

—V. Alice Hughes

Creamy Cauliflower Soup

The addition of Worcestershire sauce to this recipe gives the soup a pleasant bite. For those wishing a milder flavor, it could be omitted.

Ingredients

1 head cauliflower, cut into bite-sized pieces
¼ cup butter
1 medium onion, chopped
2 Tbsp. flour
2 cups chicken stock
2 cups milk or cream
½ tsp. Worcestershire sauce
¾ tsp. salt
1 cup grated Cheddar cheese

Directions

Cook cauliflower in about 1 cup water. Drain and reserve liquid. Set cauliflower aside. Melt butter, add onion and cook until soft.

Blend in flour, add stock and bring to a boil, stirring well. Stir in 1 cup cauliflower liquid, milk, Worcestershire sauce and salt. Add cauliflower and cheese and heat through.

Serves 6.

—Ann Kostendt

Cream of Leek Soup

The leek is considered by many to be king of the soup onions. Because of their growing method, it is essential to wash leeks extremely carefully to rid them of all the trapped dirt.

Ingredients

5 large leeks
¼ cup butter
Salt & pepper
3 cups milk
1 Tbsp. flour
2–3 egg yolks, beaten

Directions

Wash and cut up leeks and cook in butter in heavy pan until soft but not browned. Add water to cover and salt and pepper. Simmer for 15 minutes. Blend well. Add milk and flour and bring to a boil. Just before serving, add egg yolks, beating the soup well as you add the yolks.

Serves 4.

—Annick Hardie

Mushroom Bisque

Ingredients

4 cups chicken stock
½ lb. mushrooms, chopped
1 onion, minced
¼ cup butter
¼ cup flour
1 cup milk
1 tsp. thyme
Salt & pepper

Directions

Combine stock, mushrooms and onion and simmer for 20 minutes.

In another pot, melt butter and stir in flour. When smooth, gradually add milk, stirring constantly, and cook until thick. Gradually stir into soup. Add seasonings.

Serves 4.

—*Billie Sheffield*

Vegetable Chowder

Ingredients

3 slices bacon, diced
½ cup chopped onion
1 cup creamed corn
1 cup chopped green beans
1 cup tomatoes
½ tsp. salt
¼ tsp. pepper
4 cups hot milk

Directions

Fry bacon in a large saucepan, add onion and sauté until tender. Add remaining ingredients and heat to almost boiling, stirring constantly.

Serves 4.

—*Vicki deBoer*

Legume Grain Soup

Ingredients

2 cups split peas
¼ cup brown rice
¼ cup pot barley
4 Tbsp. oil
1 medium onion, chopped
3–5 cloves garlic, crushed
2 stalks celery, chopped
½ green pepper, chopped
2 pork hocks
1 Tbsp. dried parsley
1 Tbsp. tamari sauce
1½ tsp. salt
⅛ tsp. pepper
Few drops Worcestershire sauce

Directions

Bring 4 cups water to a boil. Add split peas, rice and barley; cover and simmer.

Meanwhile, in a large soup pot, heat oil. Sauté onion, garlic, celery, green pepper and pork hocks for 10 minutes. Add 10 cups hot water, split pea mixture and remaining ingredients. Simmer, covered, for 1½ to 2 hours, stirring occasionally.

Remove meat and bones from soup, discard bones, chop meat and return to pot.

Serves 12.

—*John Osborne*

Ham & Potato Chowder

Ingredients

1 large onion, chopped
3 Tbsp. butter
½ cup water
6 medium potatoes, cut in ½-inch cubes
4 Tbsp. flour blended with
½ cup milk
3½ cups milk
2 cups cubed, cooked ham
1 tsp. salt
½ tsp. thyme
¼ tsp. pepper

Directions

Sauté onion in butter until tender. Stir in water and potatoes, cover and cook for 10 to 15 minutes. Stir in flour-milk mixture. Add milk, ham, salt, thyme and pepper and stir well.

Cover and cook for 5 to 10 minutes, or until potatoes are tender and soup is hot.

Serves 6.

—Janice Chammartin

Dilled Tomato Soup

This soup can be made equally successfully with canned or frozen tomatoes as with fresh. The dill, however, must be fresh — this is what gives the soup its delicious, definitive flavor.

Ingredients

10 large ripe tomatoes
1 large onion
2 cloves garlic, minced
3 Tbsp. butter
5 Tbsp. flour
2 tsp. tomato paste
5 cups chicken stock
1 cup whipping cream
4 Tbsp. dill weed
Salt & pepper

Directions

Coarsely chop 8 tomatoes without removing skins. Chop onion and sauté with garlic and 4 of the tomatoes in butter for 3 minutes. Remove from heat. Blend in flour, tomato paste and stock and bring to a boil. Lower heat, add 4 tomatoes and simmer for 15 minutes. Add cream.

Peel and chop remaining 2 tomatoes and add to soup with dill, salt and pepper. Heat through, stirring well so cream does not curdle.

Serves 8.

—Ingrid Birker

Seafood Chowder

Ingredients

½ lb. fresh halibut or cod
½ lb. fresh salmon
½ lb. fresh crabmeat
Lobster meat
Clams
2–3 Tbsp. butter
1 onion, finely chopped
2–3 stalks celery, chopped
Celery leaves, finely chopped
1 small clove garlic, minced
3–4 potatoes, peeled & diced
2 large carrots, sliced
1 bay leaf
2 cups milk or cream
2 Tbsp. cornstarch
1 tsp. salt
¼ cup butter

Directions

Chop and combine halibut, salmon and crabmeat, adding lobster and clams to taste. Set aside.

Melt butter in large, heavy pot and sauté onion, celery, celery leaves and garlic until tender. Add potatoes, carrots and bay leaf and cover with water. Cover and simmer until vegetables are tender but crisp — 15 to 20 minutes.

Add fish mixture and continue to simmer until fish is flaky. Combine milk and cornstarch and stir into soup. Add salt and butter. Simmer until thoroughly heated.

Serves 4.

—*Donna Parker*

Ol' Magic Tomato Soup

Ingredients

28-oz. can tomatoes
1 onion
1 bay leaf
2 cloves
¼ tsp. baking soda
½ tsp. sugar
2 Tbsp. butter
2 Tbsp. flour
1 quart milk, heated
½ tsp. salt
¼ tsp. paprika

Directions

Put tomatoes, onion, bay leaf and cloves in saucepan and cook for 10 minutes. Purée and strain. Add soda and sugar.

Melt butter and add flour. Cook for 2 minutes. Add hot milk. Season with salt and paprika. Mix this cream sauce into the tomato mixture and serve immediately.

Serves 6.

—*Vera Fader*

Beet Vegetable Soup

"An exceptionally pretty soup—pink with lots of colorful vegetables. Garnish with fresh dill," says our Vermont tester.

Ingredients

1 cup cubed potatoes
1 cup cubed carrots
1 cup cubed beets
¼ tsp. salt
Pepper
1 cup sour cream

Directions

Cook potatoes, carrots and beets in 1 cup water until just done. Add salt and pepper, remove from heat and stir in sour cream.

Serves 4.

—Deborah Elmer

Beef Soup

Ingredients

2 Tbsp. butter
Beef bones
1½ cups chopped beef scraps
1 large onion, chopped
½ tsp. celery seed
6 cups water
Salt & pepper
Chopped vegetables

Directions

Melt butter in heavy pot. Add bones, chopped beef, onion and celery seed. Fry, stirring, until browned. Add water and salt and pepper.

Simmer, covered, for 2 to 3 hours. Remove bones. Add chopped vegetables.

Serves 4 to 6.

—Velma Hughes

Spicy Halibut Soup

The use of a whole, dried cayenne pepper gives this dish its distinctive hot flavor. The amount of pepper used can be varied to suit individual tastes.

Ingredients

1 cup diced onion
Butter
6 cups chicken stock
1 dried red cayenne pepper, broken into pieces
½ lb. halibut, cut in small chunks
2 Tbsp. flour
½ tsp. basil
½ tsp. chervil
Thyme

Directions

Sauté onion in butter until transparent. Add chicken stock and cayenne and bring to a boil. Add halibut, lower heat and simmer for 10 minutes.

Mix the flour with a small amount of the soup stock and then gradually stir the flour mixture into the soup. Add spices.

Serves 4.

—Nancy Newsom

Fresh Pea Soup

Soup Ingredients

4 cups peas
5 Tbsp. oil
1 tsp. salt
1 cup chopped celery heart
1 bunch parsley
2 Tbsp. flour
1 Tbsp. sweet paprika
1 tsp. pepper

Noodle Ingredients

1 egg
1 cup flour

Directions

Braise peas in 3 Tbsp. oil, stirring gently, for 5 minutes. Add salt, celery heart, parsley and 4 cups water. Cover and cook over low heat for 20 minutes, or until peas are tender.

Meanwhile, in small pot, heat remaining 2 Tbsp. oil. Stir in flour, paprika and pepper and cook gently for 2 minutes. Slowly add 1 cup water. When thickened, stir into soup and boil for 5 minutes.

Prepare noodles: Mix egg and ¼ cup cold water, adding enough flour to make a very soft dough.

Remove cover from soup, and drizzle dough into soup with a fork. Cook for 5 to 10 minutes.

Serves 4 to 6.

—Julie Herr

Lebanese Soup

This is a tasty cold soup to serve on hot summer days, when mint is plentiful in the garden.

Ingredients

**½ English cucumber, seeds removed, cut into
    small pieces**
3 cups plain yogurt
6 cups chicken stock
4 cloves garlic, minced
4 Tbsp. finely chopped mint leaves
Salt & pepper
1 ripe avocado

Directions

Salt the cucumber pieces lightly and let stand, refrigerated, for a few hours. Rinse and drain.

Combine yogurt with the stock; add cucumber, garlic and mint. Add salt and pepper to taste. Refrigerate until thoroughly chilled.

Immediately before serving, peel an avocado, cut it into small pieces and add to the soup. Serve cold.

Serves 6.

—Ulla Sterm Troughton

Creamy Celery Soup

Our Vermont tester reports, "Lovely green color—especially appropriate for spring. The cream stock and crunchy celery make for a very pleasant combination of textures."

Ingredients

4 stalks celery with leaves, chopped
¼ tsp. crushed garlic
⅛ tsp. thyme
3 leaves parsley, minced
2 Tbsp. butter
¼ cup flour
2 cups milk
½ cup chicken stock
Salt & pepper

Directions

Cover celery with water in heavy pot. Bring to a boil and cook until celery is just tender. Reduce heat to simmer and add garlic, thyme and parsley. Continue cooking until most of juice is absorbed. Remove from heat, cover and set aside.

Melt 1 Tbsp. butter and stir in flour. Remove from heat and slowly stir in milk, then stock, then remaining 1 Tbsp. butter. Return to heat and cook, stirring, until almost boiling. Remove from heat.

Return celery to heat. Slowly add cream sauce, stirring constantly. Cook for 5 minutes over low heat. Season with salt and pepper.

Serves 2.

—Deborah Elmer

Cauliflower Soup

The parsley roots and greens in this recipe aid digestion. The soup has a delicate flavor and makes a very attractive beginning to a meal.

Ingredients

1 cauliflower, broken into florets
1 tsp. salt
3 Tbsp. oil
1 clove garlic, chopped
2 parsley roots, sliced
1 bunch parsley, chopped
2 Tbsp. flour
1 Tbsp. sweet paprika
1 cup cooked rice or small noodles
½ cup sour cream

Directions

Cook cauliflower in 5 cups water with salt until tender, about 20 minutes. Meanwhile, heat oil in skillet and sauté garlic, parsley roots and parsley for 5 minutes. Stir in flour and paprika, then add 1 cup water. Cook, stirring, until thickened, then stir into cauliflower and water. Boil for 5 minutes, then add rice or noodles and sour cream.

Serves 4.

—Julie Herr

Cream of Tomato Soup

Serve this soup topped with grated cheese and garlic croutons for a dressier dish.

Ingredients

4 cups canned tomatoes
1 bay leaf
2 carrots, chopped
2 onions, chopped
2 stalks celery, chopped
5 Tbsp. butter
5 Tbsp. flour
3 cups milk
salt & pepper

Directions

Cook tomatoes, bay leaf, carrots, onions and celery until tender — 35 to 40 minutes. Discard bay leaf. Purée soup.

Melt butter and stir in flour. Stir in milk and cook, stirring, until thickened. Slowly add puréed mixture. Add salt and pepper to taste.

Serves 4.

—Caren Barry

Cream of Mushroom & Wild Rice Soup

Ingredients

½ cup dry wild rice
⅓ cup butter
3 stalks celery, finely chopped
1 bunch green onions, including tops, chopped
1½ lbs. mushrooms, sliced
¼ cup chopped fresh parsley
⅓ cup flour
3 cups chicken broth
2 13-oz. cans evaporated milk
salt & pepper

Directions

Rinse wild rice thoroughly. Cook, covered, in 1¼ cups water until tender — about 40 minutes. Melt butter in soup pot and add celery and onions. Sauté for a few minutes. Add mushrooms and parsley. Cook over high heat, stirring, until juices start to evaporate. Stir in flour and cook at least one more minute. Gradually stir in broth until smooth. Add evaporated milk, wild rice and salt and pepper to taste.

Serves 4.

—Sandy Lance

Egg Lemon Soup

Ingredients

3-4 cups chicken stock
½ cup white wine
¾ cup cooked rice or fine egg noodles
3 eggs
3 Tbsp. lemon juice
pepper

Directions

Heat stock and wine to rolling boil. Add rice or pasta. Whisk eggs and lemon juice together until frothy, then quickly whisk into boiling stock. Pepper generously and serve immediately.

Serves 4 to 6.

—Elizabeth Templeman

Mushroom & Leek Soup

Whether garnished and served formally or sipped from mugs by the fireplace, this soup is sure to satisfy.

Ingredients

6 leeks
½ cup butter
½ lb. mushrooms, sliced
¼ cup flour
1 tsp. salt
1 tsp. pepper
1 cup chicken stock
3 cups milk
1 Tbsp. sherry
lemon slices & fresh parsley

Directions

Wash white part of leeks thoroughly and slice thinly. Sauté leeks in ¼ cup butter until soft but not brown. Remove leeks. In remaining butter, sauté mushrooms until soft. Blend in flour, salt and pepper. Gradually add stock and milk and stir until mixture is thick and creamy. Add leeks and simmer for 10 minutes. Stir in sherry just before serving. Garnish with thin slices of lemon and chopped fresh parsley.

Serves 6.

—Denise Ford

Cilantro Soup

You may substitute watercress for the cilantro, but the taste will be less spicy. This soup has a lovely, delicate "green" taste.

Ingredients

4½ Tbsp. butter
1½ cups chopped onions
4½ cups sliced leeks
¾ cup chopped celery
3 cups peeled, sliced potatoes
5½ cups chicken stock
1½ tsp. salt
½ tsp. white pepper
3 cups cilantro or watercress, leaves & fine
    stems only
1½ cups light cream
sour cream & chopped cilantro for garnish

Directions

Melt butter and sauté onions, leeks and celery until tender but not brown. Cover and cook over low heat for 15 minutes. Add potatoes, stock, salt, pepper and cilantro. Simmer, covered, for 15 to 20 minutes. Purée until smooth in blender or food processor.

Return mixture to clean pot, add cream and heat but do not boil. Serve, hot or cold, garnished with a dollop of sour cream and some chopped cilantro.

Serves 8 to 10.

—Louise Routledge

Swiss Potato Soup

"This recipe has been in my family for years—it's a favorite with us after a winter day spent hiking in the woods. Creamy, but not too rich, this is a homey soup with surprising sophistication."

Ingredients

4 medium potatoes, pared
2 slices bacon, diced
¼ cup minced onion
2 Tbsp. butter
1 Tbsp. snipped parsley
2 tsp. salt
½ tsp. nutmeg
cayenne
¼ tsp. dry mustard
1 tsp. Worcestershire sauce
3 cups milk
½ cup grated Swiss cheese

Directions

Cook potatoes in boiling water until tender; drain. Meanwhile, sauté bacon and onion over low heat, stirring, until brown and tender. Mash potatoes; add bacon, onion, butter, parsley, salt, nutmeg, cayenne, mustard and Worcestershire sauce. Stir in milk. Cook over low heat, stirring. Sprinkle with cheese and serve at once.

Serves 4.

—Alyson Service

Wild Rice Soup

"This soup has a subtle savory flavor and it is an innovative way to serve wild rice to a crowd without going broke!"

Ingredients

1½ Tbsp. cornstarch
10 cups beef stock
3 Tbsp. butter
2 cups diced celery
½ cups diced carrot
½ cups diced onion
½ lb. mushrooms, sliced
1¼ cups wild rice
1 Tbsp. chopped thyme
1 bay leaf
pepper
parsley sprigs

Directions

Mix cornstarch with 1 cup stock and set aside. Melt butter in large heavy pot and sauté celery, carrot and onion until soft. Add mushrooms and sauté for 5 minutes more. Add remaining 9 cups stock, rice, thyme and bay leaf and bring to a boil. Reduce heat, cover and simmer for 45 minutes, or until rice is tender. Stir in cornstarch mixture and cook until slightly thickened. Add pepper to taste. Remove bay leaf and garnish with parsley.

Serves 12.

—Pam Collacott

Mexican Bean Soup

Our Vermont tester says, "I wholeheartedly recommend this recipe. It has just the right amount of spice, is very well balanced and is the right consistency for a soup."

Ingredients

7 oz. dry pinto beans, soaked overnight
   & drained
½ lb. ham, cubed (optional)
2½ cups water
1½ cups tomato juice
2½ cups chicken stock
2 onions, chopped
½–2 cloves garlic, minced
1½ Tbsp. chopped parsley
2 Tbsp. chopped green pepper
2 Tbsp. dark brown sugar
2 tsp. chili powder
½ tsp. salt
1 bay leaf
½ tsp. oregano
¼ tsp. cumin
¼ tsp. rosemary
¼ tsp. celery seed
¼ tsp. thyme
¼ tsp. basil
⅛ tsp. marjoram
⅛ tsp. curry
⅛ tsp. cloves
½ cup dry sherry
chopped scallions

Directions

Combine all ingredients except sherry and scallions in large heavy pot. Simmer, partially covered, for 3 hours, or until beans are tender. Remove bay leaf.

Add sherry just before serving, then sprinkle with scallions.

Serves 6.

—Beazie Larned

Golden Squash Soup

Cook and freeze squash in the fall, then use it to make this soup in the winter. If you prefer a completely smooth soup, the potatoes can be puréed as well.

Ingredients

4 Tbsp. butter
⅛ cup diced onions
1 large potato, finely diced
1 cup chicken stock
2 cups cooked squash
¼ tsp. salt
¾ tsp. curry
white pepper
¾ cup milk
paprika

Directions

Melt butter and sauté onions until softened. Add potato, stock, squash, salt, curry and pepper. Heat through over medium heat, then simmer for 10 minutes, or until potatoes are tender. Stir in milk. Sprinkle with paprika.

Serves 4.

—Linda Russell

Broccoli Soup

Made with fresh-from-the-garden broccoli, this soup is a lovely early summer lunch dish. Serve with sliced tomatoes and garlic mayonnaise.

Ingredients

6 cups chicken stock
1 head broccoli, cut into florets
1 cup chopped onion
1 Tbsp. chopped tarragon
salt & pepper
nutmeg
1 cup sour cream or yogurt

Directions

Bring stock to a boil. Add broccoli and onion and cook for 6 to 8 minutes, or until broccoli is tender. Purée soup. Reheat, then add tarragon, salt and pepper and nutmeg. Add sour cream or yogurt, whisking thoroughly. Do not allow soup to boil.

Serves 4 to 6

—Marie Blundell

Carrot, Cashew & Curry Soup

"I tasted a soup like this in a little place called The Soup Kitchen in Calgary, Canada. I liked it so much that I developed this version of it for my own use."

Ingredients

¼ cup butter
5–6 carrots, sliced
1 onion, halved & sliced
1 green pepper, chopped
4 cloves garlic, crushed
1 cup cashews
4 cups soup stock
2 tsp. curry
1 bay leaf
salt & pepper

Directions

Melt butter and sauté carrots, onion, green pepper, garlic and cashews until onion is transparent. Add remaining ingredients and simmer until carrots are tender but not mushy — 30 minutes. Remove bay leaf before serving.

Serves 4.

—Bonnie Lawson

Cabbage Soup

A zesty, spicy soup with an Italian flavor, this would be great for a hearty after-ski repast. Add crusty bread and bowls of marinated olives to round out the meal.

Ingredients

4 hot Italian sausages
3 Tbsp. olive oil
2–3 cloves garlic, crushed
1 onion, chopped
1 carrot, sliced
2 stalks celery, chopped
2 28-oz. cans crushed tomatoes
2 potatoes, peeled & cubed
2 cups cooked navy beans
2 cups coarsely chopped cabbage
½ cup white wine
½ tsp. pepper
1 Tbsp. oregano
2 tsp. basil
salt
Parmesan cheese

Directions

Cook sausages in large heavy pot. Discard fat and slice sausages; set aside. Heat oil and sauté garlic and onion until transparent. Add carrot and celery and sauté briefly. Stir in tomatoes and raise heat. Add potatoes, beans, cabbage, wine, pepper, oregano, basil, salt and sausages. Boil for 10 to 15 minutes, reduce heat, cover and simmer until potato and cabbage are tender. Sprinkle with Parmesan cheese and serve.

Serves 6 to 8.

—Elizabeth Templeman

Lamb Soup

Ingredients

1 leftover meaty lamb leg
2 cups chopped spinach
2 tomatoes, cubed
½ cup peas
½ cup corn
3 potatoes, cubed
¾ cup sliced mushrooms
salt & pepper
Worcestershire sauce
1 onion, diced
¼ cup dry barley

Directions

Simmer lamb leg in 6 to 8 cups water for 4 hours. Strain, reserving liquid. Chop meat.

Combine meat, reserved stock and remaining ingredients in large heavy pot. Simmer for 1 hour, or until vegetables are tender, adding liquid if necessary.

Serves 6.

—Patricia E. Wilson

Meal-in-a-Soup

Ingredients

1 Tbsp. butter
¾ lb. ground beef
2 onions, sliced
3 stalks celery, sliced
2 large carrots, sliced
1 potato, diced
1½ cups cauliflower florets
19-oz. can tomatoes
1½ tsp. salt
⅛ tsp. pepper
¾ cup dry macaroni

Directions

Melt butter, add ground beef and brown slightly, stirring. Add remaining ingredients, except pasta. Cover and bring to a boil. Reduce heat and simmer for 30 minutes. Add macaroni about 7 to 9 minutes before the end of cooking time.

Serves 4 to 6.

—Eileen Caldwell

Borscht

Ingredients

8 whole fresh beets
1 small onion, diced
2 Tbsp. butter
4 cups chicken stock
2 medium-sized potatoes
1½ cups sour cream
salt & pepper

Directions

Boil unpeeled beets for 30 minutes, or until tender. Peel and set aside. In large pot, sauté onion in butter for 5 minutes or until transparent. Add chicken stock, potatoes and beets and simmer for 20 minutes, or until potatoes are soft. Purée and chill for at least 3 hours. Whisk sour cream into soup just before serving and season to taste with salt and pepper. Garnish each bowl with a dollop of sour cream.

Serves 6.

Ham-Lentil Soup with Cheese Tortellini

"A richly flavored, chill-chasing soup—especially favored by the harvest crew after a cold day of combine repairs. Serve in prewarmed bowls and garnish with chives. Good accompanied by warm garlic toast and a platter of sliced fresh fruits and vegetables."

Ingredients

2 Tbsp. butter
⅓ cup chopped onion
1 clove garlic, minced
1⅓ cups dry lentils, rinsed & drained
1 cup cubed ham
1 stalk celery, sliced
1 cup peeled, seeded & chopped tomatoes
3" sprig thyme
1 tsp. salt
1 large bay leaf
Tabasco sauce
3¼ cups dry cheese-filled tortellini
snipped chives for garnish

Directions

Melt butter in large, heavy pot over moderate heat. Add onion and garlic and cook, stirring frequently, until onion is limp. Add lentils, ham and celery. Cook, stirring frequently, until lentils just start to brown. Add 8 cups water, tomatoes, thyme, salt, bay leaf and Tabasco sauce and stir to blend. Cook, covered, for 1 hour. Add tortellini and cook for another 30 minutes. Garnish with chives.

Serves 4.

—*Ellen Ross*

Mandarin Hot & Sour Soup

"I developed this recipe after living in China for two years and growing to love hot and sour soup." Hotness and sourness can be adjusted by adding to or subtracting from the amount of vinegar and chili oil.

Ingredients

6–8 cups chicken stock
¼ lb. lean pork, shredded
2–3 dried black mushrooms, soaked & shredded
3–4 dried tree ears, soaked & shredded (optional)
½ square tofu, diced
¼ cup shredded bamboo shoots
½ cup sliced mushrooms
2 green onions, chopped
1 slice cooked ham, shredded
4 Tbsp. vinegar
1 tsp. chili oil
¼ tsp. white pepper
¾ tsp. salt
½ tsp. sesame oil
½ tsp. sugar
1 Tbsp. soy sauce
3 Tbsp. cornstarch dissolved in 3 Tbsp. water
2 eggs, lightly beaten

Directions

Bring stock to a boil, add pork, black mushrooms and tree ears. Cook for 2 to 3 minutes. Add remaining ingredients except for cornstarch and eggs, reduce heat, and simmer for 2 minutes more. Slowly stir cornstarch mixture into soup and continue cooking until stock is thickened. Turn off heat. Slowly pour in eggs in a thin stream while stirring.

Serves 6 to 8.

—*Barb McDonald*

Smoky Potato & Bacon Soup with Cheddar Croutons

This is a meal-in-a-bowl soup, especially good on a cold winter's day. The croutons would be tasty in other soups as well — double or triple the recipe, and freeze the rest for later use.

Soup Ingredients
1 thick strip bacon, with rind
¼ cup butter
1 cup chopped onion
½ cup chopped celery
½ cup chopped leek
5 cups chicken stock
½ tsp. salt
½ tsp. white pepper
2 cups peeled, cubed potatoes
½ cup heavy cream

Crouton Ingredients
1 cup grated sharp Cheddar cheese
1 egg, lightly beaten
½ tsp. Dijon mustard
1 green onion, chopped
cayenne
4 slices bread

Directions

Remove rind from bacon and reserve. Chop bacon. Melt butter, then add rind, onion, celery and leek and cook for 10 minutes over medium heat, stirring. Add stock, salt and pepper and bring to a boil. Add potatoes and simmer for 25 minutes. Remove rind and discard. Purée soup, then return to pot and add cream. Fry bacon until crisp and add to soup.

To make croutons: Combine cheese, egg, mustard, onion and cayenne. Spread onto bread. Bake at 375°F for 10 to 15 minutes or until dry. Cool, then cut into cubes. Sprinkle on soup.

Serves 6 to 8.

—Terry Seed

Clam Chowder

This is a hearty soup with a velvety-smooth, nicely colored broth. Real clam aficionados could easily increase the amount of clams. This chowder combines the cream of a New England clam chowder with the tomatoes of a Manhattan chowder.

Ingredients
2 oz. salt pork or bacon, chopped
1 clove garlic, chopped
½ cup chopped onion
3 cups diced potatoes
1½ tsp. thyme
1 bay leaf
4 cloves
2 tsp. salt
½ tsp. pepper
10-oz. can clams
½ cup chopped green pepper
½ carrot, diced
¼ cup chopped celery
3 cups diced tomatoes
2 Tbsp. flour
4 cups scalded milk
2 cups cream
3 Tbsp. butter
¼ cup chopped parsley

Directions

In large heavy pot, sauté pork. Add garlic and onion and sauté until onion is golden.

Add 3 cups water, potatoes, thyme, bay leaf, cloves, salt and pepper and simmer for 15 minutes. Add clams and their juice, green pepper, carrot, celery and tomatoes. Simmer for 10 minutes.

Mix flour with ½ cup milk. Stir into soup with remaining milk and cream and simmer for 10 minutes more. Stir in butter and parsley.

Serves 8 to 10.

—Xenia Von Rosen

Salads & Vegetables

Baked Carrots

Ingredients
4 carrots
4 Tbsp. butter
Nutmeg

Directions
Grate carrots into a buttered casserole dish. Dot with butter and sprinkle with nutmeg. Bake at 350°F for 20 to 30 minutes.

Serves 4.

—Jenny MacDonald

Swiss Green Beans

Ingredients
2 Tbsp. butter
2 Tbsp. flour
1 tsp. salt
¼ tsp. pepper
½ tsp. grated onion
1 cup sour cream
4 cups green beans, cooked & drained
¼ lb. Swiss cheese, grated
1 cup bread crumbs
2 Tbsp. melted butter

Directions
Melt butter and stir in flour, salt, pepper and onion. Add sour cream gradually. Fold in green beans. Pour into greased casserole dish. Sprinkle cheese over beans. Mix bread crumbs with melted butter and sprinkle over cheese.

Bake at 400°F for 20 minutes.

Serves 6.

—Jayne Campsall

Green Bean Casserole

This recipe provides a quick and easy way to dress up an everyday vegetable.

Ingredients

1 lb. green beans, cooked
2 Tbsp. vinegar
2 tsp. honey
2 slices toast, cubed
2–4 Tbsp. Parmesan cheese

Directions

Place beans in greased baking dish. Stir in vinegar and drizzle with honey. Toss in toast. Sprinkle cheese on top.

Bake at 450°F for 15 minutes, then broil 2 minutes to brown top.

—Sharon Steele

Broccoli Medley

A pleasant and unusual way to serve either fresh or frozen broccoli, this dish can be made ahead and reheated at serving time.

Ingredients

2 heads fresh broccoli or 2 10-oz. pkgs. frozen broccoli
1 cup chicken stock
¼ lb. bacon, cut in 1-inch pieces
2 cups mushrooms, sliced
1 can water chestnuts, drained & sliced
¼ cup slivered almonds
1 tsp. salt
⅛ tsp. pepper
Pimento strips

Directions

Cook broccoli in stock until crisp-tender, about 6 minutes. Drain, reserving ⅓ cup of cooking liquid. Cut broccoli into bite-sized pieces.

Fry bacon until slightly crisp, then add re-maining ingredients except pimento, broccoli and cooking liquid. Cook and stir until bacon is crisp and mushrooms are tender, about 5 minutes. Add broccoli and reserved cooking liquid. Continue cooking until hot. Arrange on serving dish and garnish with pimento.

Serves 12.

—Pam Collacott

Stir-Fried Cauliflower

*An unusual and attractive way to cook cauli-
flower, this dish is fast and simple to prepare.*

Ingredients

2 Tbsp. oil
2 cloves garlic, minced
1 slice fresh ginger, the size of a quarter
1 head cauliflower, washed & broken into florets
1 red pepper, seeded & cut into strips
½ cup chicken stock
½ tsp. oregano
½ tsp. basil
3 tomatoes, peeled, seeded & cut into strips
1 cup peas, fresh or frozen

Directions

Heat oil in a large skillet. Add garlic, ginger and
cauliflower. Stir-fry for 3 minutes. Stir in pepper
and cook for 2 minutes. Add stock and herbs,
cover and steam for 5 minutes. Remove cover,
stir in tomatoes and peas and cook 3 to 4 more
minutes or until vegetables are tender-crisp.
Remove from heat and serve quickly.

—Ingrid Birker

Red Cabbage & Apples

Ingredients

2 lbs. red cabbage
¼ cup butter
½ cup chopped onion
1½ tsp. salt
¼ tsp. pepper
3 Tbsp. vinegar
1½ cups peeled & diced apples
Sour cream to garnish

Directions

Shred cabbage coarsely. Melt butter, add cabbage, onion, seasonings and vinegar. Cook,
covered, for 20 minutes over low heat, stirring
occasionally. Add apples, cover and cook a further
20 minutes or until tender, stirring every few
minutes.

Serve with sour cream.

Serves 6.

—Florence Graham

Marinated Broccoli

Ingredients

1 bunch broccoli
½ cup oil
6 Tbsp. vinegar
1 tsp. minced garlic
¾ tsp. salt
¼ tsp. pepper
½ tsp. tarragon
½ tsp. thyme
½ tsp. dry mustard
⅓ cup sliced green onions
½ cup slivered almonds
Pimento strips
Tomato wedges

Directions

Cut florets from stems of broccoli. Slice stems on the diagonal about 4-inch thick. Steam 3 to 5 minutes or until tender but crispy.

To make marinade, combine other ingredients, except almonds, pimento, and tomatoes, in large bowl. Add hot broccoli and toss to mix. Cover and chill for at least 4 hours.

Lift broccoli from marinade and arrange on serving dish. Garnish with almonds, pimento and tomato.

Serves 4 to 6.

—*Cheryl Peters*

Broccoli Casserole

Ingredients

2 heads broccoli, chopped
1½ cups cream of mushroom sauce, page 129
½ cup shredded Cheddar cheese
¼ cup milk
¼ cup mayonnaise
1 egg, beaten
¼ cup bread crumbs
1 Tbsp. butter

Directions

Cook broccoli and drain. Place in a casserole dish. Mix remaining ingredients together and pour over broccoli. Bake at 350°F for 45 minutes.

Serves 6 to 8.

—*Karen Brouwers*

Glazed Beets

Ingredients

Beets
Butter
Honey or maple syrup

Directions

Cook beets until tender. Drain, peel and, if beets are large, slice. Combine equal quantities of butter and honey or maple syrup in a saucepan. Add the beets and let simmer until the sauce is thickened and beets are shiny with the glaze, usually 10 to 20 minutes.

—*Donna Jubb*

Carrot Casserole

Ingredients

8 carrots
1 cup finely chopped celery
1 medium onion, finely chopped
1 Tbsp. prepared mustard
½ cup mayonnaise
½ cup buttered bread crumbs

Directions

Boil carrots until tender. Drain and mash. Combine celery, onion, mustard and mayonnaise and add to carrots. Spoon into buttered casserole dish and top with bread crumbs.

Bake at 300°F for 1 hour.

—*Grace Zomer*

Corn Fritters

Delicious with maple syrup at breakfast, corn fritters can also be served as a vegetable with dinner.

Ingredients

15-oz. can creamed corn
2 eggs, beaten
2 Tbsp. melted butter
2 cups flour
2 tsp. baking powder
1 tsp. salt
½ tsp. curry powder
4–5 cups oil for deep frying

Directions

Combine corn, eggs and butter. Sift dry ingredients together and blend in corn mixture. Drop mixture by spoonfuls into hot oil (375°F). Fry for approximately 4 minutes, turning once to cook evenly. Drain well.

Makes 15–18 fritters.

—*Janice Clynick*

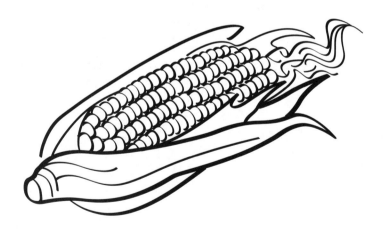

Celery Crunch with Cheese-Nut Pastry

Ingredients

⅔ cup flour
1 tsp. salt
6 Tbsp. butter
1 cup diced almonds, toasted
2¼ cups shredded Cheddar cheese
2–3 Tbsp. cold milk
2½ cups diced celery
¼ cup flour
1½ cups milk

Directions

Sift together flour and ½ tsp. salt. Cut in 3 Tbsp. butter until mixture is crumbly. Stir in ⅓ cup almonds and ¾ cup cheese. Sprinkle 2–3 Tbsp. milk over mixture, stirring with a fork until dough holds together. Flatten into a ½-inch-thick square. Roll out to fit top of baking dish. Set aside.

Cook diced celery in boiling water until tender, drain and add 3 Tbsp. butter. Stir in ¼ cup flour and ½ tsp. salt. Mix well. Gradually blend in 1½ cups milk. Cook over medium heat, stirring constantly, until thickened. Stir in remaining almonds and cheese.

Place in baking dish and top with pastry. Bake at 425°F for 20 to 25 minutes.

Serves 8.

—Susan Gillespie

Eggplant Parmesan

Ingredients

1 large eggplant
2 eggs
¼ cup milk
½ cup flour
¼ cup sesame seeds
1¼ cups grated Parmesan cheese
2–3 cups spaghetti sauce
2 cups grated mozzarella cheese

Directions

Slice eggplant into ¼-inch slices. Beat eggs with milk. Mix flour with sesame seeds and ¼ cup Parmesan cheese. Dip eggplant slices in egg mixture and then in flour mixture.

Heat oil in frying pan and fry slices until brown on both sides.

Arrange a layer of fried eggplant slices on the bottom of a greased casserole dish. Spoon some spaghetti sauce over these and then sprinkle with some of the Parmesan and mozzarella cheeses. Repeat layers twice.

Bake at 350°F for 30 to 45 minutes.

Serves 6.

—Mikell Billoki

Celery with Almonds

Ingredients

½ cup slivered almonds
2 Tbsp. butter
4 cups diced celery
½ cup chopped onion
Pepper
2 Tbsp. dry white wine

Directions

In a skillet, cook the almonds in 1 Tbsp. butter, stirring constantly, until they are lightly browned. Drain on paper towels.

Sauté the diced celery and onion in the remaining butter. Season with pepper, if desired. Cook over low heat, stirring occasionally, for about 7 minutes.

Add the wine and cook, covered, for 2 minutes. Transfer to a serving dish and garnish with the almonds.

Serves 4 to 6.

—Janet Flewelling

Greens Chinese Style

This is an interesting way to prepare all kinds of green, leafy vegetables, such as kale, Swiss chard or leaf lettuce.

Directions

Wash greens and pat dry. Plunge briefly into a pot of boiling water until wilted. Mix with a dressing of equal parts oil and tamari sauce. Serve immediately.

—Brigitte Wolf

Eggplant Casserole

Ingredients

2 medium-sized eggplants
4 strips bacon
1 onion
1 green pepper
2 cloves garlic
3 slices bread
1 cup milk
2 cups shrimp, minced clams or tuna
4 eggs, well beaten
Salt & pepper

Directions

Peel eggplants and boil until tender. Drain, mash and set aside. Fry bacon until crispy, remove from pan and crumble. Finely chop onion, pepper and garlic and fry in bacon fat until tender. Soak bread in milk then gently squeeze out excess.

Mix together eggplant, bacon, vegetables, shrimp and bread. Stir well. Add eggs and salt and pepper to taste.

Place in casserole dish and bake at 350°F for 25 to 30 minutes.

Serves 6.

—James R. Wilson

Herb Stuffed Mushroom Caps

This dish, excellent as a vegetable side dish or as an appetizer, can be assembled ahead of time, refrigerated and baked before serving.

Ingredients

24 very large fresh mushrooms (1½ lbs.)
½ cup butter
3 Tbsp. finely chopped green onion
1 cup fresh bread crumbs
½ cup chopped fresh parsley
⅛ tsp. powdered savory
⅛ tsp. pepper

Directions

Wipe mushrooms with a damp cloth. Remove stems and chop them finely. Melt ¼ cup butter in a large skillet and toss mushroom caps in this for 1 minute. Remove mushroom caps to a flat baking dish or a cookie sheet.

Melt remaining ¼ cup of butter in the same skillet. Sauté stems and onions briefly. Remove from heat and stir in bread crumbs, parsley, savory and pepper, tossing lightly. Spoon this mixture into caps.

Bake mushrooms at 350°F for 10 minutes.

—Wendy Searcy

Mushroom Loaf

Ingredients

3 Tbsp. butter
1 onion, finely chopped
1 lb. mushrooms, sliced
2 cups bread crumbs
1 egg, beaten
½ cup water or tomato juice
3 Tbsp. butter
Salt & pepper

Directions

Melt 3 Tbsp. butter in heavy pan, add onion and sliced mushrooms and cook for 10 minutes. Lift vegetables out with slotted spoon and add to bread crumbs. Mix well.

Add beaten egg, liquid, remaining butter and salt and pepper. Bake in a greased loaf pan at 375°F for 25 to 30 minutes.

Serves 4.

—Jacqueline Dysart

Stuffed Mushrooms

Ingredients

12–20 large mushrooms
6–8 slices of bacon, fried & crumbled
Parsley
Salt & pepper
½ cup Cheddar cheese
1 egg
½ cup bread crumbs
¼ cup finely chopped green pepper
2 cloves garlic, finely chopped
1 onion, finely chopped

Directions

Remove mushroom stems and chop. Mix all ingredients except mushroom caps. Place a tablespoon of mixture in each mushroom cap. Bake at 425°F for 30 minutes.

—Diane Adrian

Mushroom Bake

Ingredients

½ lb. mushrooms
½ cup butter
1 lb. tomatoes
1 cup fresh bread crumbs
1 small onion, grated
¾ cup grated Cheddar cheese
Juice & rind of ½ lemon
Cheese sauce, page 129

Directions

Wash and slice mushrooms and fry in ¼ cup butter for 5 minutes. Slice tomatoes and set aside.

Blend together the bread crumbs, onion, cheese, remaining butter and lemon rind, and press half the mixture into a casserole dish.

Spread mushrooms on top of crumb layer and follow with sliced tomatoes. Season well and sprinkle with lemon juice. Press on remaining crumb mixture.

Bake at 375°F for 30 minutes. Serve with cheese sauce.

Serves 2.

—Mrs. A.E. Nehua-Cafe

Dusty Potatoes

Ingredients

¾ cup dry bread crumbs
1½ tsp. nutmeg
½ tsp. salt
¼ tsp. pepper
4 medium potatoes, pared & quartered
⅓ cup melted butter

Directions

Mix bread crumbs and seasonings. Dip potatoes in melted butter and then roll in crumb mixture. Place on greased baking sheet. Bake at 350°F until crisp and brown about 1 hour.
Serves 4.
—Pam Collacott

Mediterranean Potato Pie

Ingredients

2 small onions, chopped
3 large potatoes, peeled
1 cup flour
½ tsp. pepper
1 tsp. salt
¼ cup olive oil
3 Tbsp. butter
3 Tbsp. flour
3 large ripe tomatoes, chopped
½ green pepper, chopped
½ bay leaf
2 cloves
1 tsp. oregano
½ lb. mozzarella cheese, diced
¼ cup grated Parmesan cheese

Directions

Sauté chopped onion in a little oil. Boil the potatoes and mash until smooth. Blend in 1 cup flour, salt and pepper. Press mixture ½-inch thick in the bottom of a shallow baking dish. Spoon olive oil on top.

Melt butter in a skillet and stir in 3 Tbsp. flour. Add tomatoes, remaining onion, green pepper, bay leaf, cloves and oregano. Simmer for 20 minutes. Remove bay leaf and cloves.

Spoon sauce over potato mixture and top with cheeses.

Bake at 350°F for 15 minutes.

Serves 4.

—Brenda Kennedy

Scalloped Onions

A pleasant change from simple baked onions, this casserole can be quickly and easily assembled with ingredients which are usually on hand.

The combination of cheese and onion provides a satisfying accompaniment to meat dishes.

Ingredients
6 medium onions
¼ cup butter
¼ cup flour
2 cups milk
½ tsp. salt
2 cups grated Cheddar cheese

Directions
Slice onions and separate into rings. Place in 1½-quart casserole dish. Melt butter and blend in flour. Slowly stir in milk and cook, stirring, until thickened. Stir in salt and grated cheese. Pour over onions. Bake, uncovered, at 375°F for 1 hour.

Serves 6.

—Wendy Fitzgerald

Scalloped Potatoes

Ingredients
3 cups peeled & sliced potatoes
1 large onion, thinly sliced
1½ cups cream of mushroom sauce, page 129
4 Tbsp. flour
1½ tsp. salt
½ tsp. pepper
4 Tbsp. butter
3 cups milk

Directions
Place a layer of potatoes in a deep casserole dish and add a layer of sliced onion. Spread half the mushroom sauce over this, sprinkle with flour, salt and pepper and dot with butter. Repeat layers.

Pour milk around the potatoes until it reaches the top layer of potatoes.

Bake, covered, at 375°F for 30 minutes. Uncover and bake another 30 to 45 minutes — until top is golden brown.

Serves 4.

—Aurora Sugden

Potato Puff

This is an easy and delicious way to use up leftover potatoes.

Ingredients
3 cups mashed potatoes
2 Tbsp. butter
1 tsp. chopped parsley
¼ tsp. salt
Few grains cayenne
1 tsp. onion juice
3 eggs, separated

Directions
Mix potatoes with butter, parsley, salt, cayenne and onion juice. Beat egg yolks, add to potatoes and mix well. Beat egg whites until stiff and fold in. Place in greased baking dish and bake at 350°F for 40 minutes or until golden brown.

—Shirley Morrish

Twice-Baked Potatoes

Almost any filling can be mixed with the cooked potatoes. Some suggestions are cooked bacon, ham, mushrooms, onions or other vegetables.

Ingredients
6 medium potatoes
½ tsp. salt
Pepper
4 Tbsp. butter
¼ cup sour cream
Shredded mozzarella cheese
Parsley

Directions
Wash potatoes and bake at 400°F until done, about 1 hour. Remove from oven, split tops and scoop out insides. Place this in a bowl and mash, combining with all other ingredients except cheese and parsley.

When well blended, scoop mixture back into potato shells. Top with cheese, sprinkle with parsley. Put back into oven at 300°F. Serve when cheese has melted.

Serves 6.

—Johanna Vanderheyden

Sweet Potato Cashew Bake

Ingredients
½ cup brown sugar
⅓ cup broken cashews
¼ tsp. ground ginger
½ tsp. salt
2 lbs. sweet potatoes, cooked, peeled & sliced
8 peaches, peeled & halved
3 Tbsp. butter

Directions
Combine sugar, cashews, ginger and salt. In a shallow baking dish, layer half the potatoes, half the peaches and half the nut mixture. Repeat layers and dot with butter.

Bake, covered, at 350°F for 30 minutes. Uncover and bake 10 minutes longer.

Serves 6 to 8.

—Elizabeth Clayton

Potato Casserole

Ingredients
6 large potatoes, cooked until just tender
1½ cups cream of mushroom sauce, page 129
1 cup chopped onion
2 cups sour cream
½ cup butter
½ lb. old Cheddar cheese, grated
Salt & pepper
½ cup bread crumbs
4 Tbsp. Parmesan cheese

Directions
Pare and grate cooked potatoes. Combine with all remaining ingredients except bread crumbs and Parmesan cheese. Place in a 9" x 13" baking dish and top with bread crumb-Parmesan cheese mixture.

Bake at 375°F for 1 hour.

Serves 12.

—Mrs. G. Fellows

Spaghetti Squash with Tomato Sauce

Ingredients

1 onion, finely chopped
1 clove garlic, minced
Butter or oil
1 lb. tomatoes, peeled seeded & chopped
Fresh parsley & basil
½ tsp. lemon juice
Salt & pepper
1 spaghetti squash

Directions

Sauté the onion and garlic in butter or oil. Add the chopped tomatoes and their juices, the herbs, lemon juice and salt and pepper. Simmer briefly.

Place the squash, whole, in a 325°F oven and bake 20 to 30 minutes, until tender. Pierce one end to test for tenderness. Cut the squash in half, gently remove the seeds, then lift out the flesh. Pile on a plate, toss with a bit of oil and pour the hot tomato sauce over it.

Serves 6.

—*Kathee Roy*

Spinach Provençale

Ingredients

2 lbs. spinach
1 large onion, sliced
1 clove garlic, minced
Olive oil
Butter
2 eggs, beaten
1 cup grated Parmesan cheese
Salt & pepper

Directions

Wash and tear spinach. Sauté onion and garlic in olive oil until the onion is transparent. Add spinach, cover and cook until spinach is wilted — about 2 minutes. Remove from heat and cool slightly.

In a baking dish, combine spinach mixture, beaten eggs and half the cheese. Season, and sprinkle the remaining cheese on top. Dot with butter and bake at 375°F for 10 to 15 minutes.

Serves 6 to 8.

— *Jean Hally*

Tomatoes Provençales

In the late summer and early fall, when tomatoes are ripening all too quickly, this dish is an appetizing complement to any meal.

Ingredients

4 large tomatoes
3 Tbsp. olive oil
½ tsp. salt
½ tsp. pepper
2 cloves garlic, crushed
1 Tbsp. chopped parsley
1 tsp. basil
½ tsp. oregano
2 Tbsp. coarse bread crumbs
2 Tbsp. Parmesan cheese

Directions

Halve tomatoes crosswise and remove seeds by pressing each half in your hand.

Heat the oil in a large frying pan. Place tomatoes in oil, cut side down, and cook over medium heat for 3 minutes. Turn, and sprinkle cut side with salt and pepper. Place crushed garlic in bottom of pan and cook another 2 minutes.

Place tomatoes on a cookie sheet and sprinkle with parsley and basil mixed together. Top with bread crumbs mixed with Parmesan cheese. Broil for 5 to 10 minutes — until tomatoes are golden brown on top but still firm.

Serves 4.

—*Carolyn Hills*

Zucchini Parmesan Loaf

Ingredients

¾ cup flour
2 tsp. salt
⅓ cup milk
2 lbs. zucchini, cut lengthwise into ¼-inch slices
Salad oil
1 cup tomato sauce, page 339
½ cup grated Parmesan cheese
1 cup grated mozzarella cheese

Directions

Combine flour and salt on a sheet of wax paper. Pour milk into pie plate. Dip the zucchini in milk, then coat with flour.

In a 12-inch skillet over medium-high heat, cook zucchini in oil, a few slices at a time, until golden. Drain on paper towels.

In a greased loaf pan arrange half the zucchini, spoon on half the tomato sauce and sprinkle with half the mozzarella and Parmesan cheeses. Repeat layers.

Bake at 350°F for 40 minutes, until browned and bubbly.

Serves 4.

—*Margaret Orr*

September Garden Zucchini

This recipe can be easily adapted to barbecue cooking. Wrap layered vegetables in a square of aluminum foil and cook on grill, turning three or four times.

Ingredients

4 Tbsp. oil
1 large onion, cut in rings
1 zucchini, sliced
1 stalk celery, sliced
1 green pepper, sliced
2 tomatoes, quartered

Directions

Heat oil in a heavy frying pan and sauté onion, zucchini, celery and green pepper. When onions are transparent, add tomatoes.

Cover and simmer until tomatoes are soft.

—Donna Gordon

Tempura

Batter Ingredients

1 cup brown rice flour
1 Tbsp. cornstarch
Salt
1 egg, beaten
½ cup cold water

Vegetable Ingredients

Use almost any vegetable that will cook quickly. When using long-cooking vegetables such as carrots, lightly steam first.

Sauce Ingredients

1 cup chicken stock
½ cup tamari sauce
⅓ cup honey
2 Tbsp. sherry

Directions

Mix flour with cornstarch, salt, egg and cold water to make a thin batter. Chill 15 minutes. To prepare vegetables, wash and dry thoroughly. Cut into small pieces and chill well. Dredge in flour before dipping into batter.

For sauce, combine all ingredients and mix well.

To cook, heat several inches of oil in a wok. Dip each vegetable piece in batter, shake and fry briefly until golden, turning often. Drain and serve immediately with sauce.

—Bryanna Clark

Zucchini Supreme

Ingredients
Small zucchini
Parmesan cheese
Butter

Directions
Wash zucchini and slice in half lengthwise. Spread with butter and sprinkle on cheese. Place on cookie sheet on bottom rack of oven. Broil for 10 minutes or until bubbly and brown on top and crisp inside.

—Beth Hopkins

Zucchini Boats

When large zucchini are in abundance, recipes such as the following provide delightful meals. Almost any combination of vegetables and cheese, with or without meat, can be used in these "boats."

Ingredients
1 large zucchini (approx. 12")
1 green pepper, cut in small squares
½ cup dry bread crumbs
½ cup grated Cheddar cheese
Butter
Salt & pepper

Directions
Cut zucchini in half lengthwise and then crosswise. Remove center, except for a piece at each end, to form a boat. Fill with green pepper. Dot with butter, add salt and pepper to taste. Sprinkle bread crumbs on top and cover with grated cheese.

Bake in covered baking dish at 350°F for 20 minutes, then remove lid and bake 10 to 15 minutes longer.

—Eleanor Bell

Zucchini Medley

Ingredients
2 small zucchini
2 slices eggplant, peeled
2 cooking onions
½ sweet red pepper
4 Tbsp. butter
Salt & pepper

Directions
Cut zucchini into ¼-inch slices, eggplant into ½-inch squares, onions into rings and pepper into 1-inch strips. Stir-fry in melted butter and season with salt and pepper.

—Eleanor Bell

Ratatouille

For a satisfying meal with Italian overtones, this succulent vegetable stew can make a complete meal when served with black olives and warm fresh bread.

Ingredients

½ cup salad oil
2 large onions, thinly sliced
2–3 cloves garlic, minced
1 eggplant, peeled & diced
4 tomatoes, peeled & diced
1 zucchini, peeled & diced
2 green peppers, cleaned & diced
3 stalks celery, diced
2 tsp. fresh basil
1 tsp. oregano
Salt & pepper

Directions

Heat oil in heavy saucepan and brown onion and garlic. Add eggplant and tomatoes and cook for a few minutes.

Add remaining ingredients, bring to a boil and lower heat. Simmer for at least 1 hour.

Serves 4 to 6.

—*Mrs. E. Imboden*

Vegetable Stew

The special appeal of this dish is that it does not use salt but rather relies upon the subtle flavors of each vegetable for seasoning.

Ingredients

¼ cup butter
4 carrots, cut into ¼-inch slices
1 large turnip, cut into strips
1 celeriac root, cut into strips
4 potatoes, cubed
2 green peppers, cut into rings
4–6 tomatoes, chopped
6 small whole onions
4 tsp. chopped parsley
½ tsp. thyme
3 soy cubes mixed in 3 cups water or 3 cups
  chicken stock
¼ cup arrowroot
½ cup water

Directions

Melt butter in stewing pot. Add carrots and turnip, cover and cook for 10 to 15 minutes. Add celeriac, potatoes, peppers, tomatoes, onions, seasonings and broth. Simmer for 1 hour.

Mix arrowroot with water and add to stew when vegetables are tender. Simmer for 10 more minutes.

Serves 4.

—*Christine Taylor*

Celery Salad

Ingredients

¼ cup olive oil
Juice of ½ large lemon
1 tsp. dried mustard
Salt
1 bunch celery, washed & sliced

Directions

Combine olive oil, lemon juice, mustard and salt. Mix well. Pour over celery, toss and marinate for at least 24 hours.

Serves 6 to 8.

—Dawn Hermann

Shrimp & Avocado Salad

Ingredients

1 avocado, peeled & chopped
½ cup shrimp, cleaned & cooked
½ English cucumber, cubed
½ head Boston lettuce, broken
1 cup alfalfa sprouts
¼ cup mayonnaise, page 130
¼ cup sour cream
1–2 Tbsp. lemon juice
Salt & pepper

Directions

Combine avocado, shrimp, cucumber, lettuce and sprouts and toss. Mix remaining ingredients. Pour over salad and toss gently.

Serves 2.

—Jane Pugh

Marinated Cucumber Salad

Ingredients

2 medium cucumbers, pared & thinly sliced
1 medium onion, thinly sliced
1 tsp. salt
3 Tbsp. vinegar
3 Tbsp. water
½ tsp. sugar
¼ tsp. paprika
¼ tsp. pepper
1–2 cloves garlic, crushed

Directions

Combine cucumbers and onion in a bowl and sprinkle with salt. Mix lightly and set aside for 1 hour.

Meanwhile, combine remaining ingredients. Drain cucumbers, pour dressing over them and toss until well mixed.

Chill for 1 to 2 hours, stirring occasionally. Discard garlic before serving and sprinkle with additional paprika.

Serves 6.

—Valerie Gillis

Carrot Salad

Ingredients

1 lb. carrots, sliced
½ Spanish onion, quartered & separated
½ green pepper, cut into rings
1 cup finely cut celery
¾ cup tomato sauce, page 339
¼ cup vinegar
½ cup granulated sugar
½ tsp. prepared mustard
½ tsp. dry mustard
½ tsp. salt
½ tsp. pepper
½ Tbsp. Worcestershire sauce
¼ cup salad oil

Directions

Boil carrots until tender, drain and cool. Add onion, green pepper and celery.

Combine tomato sauce, vinegar, sugar, mustards, salt, pepper and Worcestershire sauce in a blender. When well blended, slowly pour in oil and blend well.

Toss salad with dressing and refrigerate for at least 24 hours.

Serves 6.

—V.A. Charles

Sweet Pepper Salad

The red and green of this salad make it a colorful addition to Christmas dinner.

Ingredients

2 large red peppers, sliced
2 large green peppers, sliced
½ lb. mushrooms, sliced
3 green onions, chopped
½ tsp. salt
½ tsp. pepper
¾ cup olive oil
3 Tbsp. vinegar
½ tsp. dry mustard
1–2 cloves garlic

Directions

Place all vegetables in a large bowl. Combine remaining ingredients and whirl in a blender. Pour over vegetables. Refrigerate for at least 3 hours before serving.

Serves 6 to 8.

—Pam Collacott

Curried Potato Salad

Ingredients

2 Tbsp. butter
2 Tbsp. flour
2 tsp. curry powder
1 cup chicken stock
½ cup sour cream
½ cup mayonnaise, page 130
½ tsp. salt
½ cup sliced green onion
½ cup diced celery
½ cup sliced green olives
2 Tbsp. chopped parsley
2 Tbsp. chopped green pepper
4 cups diced cooked potatoes

Directions

Melt butter, stir in flour and curry powder. Add chicken stock and cook until thick and smooth. Stir in sour cream, mayonnaise and salt. Add remaining ingredients and combine gently.

Place in a greased baking dish and sprinkle with paprika. Bake at 375°F until hot — 20 to 30 minutes. Serve hot.

Serves 6 to 8.

—Dorothy Hurst

Potato Salad

Ingredients

3–4 hard-boiled eggs
5 cooked potatoes
2–3 Tbsp. water
1 Tbsp. tarragon vinegar
1 onion, diced
1 tsp. celery seeds
1 tsp. salt
Mayonnaise, page 130

Directions

Peel and dice eggs and potatoes. Set aside. Combine 2 to 3 Tbsp. water, vinegar, onion, celery seeds and salt in saucepan. Cook until onion is tender — about 5 minutes. Pour over the potatoes and eggs, add mayonnaise to taste and toss gently.

Serves 4.

—Nancy McAskill

Broccoli Salad

Ingredients

1 head broccoli, broken into bite-sized pieces
1 onion, quartered & separated
6–8 slices bacon
⅓ cup vinegar
⅓ cup brown sugar

Directions

Fry bacon until crisp. Remove from pan and crumble into serving bowl with broccoli. Sauté onion in bacon fat and add to broccoli. Add vinegar and brown sugar to remaining bacon fat and simmer for a few minutes.

Pour over the broccoli, toss and serve.

Serves 4.

—Margaret Robinson

Three Bean Salad

Ingredients

½ cup vinegar
¼ cup oil
1 tsp. salt
Dash pepper
Dash garlic powder
2 Tbsp. sugar
2 cups green beans, cooked, drained & chopped
2 cups wax beans, cooked, drained & chopped
2 cups red kidney beans, cooked & drained
¼ cup chopped green onions

Directions

Mix together vinegar, oil, salt, pepper, garlic powder and sugar. Add beans and onions. Toss well.

Cover and refrigerate for 3 hours or overnight, tossing occasionally.

—Wanda Gaitan

Dandelion Salad

Ingredients

2 slices bacon
½ cup unopened dandelion flower buds
2 cups young dandelion leaves
2 Tbsp. oil
1 Tbsp. vinegar
Salt & pepper
1 tsp. tarragon

Directions

Cook bacon until crisp. Remove from pan and drain.

Wash dandelion flowers and leaves and pat dry with paper towels. Cook flowers in bacon fat until the buds burst open. Drain. Crumble bacon into salad bowl. Add leaves and flowers.

Combine oil, vinegar and seasonings, pour over salad and toss.

Serves 4.

—Shirley Morrish

Coleslaw

Ingredients

1 large head cabbage
4 carrots
2–4 green onions, chopped
½ cup vinegar
⅔ cup oil
2 Tbsp. salt
3 Tbsp. sugar

Directions

Shred cabbage and carrots into a large bowl. Add green onion.

Place remaining ingredients in a saucepan and bring to a boil. Let cool and pour over cabbage and carrots. Toss gently.

Refrigerate for at least 24 hours, stirring occasionally.

—Helen Owen

Fruit Salad with Vermouth

Some suitable fresh fruit combinations for this salad are apples and pears, peaches and melon or oranges, grapefruit and grapes. Toasted sesame or sunflower seeds can also make a tasty addition.

Ingredients

½ cup raisins
½ cup grated coconut
½ cup vermouth
Fruit, whatever is in season

Directions

Soak raisins and coconut in vermouth overnight. Slice up fruit, add to raisin mixture and toss. Refrigerate until time to serve.

—Kathe Lieber

Almond Vegetables Mandarin

Ingredients

1 cup thinly sliced carrots
1 cup green beans, cut in 1-inch slices
2 Tbsp. salad oil
1 cup thinly sliced cauliflower
½ cup sliced green onion
1 cup chicken stock
2 tsp. cornstarch
Pinch garlic powder
½ cup unblanched whole almonds

Directions

Stir carrots and beans in oil over medium heat for 2 minutes. Add cauliflower and onion, and cook 1 minute longer. Add chicken stock, cornstarch and garlic. Cook and stir until thickened and vegetables are crispy tender. Add almonds.

Serves 4 to 6.

—Kathenne Dunster

Orange Bean Salad

This pungent salad serves as an excellent accompaniment to pork or lamb.

Ingredients

¾ lb. fresh green beans cut in half
½ cup honey
¼ cup cider vinegar
½ cup oil
½ cup water or chicken stock
Dash coriander
¼ cup fresh chopped parsley
2 cups cooked red kidney beans
½ cup red onion, chopped
3 oranges, peeled & sectioned

Directions

Cook green beans in boiling water for 4 minutes. Mix together honey, vinegar, oil, water or stock, coriander and parsley.

Drain beans. Combine with kidney beans, chopped onion and orange sections in large bowl. Pour ⅓ cup dressing over all ingredients and mix well. The rest of the dressing will keep in the refrigerator.

Serves 6 to 8.

—Ingrid Birker

Greek Salad

Less expensive than restaurant versions, this delicious salad may be served as a meal with warm garlic bread, or as a side dish.

Ingredients

1 head romaine lettuce, shredded
½ Spanish onion, thinly sliced & separated
    into rings
1 green pepper, cut in ½-inch squares
4 tomatoes, cut in wedges
½ cucumber, cut into 4 lengthwise, then sliced
12 or more ripe black olives
½ lb. feta cheese, crumbled
2 cloves garlic, peeled & crushed
½ cup olive oil
1 Tbsp. wine vinegar
¼ tsp. salt
Dash black pepper

Directions

Place salad ingredients in large salad bowl. When ready to serve, place oil in a small container that has a lid. Drop crushed garlic clove into the oil, add vinegar, salt and pepper, cover and shake vigorously.

Pour over salad and serve immediately.

—Don & Foley Boyd

Caesar Salad

Ingredients

1 head romaine lettuce
3 large cloves garlic
2 anchovy fillets
1 tsp. dry mustard
Juice of 1 lemon
1 egg yolk
2 Tbsp. blue cheese
Salt & pepper
¾ cup olive oil
4 Tbsp. Parmesan cheese

Directions

Wash, dry and tear up romaine lettuce. Set aside.

Crush garlic in a large wooden bowl, add anchovies, mustard, lemon juice, egg yolk and blue cheese. Stir, continuing to flatten cheese and anchovies against the bowl until a thick paste is formed. Add salt, pepper and olive oil, beating fast to make a thick and creamy dressing.

Toss in lettuce pieces and mix thoroughly. Sprinkle with Parmesan cheese.

Serves 4 to 6.

—Julienne Tardif

Spring Salad

Ingredients

2 cups watercress
2 cups dandelion leaves
3 wild leeks, chopped
¼ cup sunflower seeds
2–3 fresh basil leaves
¼ cup salad oil
¼ cup cider vinegar
1 Tbsp. lemon juice
2 tsp. sugar
½ tsp. Worcestershire sauce

Directions

Combine cleaned watercress and dandelion leaves. Add leeks, sunflower seeds and basil and toss. Combine remaining ingredients, pour over salad and toss well.

Serves 6 to 8.

—Nora Jones

Tomato Cucumber Toss

This is an ideal salad for late summer, when gardens abound with tomatoes and cucumbers.

Ingredients

3 ripe tomatoes
3 small cucumbers
¼ cup oil
¼ cup cider vinegar
Salt & pepper

Directions

Chop tomatoes and unpeeled cucumbers into chunks. Place in a shallow bowl and toss with the oil, vinegar and seasonings.

—*Mikell Billoki*

Town Hall Supper Salad

"A much-requested salad favorite at our community suppers and luncheons, this is a nutritious as well as a tasty salad."

Ingredients

¼ cup dry wild rice
4 cups broccoli florets
4 cups cauliflower florets
2 cups raisins
1⅓ cups roasted, salted peanuts
½ lb. bacon, fried crisp & crumbled
¼ cup toasted wheat germ
4 green onions, thinly sliced
2 cups mayonnaise
¼ cup sugar
1½ Tbsp. raspberry vinegar
pepper

Directions

Cook rice until tender, drain well and set aside. Blanch broccoli and cauliflower, drain, then rinse in cold running water. Combine with rice, raisins, peanuts, bacon, wheat germ and onions. Beat together mayonnaise, sugar, vinegar and pepper until smooth. Toss with salad ingredients. Chill well.

Serves 12.

—*Ellen Ross*

April Salad

Ingredients

1 cup dry chickpeas
3 cups water
1 Tbsp. garlic powder
1½ tsp. celery seed
3–4 cups alfalfa sprouts
1–2 cups fenugreek sprouts
½ lb. feta cheese

Directions

Soak chickpeas in 3 cups water for at least 4 hours. Add garlic powder, celery seed and more water, if necessary. Bring to a boil and simmer until chickpeas are chewy tender — about 1½ hours. Drain and cool.

Make a bed of alfalfa and fenugreek sprouts and crumble feta cheese over them. Top with chickpeas.

Serves 8 to 10.

—*Susan Ellenton*

Spinach, Mushroom & Bacon Salad

Ingredients

10 oz. fresh spinach, washed
1 tomato, cut into wedges
1 small red onion, thinly sliced &
   separated into rings
½ cup sliced mushrooms
⅓ cup chopped cooked bacon
⅓ cup olive oil
2 Tbsp. wine vinegar
¼ tsp. oregano
¼ tsp. pepper

Directions

Tear spinach into bite-sized pieces. Place spinach, tomato, onion rings, mushrooms and bacon in salad bowl. Toss gently.

Combine oil, vinegar, oregano and pepper in a jar. Cover and shake well. Pour over salad and toss.

Serves 10.

—Jane Cuthbert

Bean Sprout Salad

Ingredients

2 cups bean sprouts
1 clove garlic, crushed
¼ cup oil
2 Tbsp. vinegar
2 Tbsp. soy sauce
2 Tbsp. sesame seeds
Salt & pepper

Directions

Mix together all ingredients except sprouts. Pour over sprouts and toss gently.

Serves 4.

—Dawn Hermann

Basic White Sauce

Ingredients

1 cup milk or light cream
Salt & pepper
2 Tbsp. butter
2 Tbsp. flour

Directions

Melt butter and stir in flour. Cook over low heat for 3 or 4 minutes, stirring constantly. Slowly stir in milk or cream and salt and pepper. Cook, stirring, until sauce has thickened. Makes 1 cup.

Cheese Sauce

Ingredients

1 cup basic white sauce, left
½ cup grated Cheddar or Swiss cheese
1 tsp. lemon juice
Nutmeg

Directions

Warm the white sauce and gradually stir in grated cheese. Cheddar will give a tangy flavor while Swiss gives a milder, thicker sauce. Add lemon juice and nutmeg. Cook and stir until cheese is completely melted.
Makes 1½ cups.

Thousand Island Dressing

Ingredients

To basic mayonnaise add:
3 Tbsp. chili sauce
1 Tbsp. grated onion
2 Tbsp. finely chopped green pepper
2 Tbsp. chopped chives
⅓ hard-boiled egg, finely chopped

—Mrs. E. Louden

Cream of Mushroom Sauce

Ingredients

1 cup basic white sauce, above
½ cup chopped mushrooms
2 Tbsp. butter
2 tsp. tamari sauce
½ tsp. thyme

Directions

Warm white sauce. Cook mushrooms in butter for 2 minutes. Add to white sauce with tamari sauce and thyme. Stir well and heat through.
Makes 1¼ cups.

Basic Mayonnaise

Ingredients

1 egg
1 tsp. salt
½ tsp. dry mustard
2 cloves garlic, peeled
2 Tbsp. vinegar
1 cup vegetable oil

Directions

Combine egg, salt, mustard, garlic, vinegar and ¼ cup oil in blender. Cover and whirl until ingredients are blended. Remove lid and slowly pour in remaining oil, in a steady stream, until mixture has thickened. Keep refrigerated. Makes 1¼ cups.

Oil & Vinegar Dressing

Ingredients

⅔ cup oil
½ cup red wine vinegar
½ tsp. sugar
1 tsp. salt
¼ tsp. pepper
½ tsp. basil
½ tsp. tarragon
2 Tbsp. Parmesan cheese

Directions

Combine all ingredients, shake well and chill. This dressing is particularly tasty with a buttercrunch lettuce and mushroom salad.

—Beth Hopkins

Sesame Dressing

Ingredients

¼ cup olive oil
2 cloves garlic, diced
3 Tbsp. tamari sauce
3 Tbsp. lemon juice
1 tsp. honey
½ tsp. ginger
½ tsp. black pepper
3 Tbsp. toasted sesame seeds

Directions

Combine oil and garlic. Let sit at room temperature for 1 to 2 hours. Add tamari, lemon juice, honey, ginger and black pepper and shake well. At serving time, add sesame seeds.
—Shiela Alexandrovich

Guacamole

Ingredients

2 ripe avocados
Juice of 1 lemon
2 cloves garlic, minced
2 Tbsp. chili powder

Directions

Peel avocados and then mash with a fork or purée in a food processor. Add remaining ingredients and mix well. Keep covered and refrigerated until ready to serve.

Makes 1½ cups.

—Bryanna Clark

Poppy Seed Dressing

Ingredients

4 Tbsp. lemon juice
2 tsp. Dijon mustard
1 tsp. salt
Cayenne pepper
2 Tbsp. honey
6 Tbsp. olive oil
6 Tbsp. vegetable oil
1 Tbsp. poppy seeds

Directions

Combine all ingredients in a jar and shake well. Keep in refrigerator. Makes enough dressing for one large salad.

—Sherrie Dick

African Lemon Dressing

Ingredients

Grated peel of 2 lemons
¼ cup lemon juice
1½ tsp. salt
⅛ tsp. red pepper or Tabasco sauce
2 cloves garlic, chopped
⅔–¾ cup olive oil
½ tsp. ground coriander
½ tsp. ground cumin
½ tsp. dry mustard
½ tsp. honey
½ tsp. paprika

Directions

Combine all ingredients in a jar, shake well and refrigerate for several hours.

—Carol Gasken

French Dressing

Ingredients

12 Tbsp. olive oil
4 Tbsp. lemon juice
Salt & pepper
2 cloves garlic, peeled
½ tsp. dry mustard

Directions

Combine 2 Tbsp. of oil, 2 Tbsp. of lemon juice, salt, pepper and mustard and beat well with a whisk. When smooth, add 4 Tbsp. oil and beat well again. Add remaining lemon juice and oil. Place in a jar, add garlic, cover and refrigerate. Makes 1 cup.

Sour Cream Vegetable Dip

Delicious with a variety of raw vegetables, fruit or crackers, this is an easy-to-make dip which will keep well.

Ingredients

1 cup sour cream
1 cup mayonnaise, page 130
1 Tbsp. parsley flakes
1 Tbsp. minced onion
Dash lemon pepper

Directions

Mix together all ingredients and refrigerate for 2 hours.

—Martha Brown

Olga's Salad Dressing

Ingredients

½ cup oil
⅓ cup cider vinegar
2 Tbsp. honey
1 Tbsp. onion, grated
Salt & pepper
½ tsp. mustard

Directions

Combine all ingredients in a jar and shake until well blended. Let sit overnight at room temperature for best flavor.

Special Winter Salad

Ingredients

1 tsp. Dijon mustard
1 tsp. brown sugar
¾ cup vinegar
¾ cup orange juice, or juice from canned mandarin oranges
1½ cups oil
1 tsp. poppy seeds
1 tsp. curry
1 head romaine lettuce
2 ripe avocados
4 fresh (or 1 tin) mandarin oranges

Directions

Shake together mustard, sugar, vinegar, juice, oil, poppy seeds and curry. Tear romaine lettuce into bite-sized pieces. Slice avocados and oranges and arrange on lettuce. Pour dressing over top.

Serves 4.

—Kathe Lieber

Cauliflower Pecan Salad

The cauliflower is a vegetable of Asian origin, which has been cultivated in Europe since the sixteenth century. Although it is the white head that is commonly eaten either hot, or, as in these recipes, cold, the leaves and stalks are also edible. They should be prepared as broccoli would be.

Salad Ingredients

1½ cups cauliflower florets
¾ cup chopped green pepper
1 cup toasted pecan halves
1 cup grated carrots
1 cup chopped celery

Dressing Ingredients

¾ cup mayonnaise
4 Tbsp. horseradish
½ cup sour cream or yogurt
½ tsp. prepared mustard
Salt & pepper

Directions

Blanch cauliflower in boiling water for 2 minutes. Drain and chill. When ready to serve, combine all ingredients and toss with dressing.

To make dressing, combine all ingredients and mix well.

Serves 4 to 6.

—Lorraine Murphy

Hot Spinach Salad

Ingredients

1 clove garlic, peeled & slivered
¼ cup oil
1 lb. spinach, washed, drained & torn into bite-sized pieces
1 cup sliced raw mushrooms
6 slices bacon
2 green onions, finely chopped
¼ cup vinegar
½ tsp. salt
Pepper

Directions

Let garlic stand in oil for 1 hour. Discard garlic. Toss spinach and mushrooms in a bowl and refrigerate.

Fry bacon until crisp, remove from pan and crumble. Reserve 1 Tbsp. of fat. Stir in onions and sauté for 2 to 3 minutes. Add oil, vinegar, salt and pepper and bring to a boil.

Toss with spinach and mushrooms. Sprinkle with bacon.

Serves 4 to 6.

—Carol Frost

Avocado Salad

Ingredients

1 avocado
1 green pepper
2 stalks celery
10 raw mushrooms
1 cup oil
¼ cup apple cider vinegar
½ tsp. dry mustard
1 tsp. honey
½ tsp. paprika
½ tsp. salt
1 Tbsp. finely chopped onion
2 cloves garlic, finely chopped
Tarragon, thyme, basil, marjoram

Directions

Peel and dice avocado. Dice pepper, celery and mushrooms and combine with avocado. Combine remaining ingredients and mix well. Pour over vegetables and toss lightly.

Serves 2.

—Denise Hensher

Avocado Yogurt Salad Dressing

Ingredients

1 very ripe avocado
1 cup unflavored yogurt
⅓ cup diced onion
⅓ cup diced green pepper
¼ cup mayonnaise
2 tsp. fresh dill weed
½ tsp. lemon juice
2 cloves garlic, minced
Salt & pepper

Directions

Blend avocado, yogurt, onion and green pepper for 20 seconds. Add remaining ingredients and blend until smooth.

Makes 1½ to 2 cups.

—Jill Leary

Beyond Coleslaw

Ingredients

3 cups finely grated cabbage
1 cup finely chopped cauliflower
1 red or green pepper, chopped
⅔ cup oil
⅓ cup apple cider vinegar
Salt & pepper
Garlic powder

Directions

Toss together cabbage, cauliflower and pepper. Combine oil, vinegar and seasonings to taste. Pour over vegetables and toss.

Serves 4 to 6.

—Dyan Walters

Watermelon Boat Salad

Ingredients

½ watermelon
1 cantaloupe
1 honeydew melon
1 cup orange or pineapple juice
2 peaches or nectarines
2 apples
2 pears
1 bunch green grapes
6–10 large strawberries
½ cup Kirsch or Cointreau

Directions

Clean watermelon out using melon baller. Save juice. Ball cantaloupe and honeydew melons and place fruit in orange juice. Peel and slice peaches, apples and pears and add to above. Wash grapes and strawberries and add. Place fruit in watermelon boat and pour liqueur over top. Cover with plastic wrap and let marinate for 1 to 2 hours.

—Kirsten McDougall

Apple Bacon Salad

Ingredients

⅔ cup garlic oil (oil which has had 2–3 peeled, sliced garlic cloves standing in it overnight)
2 tsp. lemon juice
3 red apples, quartered, cored & thinly sliced
½ lb. bacon, cooked until crisp
1 head lettuce, torn into bitesized pieces
½ cup grated Parmesan cheese
1 bunch scallions, chopped
½ tsp. pepper
¼ tsp. salt
1 egg

Directions

Mix garlic oil and lemon juice, and drop freshly cut apples into mixture. Combine all ingredients in salad bowl and toss until all traces of egg disappear. Serve immediately.

Serves 4.

—Denise Feeley

Delicious Apple Salad

This rich salad is delicious with roast duck or turkey.

Ingredients

1 cup whipping cream
3 tsp. sugar
½ cup mayonnaise
8 medium-sized Delicious apples, diced

Directions

Whip the cream and add sugar. Add mayonnaise and mix well. Stir in the cut-up apples and mix until well coated.

Serves 5 to 7.

—Pam Stanley

Mother's French Dressing

Ingredients

1 cup oil
⅓ cup vinegar
1½ tsp. dry mustard
¼ tsp. pepper
1½ tsp. salt
1 tsp. paprika
2 cloves garlic, minced

Directions

Combine all ingredients together and beat until creamy. Place in glass jar and store in refrigerator for 1 to 2 days.

Strain dressing through sieve to remove garlic and chill.

Makes 1 cup.

—Mary Matear

Curry Vinaigrette

Ingredients

1 Tbsp. curry powder
1 Tbsp. Dijon mustard
1 Tbsp. chopped parsley
1 Tbsp. chopped green onion
9 Tbsp. wine vinegar
1 cup olive oil
Juice of 1 lemon
Salt & pepper

Directions

Combine all ingredients and shake to mix well. Store in the refrigerator.

Makes approximately 1½ cups.

—Wendy Neilson

Garden Salad Dressing

This dressing is particularly tasty tossed with a lettuce and mushroom salad.

Ingredients

½ cup oil
¼ cup vinegar
¼ cup chopped parsley
2 green onions with tops, chopped
1–1½ Tbsp. chopped green pepper
1 tsp. salt
1 tsp. dry mustard
½ tsp. sugar
Paprika
Cayenne

Directions

Combine all ingredients, shake well and refrigerate. Shake well before tossing into salad.

—Charlotte DuChene

Creamy Salad Dressing

Ingredients

½ cup mayonnaise
½ cup sour cream
1½ Tbsp. vinegar
1½ Tbsp. lemon juice
¼ cup chopped chives

Directions

Combine all ingredients and mix well. Cover and let stand, refrigerated, for 1 day.

Makes approximately 1 cup.

—Carol A. Smith

Herb and Garlic Salad Dressing

Ingredients

⅓ cup vinegar
⅔ cup salad oil
½ tsp. salt
½ tsp. sugar
1 clove garlic, chopped
¼ tsp. pepper
¼ tsp. dry mustard
¼ tsp. basil
¼ tsp. oregano
½ tsp. lemon juice
1 Tbsp. water

Directions

Combine all ingredients in a jar with tight-fitting lid. Shake well to combine. Refrigerate. Shake well before each use.

Makes 1 cup.

—Joan Morrison

Peanut Sauce

Any nut butter may be used in place of peanut butter — cashew is a favorite. Serve this sauce over rice, spaghetti, tofu, as a fondue dip or over steamed vegetables.

Ingredients

½ cup peanut butter
1 small onion, grated
1 clove garlic, crushed
¼ cup instant milk powder
½ tsp. honey
2 Tbsp. lemon juice
2 tsp. soy sauce

Directions

Blend all ingredients in saucepan over low heat, adding hot water until mixture has consistency of heavy cream. For a smoother sauce, use blender to mix.

Makes 1 cup.

—Lorna Wollner

Vegetarian Paté

Equally delicious as a cracker spread or a sandwich filling, this paté is quickly and easily prepared.

Ingredients

1 cup sunflower seeds
1 potato, peeled
½ cup whole wheat flour
1½ cups hot water
1 large onion, minced
½ cup butter, melted
1½ tsp. basil
1 tsp. thyme

Directions

Chop the sunflower seeds finely by hand or in food processor. Grate the potato. Combine all ingredients and place in greased loaf pan. Bake at 350°F for 1½ hours. Paté will be moist. Serve hot, or chill in refrigerator overnight before serving.

—Suzanne Dignard

Green Bean Casserole

Ingredients

½ cup sliced onion
1 tsp. finely chopped parsley
2 Tbsp. butter
2 Tbsp. flour
½ tsp. grated lemon peel
Squeeze of lemon juice
Salt & pepper
1 cup sour cream
5 cups green beans, partially cooked
2 Tbsp. melted butter
½ cup dry bread crumbs
½ cup grated sharp cheese

Directions

Cook together onion, parsley, butter, flour, lemon peel, lemon juice and salt and pepper, then add sour cream and green beans. Pour into greased casserole dish and spread evenly, smoothing the top. Combine melted butter and bread crumbs and sprinkle over the top, then distribute the cheese evenly. Bake at 325°F for 30 minutes, or until cheese is melted and browned.

Serves 8 to 10.

—Rebecca Gibson Spink

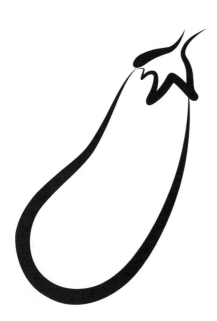

California Corn

Ingredients

1 large onion, sliced
1 clove garlic, minced
2 Tbsp. olive oil
½ cup thinly sliced green pepper
1 lb. mushrooms, sliced
1 cup minced parsley
½ cup dry bread crumbs
½ tsp. oregano
14-oz. can creamed corn
4 medium tomatoes, peeled & sliced
½ lb. sharp Cheddar cheese, grated
1 tsp. salt

Directions

Sauté onion and garlic in oil until tender. Add green pepper and mushrooms and cook over low heat for 5 minutes. Combine parsley, bread crumbs and oregano in a bowl.

To assemble, place half the creamed corn in a greased casserole dish, then add half the green pepper-mushroom mixture, half the tomatoes, half the cheese, ½ tsp. salt and half the bread crumb mixture. Repeat layers. Cover and bake at 300°F for 45 minutes. Remove cover and bake for 15 minutes more.

Serves 4.

—Enid Campbell

Cheddar Almond Broccoli Casserole

Ingredients

2 lbs. broccoli florets, steamed until barely tender
¼ cup butter
¼ cup flour
1 cup milk
¾ cup vegetable stock
2 Tbsp. lemon juice
2 Tbsp. sherry
Pepper
1 cup shredded Cheddar
¼ cup ground almonds
Parmesan cheese

Directions

While broccoli is steaming, melt butter in saucepan and blend in flour. Add milk and stock and cook, stirring, until smooth and thick. Add lemon juice, sherry and pepper. Blend in Cheddar cheese and all but 1 Tbsp. of the almonds. Place broccoli in casserole dish and pour sauce over it. Sprinkle with Parmesan cheese and remaining almonds. Bake, uncovered, at 375°F for 20 minutes.

Serves 4.

—Holly Andrews

Baked Corn

Ingredients

¼ cup chopped onion
2 Tbsp. flour
1 tsp. salt
2 Tbsp. butter
2 tsp. paprika
¼ tsp. dry mustard
Pepper
¾ cup milk
2 cups corn
1 egg

Directions

Combine all ingredients and bake at 350°F for 20 to 25 minutes.

Serves 4.

—Kathy Cowbrough

Mexican Corn Custard

Ingredients

2 eggs, beaten
3 cups creamed corn
1 cup cooked corn
½ tsp. salt
1 clove garlic, minced
½ tsp. baking powder
⅓ cup melted butter
4 oz. chopped green chilies
½ cup chopped green or red pepper
⅓ lb. sharp Cheddar cheese, grated

Directions

Combine all ingredients in order listed and pour into buttered, 2-quart casserole dish.

Bake at 375°F for 45 minutes; reduce temperature to 325°F and continue to bake for another 30 to 45 minutes, or until set.

Serves 6.

—Joyce Falkowski

Crab Stuffed Mushrooms

Ingredients

4 oz. cream cheese
2 Tbsp. chopped almonds
1 tsp. chopped chives
8 oz. chopped crabmeat
Salt & pepper
Lemon juice
16 large mushroom caps
10 oz. spinach
2 cloves garlic, minced
4 oz. butter

Directions

Mix cream cheese, almonds and chives until smooth. Add crabmeat, salt and pepper and lemon juice.

Drop mushrooms into boiling water for 2 minutes, remove and rinse in cold water. Dry and stuff with cream cheese mixture.

Drop spinach into boiling water for 1 minute, drain and rinse with cold water to stop cooking. Squeeze dry. Sauté briefly in butter, tossing until hot. Place in greased 8" x 8" casserole dish, top with stuffed mushrooms and bake at 500°F for 3 to 5 minutes. Heat garlic with butter until butter is melted. Pour over mushroom caps and serve.

Serves 4 as an appetizer.

—Estelle Lemay

Spinach Stuffed Mushrooms

Ingredients

1 lb. fresh spinach
24 medium to large mushrooms, cleaned & stemmed, reserving stems
Butter
½ cup grated Parmesan cheese
⅔ cup crumbled feta cheese
½ cup finely chopped green onion
½ cup chopped fresh parsley

Directions

Steam spinach, chop finely, then drain well in sieve, pressing out moisture with wooden spoon. Finely chop mushroom stems and sauté in small amount of butter. Combine all ingredients, except mushroom caps, in bowl and mix well.

Brush outsides of mushroom caps with butter, then fill with spinach mixture, mounding it up in center. Place on baking sheet and bake at 375°F for 20 minutes, or until mushrooms are soft. Serve warm.

Makes 24.

—Susan Gillespie

Maple Glazed Parsnips

The selection of small, uniformly sized parsnips for this recipe results in a delicious, tender dish.

Ingredients

8 small parsnips, trimmed & pared
⅓ cup maple syrup
1½ Tbsp. unsalted butter
2 tsp. lemon juice
¼ tsp. grated lemon zest

Directions

Cook parsnips, covered, in ½ inch of boiling water over medium-high heat until tender but crisp — 3 to 4 minutes. Remove from heat and drain well.

Combine remaining ingredients in same skillet and heat over medium heat until simmering. Return parsnips to skillet and cook, uncovered, turning frequently, until parsnips have absorbed the glaze — about 4 minutes.

Serves 4.

—Lucia M. Cyre

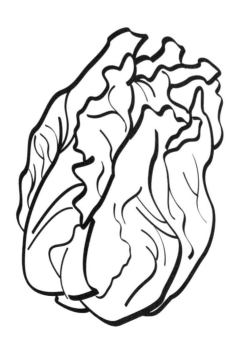

Potato Casserole

Ingredients

2 cups mashed potatoes
2 cups cottage cheese
½ cup sour cream
1 small onion, minced
1-2 eggs, well beaten
Salt & pepper
Romano or Parmesan cheese

Directions

Combine all ingredients and place in greased casserole dish, cover with grated Romano or Parmesan cheese if you wish and bake at 350°F for 1 hour.

Serves 4.

—Margaret Graham

Green Bean & Potato Salad

Ingredients

4 large russet potatoes
¾ lb. green beans, snapped in half
⅓ cup olive oil
¼ cup cider vinegar
1 clove garlic, crushed
½ tsp. basil
¼ tsp. thyme
salt & pepper
½ tsp. dry mustard
⅓ cup Parmesan cheese

Directions

Scrub and dice potatoes. Cook in boiling water. Steam green beans until bright green and crispy-tender. Combine potatoes and beans. Mix together oil, vinegar, garlic, basil, thyme, salt and pepper and mustard. Toss with vegetables. Sprinkle with cheese. Serve warm or at room temperature.

Serves 4 to 6.

—Nancy R. Franklin

Hot German Potato Salad

Ingredients

6 medium potatoes
¼ lb. bacon, chopped
¼ cup sliced green onions
⅓ cup vinegar
⅓ cup beef stock
1 Tbsp. sugar
½ tsp. salt
½ tsp. celery salt
Pepper
Parsley
Paprika

Directions

Boil potatoes until tender. Peel, slice and keep warm in serving dish. Cook bacon until crisp, remove, drain and add to potatoes, reserving fat.

In fat, fry green onions. Add vinegar, stock, sugar, salt, celery salt and pepper. Bring to a boil and pour over potatoes. Toss lightly to combine and top with parsley and paprika.

Serves 6.

—Irma Leming

Spinach & Egg Casserole

Ingredients

¼ cup butter
¼ cup flour
½ tsp. salt
¼ tsp. paprika
2 cups milk
1 cup bread crumbs
2 cups chopped, cooked spinach
4 eggs, hard boiled, peeled & sliced
4 slices Cheddar cheese

Directions

Melt butter, stir in flour, salt, paprika and milk and cook, stirring constantly, until thickened.

In greased baking dish, assemble casserole as follows: half the bread crumbs, half the spinach, half the eggs, one-third of the sauce, half the cheese, rest of spinach, rest of eggs, one-third of the sauce, rest of cheese, rest of sauce and rest of bread crumbs. Bake at 325°F for 35 to 40 minutes.

Serves 4.

—J. Kristine MacDonald

Spinach with Peanut Sauce

Ingredients

2 lbs. fresh spinach
2 Tbsp. butter
1 large onion, chopped
Cayenne
1 Tbsp. whiskey
1 tsp. soy sauce
½ cup fresh coconut milk
½ cup unsalted peanuts, crushed

Directions

Cook spinach, without water, until limp. Cool, then drain to remove all moisture. Melt butter in a pan, and when foam subsides, add onion and cayenne. Cook until onion is soft. Stir in whiskey, soy sauce, coconut milk and peanuts. Cook, stirring constantly, for 2 to 3 minutes. Add spinach to frying pan and cook until heated through, about 4 to 5 minutes.

Serves 6 to 8.

—Ingrid Birker

Green Tomato Curry

This recipe provides a delicious use for end-of-the-season unripe tomatoes. It can be frozen very successfully and does not take a great deal of time to prepare.

Ingredients

¼ cup butter
2 medium onions, chopped
4 Tbsp. curry powder
1 tsp. cumin
1 cup water
8 cups green tomatoes
½ cup brown sugar
2 Tbsp. lemon juice
½ tsp. paprika
Salt

Directions

Sauté onions in butter for 10 minutes. Add curry powder and cumin and cook for 5 minutes longer. Stir in water and remaining ingredients. Simmer for 30 minutes, stirring occasionally and adding more water if necessary. Serve over rice.

Serves 4.

—Leslie Gent

Butternut Squash with Cheese & Walnuts

Ingredients

1 small butternut squash
1 small onion, chopped
1 cup shredded hard cheese
½ cup chopped walnuts

Directions

Peel and slice squash and steam until just tender. Oil a casserole dish. Layer squash, onion, cheese and walnuts, ending with a layer of cheese and walnuts on top. Bake, uncovered, at 300°F for 15 minutes.

Serves 4.

—Brenda Thaler

Rum Squash

Ingredients

4 cups mashed, cooked squash
2 Tbsp. rum
2 Tbsp. maple syrup
½ tsp. salt
1 Tbsp. cream
½ cup well-drained, crushed pineapple
5 Tbsp. butter
½ cup brown sugar
½ cup chopped walnuts

Directions

Mix squash, rum, syrup, salt, cream, pineapple and 2 Tbsp. butter and pour into a greased, 2-quart casserole dish. Melt remaining 3 Tbsp. butter over low heat and stir in brown sugar and walnuts. Cook, stirring, until creamy and pour over squash. Bake at 350°F for 20 to 30 minutes, or until bubbly.

Serves 4.

—Joan Patricia Cox

Zucchini French Fries

Ingredients

4 medium zucchini
1½ cups flour
Salt
2 eggs
1½ Tbsp. water
1 cup Parmesan cheese
Garlic salt
Oil

Directions

Wash zucchini and remove ends, but do not peel. Cut into shoestring strips approximately 3 inches long. Sprinkle well with salt and roll lightly in ½ cup flour. Shake off excess flour and drop strips, several at a time, into eggs beaten lightly with 1½ Tbsp. water.

In wide, shallow pan, combine remaining 1 cup flour with Parmesan cheese and garlic salt. Roll zucchini in flour mixture to coat evenly and spread on paper towels to dry. Heat oil to 375°F. Fry strips, a handful at a time, until crisp and golden. Drain on paper towels and keep warm until all are fried.

Serves 4 to 5.

—*Barb Krimmer*

Zucchini Lasagne

Ingredients

2 cups cottage cheese
1 cup cooked, chopped spinach
1 lb. mozzarella cheese, grated
1½ lbs. ground beef
1 small onion, chopped
8-oz. can tomato sauce
½ tsp. salt
½ tsp. pepper
½ tsp. oregano
½ tsp. thyme
2½ lbs. zucchini, thinly sliced lengthwise

Directions

Combine cottage cheese, spinach and half the mozzarella cheese in a bowl. Brown ground beef and onion, drain off excess fat, then add tomato sauce, salt, pepper, oregano and thyme. Simmer for 5 minutes.

In a greased 9" x 13" casserole dish, layer half the meat mixture, half the zucchini, all of the spinach-cheese mixture, the rest of the zucchini, the rest of the meat and top with remaining ½ lb. of mozzarella cheese. Cover and bake at 350°F for 30 minutes. Uncover and bake for another 45 minutes.

Serves 6.

—*Christine Peterman*

Italian Vegetable Medley

This recipe is really just a guideline. Almost any garden-fresh vegetable can be added or substituted — it is the banana pepper and garlic which give the dish its distinctive flavor.

Ingredients

3 Tbsp. oil
4 medium onions, cut in half & sliced lengthwise
1 banana pepper, sliced
6 cloves garlic, crushed
1 tsp. finely chopped ginger
2 Tbsp. curry
2 sweet peppers, thinly sliced lengthwise
Juice of 1 lemon
8 tomatoes, peeled & chopped
1 cup bean sprouts

Directions

Sauté onions, banana pepper, garlic and ginger lightly in hot oil. Add curry and sweet peppers. When vegetables are cooked, but still crunchy, add tomatoes and lemon juice. Cook over low heat until tomatoes are soft. Add bean sprouts and toss. Serve with pasta or rice.

Serves 4.

—Sandra Hunter

Vegetable Pot Pie

This is a delicious alternative to the traditional beef or chicken pot pie.

Ingredients

Pastry for 9-inch pie shell
6 small white onions or 1 medium onion, cut into eighths
2 cups chopped cauliflower
1 cup sliced carrots
1 cup quartered mushrooms
1 cup peas
½ cup slivered almonds
3 Tbsp. butter
4 Tbsp. flour
1 cup milk
1 Tbsp. parsley
Salt & pepper

Directions

Cook onion, cauliflower and carrots until just tender. Drain and save 1 cup liquid. Arrange cooked vegetables in greased 8" x 8" baking dish along with mushrooms, peas and almonds.

To make sauce, melt butter, stir in flour, then gradually add cooking liquid and milk. Continue to stir and cook, adding parsley and salt and pepper, until sauce is thickened. Pour over vegetables. Top with pie crust and bake at 425°F for 20 to 25 minutes, or until crust is lightly browned. Cool for 10 minutes before serving.

Serves 4.

—Julie Pope

Almond Butter Carrots

Carrots deserve better treatment than the slicing and boiling they generally get. This is a simple but tasty method of dressing up the nutritious, inexpensive vegetable.

Ingredients

6 carrots, scraped & julienned
3 Tbsp. butter
⅓ cup slivered almonds
¼ tsp. curry
1 Tbsp. lemon juice

Directions

Steam carrots until crispy-tender. Melt butter until lightly browned, add almonds and sauté until golden brown, stirring constantly. Stir in curry and lemon juice and cook over low heat for 1 to 2 minutes. Pour over carrots and serve.

Serves 4 to 6.

—Jayne Simms-Dalmotas

Potato Pancakes (Latkes)

Ingredients

3 eggs, separated
4½ cups grated potatoes, well drained
6 Tbsp. grated onion
1–1½ tsp. salt
¼ tsp. pepper
3 Tbsp. matzo meal or potato flour or dry bread crumbs
oil

Directions

Beat together everything but egg whites and oil. Beat whites until stiff, then fold into potato mixture. Fry in about ½ inch hot oil, using a heaping tablespoonful of batter for each pancake. Turn when edges are golden brown. Keep pancakes hot until all are fried.

Makes 14 to 16 pancakes.

—Lynne Roe

Baked Hash Browns

"This is an easy way to make delicious, crispy hash browns. I serve it for special breakfasts or brunch with eggs and broiled tomatoes. It is also good for supper with smoked pork chops."

Ingredients

4 slices bacon
4 potatoes, grated
1 onion, grated
⅓ cup bread crumbs
1 egg
⅛ tsp. pepper
⅛ tsp. salt

Directions

Cook bacon lightly, so that fat is cooked out but bacon is not yet crisp. Drain, reserving fat. Dice bacon. Put bacon fat into a 9" x 9" baking pan. Heat at 400°F.

Combine remaining ingredients, including bacon, and spread in the hot dish. Bake at 400°F, uncovered, for about 45 minutes.

Serves 2.

—*Ruth Ellis Haworth*

Italian Spinach Dumplings

Ingredients

1 pkg. spinach
4 tsp. salt
½ tsp. ground nutmeg
¼ tsp. pepper
1 egg, lightly beaten
½ cup ricotta cheese
6 Tbsp. flour
1 Tbsp. butter

Directions

Cook spinach and drain thoroughly, pressing with spoon to squeeze out all liquid. Chop finely or purée. Combine spinach, 1 tsp. salt, nutmeg, pepper, egg and ricotta cheese in large bowl. Gradually add flour, using enough to make a firm mixture. Shape into 1-inch balls. Place on a plate and chill for at least 30 minutes.

Combine 8 cups water, butter and remaining 3 tsp. salt in large saucepan. Bring to a boil. Drop balls gently into water, several at a time, and cook, uncovered, for 8 minutes, or until balls rise to top and are tender. Lift out with a slotted spoon and keep warm.

Serves 4.

—*Ingrid Birker*

Orange Squash

Ingredients

1–2 Tbsp. grated gingerroot
juice and grated rind of 2 oranges
1 Tbsp. coriander
¼ cup butter, softened
salt
3 small squash, halved & seeded

Directions

Combine ginger, orange rind, juice of 1 orange, coriander, butter and salt and mix well. Place in squash halves. Bake in covered casserole dish with juice of other orange at 350°F for 45 minutes.

Serves 6.

—Wendy Vine

Turnips & Apples

Filling Ingredients

1 large turnip
1 Tbsp. butter
2 apples
¼ cup brown sugar
½ tsp. cinnamon

Crust Ingredients

⅓ cup flour
⅓ cup brown sugar
2 Tbsp. butter

Directions

Cook turnip, then mash with butter. Peel and thinly slice apples. Toss with sugar and cinnamon. In greased casserole dish, arrange turnip and apples in layers, beginning and ending with turnip.

Combine crust ingredients until texture is crumbly. Pat on top of turnip. Bake, uncovered, at 350°F for 45 minutes.

Serves 4.

—Pat de la Ronde

Tomato Curry

This curry can also be made with half ripe and half unripe tomatoes, although the result will not be as smooth. Serve with rice, noodles, meatloaf, fish or hard-cooked eggs.

Ingredients

2 Tbsp. oil
2 onions, chopped
1 Tbsp. chopped coriander
1 tsp. toasted cumin seed
2 cloves garlic, crushed
2 lbs. ripe tomatoes, peeled & chopped
1 Tbsp. brown sugar
salt

Directions

Heat oil and sauté onions until golden. Add coriander and cook, stirring, for 1 minute, then add remaining ingredients. Cook for 30 minutes over medium heat.

Serves 6 as a sauce.

—*Ethel Hunter*

Herbed Tomatoes

Ingredients

4 ripe tomatoes
salt
¼ cup butter
⅛ tsp. pepper
1 tsp. brown sugar
1 Tbsp. lemon juice
½ cup diced celery
3 Tbsp. finely chopped chives or green onion
3 Tbsp. chopped parsley
½ tsp. oregano

Directions

Core tomatoes and sprinkle with salt. Melt butter in frying pan, add pepper and brown sugar, then place tomatoes in pan, cored side down. Cover and simmer slowly for 5 minutes. Turn tomatoes over and spoon butter mixture into hollow. Add remaining ingredients to pan and sauté for 2 minutes. Cover and simmer until tomatoes are just tender — 8 minutes. Spoon mixture into tomatoes and lift carefully from pan. Pour any remaining pan liquids over tomatoes and serve.

Serves 4.

—*Lynn Tobin*

Calzone

Calzone is basically a pizza turnover. It can be made as one large turnover or as individual turnovers. The filling possibilities are limited only by the cook's imagination — try pesto, chicken cacciatore, seafood, a meat spaghetti sauce, ricotta cheese and spinach and so on. For this version, we suggest a combination of onion, mushrooms, olives and zucchini. Calzone can also be eaten cold, without the sauce, as picnic fare.

Sauce Ingredients
8-oz. can tomato sauce
6½-oz. can tomato paste
¼ cup minced onion
3 cloves garlic, crushed
¼ tsp. pepper
¼ tsp. oregano
¼ tsp. basil
10 fennel seeds, crushed

Crust Ingredients
½ tsp. sugar
½ tsp. pepper
½ tsp. parsley
1½ tsp. yeast
1 egg, beaten
2–3 cups flour

Filling Ingredients
4 cups partially cooked vegetables
1 tsp. parsley
1 tsp. basil
1 tsp. oregano
1 cup grated mozzarella cheese
1 egg, beaten

Directions

Combine sauce ingredients in saucepan and simmer for 45 minutes.

For crust: Mix ⅔ cup hot water with sugar, pepper and parsley. Add yeast and beaten egg. Stir in flour to make a soft dough and set in warm place to rise.

Toss vegetables in lightly oiled skillet with parsley, basil and oregano for 10 minutes. Stir in cheese.

Shape dough into oval the thickness of pizza crust. Lay half on and half off a greased cookie sheet. Mix filling ingredients together and arrange on half of dough that is on cookie sheet. Trickle ¼ cup sauce over filling. Fold dough over and pinch edges closed. Bake calzone at 350°F for 3 minutes. Remove from oven and glaze with beaten egg. Cut steam vents and bake for 30 minutes, then broil until golden. Serve with sauce.

Serves 4 to 6.

—*E. K. Molitor*

Vegetables Parmigiana

Ingredients

2 Tbsp. oil
1 Tbsp. butter
1 lb. eggplant, peeled & sliced ½" thick
1 lb. zucchini, sliced ½" thick
1 onion, halved & sliced
1 tsp. salt
1 tsp. oregano
½ tsp. pepper
1½ cups tomato sauce
2 cloves garlic, crushed
½ lb. mozzarella cheese, sliced
2 Tbsp. Parmesan cheese

Directions

Heat oil and butter and sauté eggplant, zucchini and onion for 10 minutes. Stir in salt, oregano and pepper, then spoon into greased 2-quart baking dish. Mix tomato sauce with garlic and pour over vegetables. Tuck mozzarella cheese slices into vegetables so half of each slice is on surface. Sprinkle with Parmesan cheese and bake, uncovered, at 375°F for 25 minutes.

Serves 4.

—*Nancy R. Franklin*

Tomato Green Pepper Salad

Ingredients

1 large onion, finely chopped
2–3 green peppers, thinly sliced
½ tsp. basil pepper
3 Tbsp. red wine vinegar
3–4 Tbsp. olive oil
4–5 tomatoes, sliced

Directions

Toss together onion and peppers. Combine basil, pepper, vinegar and oil and pour over onion and peppers. Toss, then chill for 1 to 2 hours. Stir in tomatoes just before serving.

Serves 6.

—*Trudi Keillor*

Summer Bean Salad

A well-rounded and appealing salad—the beans complement each other in color and flavor without compromising texture.

Ingredients

2 cups cooked sliced green beans
2 cups cooked sliced wax beans
2 cups cooked kidney beans
2 cups cooked chickpeas
½ red onion, chopped
2 Tbsp. chopped parsley
1 stalk celery, chopped
1 cup quartered artichoke hearts
6 Tbsp. peanut oil
3 Tbsp. cider vinegar
1 clove garlic, minced
salt & pepper

Directions

Combine beans, chickpeas, onion, parsley, celery and artichoke hearts in large bowl. Combine remaining ingredients and toss with salad. Chill for at least 2 hours to blend flavors.

Serves 6 to 8.

—Lynne Roe

Mom's Potato Salad

"Our family of 11 children grew up on this. With so many people, it was easiest to have buffet-style meals. This dish is easy to enlarge."

Salad Ingredients

6 potatoes, cooked & diced
5 hard-cooked eggs, diced
1 cup chopped parsley
2 stalks celery, chopped
½ cup chopped chives
½ cup chopped radishes
¼ cup chopped red onion

Dressing Ingredients

¼ cup sugar
¼ cup flour
2 tsp. salt
1½ tsp. dry mustard
¾–1 tsp. cayenne
4 egg yolks, lightly beaten
1½ cups milk
½ cup vinegar
1 Tbsp. butter

Directions

To make dressing: In top of double boiler, mix sugar, flour, salt, mustard and cayenne. Stir in yolks and milk and cook, stirring, until thickened. Add vinegar and butter, mix well, then cool. Combine remaining ingredients and toss with cooled dressing. Chill.

Serves 8 to 10.

—Penny Tognet

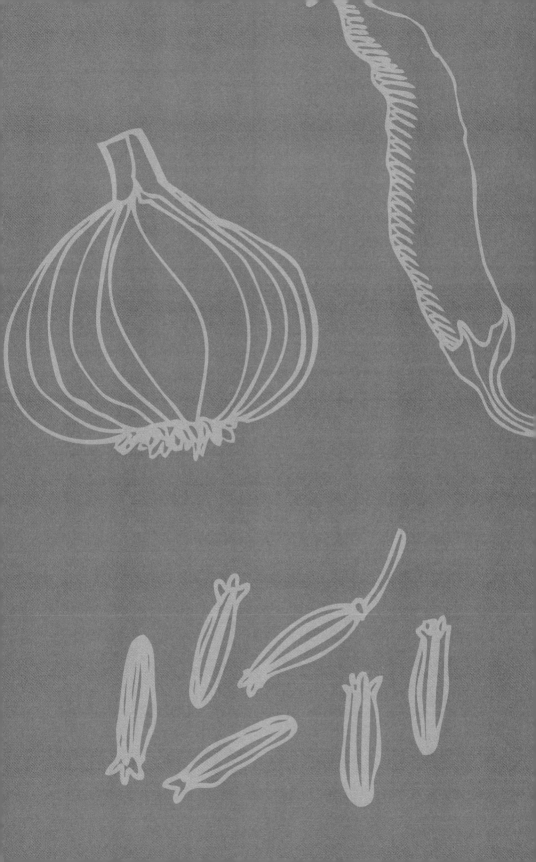

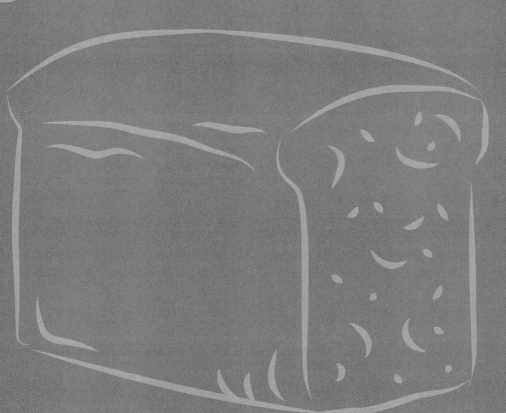

Beans
& Grains

Mushroom Barley Casserole

Ingredients

½ lb. mushrooms
1 large onion, chopped
1 cup pot barley
¼ cup butter
½ tsp. salt
⅛ tsp. pepper
4 cups chicken stock

Directions

Sauté mushrooms, onion and barley in melted butter. Place in a casserole dish and add remaining ingredients. Mix well.

Bake, covered, 1½ hours at 350°F. If there is too much liquid, remove lid for last 20 minutes.

Serves 6 to 8.

—Eileen Deeley

Refried Beans

Ingredients

2 Tbsp. oil
5 cups cooked kidney beans
1½ Tbsp. oregano
1½ Tbsp. minced garlic
1 Tbsp. crushed chili peppers
½ lb. Cheddar cheese, grated

Directions

Place oil, beans, oregano, garlic and chili peppers in a heavy, deep frying pan. Simmer for 10 minutes. Mash until all the beans are broken up.

Stir in cheese and cook until it melts. Serve in tortillas.

Serves 6 to 8.

—Donna Schedler

Polenta

This variation of a traditional Italian dish, polenta, with a mush-like consistency, is good topped with cheese and stew.

Ingredients

5 cups water
1 tsp. salt
3 cups cold water
3 cups corn meal

Directions

Bring 5 cups of salted water to a boil. Combine cold water with corn meal and add to boiling water. Cook, stirring, over medium heat for 30 minutes — until mixture thickens.

Serves 4.

—Anne Erb Panciera

Bean Filling for Pita Bread

Ingredients

4 cups cooked white navy beans
5 Tbsp. oil
2 Tbsp. lemon juice
1 tsp. oregano
½ tsp. salt
½ tsp. cumin
¼ tsp. ground pepper
4 oz. cream cheese, cubed
2 medium tomatoes, chopped
1 medium cucumber, diced
2 Tbsp. chopped parsley
Pita bread for 4 (page 382)

Directions

Toss beans, oil, lemon juice and spices in a large bowl. Gently stir in cheese, tomato and cucumber. Cover and chill for 2 hours.

Cut bread in half and fill with bean mixture. Sprinkle with parsley.

Serves 4.

—Margaret Silverthorn

Betty's Baked Beans

Ingredients

1 cup navy beans
1 tsp. dry mustard
1 tsp. salt
¼ tsp. pepper
¾ cup brown sugar
2 cups tomato juice
½ cup chopped onion
1 cup bacon pieces
3 medium-sized apples

Directions

Cook beans in boiling water until tender. Add mustard, salt, pepper, brown sugar, tomato juice, onion, bacon and apples.

Place in bean pot or casserole dish, cover and bake at 300°F for 1 hour.

Serves 4.

—Catherine Rupke

Lentil Burgers

Ingredients

1 cup uncooked lentils, rinsed
½ cup uncooked rice
3 cups water
1½ Tbsp. salt
1 cup bread crumbs
½ cup wheat germ
1 large onion, chopped
½ tsp. celery seed
½ tsp. marjoram
¼ tsp. thyme
1 tsp. salt
½ tsp. pepper
1 Tbsp. chopped fresh parsley
Wheat germ

Directions

Combine lentils, rice, water and salt in a saucepan. Bring to a boil, lower heat, cover and simmer for 35 to 45 minutes or until rice is tender. Remove from heat, let stand 10 minutes and then mash together with any remaining liquid in pan.

Place in a large bowl with bread crumbs, wheat germ, onion, celery seed, marjoram, thyme, salt, pepper and parsley. Mix well and shape into patties.

Coat with wheat germ and fry in vegetable oil until golden brown on both sides.

Makes 24 patties.

—Barbara J. Spangler

Hummus

A chick pea paté of Middle Eastern origin, hummus makes a flavorful and protein-rich sandwich spread or appetizer dip.

Ingredients

2 cups cooked chickpeas
⅓ cup water
Juice of 2 lemons
½ cup tahini (ground sesame seeds)
2 cloves garlic, crushed
½ tsp. salt
Cayenne pepper

Directions

Whir all ingredients in a blender until smooth. Serve as a dip for pita bread or raw vegetables.

Makes 2½ cups.

—Sandra James-Mitchell

Vegi-Burgers

There are many good recipes for meatless burgers. Most grains can be used, but it is important to add sufficient seasoning, otherwise the finished product will be bland and pasty. Toppings can include regular hamburger sauces, sprouts, yogurt, chili sauce and so on.

Ingredients

1 cup grated Cheddar cheese
1 cup sunflower seeds
2 cups bread crumbs
¼ cup bran
¼ cup wheat germ
¼ cup oats
1 cup onion, finely chopped
1 tsp. salt
1 tsp. sage
6 eggs

Directions

Mix all ingredients together and form into patties. Fry on both sides in vegetable oil. Makes 12 patties.

—Brenda Kennedy

Curried Lentil Spaghetti Sauce

Despite our initial hesitation about this recipe — primarily because it does not call for browning the beef and vegetables — this spaghetti sauce was a delicious hit. It can be assembled first thing in the morning and left to simmer all day, with only an occasional stir.

Ingredients

2 28-oz. cans tomatoes
1 cup dry lentils
1 lb. ground beef
½ cup tomato paste
1 clove garlic, crushed
½ cup chopped green pepper
½ cup chopped mushrooms
1 onion, chopped
1½ Tbsp. curry
2 tsp. cumin
1 tsp. oregano
1 tsp. basil
1 Tbsp. parsley
salt & pepper

Directions

Combine all ingredients in heavy pot. Bring to a boil, stir thoroughly, reduce heat to lowest setting, cover and simmer for 1½ to 2 hours.

Serves 6 to 8.

—Judie Wright

Cheese Nut Loaf

Ingredients

1 medium onion, chopped
1 clove garlic, chopped
3 Tbsp. oil
1 cup cooked rice
½ cup wheat germ
½ cup chopped walnuts or cashews
½ cup thinly sliced mushrooms
¼ tsp. salt
¼ tsp. pepper
½ lb. Cheddar cheese, grated
2 eggs, beaten

Directions

Sauté onion and garlic in oil. Combine with rice, wheat germ, nuts, mushrooms, salt, pepper and all but half a cup of cheese. Mix well, add eggs and mix again.

Place in a greased loaf pan and bake at 350°F for 50 minutes. Sprinkle with remaining cheese after 30 minutes.

Serves 4.

—Carol Bomke

Nut Loaf

Ingredients

2 cups uncooked red river cereal
1 cup boiling water
1 cup light cream
1 small onion, chopped
1 cup Cheddar cheese, cubed
1 cup walnuts, chopped
3 Tbsp. Worcestershire sauce
1 tsp. sage
1 egg

Directions

Pour boiling water over the cereal, stir in the cream and let stand.

Combine remaining ingredients, add to cereal mixture, and pack into a loaf pan coated with ⅛-inch of vegetable oil.

Bake at 350°F for 1 hour.

Serves 4.

—Norma Stellings

Cheese & Broccoli Casserole

Ingredients

1 cup chopped onion
1 Tbsp. butter
1½ cups white sauce, page 129
½ cup sliced mushrooms
Salt & pepper
2 tsp. tamari sauce
1 cup grated Cheddar cheese
1 cup cooked rice
½ tsp. dry mustard
4 hard-boiled eggs, quartered
1 bunch broccoli, cooked

Directions

Sauté onion in butter until soft, then gradually stir in white sauce, mushrooms, salt, pepper and tamari sauce. Add cheese, rice and mustard and cook, stirring, until cheese is melted. Fold in quartered eggs.

Place broccoli in greased 2-quart baking dish and pour sauce over it.

Bake at 350°F for 20 minutes.

Serves 6 to 8.

—Signe Dickerson

Browned Rice

Ingredients

2 cups uncooked rice
¼ cup butter
1 cup sliced mushrooms
¼ cup chopped green onions
½ lb. slivered almonds
3 cups chicken stock

Directions

Brown rice in butter in large saucepan. Sauté mushrooms, onion and almonds in butter in a frying pan. Boil stock and pour over rice. Boil again, reduce heat, cover and cook for 15 minutes.

Add mushrooms, onions and almonds and leave on low heat until ready to serve.

Serves 8 to 10.

—Jacquie Gibson

Herbed Rice

Ingredients

3 Tbsp. butter
¼ cup finely chopped chives or green onions
1 cup uncooked rice
½ tsp. marjoram
½ tsp. rosemary
½ tsp. salt
2 cups chicken stock

Directions

In a heavy saucepan, melt butter and sauté chives or onions until softened. Add rice and cook, stirring constantly, until the rice is lightly browned. Add the herbs, salt and chicken stock.

Cover tightly and bring to a boil, then lower heat and simmer until rice is tender.

Makes 3 cups.

—Kathy Christie

Mushroom Brown Rice

Ingredients

1 cup bread crumbs
1½ cups melted butter
2 cups mushrooms, sliced
6 cups cooked brown rice
Salt & pepper
1 cup grated Cheddar cheese
¼ cup minced parsley

Directions

Sauté bread crumbs in ½ cup melted butter. Remove crumbs from pan, then sauté mushrooms.

Place rice in a casserole dish and toss lightly with remaining butter. Add mushrooms, bread crumbs and salt and pepper to taste. Mix well and top with cheese and parsley.

Bake at 350°F for 20 to 30 minutes.

Serves 8 to 10.

—Winona Heasman

Spanish Rice

Quickly and easily assembled, this dish can be served as a meatless main dish or as a side dish.

Ingredients

1 cup uncooked brown rice
2 cups water
1 onion
1 green pepper
3 stalks celery
3 cloves garlic
4 Tbsp. oil
28-oz. can tomatoes
1 tsp. salt
Dash of pepper
3 whole cloves or ½ tsp. ground cloves
1 cup grated Cheddar cheese

Directions

Cook rice in boiling water for 45 minutes. Meanwhile, chop onion, green pepper and celery and sauté with garlic in oil until onion becomes translucent. Add tomatoes and seasonings to vegetables and simmer for 10 minutes.

Combine with cooked rice in casserole dish and top with grated cheese. Bake at 350°F for 15 to 20 minutes.

Serves 4.

—Rae Anne Huth

Curried Rice Salad

Ingredients

1½ cups uncooked rice
2 Tbsp. diced green pepper
2 Tbsp. raisins
1 small onion, finely chopped
2 Tbsp. snipped parsley
⅔ cup olive oil
⅓ cup wine vinegar
Salt & pepper
½ tsp. dry mustard
1 clove garlic, mashed
1 Tbsp. curry powder
Green pepper rings & tomato wedges to garnish

Directions

Cook rice and cool. Add green pepper, raisins, onion and parsley and mix well.

Combine oil, vinegar, salt, pepper, mustard and garlic in a small bowl.

When ready to serve, pour dressing over salad, add curry powder and mix well. Garnish with green pepper rings and tomato wedges.

Serves 6.

—Sandra Kapral

Chinese Rice Salad

Ingredients

1 cup cold cooked rice
1 cup cooked peas
¼ cup chopped green onion
½ cup shrimp
1½ cups chopped celery
1 tsp. salt
1 Tbsp. soy sauce
3 Tbsp. vinegar
1 tsp. curry powder
⅓ cup oil
½ tsp. sugar

Directions

Combine rice, peas, onion, shrimp and celery.

Combine remaining ingredients to make a dressing and pour over rice mixture. Mix well and refrigerate for several hours.

Serves 6 to 8.

—*Beth Hopkins*

Rice Cakes

Ingredients

2 eggs, well beaten
3 cups cooked brown rice
3 Tbsp. flour
2–3 Tbsp. finely chopped onion
½ cup milk
1 tsp. salt
1–2 tsp. parsley

Directions

Blend eggs into cooled rice. Add flour, onion, milk and seasonings. Mix well.

Drop by spoonfuls onto hot frying pan. Flatten, brown and flip.

—*Pat Dicer*

Pesto Bean Salad

"Pesto adds a wonderful flavor to almost everything. It is most commonly associated with pasta, but I developed this easy salad one summer day, when confronted with leftover pesto and beans."

Salad Ingredients

3 cups cooked navy beans
2 cups cooked white kidney beans
¾ cup garlic mayonnaise

Dressing Ingredients

1 cup fresh basil
1 clove garlic
¼ cup parsley
¼ tsp. salt
¼ cup olive oil
¼ cup Parmesan cheese
2 Tbsp. pine nuts
salt & pepper

Directions

Combine beans and mayonnaise and toss to coat beans completely.

Make pesto by placing first seven ingredients in blender or food processor and processing to make a chunky paste. Toss into salad. Add salt and pepper and chill thoroughly.

Serves 6 as a side dish.

Crunchy Granola

Ingredients

1 cup butter
½ cup honey
1 Tbsp. milk
1 tsp. salt
4 cups rolled oats
1 cup wheat germ
1 cup coconut
¼ cup sesame seeds
½ cup sunflower seeds
½ cup raisins

Directions

Heat butter, honey, milk and salt. Combine rolled oats, wheat germ, coconut, sesame seeds and sunflower seeds. Mix in honey-butter mixture until well combined.

Place in a large shallow pan and bake at 350°F for 20 minutes, stirring from time to time.

Stir in raisins and cool.

Makes 7 cups.

—Carol Frost

Sweet & Sour Beans

Ingredients

½ cup maple syrup
¼ cup lemon juice
3 Tbsp. soy sauce
1 cup unsweetened pineapple chunks,
    drained with juice reserved
2–3 Tbsp. cornstarch
1 cup thinly sliced carrots
1 cup thinly sliced celery
1 onion, thinly sliced
2 cups cooked kidney beans
2 cups cooked garbanzo beans
Salt
4 cups steamed rice

Directions

Combine maple syrup, lemon juice and soy sauce with reserved pineapple juice in a saucepan. Add cornstarch dissolved in 2–3 Tbsp. water. Heat, stirring, until mixture boils. Add carrots and celery and simmer, covered, for 10 minutes, or until vegetables are tender but still crisp. Stir in pineapple, onion and beans and heat through. Season with salt to taste. Serve on rice.

Serves 4 to 6.

—Patricia McKay

Vegetarian Chili

Ingredients

1 cup pinto beans
1 cup navy beans
1 cup kidney beans
9 cups water
1 large onion, chopped
2 cloves garlic, minced
2 Tbsp. oil
2 stalks celery, chopped
1 large green pepper, chopped
2 26-oz. cans tomatoes
1 cup chopped mushrooms
Chili powder

Directions

Soak beans in water overnight. Sauté onion and garlic in oil. Add celery and green pepper and cook for 5 minutes. Add tomatoes, mushrooms and beans, bring to a boil and simmer for at least 2 hours. Season with chili powder to taste.

Serves 6.

—*Lynn Bakken*

Bean Lentil Stew

This vegetarian stew is flavorful and hearty. It is very easy on the budget, especially in summer, when fresh vegetables are in abundance.

Ingredients

1 cup navy beans, rinsed
1 cup brown lentils, rinsed
28 oz. canned tomatoes
2 onions, chopped
2 stalks celery, chopped
½ cup diced green pepper
1–2 cloves garlic, minced
1 Tbsp. butter or oil
3 large carrots, cut into chunks
1 large potato, cut into chunks
1 cup diced turnip
2 tsp. salt
¼ tsp. pepper
1 tsp. crushed savory
½ tsp. crushed basil
¼ cup finely chopped parsley

Directions

Place navy beans in a large pot, cover with 4 cups water and bring to a boil. Boil for 2 minutes, turn off heat and let sit for 1 hour. Then simmer beans gently for about 2 hours, or until almost tender. Add lentils and tomatoes.

In heavy pan, sauté onions, celery, green pepper and garlic in oil. Add this to the bean mixture. Add remaining ingredients and simmer until lentils and vegetables are cooked, adding liquid as necessary.

—*Jan Gilbert*

Indonesian Fried Rice

For a vegetarian meal, the meat can be easily omitted from this recipe.

Ingredients

1 onion, chopped
3 cloves garlic
½ tsp. ginger
½ tsp. cardamom
½ tsp. turmeric
½ tsp. crushed red pepper
1 tsp. salt
¼ tsp. pepper
2 Tbsp. oil
2 Tbsp. lemon juice
1 Tbsp. soy sauce
1 cup cubed, cooked meat
3 Tbsp. chopped green pepper
3 Tbsp. chopped celery
¼ cup coconut milk
4 cups cooked rice

Directions

Crush together onion, garlic, ginger, cardamom, turmeric, red pepper, salt and pepper. Sauté in oil for 2 to 3 minutes. Add lemon juice, soy sauce and meat and cook for a few minutes longer. Add green pepper, celery, coconut milk and rice. Stir-fry until hot.

—*Susan Bates Eddy*

Sesame Rice

This is a slightly dressed-up version of fried rice. Cashews or other nuts or seeds may be used in place of sesame seeds.

Ingredients

1½ cups sesame seeds
½ tsp. cayenne
1 bay leaf
4 Tbsp. butter
1 tsp. salt
4 cups cooked rice
Juice of ½ lime

Directions

Sauté sesame seeds, cayenne and bay leaf in butter until seeds are golden. Stir in salt and rice and cook over high heat, stirring constantly, until rice is heated through. Sprinkle with lime juice and serve.

Serves 4.

—*Susan Bates Eddy*

Herbed Rice & Lentil Casserole

Ingredients

2⅔ cups water
¾ cup lentils
¾ cup chopped onion
½ cup rice
¼ tsp. salt
⅛ tsp. garlic powder
⅛ tsp. pepper
¼ tsp. oregano
2 Tbsp. chopped dill weed
1 cup grated Cheddar cheese

Directions

Combine all ingredients in a greased casserole dish and bake at 325°F for 1½ to 2 hours, stirring twice.

Serves 2.

—Rose Strocen

All in-one Cereal

Ingredients

2 cups cracked wheat
1 cup rolled oats
½ cup toasted wheat germ
½ cup raw wheat germ
½ cup soy grits
½ cup wheat germ
1 cup coarse cornmeal

Directions

Combine all ingredients and store in cool place in jar with tight-fitting lid.

To cook, use 1 cup cereal to 4 cups water, adding ¼ to ½ tsp. salt to taste for each cup of grain. Bring salted water to a boil and stir in cereal slowly. Cook and stir for 1 to 2 minutes, then cover and cook on very low heat for 20 to 25 minutes.

Makes 6 cups of dry cereal.

—Kathy Cowbrough

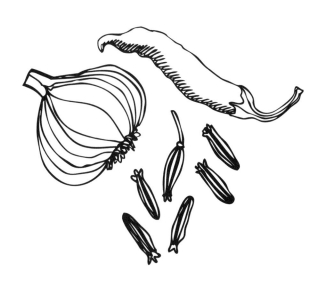

Healthy Breakfast Cookies

These cookies are sold at the Saturday morning Kamloops farmers' market. Packed full of grains and nuts, they provide a nutritious, if unusual, breakfast.

Ingredients

½ cup butter or oil
½ cup peanut butter
1½ cups honey
2 eggs
½ tsp. vanilla
1½ cups flour
1 tsp. salt
1 tsp. baking soda
3 cups rolled oats
1 cup coconut
¾ cup bran
¼ cup wheat germ
1 cup raisins
½ cup chopped peanuts

Directions

Cream butter or oil, peanut butter and honey. Add eggs and vanilla, then beat well. Stir in flour, salt and baking soda until very smooth. Add remaining ingredients and blend well.

Drop by teaspoonful onto greased cookie sheets. If a large, meal-sized cookie is desired, use ¼ cup of dough for each cookie. Bake at 375°F for 10 to 20 minutes, depending on size of cookies.

—Dianne Lomen

Vegetable Paella

There are as many paella recipes as there are Spanish cooks. The essential ingredients are rice and saffron — after that, it is up to the imagination of the cook and the ingredients that are available. Almost all paellas include chicken and seafood (we include such a recipe on page 194); we present this as a tasty vegetarian alternative.

Ingredients

2 cups dry basmati rice
4 Tbsp. olive oil
2 onions, sliced fine
4 cloves garlic, crushed
3 green peppers, sliced
2 tomatoes, sliced
1 bay leaf
½ tsp. saffron threads
salt
2 cups snow peas, steamed just until
    color changes
2 pimientos, diced

Directions

Boil rice until tender but firm. Meanwhile, heat oil in large heavy pot, then sauté onions, garlic, peppers and tomatoes. Combine rice with vegetables, add 2½ cups water, bay leaf, saffron and salt. Cover and cook over low heat until water is almost absorbed. Add peas and pimientos and heat through.

Serves 4.

Asian Rice Salad

Ingredients

⅓ cup oil
2 Tbsp. orange juice
1 Tbsp. brown sugar
2 tsp. soy sauce
½ tsp. dry mustard
salt & pepper
1 cup dry rice, cooked
4 green onions, sliced
1 cup chopped water chestnuts
2 cups sliced celery
1 tomato, chopped

Directions

Combine oil, orange juice, sugar, soy sauce, mustard and salt and pepper in large bowl and mix well. Stir in warm rice. Add onions, water chestnuts, celery and tomato and toss lightly. Chill well.

Serves 4 to 6.

—Rose Strocen

Cabbage & Rice

This was a big hit — even with the doubters in the crowd — when we tested it in our Vermont office. It is easy to prepare and has a subtle sweetness.

Ingredients

3 Tbsp. oil or butter
6 cups chopped cabbage
1 onion, chopped
1½ cups cooked brown rice
¾ cup grated Swiss cheese
¾ cup sliced mushrooms, sautéed
½ tsp. savory
1 egg
½ cup wheat germ
2 Tbsp. butter, melted

Directions

Heat oil or butter in heavy pot and sauté cabbage and onion until cabbage is tender. Keep covered with the heat low. Combine remaining ingredients except wheat germ and melted butter. Layer half cabbage mixture in greased casserole dish. Spread rice mixture over this. Top with remaining cabbage.

Combine wheat germ and melted butter and drizzle over casserole. Bake, uncovered, at 350°F for 30 to 40 minutes.

Serves 3 to 4.

—Susan O'Neill

Wild Rice

Ingredients

6 Tbsp. butter
½ cup chopped parsley
½ cup chopped onion
1 cup sliced celery
1½ cups dry wild rice
3 cups hot chicken stock
1 tsp. salt
½ tsp. marjoram
½ cup sherry

Directions

Combine butter, parsley, onion and celery in heavy skillet and cook for 10 minutes, or until soft but not brown. Add remaining ingredients except sherry. Bring to a boil, reduce heat, cover and cook for approximately 45 minutes, stirring occasionally. Add hot water if mixture gets too dry. When rice is tender, stir in sherry and cook, uncovered, for 5 more minutes.

Serves 6 to 8.

—Rose Strocen

Cashew Nut Fried Rice

This is a wonderful dish — beautiful to look at, full of different textures and very tasty. It does not take long to prepare once the rice is cooked.

Ingredients

6 Tbsp. peanut oil
8 eggs
½ head cabbage, shredded
6 green onions, sliced
½ lb. bacon, fried & crumbled
1½ cups roasted cashews
2 slices gingerroot
3 Tbsp. sesame oil
3 Tbsp. soy sauce
3 Tbsp. sherry
2 cups cooked brown rice
2 cups cooked basmati rice
2 cups cooked wild rice

Directions

Heat wok, then add peanut oil. Add eggs, stir quickly to scramble, then remove and keep warm. Stir-fry remaining ingredients until crispy-tender and heated through. Remove ginger slices and add eggs.

Serves 10.

—Sandra K. Bennett

Broccoli Nut Casserole

Ingredients

1½ cups dry brown rice
2–3 Tbsp. oil
1 large onion, chopped
2 cloves garlic, crushed
½ tsp. dill
1 tsp. thyme
1 tsp. oregano
½ bunch parsley, chopped
½ lb. mushrooms, sliced
1 green pepper, sliced
1 head broccoli, cut into florets
½ cup cashews
½ lb. Swiss or Gruyère cheese, grated
2 Tbsp. Parmesan cheese

Directions

In heavy pan with tight-fitting lid, combine rice, 3 cups water and dash of salt. Bring to a boil, reduce heat and simmer, covered, until water is absorbed — about 45 minutes. Heat oil in large skillet. Add onion, garlic, dill, thyme and oregano and cook until onions are limp. Add parsley, mushrooms, green pepper and broccoli and cook, stirring often. When broccoli becomes deep green but is still crisp, toss in nuts and remove from heat. Spread rice in greased casserole dish. Cover with vegetable-nut mixture, mix well and sprinkle with cheeses. Bake, uncovered, at 350°F for 15 minutes, or until bubbly.

Serves 8.

—*Sandra K. Bennett*

Fiesta Pilaf

Ingredients

¼ cup butter
3 cloves garlic, finely chopped
1 cup finely chopped green onions
1 cup sliced mushrooms
½ cup diced red pepper
½ cup diced green pepper
1 cup dry wild rice
¼ tsp. thyme
⅛ tsp. cloves
4 cups chicken stock
pepper

Directions

Melt butter and add garlic, onions and half the mushrooms. Cook over low heat for about 3 minutes. Add peppers and remaining mushrooms. Increase heat and cook for 2 to 3 minutes. Stir in wild rice, coating well with buttery mixture. Season with thyme and cloves. Pour in stock and bring to a boil; cover and simmer over low heat for 45 to 50 minutes. Season with pepper.

Serves 4.

—*Mo'e Howard-Samstag*

Mushroom Rice

Equally delicious as a side dish or as a poultry stuffing, this will keep you from ever using commercially prepared rice dishes. For a 12-to-14 lb. turkey, double the recipe.

Ingredients

2 Tbsp. butter
1 onion, chopped
6 mushrooms, sliced
⅔ cup dry brown rice
⅓ cup dry wild rice
2 cups hot chicken stock
1 Tbsp. chopped parsley
¼ tsp. thyme
pepper to taste

Directions

In heavy pot with tight-fitting lid, melt butter over medium heat. Sauté onion and mushrooms until limp. Add rice. Cook, stirring, until rice browns. Pour in stock. Stir in parsley, thyme and pepper. Cover pot and bring to a boil. Reduce heat and simmer for 35 to 45 minutes. Turn off heat and let stand, covered, for 10 minutes.

Serves 4 to 5.

—*Lynne Roe*

Indonesian Rice Salad

Salad Ingredients

2 cups cooked rice (basmati, brown, wild or a combination)
¼ cup raisins
3 green onions, chopped
¾ cup sliced water chestnuts
1 cup bean sprouts
1 green pepper, chopped
2 stalks celery, chopped
1 cucumber, chopped
⅓ cup sliced radishes
⅓ cup sesame seeds, toasted
⅓ cup cashews, toasted

Dressing Ingredients

¾ cup oil
⅓ up lemon juice
2 tbsp. soy sauce
1 tbsp. sherry
2 cloves garlic, crushed
1 slice gingerroot
salt & pepper

Directions

Combine salad ingredients and toss gently. Place dressing ingredients in jar with lid and shake until blended. Pour over salad and toss. Chill well.

Serves 6.

Wild Rice Cake

"My friend Grace Milashenko of Saskatoon presented me with a gift of Saskatchewan wild rice, and I set forth to experiment. The wild rice cake was daring in that, if it didn't work, I would have wasted many expensive ingredients. Fortunately, it produced a moist, delightful cake with a curious tang of the outdoors."

Cake Ingredients

1 cup dry wild rice, washed, soaked in cold water overnight & drained
2–3 strips orange zest
1 tsp. sugar
1 pkg. yeast
¼ cup melted butter
½ cup maple syrup
1 tsp. salt
½ tsp. cinnamon
2 eggs
½ cup brown sugar
1½ cups whole wheat flour
2 cups unbleached white flour
¼ cup wheat germ
⅓ cup buttermilk or sour milk
handful crushed walnuts

Directions

Cook drained rice in 2½ cups water, adding zest strips when water comes to a boil. Reduce heat to medium and cook for 45 minutes to 1 hour, or until rice is fluffy.

Mix sugar with ½ cup warm water. Stir in yeast and set aside for 10 minutes. Meanwhile, combine melted butter, maple syrup, salt and cinnamon with cooked rice. Beat in eggs, then add brown sugar. Stir in flours, wheat germ and buttermilk. Add walnuts. Stir in yeast mixture. Mix well and let rise for 1 hour.

Stir down dough. Grease tube pan and pour in dough. Let rise for another hour. Bake at 400°F for 15 minutes, lower heat to 375° and bake for an additional 45 minutes, or until done. Let cool slightly and top with praline topping.

Topping Ingredients

¼ cup brown sugar
½ cup chopped walnuts
¼ tsp. nutmeg
1 Tbsp. melted butter
2 Tbsp. cream

Directions

Mix all ingredients together. Pour over hot or cooled cake. Broil about 3 inches from direct heat for 2 to 3 minutes, or until amber-brown.

—*Mo'e Howard-Samstag*

Vegetarian Couscous

Cook couscous by pouring 4 cups boiling water over 2 cups dry couscous. Cover and let stand for 5 minutes. Mix in 4 tablespoons butter and fluff up with a fork.

Ingredients

3 Tbsp. oil
1 onion, chopped
1 red pepper, chopped
1 green pepper, chopped
1 tsp. allspice
2 sweet potatoes, peeled & cubed
2 tomatoes, peeled & chopped
1 Tbsp. lemon juice
½ tsp. saffron threads
4-5 cumin seeds
2 cups cooked chickpeas
salt
2 zucchini, chopped
4 cups hot cooked couscous
hot pepper sauce

Directions

Heat oil over medium heat. Add onion, peppers and allspice and cook until onion is soft — 5 minutes. Stir in sweet potatoes and cook, stirring often, for 2 minutes. Add tomatoes, ¼ cup water, lemon juice, saffron, cumin and chickpeas. Season with salt, cover, reduce heat and simmer for 15 minutes. Mix in zucchini and cook for 5 minutes more.

To serve, spread couscous around edge of deep platter and spoon vegetables into center. Serve with hot pepper sauce.

Serves 6

—*Helene Gaufreau*

Tabouli

This is a delicious version of tabouli. We had not tried one before that did not cook the bulgur, but our concern was unnecessary. The bulgur "cooks" by soaking overnight in the dressing.

Ingredients

½ cup dry bulgur
3 cups packed, chopped parsley
6 4" mint tops (leaves only), chopped
½ cucumber, chopped
1 onion, chopped
2-3 tomatoes, chopped
½ green pepper, chopped
juice of 2 lemons
1 shallot, chopped
½ cup oil
salt & pepper

Directions

Combine all ingredients and mix well. Let stand, refrigerated, overnight. Toss gently before serving.

Serves 6 to 8.

—*Penny Tognet*

Mexican Bean Dip

Ingredients

½ cups dry pinto beans, cooked, drained & mashed
3 cloves garlic, minced
1 cup minced onion
1 tsp. salt
pepper
½ tsp. crushed hot red peppers
⅓ tsp. cumin
¼ tsp. dry mustard

Directions

Combine all ingredients and mix well. Chill.

Makes approximately 3 to 4 cups.

Black Bean & Tomato Salad

Ingredients

1 cup cooked black turtle beans
1 Tbsp. cider vinegar or lemon juice
2 Tbsp. olive oil
salt & pepper
1 large onion, chopped
2 large tomatoes, chopped, or
    1½ cups cherry tomatoes
2 cloves garlic, chopped

Directions

While beans are still warm, mix with vinegar, oil and salt and pepper. Chill, then add onion, tomatoes and garlic, combining well. Chill overnight.

Serves 4.

—Judith Almond Best

Baked Beans with Pizzazz

Ingredients

2 cups dry navy beans
4 Tbsp. butter
2 large onions, chopped
4 cloves garlic, crushed
½ tsp. salt
1 tsp. allspice pepper
2 tsp. dill
5 Tbsp. light molasses
5 Tbsp. Poupon mustard
4 cups tomato juice
2 Tbsp. lemon juice
1 Tbsp. soy sauce
1 green pepper, chopped
1 stalk celery, chopped
2 carrots, diced

Directions

Cover beans with water. Bring to a boil, reduce heat, cover and simmer for 1 to 2 hours, or until beans are tender. Add water during cooking if necessary. When cooked, drain.

Meanwhile, melt butter and sauté onions and garlic until limp. Add salt, allspice, pepper, dill, molasses, mustard, tomato juice, lemon juice and soy sauce. Bring to a boil, reduce heat and simmer, covered, for 45 minutes.

In large, greased casserole dish, combine beans, sauce and vegetables. Bake, covered, at 325°F for 1 to 2 hours, or until liquid is absorbed.

Serves 6 to 8.

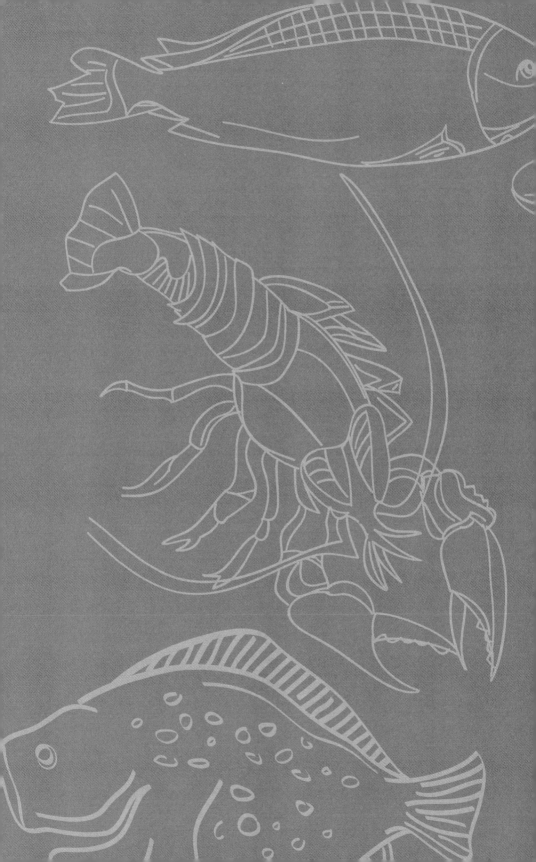

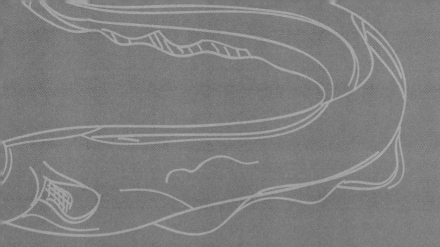

Fish & Seafood

Salmon Mediterranean

Ingredients

1 qt. tomatoes
¼ cup olive oil
4-6 cloves garlic, minced
1 Tbsp. basil
1 tsp. oregano
Salt & pepper
Large bunch parsley, chopped
4 lbs. salmon, cut into 1½ inch steaks
2 onions, thinly sliced
1 large lemon, thinly sliced

Directions

Combine tomatoes, olive oil, garlic, basil, oregano, salt, pepper and p arsley in a saucepan and cook for 15 minutes. Transfer to a baking dish.

Place salmon steaks in baking dish so that at least half of each steak is submerged in sauce. Arrange onion and lemon slices among the steaks. Cover and bake at 325°F for 30 minutes, uncover and bake a further 30 minutes.

Serves 6 to 8.

—Chris Ferris

Canadian Smoked Salmon

Ingredients

1 lb. smoked salmon
Juice of 1 lemon
2 Tbsp. mayonnaise, page 130
1 dill pickle, finely chopped
1 large green onion, finely chopped
Salt & pepper
Salad greens
Tomato, radishes, cucumbers & green peppers to garnish.

Directions

Slice salmon thinly, removing bones and skin. This is most easily done if the salmon has been placed in the freezer for a few hours first.

Toss in lemon juice and mayonnaise. Add dill pickle, onion, salt and pepper. Toss again and refrigerate.

Serve on a bed of greens, garnished with raw vegetables.

Serves 6 as an appetizer.

—Nita Hunton

Salmon Cakes

Ingredients

2 cups cooked salmon
1 medium onion, chopped & sautéed
1 egg
¼ cup chopped parsley
1 tsp. dry dill weed
½ tsp. sweet basil
4 Tbsp. flour

Directions

Combine all ingredients except flour in a bowl and shape into patties. Coat well with flour. Fry, turning once, until crisp and golden.

Makes 8 large patties.

—Chris Ferris

Poached Cod

Ingredients

1 lb. fish fillets
1¼ cups milk
½ tsp. salt
1 small bay leaf
3 peppercorns
1 whole clove
2 Tbsp. butter
3 Tbsp. chopped green onion
2 Tbsp. flour
⅛ tsp. pepper
2–3 Tbsp. Lemon juice

Directions

Cut fish into serving-sized pieces. Heat milk, salt, bay leaf, peppercorns and clove to boiling in a large skillet. Add fish, bring just to a boil, lower heat, cover and simmer until flaky — 5 to 10 minutes. Lift fish out and keep warm.

Meanwhile, melt butter and add onion. Cook, stirring, for 3 minutes. Sprinkle in flour and pepper, stirring to blend. Remove from heat and stir into fish liquid.

Return pan to heat and stir sauce until boiling, thickened and smooth. Add lemon juice. Pour the sauce over the fish and garnish with more green onion.

Serves 4.

—*Sharron Jansen*

Breaded Cod Fillets

Ingredients

1 lb. cod fillets
1 egg
¼ cup milk
8–10 crushed crackers
¼ tsp. sea salt
Pinch of pepper
¼ tsp. garlic powder
¼ tsp. sweet basil
¼ tsp. dill weed

Directions

Dip fillets in egg and milk beaten together. Combine remaining ingredients and coat fillets with this mixture.

Fry fillets in oil for about 5 minutes on each side.

Serves 4.

—*Diane Schoemperlen*

Sole Amandine

With its subtle flavors and contrasting textures, this simple but elegant dish can only be described as delectable.

Ingredients

½ cup flour
1 tsp. salt
¼ tsp. pepper
1 tsp. paprika
2 lbs. sole fillets
3 Tbsp. butter
3 Tbsp. slivered almonds
3 Tbsp. lemon juice
1 tsp. grated lemon rind
3 Tbsp. chopped chives
⅓ cup salad oil

Directions

Combine flour, salt, pepper and paprika in a flat dish. Cut fish into serving-sized pieces and dip into flour mixture to coat both sides.

Heat butter in a small skillet. Add almonds and cook gently, stirring, until golden. Stir in lemon juice, lemon rind and chives.

Heat oil in large heavy skillet and fry fish quickly on both sides until golden. Lift out onto a hot platter and pour almond mixture over fish. Serve immediately.

Serves 6.

—*Patricia Burley*

Sole Florentine

Ingredients

1½ lbs. spinach, cooked,
    drained & chopped
2 lbs. sole fillets, wiped dry
3–4 green onions, chopped
2 cups sliced mushrooms
4 Tbsp. butter
½ cup butter
½ cup flour
2 cups milk
Salt & pepper

Directions

Place spinach in buttered casserole dish and lay fish fillets on top.

Sauté mushrooms in 4 Tbsp. butter. Sprinkle green onion and mushrooms on top of fish.

Melt remaining ½ cup butter in heavy saucepan. Stir in flour and cook for about 2 minutes. Gradually add milk, stirring constantly. Bring to a boil and cook for 1 to 2 minutes or until thick. Add salt and pepper to taste.

Pour over fish and bake at 425°F for 15 to 20 minutes.

Serves 6.

—*Sheila Bear*

Haddock Fillets with Mushroom Sauce

Ingredients

2½ lbs. haddock fillets
1 tsp. salt
Pinch pepper
Pinch cayenne
5 Tbsp. flour
5 Tbsp. butter
1 Tbsp. oil
Pinch white pepper
2 cups milk
½ cup finely chopped
   mushrooms
1 tsp. chopped fresh dill

Directions

Pat fillets dry with a paper towel, season on both sides with ½ tsp. salt, pepper and cayenne, and dust lightly with 1 Tbsp. flour.

Place 1 Tbsp. butter and oil in a heavy frying pan, heat and brown fillets, one at a time, on both sides. Place on a heated serving platter to keep warm.

Melt 4 Tbsp. butter in heavy saucepan and stir in 4 Tbsp. flour, white pepper and remaining salt. Slowly stir in milk until sauce is smooth and creamy. Add mushrooms.

Pour mushroom sauce over fish and garnish with dill.

Serves 4 to 6.

—Brenda Eckstein

Tuna Casserole

Ingredients

3 Tbsp. butter
3 Tbsp. flour
1 cup milk
Pinch each: celery salt, dry mustard, paprika
¼ tsp. garlic powder
¼ tsp. basil
½ cup grated Cheddar cheese
1 cup uncooked macaroni
1 small onion, chopped
1 green pepper, chopped
2 stalks celery, chopped
½ cup chopped mushrooms
1 large tin tuna

Directions

Melt butter, blend in flour and cook on low heat for 5 minutes. Slowly blend in milk and seasonings. Add cheese and cook, stirring, until thick and smooth. Remove from heat and set aside.

Cook macaroni in boiling water until tender.

In a casserole dish, mix together the vegetables, macaroni, cheese sauce and tuna. Bake at 350°F for 45 minutes.

Serves 6.

—Diane Schoemperlen

Baked Scallops

Ingredients

1 cup bread crumbs
Salt & pepper
1 lb. scallops
½ cup melted butter

Directions

Butter a casserole dish and layer the crumbs, seasoned with salt and pepper, and scallops, finishing with a layer of crumbs. Pour melted butter over all and bake at 375°F for 15 to 20 minutes.

Serves 2.

—Audrey Moroso

Shrimp Tarts

Ingredients

Pastry for 9-inch pie crust
1½ cups shrimp
½ cup chopped green onion
½ lb. Swiss cheese, grated
1 cup mayonnaise, page 130
4 eggs
1 cup milk
½ tsp. salt
½ tsp. dill weed

Directions

Roll out pastry and cut into six 4-inch circles. Place in muffin tins. Combine shrimp, green onion and cheese and place in pastry shells. Beat together mayonnaise, eggs, milk, salt and dill weed. Pour over mixture in shells.

Bake at 400°F for 15 to 20 minutes.

Makes 6 tarts.

—Linda Fahie

Crab Tarts

Ingredients

2 loaves thin sandwich bread
½ cup melted butter
3 Tbsp. butter
¼ cup flour
1½ cups milk
1 cup grated Cheddar cheese
6-oz. can crabmeat, drained & flaked
1 Tbsp. green onion, finely chopped
1 Tbsp. lemon juice
2 Tbsp. minced parsley
1 tsp. Worcestershire sauce
1 tsp. prepared mustard
½ tsp. salt
Dash Tabasco sauce

Directions

To make toasted shells, cut circle out of bread using a medium-sized cup. Brush melted butter on both sides of the bread circles. Press bread gently into muffin tins to form a shell. Bake at 425°F for 5 minutes, or until edges are crisp and golden brown.

To make filling, melt butter in medium saucepan over medium heat. Let butter bubble, then stir in flour to form a smooth paste. Let bubble and add milk. Bring to a boil, stirring frequently, then turn heat to low. When mixture forms a thick, creamy sauce, add the cheese, stirring until melted.

Add the remaining ingredients one at a time, stirring after each addition. Remove from heat. Spoon filling into toasted shells and place on a cookie sheet. Bake at 350°F for 15 minutes.

Makes 3 dozen.

—Cathy Davis

Seafood Casserole

Ingredients

1 lb. scallops
2 cups milk
¼ cup butter
¼ cup flour
½ tsp. salt
Pepper
1 tsp. curry powder
1 can cream of shrimp soup
½ cup shrimp

Directions

Cover scallops with milk and simmer for 10 minutes. Drain and reserve 1½ cups of milk.

Meanwhile, melt butter and stir in flour and seasonings. Add reserved milk and cook, stirring, until thickened. Stir in curry powder and shrimp soup.

Pour into serving dish and add shrimp and scallops.

Serves 4.

—J.E. Riendl

Shrimp Curry

Ingredients

1 stalk celery, finely chopped
½ green pepper, finely diced
2 green onions, finely chopped
¼ cup butter
1 lb. shrimp, cleaned & deveined
¼ cup flour
2 cups light cream
Salt & pepper
2 Tbsp. curry powder

Directions

Sauté celery, green pepper and onions in butter. When celery is slightly softened, stir in shrimp and continue to sauté, stirring constantly, until shrimp is bright pink. Remove shrimp and vegetables from pan.

Stir flour into remaining liquid, adding butter, if needed, to make a roux. Slowly stir in cream to make a thick cream sauce. Add salt, pepper and curry powder. Return shrimp and vegetables to sauce and heat through.

Serves 2.

Shrimp Salad

Ingredients

1½ cups cooked rice
1½ cups raw peas
1½ cups chopped celery
¼ cup chopped green onion
1 cup shrimp
½ cup salad oil
1 Tbsp. soy sauce
1 tsp. celery seed
2 Tbsp. cider vinegar
Salt
½ Tbsp. sugar

Directions

Combine rice, peas, celery, onion and shrimp. For dressing, blend remaining ingredients well. Pour over shrimp mixture. Toss and chill.

Serves 4.

—Trudy Mason

Shrimp Dip

Ingredients

8 oz. cream cheese
Juice of 1 lemon
½ cup basic mayonnaise, page 130
2 Tbsp. ketchup
1 small onion, grated
Dash Worcestershire sauce
Dash salt
1 cup chopped shrimp

Directions

Cream cheese with lemon juice and add remaining ingredients. Chill well before serving.

Makes 2 cups.

—A. H. McInnis

Herring Salad

Herring is a traditional Yuletide dish for many, and this salad provides a colorful and flavorful method of serving it. Milter herring are the male fish during breeding season.

Ingredients

6 milter herring
1 cup dry red wine
2 hard-boiled eggs, cubed
1 cup cooked veal, cubed
2 cups pickled beets, cubed
½ cup chopped onion
2 stalks celery, chopped
½ cup chopped boiled potatoes
3 cups diced apples
1 cup shredded almonds
1 cup sugar
2 Tbsp. horseradish
2 Tbsp. parsley
Olives to garnish

Directions

Soak the herring in water for 12 hours. Skin them and remove the milt and bones. Rub the milt through sieve with wine.

Cube the herring and mix with eggs, veal, beets, onion, celery, potatoes, apples and almonds.

Combine milt mixture with sugar, horseradish and parsley. Pour over salad and mix well. Shape into mound and garnish with olives.

Serves 12.

Fillets of Sole with Leeks & Shrimp

Ingredients

2 cups sliced leeks, white part only
½ cup butter
8 oz. shrimp, cooked, shelled & chopped
2 Tbsp. chopped dill weed
1 cup whipping cream
⅔ cup dry white wine
Salt & white pepper
Lemon juice
4 sole fillets
Flour

Directions

Cook leeks in ¼ cup butter over medium heat for 5 minutes. Stir in shrimp and dill and cook for 1 minute. Add cream, wine, salt and pepper and lemon juice to taste and simmer for 10 minutes, or until thickened. Set aside and keep warm.

Dust sole with flour and sauté in remaining ¼ cup butter over medium-high heat until golden and flaky. Transfer to heated platter and pour sauce over.

Serves 4.

—Pam Collacott

Creamy Fillet of Sole

Ingredients

4 sole fillets
1 green onion, chopped
1 Tbsp. chopped parsley
6 large mushrooms, sliced
1 tsp. salt
⅛ tsp. pepper
3 Tbsp. apple juice
2 Tbsp. butter, cut into pieces
3 Tbsp. cream
1 tsp. lemon juice

Directions

Place sole in buttered dish. Sprinkle with onion and parsley. Top with mushrooms and salt and pepper. Add apple juice and dot with 1 Tbsp. butter. Top with a piece of brown paper and bake at 500°F for 15 minutes. Drain liquid and reduce to half by cooking over high heat. Add cream, lemon juice and remaining 1 Tbsp. butter. Mix and pour over fillets and place in hot oven or under broiler for 5 minutes to brown.

Serves 4.

—Andrea Stuart

Smoked Salmon

Smoked salmon can serve as the base for a number of delicious hors d'oeuvres. Of course, it is best known served as lox, with bagels and fresh cream cheese. Smoked salmon should be pale pink and should not be salty in taste. If it is red in color and tastes salty, a smoke salt extract has been used in the processing.

It is easiest to slice smoked salmon if it is partially frozen — it should be sliced across the grain as thinly as possible. A few suggestions for serving smoked salmon as a canape follow.

Directions

1. Place on crackers or squares of toast, dust with freshly ground pepper and sprinkle with lemon juice.
2. Top salmon with a slice of stuffed olive.
3. Top with guacamole and serve on toast.

Baked Trout with Almond Cream

Ingredients

⅓ cup slivered almonds
3 Tbsp. butter
1 Tbsp. minced green onion
3 rainbow trout, boned
Parsley
6 Tbsp. white wine
½ cup whipping cream
1 Tbsp. sour cream
1½ tsp. cornstarch
Salt & pepper
Lemon juice

Directions

Brown almonds in butter and set aside. Butter a piece of aluminum foil large enough to wrap around fish. Sprinkle with green onion and place fish on top. Stuff each fish with parsley, then pour over wine and butter from cooking almonds. Tightly close foil over fish and bake at 425°F for 10 minutes per inch of thickness of fish.

Meanwhile, remove almonds to paper towel. Combine whipping cream, sour cream and cornstarch in saucepan. When fish is cooked, pour fish liquid into cream mixture and bring to a boil, stirring constantly. Cook until thickened and smooth. Add salt and pepper and lemon juice to taste.

To serve, remove parsley from fish. Top each fish with small ribbon of sauce and almonds. Serve remaining sauce separately.

Serves 6.

—The Art of Cooking School

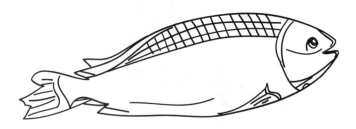

Fish Spinach Casserole

Ingredients

6 oz. fine egg noodles
3 cups vegetable stock
4 Tbsp. butter
4 Tbsp. flour
½ cup yogurt or sour cream
1½ cups cooked spinach
1 cup cooked, flaked fish
3 eggs, hard-boiled & sliced
5 Tbsp. Parmesan cheese

Directions

Cook egg noodles in stock until just tender. Drain and reserve liquid.

Melt butter until it foams, add flour and stir until combined. Add warm stock and stir until thickened. Remove from heat and add yogurt or sour cream.

Assemble in a casserole dish by layering as follows: noodles, spinach, half the sauce, fish and eggs. Add 4 Tbsp. Parmesan cheese to remaining sauce and pour over top. Bake at 350°F for 20 minutes. Sprinkle remaining tablespoon of cheese over top and broil until browned.

Serves 4.

—Ann R. Jeffries

Greek Pastry Stuffed with Fish & Spinach

This recipe takes a bit of time to prepare, but the resulting dish is well worth the effort. Filo pastry can be found in most Italian and Greek specialty stores. It can be stored in the freezer for several months if necessary.

Filling Ingredients

1½ lbs. spinach, washed & coarsely chopped
Butter
1 bunch green onions, sliced
¾ lb. Boston bluefish, minced
½ green pepper, minced
4 eggs, lightly beaten
¼ cup lemon juice
Salt & pepper
1½ tsp. dill weed
1 tsp. garlic powder

Pastry Ingredients

2 cups butter
⅓ cup lemon juice
1 Tbsp. garlic powder
1 lb. filo pastry

Directions

To make filling, sauté spinach in butter until limp. Combine with remaining ingredients in bowl and set aside.

For dough, combine butter, lemon juice and garlic powder in saucepan. Cook over low heat until melted. Unwrap filo dough on large working area. Fold one sheet lengthwise in thirds and brush with butter mixture. Fold and butter a second sheet similarly. Place strips end to end, overlapping by ½ inch. Place 2 Tbsp. filling near one end and fold pastry into triangle shape, folding over and over until all dough is used. Place on greased cookie sheet. Repeat with remaining dough and filling. Drizzle with remaining butter mixture and bake at 350°F for 30 minutes, or until golden brown and puffed.

Makes 12 triangles.

—Titia Posthuma

Herring in Sour Cream

Ingredients

16-oz. jar herring, whole or fillets
6 large onions
6 apples
1 quart sour cream
3 Tbsp. vinegar
Salt & pepper
¼ cup crushed walnuts

Directions

Drain liquid from jar of herring, discarding spices, onion rings, etc. Dice herring and place in 4-quart porcelain or glass bowl. Peel onions and apples. Cut onions into thinly sliced rings; core and cube apples into ¼-inch cubes. Add to herring. Pour sour cream over top and mix well. Add vinegar, salt and pepper and walnuts. Cover and let stand for 8 hours at room temperature, then refrigerate.

Serves 12 as an appetizer.

—Wido J. Heck

Seaside Manicotti

Ingredients

6 manicotti shells
10 oz. spinach
½ cup chopped onion
1 clove garlic
2 Tbsp. butter
3 Tbsp. flour
2 cups milk
1 cup Swiss cheese
¼ cup grated Parmesan cheese
2 Tbsp. butter, melted
½ tsp. salt
1 lb. perch fillets, cooked & flaked
Ground nutmeg

Directions

Cook manicotti shells and drain. Cook spinach and drain.

Meanwhile, prepare cheese sauce. Cook onion and garlic in 2 Tbsp. butter until tender but not brown. Blend in flour. Add milk all at once. Cook and stir until thick and bubbly. Stir in Swiss cheese until melted.

Combine ½ cup of sauce with the spinach, Parmesan cheese, 2 Tbsp. melted butter and salt. Fold in flaked fish. Stuff manicotti shells with this mixture.

Pour half of remaining sauce into baking dish. Put manicotti on top and pour remaining sauce over.

Cover and bake at 350°F for 30 to 35 minutes. Sprinkle nutmeg over top before serving.

Serves 6.

—Mary Ann Vanner

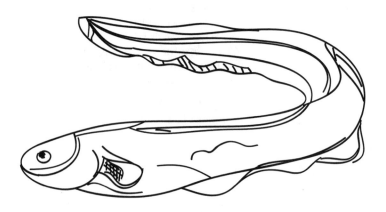

Stir-Fried Prawns

The prawns are cooked in their shells in this recipe. To enjoy all the delicious flavor, suck the shells before removing them to eat the prawns.

Ingredients

3 Tbsp. peanut oil
2 Tbsp. finely chopped ginger root
2 cloves garlic, chopped
1 lb. fresh prawns, deheaded & washed
1 Tbsp. soy sauce
1 Tbsp. dry sherry
½ tsp. salt
Pepper
Coriander

Directions

Heat oil in wok and stir-fry ginger root and garlic for 30 seconds. Add prawns and cook for 2 more minutes to brown shells lightly. Add soy sauce, sherry, salt and pepper and cook for another 2 minutes. Transfer to warm serving dish and garnish with coriander.

Serves 3 to 4.

—Helen Campbell

Shrimp Cooked in Beer

This dish makes an excellent cold appetizer or party snack.

Ingredients

2 bottles beer
2 bay leaves, crumbled
½ tsp. crushed red pepper
½ tsp. cayenne
2 Tbsp. mustard seeds
1½ lbs. jumbo shrimp, shelled & deveined
¼ cup wine vinegar
1 large clove garlic, peeled

Directions

Combine beer, bay leaves, red pepper, cayenne and mustard seeds in saucepan. Bring to a boil and simmer for 5 minutes. Add shrimp and simmer for 8 to 10 minutes, or until shrimp turns pink.

Remove from heat and add vinegar and garlic. Let stand for 30 minutes. Strain and chill well before serving.

Serves 8 to 10 as an appetizer.

—Mary Carney

Mama's Scampi

Ingredients

1½ lbs. shrimp
½ cup melted butter
½ tsp. salt
Pepper
1 clove garlic, chopped
1 cup sliced mushrooms
¼ cup chopped parsley
¼ cup chopped chives

Directions

Shell and devein shrimp. In large heavy pot, melt butter and sauté shrimp for 5 minutes, or until shrimp are pink. Sprinkle with salt and pepper, place on heated platter and keep warm. Sauté garlic and mushrooms for 1 to 2 minutes, then add parsley and chives and cook for 1 minute longer. Pour over shrimp. Serve with rice.

Serves 4.

—Kirsten McDougall

Guyanese Cook-up

Make the coconut milk for this recipe by combining 3 cups boiling water with 1 cup grated coconut — preferably fresh. When mixture is cool enough to handle, squeeze out all the liquid and discard the coconut.

Ingredients

1½ cups raw brown rice
3 cups coconut milk
½ tsp. salt
¾ cup sliced green beans
½ cup shrimp

Directions

Cook rice in coconut milk with salt for 25 minutes. Place green beans and shrimp on top of rice to steam for remaining cooking time — about 20 minutes. Stir when cooked and serve.

Serves 4.

—Shiela Alexandrovich

Fillets au Gratin

Ingredients

2 Tbsp. butter
2 Tbsp. flour
½ tsp. salt
1 cup milk
1 cup grated cheese
1 lb. fish fillets
1 cup bread crumbs tossed with 4 Tbsp. melted butter

Directions

Melt butter, remove from heat, blend in flour and salt. Add milk slowly. Return to heat when well blended. Cook until smooth and thickened. Add cheese and remove from heat.

Meanwhile, steam the fillets gently for about 5 minutes. Break them up into a baking dish. Pour cheese sauce over fish. Sprinkle with bread crumbs. Bake at 350°F for 20 minutes.

Serves 4.

—Anne White

Manicotti with Shrimp Filling

Ingredients

18 manicotti noodles
2 cups ricotta cheese
1½ cups cottage cheese
½ cup Parmesan cheese
2 eggs
1 green pepper, chopped
3–4 green onions, chopped
¼ cup finely chopped fresh parsley
½ tsp. salt
½ tsp. pepper
1½ cups shrimp
2 cups white sauce (page 129)

Directions

Cook noodles in boiling water for 6 minutes, stirring so they do not stick to one another.

Combine cheeses, eggs, green pepper, onions, parsley, salt, pepper and shrimp. Carefully stuff the manicotti shells with this mixture. Arrange filled noodles in single layers in two greased 9″ x 13″ baking pans. Pour one cup of white sauce over each.

Bake, covered, at 350°F for 45 minutes.

Serves 4 to 6.

—*Lorraine McFarland*

Curried Crab

Ingredients

2 coconuts
1 cup water
1 small onion, chopped
2 cloves garlic, minced
1 inch ginger, peeled & grated
2 Tbsp. olive oil
Salt
1 Tbsp. curry
2 or more crabs, cleaned

Directions

Crack coconuts and save milk. Chop or shred coconut meat and place in blender. Add ¾ cup water and blend thoroughly. Remove from blender and squeeze all liquid from pulp, save and add to coconut milk. Replace pulp in blender and add remaining ¼ cup water. Blend, save liquid and discard pulp. Fry onion, garlic and ginger in oil until light brown. Add coconut liquid, pinch of salt and curry. Add crabmeat, bring liquid to boil, then reduce heat and cook until liquid thickens about 10 minutes.

Serves 2.

—*Pieter Timmermans*

Angels on Horseback

Ingredients

12 oysters, shucked & rinsed
Flour
Salt & pepper
12 strips bacon, fried until almost crisp

Directions

Dust oysters with flour and salt and pepper. Wrap bacon strip around each oyster and hold together with a toothpick. Broil for 4 to 6 minutes, or until bacon is crisp.

Serves 3.

—Nina Christmas

Fish in Beer Batter

Ingredients

12–14 oz. flat beer
3 Tbsp. Thousand Island dressing
Whole wheat flour
White flour
1 tsp. baking powder
¼ tsp. tarragon
¼ tsp. paprika
¼ tsp. parsley
¼ tsp. dill
Salt & pepper
9 fillets fish (bass, perch, pickerel)

Directions

Pour beer into a large mixing bowl, add the dressing and beat until it breaks into tiny particles.

Slowly mix in flour, using white and whole wheat in proportion to suit your taste, breaking up lumps until batter is thick, not runny, and adheres to a wooden spoon. Add baking powder and seasonings and let sit for 30 minutes.

Dip fillets in batter and fry or deep fry until golden brown and crisp. Drain well and serve.

Serves 4.

—Roly Kleer

Oystacado

Ingredients

2 avocados
¼ cup mayonnaise
1 tsp. Dijon mustard
Salt & pepper
1 can smoked oysters, drained & chopped
1 Tbsp. lemon juice
1 cup sour cream
4 almonds

Directions

Cut avocados in half, scoop out pulp and mash. Add mayonnaise, mustard, salt and pepper, oysters and lemon juice. Fill each avocado shell with mixture and top with dollop of sour cream and an almond.

Serves 4.

—Gillian Barber-Gifford

Marinated Oysters

Ingredients

10 oysters
3 Tbsp. olive oil
2 Tbsp. tarragon vinegar
2 Tbsp. lemon juice
3–4 Tbsp. diced onions
2 Tbsp. chopped parsley
2–3 Tbsp. chopped chives
1 Tbsp. grated lemon peel
1 tsp. salt
½ tsp. white pepper
1–2 cloves garlic, crushed
Pumpernickel bread

Directions

Steam oysters in salt water until plump — 5 to 10 minutes — then cut into quarters. Combine remaining ingredients, except bread, for marinade and pour over oysters. Refrigerate for at least 4 hours. Serve on pumpernickel bread.

Serves 4.

—*Berit Christensen*

Clam or Mussel Pie

Ingredients

Pastry for double 9-inch pie shell
1½ cups clams or mussels
¾ cup diced potatoes
1 onion, chopped
2 cloves garlic, chopped
¼ cup chopped celery
3 Tbsp. butter
2 Tbsp. flour
Thyme
Salt & pepper

Directions

Scrub clams or mussels and cook in boiling water for 10 minutes, then shuck. Reserve liquid. Cook potatoes in fish liquid. Remove and set aside. Sauté onion, garlic and celery in butter. Stir in flour, thyme, salt and pepper and cook for 2 minutes. Slowly add cooking liquid and cook until thickened. Add potatoes and clams or mussels.

Place in pastry-lined pie plate and top with pastry. Bake at 400°F until crust is browned.

Serves 4.

—*Rachelle Poirier*

Seafood Casserole

Ingredients

¾ cup crabmeat, cooked
¾ cup small shrimp, cooked & shelled
2 Tbsp. grated sharp Cheddar cheese
2 sole fillets, split in half down the center
1½ cups white sauce (page 129)
1 Tbsp. Parmesan cheese
1 Tbsp. parsley

Directions

Toss crabmeat and shrimp with cheese and place half in each of two greased individual casserole dishes. Mound mixture into loaf shapes and place one half split fillet on each side of each mound. Cover with warm white sauce and sprinkle with Parmesan cheese and parsley. Bake at 325°F for 20 minutes.

Serves 2.

—June McKinnell

Paella

An elegant party dish, this version of paella uses only seafood, whereas there are some that also include chicken. After the baking, any clams and mussels that did not open should be discarded.

Ingredients

4–5 cups stock, half clam & half chicken
1 tsp. saffron
⅓ cup oil
2 cloves garlic
1 large onion, finely chopped
1 green pepper, cut into thin strips
2 lbs. white fish, cut into 2-inch pieces
Salt & pepper
2 cups raw rice
2 large tomatoes, peeled, seeded & diced
12 shrimp, shelled & deveined
12 scallops
1–2 cups partially cooked vegetables (peas, green beans, zucchini, artichoke hearts)
12 mussels or clams, scrubbed in shells

Directions

Bring stock to a boil, add saffron and set aside. In a large casserole dish, heat ¼ cup oil, fry garlic until browned, then remove and discard. Add onion, green pepper and white fish and cook until slightly browned. Season with salt and pepper. Add remaining oil and the rice and cook, stirring, for 2 to 3 minutes until rice is slightly browned. Add tomatoes and simmer for 2 to 3 minutes. Add stock and stir once.

Bury shrimp and scallops in rice, then add vegetables. Arrange mussels or clams around edge of dish, cover and simmer for 15 minutes, or until rice is cooked, adding stock as necessary. Uncover and bake at 450°F for 10 minutes.

Serves 8.

—Alice J. Pitt

Shrimp & Crabmeat Crêpes

Ingredients

Crêpe batter (page 37)
6 Tbsp. butter
3 Tbsp. flour
1 cup milk
¼ tsp. garlic powder
¼ tsp. basil
¼ lb. mushrooms, finely chopped
1 small onion, finely chopped
6 oz. can crabmeat, drained
1 cup small shrimp, cooked

Directions

Prepare and cook crêpes as recipe indicates. Cover, set aside and keep warm.

Make a white sauce by melting 3 Tbsp. butter. Blend in flour and cook over low heat for 5 minutes. Slowly add milk, garlic powder and basil. Set aside.

Sauté mushrooms and onion in remaining 3 Tbsp. butter. Add crabmeat and shrimp and heat through. Add to white sauce, fill crêpes, place in a greased, shallow baking dish, cover and bake at 300°F for 30 minutes.

Serves 2 to 3.

—Diane Schoemperlen

Fresh Salmon Paté

"My recipe was inspired by a salmon paté I had at The Pilgrim's Inn, Deer Isle, Maine. Their version was coated with finely chopped pistachios." This paté has a delicate flavor — be sure to serve with a light, mild cracker.

Ingredients

⅔ lb. salmon steak
salt
4 oz. cream cheese
1 Tbsp. heavy cream
1 tsp. lime juice
¼–½ tsp. dill
pepper
⅓ cup whole almonds
⅓ cup parsley

Directions

Poach salmon in 2 Tbsp. water with dash of salt until just done — pink through. Cool slightly, then remove bones and skin. Crumble salmon into bowl. Add cream cheese and mix thoroughly. Add cream, stirring until smooth. Add lime juice, dill and pepper and mix well. Chill for 1 to 2 hours.

To serve, finely chop almonds and parsley in shallow bowl. Spoon chilled paté into center. Pat into ball, then turn to coat with almonds and parsley.

Serves 8 to 10 as an appetizer.

—Jane Crosen

Salmon Barbecue

Ingredients

1 cup dry vermouth
¾ cup oil
⅓ cup lemon juice
2 Tbsp. chopped chives
½ tsp. celery salt
½ tsp. thyme
1½ tsp. salt
½ tsp. pepper
4 salmon steaks

Directions

Combine all ingredients except salmon steaks and mix well. Pour over salmon and marinate, refrigerated, for 4 hours. Barbecue for approximately 10 minutes on each side, depending on thickness of steaks.

Serves 4.

—*Debra Gaudreau*

Baked Whitefish

Ingredients

½ cup milk
2 tsp. Dijon mustard
4 tsp. mayonnaise
20 oz. whitefish fillets
1 clove garlic, crushed
¼ tsp. salt
⅛ tsp. thyme
white pepper
½ tsp. tarragon
½ tsp. chopped chives

Directions

Pour milk in bottom of greased casserole dish. Combine mustard and mayonnaise and spread over fish. Sprinkle with garlic, salt, thyme, pepper, tarragon and chives. Place fillets in casserole and bake, covered, at 400°F for 20 to 25 minutes, or until fish flakes easily.

Serves 4.

—*Linda Humphrey*

Haddock in Fennel & Yogurt

Fried coconut flakes are available in cans in many ethnic food stores. If not available, simply dry-roast coconut flakes in a heavy saucepan.

Ingredients

3 Tbsp. olive oil
2 onions, chopped
2 cloves garlic, minced
1 small hot green chili, chopped
1 Tbsp. fennel seeds, crushed
2 Tbsp. fried coconut flakes
1 cup plain yogurt
½ tsp. salt
2 lbs. haddock fillets, cut into 2-3" pieces
2 sprigs coriander, chopped

Directions

Heat oil in heavy pot and sauté onions, garlic and chili until mixture turns light brown. Add crushed fennel and coconut and sauté for 3 minutes more.

Lightly beat together yogurt with 1 cup water. Add to pot and stir. Add salt and simmer for 5 minutes. Add fish and simmer for 5 to 7 minutes, or until fish is tender and flaky. Garnish with coriander.

Serves 4.

— Ingrid Birker

Shrimp-Stuffed Sole

Ingredients

1 clove garlic, minced
1 large shallot, diced
3 Tbsp. butter
⅔ cup chopped parsley
⅛ tsp. dill
3 fresh basil leaves, chopped
juice of ½ lemon
salt & pepper
¼ cup bread crumbs
1 cup cooked, chopped shrimp
1 tomato, peeled, seeded & diced
4 sole fillets
2 tsp. butter
6 thin slices lemon
3 Tbsp. chicken stock
2 Tbsp. white wine

Directions

Sauté garlic and shallot in 3 Tbsp. butter, but do not brown. Add ⅓ cup parsley, dill, basil, lemon juice and salt and pepper, and cook gently for 2 minutes. Stir in bread crumbs and shrimp and let stand for 2 minutes. Stir in tomato.

Place sole in greased shallow casserole dish, with half of each fillet lining pan edge. Place ⅓ to ½ cup stuffing on each fillet. Fold other half of fillet over stuffing and tuck end under. Dot fish with 2 tsp. butter, lay lemon slices on top and sprinkle with remaining ⅓ cup parsley. Combine stock and wine and pour over fillets.

Bake, covered, at 350°F for 20 minutes, or until flaky but still moist

Serves 4.

—Laurie D. Glaspey

Szechuan Shrimp

Ingredients

1 lb. small shrimp, peeled & deveined
1½ Tbsp. cornstarch
1 egg white
¼ cup diced bamboo shoots
¼ cup chopped green onions
¼ cup chopped green pepper
½ tsp. crushed hot red pepper
1 clove garlic, minced
1 Tbsp. grated gingerroot
½ cup chicken stock
5 Tbsp. tomato paste
½ tsp. soy sauce
2 Tbsp. dry sherry
½ tsp. sesame oil
2 cups plus 2 Tbsp. peanut oil
salt

Directions

Rinse shrimp in cold water and pat dry. Combine cornstarch and egg white and mix well. Add shrimp and stir to coat. Let stand for 5 hours. Combine bamboo shoots, green onions, green pepper, hot red pepper, garlic and ginger. Set aside.

Blend together stock, tomato paste, soy sauce, sherry and sesame oil. Set aside. Heat 2 cups peanut oil in wok. Cook shrimp for 1 minute, then remove shrimp from oil. Drain oil from wok. Heat remaining 2 Tbsp. oil in wok. Cook shrimp and vegetable mixture quickly over high heat. Add tomato paste mixture and cook until shrimp are coated and mixture is heated through. Add salt to taste.

Serves 2.

—Trudy McCallum

Seafood Casserole

Ingredients

½ lb. crabmeat
½ lb. shrimp
½ lb. scallops
⅓ cup butter
½ lb. mushrooms, sliced
2 onions, chopped
½ cup flour
1 tsp. dry mustard
2 cups milk
1 cup heavy cream
salt & pepper
2 Tbsp. sherry
1 cup grated Swiss cheese

Directions

Boil crabmeat, shrimp and scallops together for 5 minutes. Drain and set aside.

Melt butter, then sauté mushrooms and onions until tender. Stir in flour and mustard, and cook for 1 to 2 minutes. Slowly stir in milk and cream and cook until thickened. Add salt and pepper, seafood and sherry. Remove from heat and allow to cool. Spoon into greased casserole dish and cover with grated cheese.

Bake, uncovered, at 300°F until browned — 30 minutes.

Serves 4.

Halibut Paella

Like most regional dishes, paella varies in ingredients from cook to cook. This version combines meat and seafood in a colorful, festive presentation. Other possible ingredients include sausage, octopus, clams and crayfish or lobsters.

Ingredients

2 cups fresh peas or green beans
2 lbs. halibut, cut into chunks
1 lb. mussels, scrubbed
1 lb. shrimp, shelled & deveined
½ lb. squid, cleaned & cut into rings
1 tsp. saffron threads
½ cup olive oil
½ lb. ham, cubed
1 whole chicken breast, boned & cut into chunks
2 tomatoes, sliced
1 large clove garlic, sliced
2 Tbsp. sweet paprika
3 cups dry rice
2 red peppers, roasted, peeled & cut into strips

Directions

Cook peas or beans in water until just tender. Drain, saving water. Add enough water to vegetable water to make 5 cups, bring to a boil, add fish, mussels, shrimp and squid and simmer for 5 minutes. Remove mussels and set aside.

Lift out remaining seafood and set aside. Add saffron to cooking water and let stand. In large ovenproof skillet, heat olive oil. Sauté ham and chicken until just done and set aside. In same oil, sauté tomatoes and garlic. Add paprika and cook gently for a couple of minutes. Sprinkle rice into pan, cover with peas or beans, halibut, shrimp, squid, ham and chicken. Pour water with saffron over top and bring to a boil. Continue boiling while arranging mussels and strips of pepper on top.

Bake, uncovered, at 400°F for 15 minutes. Remove from oven and cook on top of stove for 1 to 2 minutes.

Serves 8.

Cheesy Crab in Filo

Made as directed, in two long rolls, this works well as a main course. To serve as an appetizer, cut the filo and roll individually. Leftover filo dough can be well wrapped and frozen.

Ingredients

½ cup chopped green onions
½ cup butter
1 cup dry white wine
12 oz. crabmeat
4 oz. cream cheese
¼ cup chopped parsley
4 egg yolks, lightly beaten
1 tsp. salt
½ tsp. pepper
1 pkg. filo dough
melted butter
1 egg, beaten

Directions

Sauté onions in butter for 3 to 4 minutes. Add wine and bring to a boil. Boil for 3 to 5 minutes until liquid is reduced by half, then remove from heat. Stir in crabmeat, cheese, parsley, egg yolks, salt and pepper. Stir until cheese is melted, then set aside to cool.

Place 1 filo leaf on waxed paper. Brush with melted butter. Repeat 3 more times. Place half the crab mixture on the filo, close to the bottom, leaving a 2-inch border. Roll up, folding in ends. Repeat with more filo and remaining crab mixture.

Place on greased cookie sheet. Brush with beaten egg. Bake at 350°F for 15 minutes, then at 450°F for 10 minutes.

Serves 4 to 6.

—*Nancy Blenkinsop*

Scallops Provençale

Since sea scallops are larger than bay scallops, the cooking time will need to be adjusted accordingly if one is substituted for the other.

Ingredients

2 Tbsp. peanut oil
1 lb. Atlantic scallops
1 tsp. butter
1 Tbsp. finely chopped shallots
1 clove garlic, crushed
1 cup sliced mushrooms
½ cup diced tomato
sesame oil
1 tsp. Pernod
½ tsp. paprika
juice of ½ lemon
garnish of chopped green onion & dill

Directions

Heat oil until very hot. Add scallops and sauté for 1 minute. Drain off all liquid, then add butter, shallots and garlic. Sauté for 1 minute more, then add mushrooms and tomato. Season with sesame oil, Pernod, paprika and lemon juice and cook until liquid is reduced. Serve in scallop shells with garnish.

Serves 2.

—A. Camm

Prawns in Coconut Milk

"My husband and I work at a large open-pit coal mine. This recipe came from a Fijian family working at the mine. We serve it with basmati rice, raita and chutney. Coconut milk can be bought at specialty food marts and ethnic food stores. It can also be made by pouring hot milk over grated coconut."

Ingredients

½ cup butter
1 onion, chopped
3 large cloves garlic, crushed
2 tsp. coriander
2 tsp. turmeric
½ tsp. cayenne
1 tsp. chili powder
½ tsp. ginger
salt & pepper
2 Tbsp. white vinegar
1 cup coconut milk
1½ lbs. large prawns, shelled & deveined

Directions

Melt butter in a wok and add the onion and garlic. Sauté over low heat until soft. Mix spices and vinegar into a paste with mortar and pestle. Add to mixture in pan and sauté for another few minutes, stirring constantly. Add coconut milk and turn up heat. Cook until thickened — 5 minutes. Add prawns and stir until coated. Simmer for a few minutes until prawns are just cooked.

Serves 4 to 5.

— Tracy Carroll

Broiled Lemon Sole with Cucumber Dill Topping

Ingredients

2 lbs. lemon sole
1 cup mayonnaise
½ cup chopped cucumber
1 Tbsp. chopped dill
3 green onions, sliced
Tabasco sauce
salt & pepper

Directions

Arrange fish in single layer on greased tray. Combine remaining ingredients and spread evenly over fish. Broil 3 to 5 inches from heat for 5 to 7 minutes.

Serves 4.

Salmon Cheese Ball

Ingredients

2 6½-oz. cans salmon
8 oz. cream cheese, softened
1 Tbsp. lemon juice
2 tsp. grated onion
¼ tsp. salt
Dash Worcestershire sauce
6 Tbsp. mayonnaise, page 130
3 Tbsp. snipped fresh parsley

Directions

Drain and flake salmon, removing bones. Mix all ingredients thoroughly except the parsley. Chill several hours. Shape into a ball or log, roll in parsley and chill.

Makes 2½ cups.

—Marva Blackmore

Tarragon Mussels

For tarragon lovers only, this dish makes a tasty appetizer. "I am a potter and I made some pots to serve this dish in. Just an ordinary pot with a lid, but the lid serves as a bowl in which to discard the shells."

Ingredients

4 Tbsp. butter
4–5 green onions, chopped
4 dozen mussels, scrubbed
2 tsp. flour
½ cup white wine
2 tsp. tarragon
cayenne

Directions

Melt butter and sauté green onions. Add mussels, then stir in flour, wine, tarragon and cayenne. Cover and cook over medium heat for 6 minutes.

Serves 8 as an appetizer.

—Doris McIlroy

Poultry
& Game

Chicken Breasts in Maple Syrup

Ingredients

4 chicken breasts, boned
Seasoned flour
3 large mushrooms, finely chopped
½ cup finely diced ham
½ tsp. dried chives
2 Tbsp. butter
¼ cup butter
1 cup thinly sliced onion
Savory
4 Tbsp. maple syrup

Directions

Roll each breast in seasoned flour. Fry mushrooms, ham and chives in 2 Tbsp. butter for 2 to 3 minutes or until mushrooms are tender.

Slit thick portion of each breast and insert spoonful of ham mixture. Pinch edges together to seal. Brown stuffed breasts in ¼ cup butter. Remove from pan, add onion to pan and fry until golden brown.

Arrange breasts in casserole dish. Top with onion and sprinkle with savory. Spoon maple syrup over chicken breasts. Rinse frying pan with ½ cup water, then pour over chicken.

Bake, uncovered, at 350°F for 30 minutes.

Serves 4.

—*Mary Rogers*

Chicken Breasts Alfredo

Ingredients

3 eggs, beaten
3 tsp. water
½ cup grated Romano cheese
¼ cup snipped parsley
½ tsp. salt
3 whole chicken breasts, split & boned
½ cup flour
1 cup fine dry bread crumbs
3 Tbsp. butter
3 tsp. oil
1 cup whipping cream
¼ cup water
¼ cup butter
½ cup grated Romano cheese
¼ cup snipped parsley
6 slices mozzarella cheese

Directions

Mix together eggs, water, Romano cheese, parsley and salt. Dip chicken in flour, then egg mixture and then bread crumbs.

Melt butter and oil in large skillet. Cook chicken over medium heat until brown — about 15 minutes. Remove to baking dish.

Heat cream, water and butter in 1-quart saucepan until butter melts. Add cheese, cook and stir over medium heat for 5 minutes. Stir in parsley. Pour over chicken.

Top each piece with a slice of mozzarella cheese. Bake at 425°F until cheese melts and chicken is tender, about 8 minutes.

Serves 4 to 6.

—*Pam Collacott*

Parmesan Chicken

Ingredients

1 cup bread crumbs
1½ cups grated Parmesan cheese
3 Tbsp. parsley
¼ tsp. salt
1 tsp. dry mustard
½ tsp. Worcestershire sauce
¼ tsp. garlic salt
½ cup melted butter
8–10 boned chicken breasts

Directions

Combine bread crumbs, cheese, parsley and salt and set aside. Combine remaining ingredients except chicken. Dip chicken, one piece at a time, into butter mixture, then into bread crumbs.

Place in shallow baking pan and bake at 350°F for 40 to 50 minutes. Garnish with pitted, sliced black olives and sliced mushrooms.

Serves 4 to 5.

—Barbara Johnson

Chicken in Bacon Roll with Cheese

Ingredients

4 whole chicken breasts, skinned & boned
4 slices ham
4 2-inch cubes mozzarella cheese
12 slices bacon

Directions

Pound chicken breasts between sheets of wax paper until quite thin — ¼ inch.

Wrap each piece of cheese in a slice of ham and place in the center of each breast. Fold edges of chicken over ham and cheese. Wrap 3 slices of bacon around each breast.

Place on a baking sheet and bake at 375°F for 30 minutes.

Serves 4.

—Kathee Roy

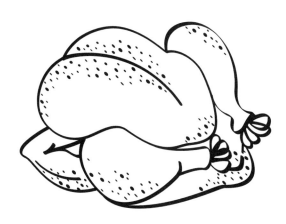

Creamy Breast of Chicken with Shrimp

Ingredients

2 large chicken breasts
Salt
Pepper
Nutmeg
1 clove garlic, minced
½ cup flour
¼ cup butter
½ cup celery
1½ cups fresh mushrooms, sliced
½ cup chopped onions
¾ cup dry white wine
1½ cups shrimp
2 Tbsp. chopped parsley
½ cup sour cream

Directions

Cut each breast into bite-sized pieces. Sprinkle with seasonings and garlic and let sit for half an hour. Coat chicken pieces with flour and brown in half the butter until crisp. Add celery, mushrooms, onions and white wine. Simmer, covered, for 30 minutes.

Sauté shrimp in remaining butter for 5 minutes and add to chicken mixture. Add parsley and sour cream and bring to a boil.

Serve over rice.

Serves 4.

—Shirley Gilbert

Cranberry Glazed Chicken

Ingredients

3 lbs. frying chicken, cut into pieces
1 cup flour
2 tsp. paprika
Garlic salt
Pinch rosemary, thyme & sage
2 Tbsp. brown sugar
¼ tsp. ginger powder
½ cup cranberry jelly
¼ cup orange juice
1 Tbsp. Worcestershire sauce
1 tsp. grated orange rind

Directions

Rinse and pat dry chicken. Coat with flour, mixed with paprika, garlic salt, rosemary, thyme and sage. Bake at 400°F for 35 minutes.

Combine sugar, ginger, cranberry jelly, orange juice, Worcestershire sauce and orange rind in small saucepan. Bring to a boil, stirring constantly. Spoon over chicken and bake 10 to 15 minutes longer until chicken is tender.

Serves 4.

—Mrs. K. Love

Chicken Divan

Ingredients

1 cup white sauce, page 129
1 egg yolk
2 Tbsp. cream
2 Tbsp. grated Parmesan cheese
2 Tbsp. grated Gruyère cheese
3 Tbsp. sherry
3–4 lbs. chicken breasts, skinned & boned
2 lbs. broccoli
Parmesan cheese to garnish

Directions

Warm the white sauce. Beat together the egg yolk and cream until well blended. Add a little of the warm sauce to the egg and cream, stir, then return mixture to the rest of the sauce. Heat through, then add cheeses and sherry and continue cooking and stirring until sauce thickens. Set aside.

Poach chicken breasts until tender but still juicy. Cook broccoli until crispy-tender. Drain.

Arrange broccoli on a heatproof platter. Place chicken pieces on top of the broccoli and pour the sauce over it all. Sprinkle with Parmesan cheese.

Bake at 350°F for 20 minutes, or until bubbly.

Serves 6.

—Cary Elizabeth Marshall

Chicken Kiev

Ingredients

½ cup soft butter
2 Tbsp. chopped parsley
1 clove garlic, chopped
2 Tbsp. lemon juice
¼ tsp. cayenne pepper
6 chicken breasts, skinned & boned
½ cup flour
2 eggs, beaten
½ cup bread crumbs

Directions

Combine butter, parsley, garlic, lemon juice and pepper. Mix well and chill until firm.

Halve chicken breasts and flatten. Salt and pepper lightly. Place a piece of butter mixture on each chicken breast, roll and secure with toothpicks. Coat each roll with flour, dip in beaten eggs and then bread crumbs.

Chill for 1 hour, then deep fry until golden — 15 minutes.

Serves 6.

—Marney Allen

Chicken Royale

Ingredients

2 chicken breasts, boned
2 pork sausages
¼ cup oil
3 potatoes, thinly sliced
2 cups broccoli pieces

Directions

Stuff boned chicken breasts with sausages, roll and fasten with a toothpick. Heat oil in an electric frying pan and brown breasts. Lower heat, add vegetables and cook for 20 minutes.

Serves 4.

—Hazel R. Baker

Soy Butter Baked Chicken

Ingredients

3 Tbsp. soy sauce
1 tsp. crushed chili peppers
⅛ tsp. pepper
1½ tsp. lemon juice
½ cup butter
⅓ cup water
½ tsp. salt
3 lbs. chicken, cut up

Directions

Combine all ingredients except the chicken in saucepan, bring to a boil, reduce heat and simmer for 10 minutes.

Place chicken in single layer in baking dish. Pour sauce over chicken and bake at 400°F for 45 to 55 minutes, basting occasionally and turning chicken once.

Serves 4 to 6.

—June Plamondon

Lemon Chicken

This dish may be assembled up to one day ahead and refrigerated until ready to cook.

Ingredients

2 lbs. chicken pieces
¼ cup lemon juice
2 Tbsp. melted butter
1 small onion, chopped
½ tsp. salt
½ tsp. celery salt
½ tsp. pepper
½ tsp. rosemary
¼ tsp. thyme

Directions

Arrange chicken in a baking dish. Mix together remaining ingredients and pour over chicken. Marinate for three hours, then bake at 325°F, covered, for 45 minutes to 1 hour.

Serves 4.

—Gena Hughes

Baked Chicken with Apples

Ingredients
3 lbs. chicken pieces
Seasoned flour
2 Tbsp. butter
2 Tbsp. oil
1 clove garlic, crushed
3 apples, cored & quartered
2 Tbsp. brown sugar
½ tsp. ginger
1½ cups unsweetened apple juice
½ cup water or dry sherry
2 Tbsp. cornstarch
¼ cup cold water

Directions

Dredge chicken in flour. Brown in butter and oil with garlic. Remove chicken and discard garlic. Add apples to drippings. Sprinkle with brown sugar and brown the apples.

Place chicken and apples in a casserole dish, sprinkle with ginger and pour drippings, apple juice and water or sherry over them. Cover and bake for 45 minutes at 350°F.

Remove chicken from sauce and keep warm. Blend cornstarch with water and stir into pan juices. Cook over high heat, stirring until thickened. Pour over chicken and serve.

Serves 4 to 6.

—Bryanna Clark

Sweet & Sour Orange Chicken

Ingredients
5–6 lb. chicken, cut up
1 cup flour
6 Tbsp. oil
1½ cups orange juice
3 medium onions, thinly sliced
4 cloves garlic, crushed
⅓ cup soy sauce
⅓ cup cider vinegar
3 Tbsp. honey
2 Tbsp. water
1 large green pepper, sliced

Directions

Dredge chicken pieces in flour. Heat oil in deep frying pan and brown chicken slowly over medium heat.

Transfer to a casserole dish. Add orange juice, onions and garlic. Cover and cook at 350°F for 20 minutes. Mix together soy sauce, vinegar, honey and water and pour over chicken. Add sliced pepper. Cover and continue cooking for 25 minutes.

Serves 6.

—Ingrid Birker

Hawaiian Chicken

Ingredients

1 Tbsp. oil
1 cup uncooked rice
2 cups chicken stock
1 cup coarsely chopped onion
½ cup chopped green pepper
2 cups chopped celery
1½ cups cooked chicken
1 Tbsp. soy sauce
1 cup pineapple juice
Salt & pepper
1 cup pineapple chunks

Directions

In a heavy frying pan, brown rice in oil, stirring frequently, for about 12 minutes. Add chicken stock, cover and cook for about 3 minutes. Add remaining ingredients, except pineapple chunks, mix well and spoon into casserole dish. Top with pineapple chunks. Bake at 350°F for 30 to 35 minutes.

Serves 4.

—A.H. McInnis

Chicken with Sour Cream

Ingredients

¼ cup flour
1 tsp. salt
Pepper
1 tsp. paprika
½ tsp. poultry seasoning
1½ lbs. boned chicken, cut into bite-sized pieces
Cooking oil
1 cup soft bread crumbs
2 Tbsp. butter
½ cup grated Parmesan
    cheese
¼ cup sesame seeds
½ cup hot water
1½ cups cream of mushroom sauce, page 129
1 cup sour cream

Directions

Mix flour, salt, pepper, paprika and poultry seasoning. Dredge meat in this mixture and brown slowly in hot oil. Arrange meat in baking dish. Combine bread crumbs, butter, cheese and sesame seeds. Spoon over meat. Stir water into meat drippings. Pour around meat. Bake at 350°F until tender — 45 to 50 minutes. Heat mushroom sauce and blend in sour cream. Serve with chicken.

Serves 4.

—Elizabeth Clayton

Chicken with Pineapple

The delightful idea of combining pineapple with meat is popular in many parts of the world — even in areas where only the tinned variety is regularly available.

Ingredients

8-oz. can pineapple tidbits
¼ cup brown sugar
2 Tbsp. cornstarch
½ cup water
1 Tbsp. cider vinegar
1 Tbsp. soy sauce
4 lbs. chicken pieces

Directions

Drain pineapple and reserve syrup. Combine sugar, cornstarch and syrup in medium saucepan. Blend in water, vinegar and soy sauce.

Cook over low heat until thick and bubbly, stirring occasionally.

Place chicken pieces in a baking dish and cover with sauce. Add the pineapple tidbits. Bake at 350°F for 40 to 45 minutes, basting chicken with sauce at 10 minute intervals.

Serves 4.

—Christine Collis

Chicken with Olives & Lemon

Ingredients

1 large onion, thinly sliced
1 clove garlic, minced
1 Tbsp. minced parsley
1 Tbsp. ground coriander
1 tsp. salt
½ tsp. pepper
⅛ tsp. turmeric
2–3 Tbsp. olive oil
2½–3 lbs. chicken pieces
⅓ cup sliced green olives

Directions

Sauté onion, garlic, parsley, coriander, salt, pepper and turmeric in olive oil. Add chicken and brown. Place lemon slices on top of chicken. Cover and simmer for 30 minutes. Stir in olives.

Remove chicken to a platter and keep warm. Boil down juices and pour over chicken.

Serves 4 to 6.

—Bryanna Clark

Chicken with White Wine

Ingredients

3 lbs. chicken pieces
Salt & pepper
3 Tbsp. cooking oil
Few pinches basil
½ cup dry white wine
4 cups cooked rice

Directions

Season chicken pieces with salt and pepper and brown in oil in large skillet. Sprinkle with basil. Cover and cook for 30 minutes on low heat. Pour wine over chicken and cook, covered, until chicken is very tender.

Remove chicken and keep warm. Reduce pan juices and stir in rice, scraping bottom of pan. Add chicken and mix well.

Serves 4 to 6.

—*Bryanna Clark*

Chicken Marengo

Ingredients

3 lbs. chicken pieces
1 cup flour
Salt & pepper
¼ cup olive oil
1 clove garlic, crushed
1 small onion, chopped
4 tomatoes, quartered
1 cup dry white wine
1 bay leaf
Pinch thyme
1 Tbsp. minced parsley
¼ lb. mushrooms, sliced
2 Tbsp. butter
½ cup sliced olives
2 Tbsp. flour
½ cup cold broth

Directions

Dredge chicken in flour seasoned with salt and pepper. Brown in oil. Add garlic, onion, tomatoes, wine, bay leaf, thyme and parsley. Cover and simmer for 30 minutes.

Meanwhile, sauté mushrooms in butter. Add to chicken after 30 minutes along with olives. Discard bay leaf and remove chicken mixture to warm platter. Keep warm.

Thicken liquid with flour mixed with broth. Boil for 3 to 5 minutes, stirring, until thickened. Return chicken to sauce and simmer for 10 minutes.

Serves 4 to 6.

—*Bryanna Clark*

Chicken Cacciatore

Ingredients

4 lb. chicken, cut up
3 Tbsp. flour
2 Tbsp. chopped onion
1 clove garlic, minced
¼ cup olive oil
¼ cup tomato paste
½ cup white wine
1 tsp. salt
¼ tsp. pepper
¾ cup chicken stock
1 bay leaf
⅛ tsp. thyme
½ tsp. basil
⅛ tsp. marjoram
½ tsp. oregano
2 Tbsp. chopped parsley
Parmesan cheese

Directions

Dredge chicken pieces with flour and brown with onion and garlic in oil. Add remaining ingredients except cheese. Simmer, covered, for 1 to 2 hours. Serve over spaghetti or baby potatoes and top with grated Parmesan cheese.

Serves 6.

—Carolyn Hills

Paprika Chicken

Ingredients

4 Tbsp. butter
1 large onion, chopped
2 Tbsp. paprika
2½–3 lbs. chicken pieces
Salt
2 green peppers, chopped
2 tomatoes, chopped
2 Tbsp. flour
½ cup cold water
½ cup sour cream

Directions

Heat butter in casserole dish, add onion and fry until translucent. Sprinkle with paprika and stir. Add a few tablespoons of water and cook until liquid is almost evaporated.

Add the chicken and salt and cook for 5 minutes, stirring frequently. Add a little water and cover. Continue cooking over low heat. Add peppers and tomatoes after 20 minutes. Continue cooking until chicken is tender, about 20 minutes.

Stir flour into ½ cup cold water and mix with sour cream. Add to chicken and stir until smooth. Cook for 5 more minutes.

Serves 6.

— Anton Gross

Honey Mustard Chicken

Quick and easy to prepare, this chicken dish has a slightly sweet-and-sour flavor.

Ingredients

¼ cup butter
½ cup honey
¼ cup prepared mustard
10 chicken drumsticks
Salt & pepper

Directions

Melt butter, honey and mustard together. Dip chicken pieces into the mixture, then bake in a shallow casserole dish at 350°F for 35 minutes.

Serves 5.

—*Ingrid Birker*

Florida Fried Chicken

This recipe produces golden delicious pieces of honey fried chicken. Just make sure that the oven is not too hot after the sauce is added or the honey will burn.

Ingredients

½ cup flour
1 tsp. salt
¼ tsp. pepper
2 tsp. paprika
4–6 lb. frying chicken, cut up
⅓ cup butter
¼ cup butter
¼ cup orange blossom honey
  (or any pure honey)
⅕ cup orange juice

Directions

Combine flour, salt, pepper and paprika in a clean paper bag. Add chicken 1 piece at a time and shake to coat well. Melt ⅓ cup butter in a large shallow baking dish in the oven at 400°F. Remove from oven and roll coated chicken pieces in butter. Leave in pan, skin side down. Bake for 30 minutes at 400°, then cool oven to 300° while making sauce.

In a small saucepan, melt ¼ cup butter, stir in honey and orange juice. Remove chicken from oven, turn pieces of chicken skin side up and pour sauce over all. Continue cooking another 30 minutes or until chicken is done.

Serves 6.

—*Cheryl Suckling*

Chicken Casserole

Ingredients

1 large chicken
6 onions, chopped
1 bunch celery, chopped
1 lb. mushrooms, chopped
1 green pepper, chopped
1 can pimento
¼ lb. butter
3 cups tomato sauce, page 339
Salt, pepper & any other seasoning desired
8-oz. package egg noodles (medium-sized)

Directions

Boil chicken, half-covered with water, until tender. Cool slightly, remove meat from the bones and cut into bite-sized pieces. Reserve broth.

Sauté onions, celery, mushrooms, green pepper and pimento in butter until vegetables are tender. Add tomato sauce, seasonings and chicken. Cook noodles in boiling salted water, drain and add to mixture.

Bake at 375°F until hot and bubbling — 20 to 30 minutes.

Serves 6.

—J. Elizabeth Fraser

Jambalaya

Ingredients

3 lb. roasting chicken, cut up
1 onion, finely chopped
1 green pepper, finely chopped
1 clove garlic, finely chopped
1 carrot, thinly sliced
19-oz. can tomatoes, cut up
½ tsp. oregano
½ tsp. basil
1 tsp. salt
½ tsp. pepper
8-oz. tin of shrimp
2 cups cooked rice

Directions

Combine chicken, onion, green pepper, garlic, carrot, tomatoes, oregano, basil, salt and pepper in a slow cooker. Cover and cook on low for 8 hours.

Approximately 1 hour before serving, add shrimp and rice. Cover and continue cooking for 1 hour or until heated through.

Serves 4.

—Ruth Faux

Chicken, Rice & Dumplings

Ingredients
1½ cups cooked rice
2 cups diced cooked vegetables
2 cups chicken broth or gravy
1 cup diced cooked chicken
1 cup flour
2 tsp. baking powder
½ tsp. salt
1 egg
¼ cup cold milk
Parsley
Pepper

Directions

Combine rice and vegetables with broth. Simmer for 5 minutes. Add chicken.

To make dumplings, mix flour, baking powder and salt together. Beat egg, mix with milk and add to dry ingredients. Stir until all the flour is moistened.

Dip a spoon into the broth, then take a spoonful of the batter and drop it onto the top of the broth. Repeat, leaving a small space between each dumpling, until the batter is gone.

Cover and simmer for 10 to 15 minutes, or until dumplings are cooked. Sprinkle with parsley and pepper and serve.

Serves 4.

—*Joan Southworth*

Crispy Chicken

Ingredients
½ cup flour
¼ cup corn meal
2 Tbsp. soy flour
2–3 Tbsp. wheat germ
½ tsp. sage
½ tsp. thyme
Curry powder
Pepper
1 egg, beaten
½ cup milk
1 chicken, cut up

Directions

Combine dry ingredients and liquid ingredients separately. Dip chicken pieces in liquid then coat with flour mixture. Place on a cookie sheet and bake at 375°F for 45 minutes to 1 hour.

Serves 4 to 6.

—*Karen Armour*

Country Chicken

Ingredients

¾ cup sour cream
1 Tbsp. lemon juice
1 tsp. salt
1 tsp. paprika
½ tsp. Worcestershire sauce
Garlic powder
2½–3 lb. chicken, cut up
1 cup fine dry bread crumbs
¼ cup butter

Directions

Combine sour cream, lemon juice, salt, paprika, Worcestershire sauce and garlic powder.

Dip chicken in mixture, roll in bread crumbs and place in shallow baking dish. Dot with butter.

Bake, covered, at 350°F for 45 minutes. Remove cover and cook 45 to 50 minutes longer.

Serves 5 to 6.

—Donna Jubb

Chicken Curry

An excellent authentic Indian recipe for an easy popular dish, this can be made with leftover chicken meat, chicken pieces or a whole chicken.

Ingredients

4 lb. stewing chicken
1½ cups ghee (clarified butter)
1½ lbs. onions, sliced
1 cup chopped fresh ginger
1 head garlic (7 or 8 cloves)
2½ cups water
2 tsp. turmeric
2 tsp. garam masala
1 Tbsp. salt
1 Tbsp. cumin
½ tsp. ground black pepper
1 tsp. hot chili powder
10 cardamoms
10 cloves
4 bay leaves
5 sticks cinnamon
1¼ cups yogurt

Directions

Skin chicken and cut into pieces.

Melt ghee in large heavy saucepan, add half the onions. While they are frying on low heat, liquidize in a blender the ginger, garlic and remaining onions with water. When the onions are fried to golden brown, add spice mixture and stir over low heat for 10 minutes.

Add turmeric, garam masala, salt, cumin, pepper, chili powder, cardamoms, cloves, bay leaves and cinnamon. Cook, stirring, for a further 10 minutes.

Add chicken pieces and yogurt. Cover the pan and cook on low heat for 3 hours.

Serves 6 to 8.

—Sheila Bear

Old-Fashioned Chicken Pot Pie

Ingredients

3 lb. chicken
3 cups water
2 tsp. salt
½ tsp. peppercorns
1 medium onion, chopped
⅓ cup butter
¼ cup flour
¼ tsp. celery salt
⅛ tsp. pepper
1 cup cooked peas
1 cup cooked carrots
2 cups mashed potatoes

Directions

Cut chicken into pieces. Place in a large pot with water, 1 tsp. of salt and peppercorns. Bring to a boil, then simmer for 45 minutes, or until tender. Remove chicken. Strain broth and discard peppercorns. Cool the chicken, remove skin and bones and cut up the large pieces. Sauté onion in butter in a medium saucepan until tender. Add flour and blend well. Cook for 1 minute. Gradually add 2 cups of broth, stirring until smooth. Cook over low heat, stirring constantly until thickened and bubbly. Add 1 tsp. salt, celery salt and pepper. Remove from heat.

Arrange chicken, peas and carrots in a 2½-quart casserole dish. Spoon sauce over and top with mashed potatoes.

Bake at 425°F for 20 minutes.

Serves 4.

—Sharron Jansen

Barbecued Chicken

Ingredients

¼ cup vegetable oil
1 tsp. minced garlic
2 medium onions, finely chopped
6-oz. can tomato paste
¼ cup white vinegar
1 tsp. salt
1 tsp. basil or thyme
¼ cup honey
½ cup beef stock
½ cup Worcestershire sauce
1 tsp. dry mustard
1 chicken, cut up
Salt & pepper
2 Tbsp. oil
1 clove garlic, crushed

Directions

Heat oil in a 12-inch skillet. Add minced garlic and onions and cook, stirring frequently, until onion is soft. Lower heat and add remaining ingredients, except chicken, salt, pepper, garlic, and oil. Simmer, uncovered, for 15 minutes.

Season chicken with salt, pepper and garlic. Brown in oil at a high temperature. Remove to a large deep, cast-iron frying pan. Pour barbecue sauce over the chicken, cover and cook over medium heat until sauce is lightly boiling. Reduce heat and simmer for 1½ to 2 hours.

Makes 2½ cups.

—Marilyn & Patricia Picco

Cold Barbecued Chicken

Ingredients

4 lb. chicken, cut in pieces
4 Tbsp. salad oil or shortening
1 large onion, sliced
3 Tbsp. brown sugar
3 Tbsp. cider vinegar
¼ cup lemon juice
1 cup ketchup or tomato sauce
3 Tbsp. Worcestershire sauce
1 Tbsp. prepared mustard
½ cup diced celery
1¼ cups water
½ tsp. salt
½ tsp. oregano
¼ tsp. pepper

Directions

In a large frying pan, brown the chicken in salad oil. As pieces are done, place them in a 3-quart casserole dish.

Add remaining ingredients to pan and bring to a boil. Pour sauce over chicken. Cover and bake for 1 hour at 350°F. Cool. Uncover and refrigerate until needed. Serve at room temperature.

Serves 4.

—Mrs. J. Hall-Armstrong

Chicken Beer Barbecue

Ingredients

3 lbs. chicken pieces
12 oz. beer
1 tsp. salt
¼ tsp. pepper
2 Tbsp. lemon juice
½ tsp. orange extract
1 tsp. grated orange rind
1 Tbsp. brown sugar
1 Tbsp. dark molasses
Generous dash Tabasco sauce

Directions

Place chicken in large bowl. Mix together remaining ingredients. Pour over chicken and marinate for several hours or overnight. Barbecue over hot coals, brushing frequently with marinade.

Serves 4 to 6

—Cynthia Stewart

Chicken Enchiladas

Ingredients
12 tortillas
3 cups chopped cooked chicken
¾ cup sliced almonds
2 cups shredded Jack cheese
3 cups chicken stock
2 Tbsp. cornstarch
½ tsp. chili powder
¼ tsp. garlic powder
¼ tsp. cumin

Directions
Fry tortillas quickly on both sides in hot oil. Stack and keep warm. Combine chicken, almonds and ½ cup cheese.

To make sauce, bring chicken stock to a boil. Mix cornstarch with a little cold water and stir into stock. Add seasonings and boil for 1 minute.

Add ½ cup of sauce to chicken mixture. Dip each tortilla in sauce to soften, put some chicken mixture on it and roll up. Place tortillas in greased casserole dish in a single layer. Top with remaining 1½ cups cheese and pour remaining sauce around tortillas.

Bake at 350°F for 20 to 25 minutes.

Serves 4.

—Linda Townsend

Chicken Wings

Ingredients
5 lbs. chicken wings
2 Tbsp. vegetable oil
1 medium onion, chopped
2 cloves garlic, minced
½ cup brown sugar
1 cup chili sauce
1 Tbsp. Worcestershire sauce
½ cup lemon juice
½ cup water
2 Tbsp. vinegar

Directions
Cook wings in oil in casserole dish at 350°F for 30 minutes. Remove wings from oven. Combine remaining ingredients and pour over wings. Return to oven for 1 to 1½ hours.

Serves 4 to 6.

—Reo Belhumeur

Blanketed Chicken

Ingredients
4-6 lbs. chicken, cut up
2 Tbsp. finely chopped green pepper
Salt & pepper
1 Tbsp. finely chopped chives
6 strips bacon
4 Tbsp. flour
1½ cups light cream

Directions
Place chicken pieces in roasting pan and add green pepper, salt, pepper and chives. Cover with bacon. Bake at 400°F for 40 to 50 minutes. Combine 3 Tbsp. fat from roasting pan, flour and cream and cook slowly until thickened. Season with salt and pepper. Place chicken in serving dish and cover with sauce.

Serves 6.

—Judy Bell

Cantonese Chicken Wings

Ingredients
3 lbs. chicken wings
1 Tbsp. cooking oil
1 Tbsp. soy sauce
½ tsp. salt
¼ cup brown sugar
1 tsp. chili powder
¾ tsp. celery seed
¼ cup vinegar
1 cup tomato sauce, page 339

Directions
Pat chicken wings dry. Place on broiler pan. Mix oil and soy sauce and brush over each wing. Mix salt, sugar, chili powder and celery seed and sprinkle over top. Place 5 inches below broiler and cook for approximately 10 minutes.

Remove from oven, place in casserole dish. Combine vinegar with tomato sauce and pour over casserole.

Bake at 350°F for 1 hour.

Serves 4.

—Irene MacPhee

Pauline's Chicken Wings

Ingredients
4 lbs. chicken wings
½ tsp. salt
½ tsp. garlic powder
¼ tsp. pepper
½ cup brown sugar
½ tsp. cornstarch
¼ cup vinegar
2 Tbsp. ketchup or tomato paste
½ cup chicken stock
1 Tbsp. soy sauce

Directions
Combine all ingredients but chicken and pour over wings. Bake, uncovered, at 400°F for 35 to 40 minutes, glazing every 10 minutes.

Serves 4.

—Mary Anne Vanner

Chicken Chow Mein

Ingredients

2 Tbsp. butter
¼ cup chopped onion
½ cup celery
4 cups bean sprouts
1 cup diced cooked chicken
½ cup water
4 cups Chinese noodles
Salt & pepper

Directions

Melt butter in a large pot and add onion and celery. Sauté for 3 to 5 minutes. Add bean sprouts, chicken, water, noodles and seasonings. Stir. Place in casserole dish and bake at 325°F for 30 minutes.

Serves 2.

Chicken Wings in Beer

Ingredients

36 chicken wings
¼ cup sugar
2 Tbsp. minced onion
1 clove garlic, minced
½ tsp. ginger
1 cup beer
1 cup pineapple or orange juice
¼ cup vegetable oil

Directions

Cut tips off wings and discard. Wash wings well. Marinate, refrigerated, in remaining ingredients overnight, turning a few times.

Place in baking pan with marinade and bake, uncovered, for 2 hours at 350°F.

Serves 8.

—Anne Lawrence

Almond Chicken

Ingredients

½ cup whole almonds
2–3 Tbsp. butter
3–4 stalks celery, thinly sliced
1 onion, sliced
1 green pepper, cut in strips
1½ cups peas
1 cup sliced mushrooms
2 cups cooked chicken, cut into bite-sized pieces
1 tsp. sugar
2 Tbsp. cornstarch
1½ cups chicken stock
1 tsp. soy sauce

Directions

Brown almonds in butter and set aside. To the remaining butter, add celery, onion and green pepper and brown slightly. Add peas. Cook about 1 minute, then stir in mushrooms and chicken. Blend sugar, cornstarch and stock. Add to pan, cooking until clear. At the last moment before serving, add soy sauce and almonds. Serve with rice.

Serves 4 to 6.

—Adele Dueck

Chicken Salad

Ingredients

½ cup mayonnaise, page 130
1 Tbsp. fresh lemon juice
¼ tsp. salt
⅛ tsp. pepper
⅛ tsp. diced marjoram
2 Tbsp. heavy cream
3 cups chopped chicken, in large pieces
Ripe olives
Tomato slices

Directions

Combine mayonnaise with lemon juice, salt, pepper, marjoram and cream, mix chicken into dressing. Arrange on plate with olives and tomatoes.

Serves 4.

—*Winona Heasman*

Chicken Tetrazzini

Ingredients

1 cup sliced mushrooms
1 cup chopped celery
½ cup chopped green pepper
1½ cups slivered almonds
¼ cup butter
¼ cup flour
1 cup chicken stock
2 cups light cream
Salt & pepper
1 cup grated Swiss cheese
3-4 cups cooked chicken, cut into bite-sized pieces
12 oz. spaghetti, cooked
½ cup Parmesan cheese

Directions

Sauté mushrooms, celery, green pepper and 1 cup almonds in butter for 5 minutes. Remove with slotted spoon. To butter in frying pan, add flour and stir until smooth. Slowly add chicken stock and cream, stirring constantly. Cook until slightly thickened. Add salt, pepper and cheese.

When sauce has thickened, remove from heat. In large casserole dish, combine cooked spaghetti, vegetables, chicken and sauce. Mix well and top with Parmesan cheese and remaining almonds.

Bake at 350°F for 20 to 30 minutes.

Serves 8 to 10.

Mushroom Sausage Dressing

Ingredients

¾ cup chopped mushrooms
¾ cup chopped onion
⅓ cup chopped celery
⅓ cup butter
½–¾ cup crumbled cooked sausage meat
4 cups dry bread cubes
1 Tbsp. parsley
1 tsp. salt
Pepper
Savory
Thyme
Chicken stock to moisten dressing

Directions

Sauté vegetables in butter. Add sausage meat, bread cubes and seasonings. Taste and adjust seasoning if necessary. Add enough stock to moisten.

Makes enough dressing to stuff a 10–12 lb. bird.

—Lynn Shelley

Orange Cranberry Dressing

Ingredients

10–12 cups coarse bread crumbs
1 Tbsp. grated orange rind
2 oranges in segments
1 cup thick cranberry sauce
1 cup finely chopped celery
1 cup finely chopped onion
2 tsp. salt
½ tsp. pepper
½ cup soft butter

Directions

Toss all ingredients together lightly.
Sufficient to stuff a 10–12 lb. turkey.

—Sherri Dick

Rice Dressing

Ingredients

2 cups cooked rice
2–3 green onions, chopped
1 cup mushrooms, chopped
½ tsp. thyme
½ tsp. sage

Directions

Combine all ingredients and place in an oven-proof dish. When poultry is nearly cooked, take 2 Tbsp. of drippings from roasting pan and add to dressing to moisten. Cover and bake for 30 minutes.

Serves 4.

—Lydia Nederhoff

Breading for Fried Chicken

Ingredients
2 cups flour
1 tsp. salt
1 Tbsp. celery salt
1 Tbsp. pepper
2 Tbsp. dry mustard
2 Tbsp. paprika
2 Tbsp. garlic powder
1 tsp. ginger
½ tsp. thyme
½ tsp. sweet basil
½ tsp. oregano

Directions
Mix thoroughly and store tightly sealed. Coat chicken pieces before frying.

Makes 2½ cups.

—Shirley Morrish

Sausage Dressing

Ingredients
1 lb. sausage meat
3 Tbsp. minced onion
4 Tbsp. minced parsley
4 Tbsp. minced celery
3 Tbsp. melted butter
Salt & pepper
5–6 cups bread crumbs

Directions
Fry sausage meat just until it loses the pink color, and drain. Combine with remaining ingredients and mix well.

Makes enough dressing to stuff a 14–17 lb. bird.

—Mary Reid

Liver Paté

Ingredients

1 medium onion, chopped
1 clove garlic, chopped
2 eggs
1 lb. chicken livers
¼ cup flour
½ tsp. ginger
½ tsp. allspice
1 cup heavy cream
1 Tbsp. salt
1 tsp. pepper
¼ cup butter

Directions

Blend onion, garlic and eggs in a blender for 1 minute. Add liver and blend for 2 more minutes. Remove to a large bowl. Combine remaining ingredients, then add to liver mixture.

Place in greased loaf pan and cover with butter. Butter aluminum foil and cover pan with it. Set in a larger pan of water and bake at 325°F for 3 hours.

Remove paté from pan and cool. Wrap and refrigerate.

—Lisa Brownstone

Rabbit with Dressing

Ingredients

2–3 lbs. rabbit meat, cut up
1 onion, sliced
5–6 cups chicken stock
3 peppercorns
¼ cup minced onion
⅓ cup butter, melted
6 cups dry bread cubes
½ tsp. sage
Salt & pepper
4 Tbsp. butter
¾ cup flour
4 egg yolks, well beaten

Directions

Place rabbit pieces, onion slices, chicken stock and peppercorns in heavy saucepan. Simmer, covered, for 1½ hours, or until rabbit is tender. Remove rabbit from broth and cool. Set broth aside. Bone meat, cut up and arrange in a 3-quart casserole dish.

Sauté minced onion in melted butter. Combine with bread cubes, sage, salt and pepper and mix lightly. Sprinkle over rabbit pieces.

Strain broth. Heat 4 Tbsp. butter in skillet, stir in flour and blend in broth. Cook, stirring constantly, until thickened. Pour a little sauce into the egg yolks, then stir yolks back into the hot mixture. Cook for 1 minute, then pour over casserole.

Bake at 375°F for 35 minutes or until dressing is set and golden brown.

Serves 8.

—Charlene Bloomberg

Rabbit Sausage Casserole

Ingredients
1 rabbit
Flour
4 Tbsp. oil
1 lb. pork sausage
1 cup beer
¼ cup cider vinegar
1 cup chicken stock
1 cup browned bread crumbs
1 tsp. caraway seeds
1 tsp. grated lemon peel
1 tsp. brown sugar
Salt & pepper

Directions

Skin, clean and cut up the rabbit. Dust with flour and brown in hot oil. Place in a large, deep pot and add remaining ingredients. Bring to a boil, reduce heat, cover and simmer gently for 2 hours. If a thicker sauce is desired, blend 2 Tbsp. flour into a little water and stir into sauce.

Serves 6.

—*Carolyn Hills*

Barbecued Wild Duck

Ingredients
¾ cup oil
½ cup vinegar
¼ cup soy sauce
1 sprig rosemary
1 Tbsp. celery seed
1 tsp. salt
¼ tsp. pepper
4 small wild ducks, cleaned, dressed & cut up

Directions

Combine all ingredients except ducks and simmer for 10 minutes. Put duck pieces in sauce and simmer for another 10 minutes, turning so that all sides are covered. Place in roasting pan and roast, uncovered, at 350°F for 50 to 60 minutes, basting often.

Serves 4

—*Adele Moore*

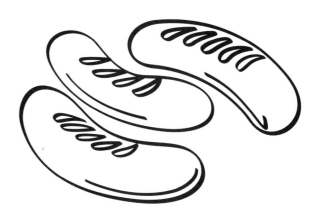

Glazed Duck

Ingredients

½ cup butter
½ cup lemon juice or wine vinegar
2 cups hot water
1 duck
Flour
2 Tbsp. cranberry jelly
Water
Salt & pepper

Directions

Combine butter, lemon juice and hot water. Pour over duck in roasting pan. Cover and bake at 350°F for 20 minutes per pound, basting several times.

For gravy, cool drippings and remove fat. Blend remaining juices with flour to make a paste, then add cranberry jelly and water until desired consistency is reached. Add salt and pepper to taste.

Serves 4.

—*Goldie Connell*

Moose Steak Roast

Ingredients

½ cup flour
Salt & pepper
2 medium-sized moose steaks
2 eggs, beaten
1 cup bread crumbs
Oil
1 cup tomato juice
2 onions, chopped
Dash soy sauce
Stalk of celery, chopped
½ green pepper, chopped

Directions

Combine flour, salt and pepper and sprinkle on both sides of meat. Pound with a meat hammer. Continue to sprinkle and pound until flour mixture is used up. Brush both sides of meat with eggs, then coat in bread crumbs. Sear gently in oil. Place meat in roasting pan and pour tomato juice over it. Sprinkle remaining ingredients on top. Roast at 350°F until tender. Baste frequently and add more tomato juice if necessary.

Serves 2 to 4.

—*H. Miller*

Gourmet Venison Chops

Ingredients
6 venison chops
½ cup brandy
½ cup olive oil
1 clove garlic, crushed
Freshly ground pepper

Directions
Marinate chops in brandy for 2 to 3 hours, turning once so brandy has a chance to soak into both sides. Combine olive oil and garlic and let sit while the meat is marinating.

Discard garlic and heat olive oil in a large frying pan. Sprinkle chops with pepper and brown in oil at a high temperature. Turn heat down to medium-low and cook, covered, for 5 minutes on each side. Serve immediately.

Serves 6.

—Nancy Russell

Roast Venison

Directions
Be sure the meat has been properly hung and aged. Wipe the roast with a damp cloth. Make several cuts in the top and insert pieces of salt pork, bacon or fat.

Bake in roasting pan in moderate oven, allowing 40 minutes per pound. Baste occasionally. Sprinkle with salt and pepper 30 minutes before time is up. To brown, raise the temperature to 450°F for the last 10 minutes of cooking time.

—Goldie Connell

Smothered Pheasant

Ingredients
Salt
Pepper
Thyme
Basil
Seasoned salt
½ cup flour
2 or 3 pheasants, cut up
Oil
1 cup sliced onions
1 cup chopped mushrooms
1½ cups cream of mushroom sauce, page 129
1 pint sour cream

Directions
Add seasonings to flour and coat pheasant. Brown in oil. Put in roaster and top with onions, mushrooms and mushroom sauce. Cook for 1 hour at 350°F. Add sour cream and cook for another 30 minutes.

—Gail Cool

Roast Canada Goose

Directions

Cut off the oil sack, then wash and dry the goose. Brush the cavity with lemon juice. Insert stuffing and close cavity.

Brush 2 Tbsp. seasoned melted butter over skin of goose. Pour water into base of roasting pan and place goose on tray. Bake at 450°F for 15 minutes, reduce heat to 350° and roast 20 minutes per pound.

If the goose is very fatty, pierce the flesh several times during roasting to drain excess fat.

—Goldie Connell

Sidney Bay Rabbit

Ingredients

¼ cup butter
¼ cup honey
1 Tbsp. soy sauce
3-4 lbs. rabbit, cut up
2 Tbsp. chopped ginger root

Directions

Melt butter, honey and soy sauce together. Spread half this mixture over rabbit in a roasting pan.

Cover with foil and bake for 45 minutes at 375°F. Remove foil, add ginger root, turn rabbit over and add remaining sauce.

Bake for 1 more hour, basting frequently, until rabbit is tender and sauce is thick and shiny.

Serves 4 to 6.

—Helen Campbell

Curried Moose

Ingredients

2 Tbsp. butter
1 medium onion, chopped
2 cups beef stock
2 lb. moose roast, cubed while still partly frozen
12 oz. tomato paste
3 Tbsp. curry powder
Handful dark raisins
2 medium potatoes, cubed

Directions

Melt butter in skillet, sauté onion in it, then combine onion with beef stock in a large saucepan.

Sear meat in skillet until brown on all sides, about 10 minutes, then add to stock and onion in saucepan, leaving juices in skillet.

Combine tomato paste and curry powder in skillet. Cook briefly, stirring, over medium heat, then add to contents of saucepan.

Stir in raisins and simmer for 2 to 3 hours. Add potatoes, and continue to simmer for another 1½ hours.

Serves 2 to 4.

—John Mortimer

Moose Pepper Steak

Ingredients
Cooking oil
1 onion, chopped
1 stalk celery, thinly sliced diagonally
2 lbs. moose meat
3 or 4 carrots, thinly sliced diagonally
1 potato, diced
Salt & pepper
1 cup chopped mushrooms
2 cups snow peas
2 Tbsp. tapioca, softened in 2 Tbsp. water

Directions

Pour a few teaspoons of oil into a heated wok. Add onions and celery, and stir until the onions are transparent. Add the meat and stir until browned. Stir in carrots, potato, salt and pepper.

Add about ½ cup water and cover until steam rises around edges of lid. Stir in mushrooms and snow peas, then tapioca. Cook, stirring, only until vegetables are glossy and sauce thickens. Serve immediately over cooked rice.

Serves 4.

—Angela Denholm

Saddle of Elk

Ingredients
6 lb. saddle of elk
Salted pork, cut into 2-inch strips
Garlic, peeled & cut in half
Butter

Directions

Preheat oven to 550°F.

Lard the elk with pork strips — draw through meat surface with a larding needle, or make slits with a knife and insert pork.

Rub elk with garlic and then butter. Place, fat side up, in a roasting pan in oven, reduce heat to 350°F and bake for 20 minutes per pound.

Serve with wild rice and gravy.

Serves 8.

Wild Chili

Ingredients

6 cups water
2 lbs. chicken necks
2 bay leaves
¾ tsp. rosemary
Freshly ground pepper
1 cup chopped celery & leaves
2 medium carrots, cut in half
¾ cup cubed turnip
1–1½ lbs. ground moose meat
1½ medium onions, chopped
2 cloves garlic, minced
½ lb. mushrooms, in thick slices
20-oz. can tomatoes
6-oz. can tomato paste
1½ cups cooked chickpeas or kidney beans
2 cups cranberries
3 Tbsp. chili powder
Salt
½ cup uncooked bulgur
1 medium zucchini, sliced

Directions

In water, simmer chicken necks, bay leaves, rosemary, pepper, celery, carrots and turnip for about 2½ hours or until chicken comes away from the bone. Remove bay leaves and necks and let broth cool in refrigerator overnight. Remove excess fat and put broth and vegetables through blender.

Cook ground moose meat, onion, garlic and mushrooms in large casserole dish. Add broth and remaining ingredients. Simmer for 1½ to 2 hours.

Serves 8.

—*Nicol Séguin*

Chicken Lemonese

Ingredients

4 chicken breasts
1 egg, beaten with 2 Tbsp. water
½ cup flour
½ cup grated Monterey jack cheese
½ cup Parmesan cheese
Garlic powder
¼ cup chopped parsley
1 tsp. paprika
Salt
3 Tbsp. butter
1 clove garlic, minced
3 lemons

Directions

Skin, debone and cut chicken breasts into bite-sized pieces. Place egg and water in shallow bowl. Mix together flour, cheeses, garlic powder, parsley, paprika and salt in another shallow bowl. Drop chicken pieces first into flour-cheese mixture, then into egg mixture, then back into flour-cheese mixture, coating well.

Melt butter and add garlic. Sauté chicken pieces until golden brown on both sides. Remove from pan and set aside. To liquid in pan add the juice of 2 lemons and simmer briefly. Add 1 sliced lemon, pour over chicken and serve.

Serves 4.

—*Francie Goodwin-Rogne*

Dijon Chicken

Ingredients
3 Tbsp. milk
2 Tbsp. Dijon mustard
2 chicken breasts
¼ cup bread crumbs
1 tsp. tarragon leaves, crushed or crumbled

Directions
Whisk milk and mustard together. Dip chicken in mixture, then coat with mixture of bread crumbs and tarragon. Place in shallow baking dish and bake at 375°F for 30 minutes, covered, then 15 minutes, uncovered.

Serves 2.

—Beth Rose

Brandied Chicken Breasts

Ingredients
4 chicken breasts, skinned, deboned & halved
¼ cup brandy
Salt & pepper
Marjoram
Thyme
6 Tbsp. unsalted butter
½ cup dry sherry
4 egg yolks
2 cups light cream
Nutmeg
Grated Gruyère cheese

Directions
Soak chicken in brandy, seasoned with salt and pepper, marjoram and thyme, for about 20 minutes.

Heat butter in large skillet and sauté chicken over medium heat for 6 to 8 minutes on each side. Remove to heated ovenproof platter and keep warm. To remaining butter in pan add sherry and the brandy that the chicken soaked in. Simmer over low heat until reduced by half.

Beat egg yolks into cream and add to pan juices, stirring constantly. Season with salt, pepper and nutmeg and cook, stirring, until slightly thickened. Pour sauce over chicken breasts, sprinkle with cheese and brown under broiler.

Serves 4.

—Jim Boagey

Herbed Chicken Breasts

Ingredients
2 chicken breasts, deboned & halved
1 Tbsp. flour
¼ cup plain yogurt
¼ tsp. lemon juice
1 tsp. grated onion
Sage, thyme & basil
¼ tsp. salt
Pepper
3 Tbsp. grated Cheddar cheese
¼ tsp. paprika
⅓ cup fine cracker crumbs

Directions
Sprinkle chicken with flour to lightly coat both sides. Mix yogurt, lemon juice, onion, spices and salt and pepper in a bowl. Mix cheese, paprika and crumbs in a flat dish.

Dip chicken in yogurt mixture, then in crumb mixture to coat all sides. Put in greased baking dish, cover with foil and bake at 350°F for 30 minutes. Uncover and bake until tender — about 15 minutes.

Serves 2.

—Maureen Thornton

Sesame Yogurt Chicken

Ingredients
½ cup yogurt
2 Tbsp. Worcestershire sauce
2 Tbsp. lemon juice
½ cup sesame seeds
½ cup bread crumbs
½ tsp. paprika
Salt & pepper
6 chicken legs or breasts

Directions
Combine yogurt, Worcestershire sauce and lemon juice in shallow bowl. In another bowl, mix sesame seeds, bread crumbs, paprika and salt and pepper.

Dip chicken in yogurt mixture, then coat with crumb mixture. Place in greased shallow pan in a single layer. Bake at 350°F for 50 to 60 minutes, or until chicken is tender and surface crisp.

Serves 6.

—Jane Lott

Chicken Larousse

Ingredients

3 large chicken breasts, cut in half
Salt
Paprika
1 cup Parmesan cheese
1 lb. green beans, trimmed & Frenched
½ cup slivered almonds
1½ cups raw wild rice
¾ cup butter
1 small onion, chopped
1 small green pepper, chopped
1 cup chopped celery
Mushrooms, halved
Pepper
1 cup dry white wine

Directions

Sprinkle chicken with salt and paprika, roll in Parmesan cheese and set aside. Place green beans and almonds in shallow casserole dish. Cook wild rice according to package directions. Melt ½ cup butter, add onion, green pepper and celery and sauté until soft. Stir in mushrooms, wild rice and salt and pepper to taste. Place chicken over beans and almonds and spoon wild rice mixture around sides of casserole. Pour white wine over all, dot chicken with remaining butter and bake at 350°F for 45 to 50 minutes.

Serves 6.

—*Sandra Binnington*

Chicken Parmesan

Ingredients

2 chickens, cut up
Oil
1 small onion, grated
4 Tbsp. butter
3 Tbsp. flour
1 cup Parmesan cheese
2 cups milk
2 egg yolks

Directions

Lightly brown chicken in hot oil, but do not cook right through. Remove from oil, drain on paper towels, then place in large baking dish.

Cook onion in butter, add flour and stir in well. Add ¾ cup cheese, then gradually stir in milk and cook over low heat, stirring constantly, until sauce is thick. Beat egg yolks slightly and add a little of the sauce to the yolks. Stir back into sauce gradually. Cook over low heat for 10 minutes, pour over chicken and sprinkle with remaining ¼ cup cheese. Bake, covered, at 325°F for 1 hour.

Serves 6.

—*Dorothy Hurst*

Southern Baked Chicken

Ingredients

½ cup butter
1 small onion, finely chopped
1 clove garlic, finely chopped
¼ cup Parmesan cheese
¾ cup bread crumbs
¾ cup corn meal
3 Tbsp. minced fresh parsley
1 tsp. salt
1 tsp. pepper
2 chickens, cut up

Directions

Melt butter and sauté onion and garlic until tender. Combine cheese, bread crumbs, corn meal, parsley, salt and pepper. Dip chicken in butter and then roll in coating.

Bake at 350°F for 1 hour.

Serves 8.

—*Valerie Marien*

Chicken Bolero

Ingredients

2 chicken breasts
1 large green pepper
1 large onion
3 Tbsp. oil
1½ Tbsp. dill weed
2½ cups sour cream
Salt & pepper
4 cups cooked rice

Directions

Debone chicken and slice into narrow strips. Slice pepper and onion into narrow strips. Sauté in hot oil until chicken is golden and vegetables are tender. Add dill weed, sour cream and salt and pepper. Cook over low heat for 10 minutes without boiling. Serve with rice.

Serves 3 to 4

—*Katie Larstone*

Italian Style Chicken Casserole

Ingredients

1 onion, sliced
6–8 medium potatoes, peeled & sliced
1 chicken, cut up
1 head broccoli, cut into bite-sized pieces
1 green pepper, sliced
19-oz. can tomatoes
¼ tsp. oregano
¼ tsp. basil
¼ tsp. parsley
¼ tsp. pepper
½ tsp. salt

Directions

In greased casserole dish, arrange layers of onion, potatoes, chicken and broccoli. Cover with slices of green pepper and tomatoes. Sprinkle with spices. Cover and cook at 350°F for about 2 hours. Remove cover for last 10 minutes to brown meat and potatoes.

Serves 4 to 6.

—*Julie Herr*

Balkan Chicken Stew

Ingredients

4-5 lbs. chicken pieces
Salt & pepper
3 medium onions, thinly sliced
1 clove garlic, crushed
4 Tbsp. butter
1 cup white wine
2 cups sour cream
1 cup pitted ripe olives

Directions

Pat chicken dry and season with salt and pepper. Sauté onions and garlic in butter until transparent. Remove onions, add chicken and sauté until brown. Return onions to skillet, add wine and simmer for 1 hour. Cool to room temperature, then stir in sour cream and olives. Simmer gently for 20 minutes.

Serves 5 to 6.

—*Midge Denault*

Spanish Chicken

Ingredients

¼ cup chopped onion
1 Tbsp. brown sugar
½ tsp. salt
1 tsp. prepared mustard
1 Tbsp. chili sauce
1 tsp. Worcestershire sauce
¼ cup vinegar
1 cup tomato juice
¼ cup water
½ cup sliced, stuffed green olives
Flour
Salt & pepper
3½ lbs. chicken pieces
½ cup butter

Directions

Combine onion, sugar, salt, mustard, chili sauce, Worcestershire sauce, vinegar, tomato juice and water. Cook over low heat for 10 minutes, then add olives.

Meanwhile, combine flour and salt and pepper. Dredge chicken pieces in this. Melt butter, add chicken and brown well.

Arrange chicken in 9" x 13" baking dish and cover with sauce. Cover and bake at 350°F for 45 minutes.

Serves 4.

—*Barbara Taylor*

Chicken Supreme

Ingredients

1 chicken, cut up
Juice of 1 lemon
¼ cup flour
¼ cup butter
1 clove garlic, minced
3 carrots, sliced
2 onions, sliced
1 stalk celery, sliced
¼ cup white wine or chicken stock
1 cup cream sauce
½ tsp. paprika
¼ tsp. basil
¼ tsp. rosemary
2 Tbsp. parsley
Salt & pepper

Directions

Brush chicken with lemon juice and coat with flour. Melt butter and brown chicken in skillet. Place in casserole dish and top with vegetables.

Pour wine into skillet with chicken drippings, add sauce and seasonings, mix well and pour over chicken. Bake at 350°F for 1½ hours.

Serves 4.

—*Pat Dicer*

Baked Almond Chicken

Ingredients

3½ lbs. chicken pieces
Flour
1 tsp. celery salt
1 tsp. paprika
1 tsp. salt
½ tsp. curry
½ tsp. oregano
½ tsp. freshly ground pepper
7 Tbsp. melted butter
¾ cup sliced almonds
1½ cups light cream
½ cup sour cream
3 Tbsp. fine, dry bread crumbs

Directions

Coat chicken pieces with flour. Blend celery salt, paprika, salt, curry, oregano and pepper with 6 Tbsp. melted butter. Roll chicken pieces in this, coating all sides. Arrange chicken in single layer in 9" x 13" baking dish and sprinkle evenly with almonds. Pour light cream between pieces.

Bake, covered, at 350°F for 45 minutes. Uncover, add about ½ cup sauce from pan to sour cream, mix together and pour evenly over chicken. Combine bread crumbs with remaining 1 Tbsp. melted butter and sprinkle over chicken. Bake, uncovered, for 15 minutes longer, or until chicken is tender.

Serves 6.

—*Marilyn Nichols*

Sherried Chicken

Ingredients
1 chicken, cut up
½ tsp. salt
⅛ tsp. pepper
½ tsp. paprika
Butter
1 cup chicken stock
½ cup sherry
Savory
Thyme
Rosemary
Parsley
Marjoram
1 bay leaf
¼ cup butter
1 cup sliced mushrooms

Directions

Sprinkle chicken on both sides with salt, pepper and paprika and brown in butter. Add stock and sherry and sprinkle with herbs. Cover and simmer for 45 minutes, turning chicken over during cooking. Add a little water if too dry. Stir in mushrooms 5 minutes before serving.

Serves 4.

—*Lori Davies*

Chicken Adobe

Ingredients
1 chicken, cut up
2–3 cloves garlic
Soy sauce
15–20 peppercorns
2–3 bay leaves
½ onion, finely chopped
⅓ cup vinegar
Flour

Directions

Place chicken in pot and cover with water. Heat water to boiling, add garlic, soy sauce, peppercorns and bay leaves. Cover and simmer for 30 minutes. Add onion and vinegar. Use sufficient flour to thicken the water to a gravy and simmer for another 20 minutes.

Serves 4.

—*Bette Warkentin*

Poulet Framboise

Ingredients
2 medium onions, thinly sliced
2 Tbsp. water
3 Tbsp. unsalted butter
2-3 lbs. chicken pieces
Salt & pepper
1 large tomato, peeled, seeded & chopped
2 cloves garlic, crushed
2 cups raspberry vinegar
1 cup whipping cream
2 Tbsp. Cognac or Armagnac

Directions
Cook onions, water and 1 Tbsp. butter in large frying pan over low heat for 30 minutes. While onions are cooking, season chicken pieces with salt and pepper. Heat remaining 2 Tbsp. butter in another frying pan and cook chicken until golden on both sides. Add tomato and garlic to onions. Place chicken pieces on top of onion mixture and cook, covered, over low heat for 30 minutes, or until chicken is tender.

Remove any excess butter from pan used to brown chicken. Add raspberry vinegar and simmer gently until only ½ cup remains. Place cooked chicken on a warm serving platter. Purée the onion and tomato mixture and add to reduced vinegar in frying pan. Place chicken in the pan and reheat with vinegar mixture for 10 to 15 minutes. Stir in cream and liquor and serve.

Serves 4.

—Ingrid Birker

Mexican Chicken Pie

Quite different from the usual crusted chicken pie, this is a flavorful and multi-textured dish.

Ingredients
3 lbs. chicken pieces
12 corn tortillas
3 cups cream of mushroom sauce (page 129)
7-oz. can green chili salsa
1 cup grated Cheddar cheese

Directions
Bake chicken pieces, covered, at 400°F for 1 hour in a 9" x 13" casserole dish. Remove chicken and debone. Do not wash dish.

Break up 4 tortillas into 2-inch pieces and place in bottom of same casserole dish. Place half the chicken on the tortillas. Combine mushroom sauce with green chili salsa, then pour one-third of this over the chicken. Cut 4 more tortillas into 2-inch pieces and place on top of sauce. Top with remaining chicken and another third of sauce. Cut up remaining tortillas and place on top of sauce. Top with remaining sauce and the cheese. Bake at 375°F for 1 hour.

Serves 6.

—Linda Stanier

Chicken Rice Pie

Ingredients

2 cups cooked rice
⅓ cup butter, melted
1 tsp. salt
¼ tsp. pepper
2 Tbsp. flour
1 cup milk
2 cups diced, cooked chicken
2 large tomatoes, peeled & chopped
3 stalks celery, chopped
1 small green pepper, chopped
3 Tbsp. dry bread crumbs

Directions

Combine rice, 2 Tbsp. butter, half the salt and half the pepper and mix well. Press into deep pie plate to form shell and set aside.

Melt 2 Tbsp. butter, stir in flour and cook until bubbly. Gradually stir in milk until thickened and smooth. Season with remaining salt and pepper. Stir in chicken, tomatoes, celery and green pepper. Pour into rice shell. Mix bread crumbs with remaining melted butter and sprinkle over pie. Bake at 350°F for 25 minutes, or until golden brown.

Serves 6.

—Inez Atkins

Skillet Chicken

Ingredients

6 chicken legs
2–3 Tbsp. oil
1 cup tomato sauce (page 339)
2 Tbsp. finely chopped onion
1 Tbsp. vinegar
2 tsp. Worcestershire sauce
2 tsp. prepared mustard
¼ cup molasses
½ cup water

Directions

Split chicken legs in half through joint. Heat oil and brown chicken gently on all sides. Combine tomato sauce, onion, vinegar, Worcestershire sauce, mustard, molasses and water. Drain off excess fat from skillet and add sauce. Cover and simmer gently for 35 minutes, turning occasionally. Remove chicken to warm platter and boil sauce briskly to reduce and thicken it. Pour over chicken and serve.

Serves 4 to 6.

—Linda Russell

Chinese Walnut Chicken

Ingredients

1 cup coarsely broken walnuts
¼ cup oil
2 chicken breasts, deboned and cut into thin
   strips
½ tsp. salt
1 Tbsp. cornstarch
¼ cup soy sauce
2 Tbsp. sherry
1¼ cups chicken stock
1 cup onion slices
½ cups celery slices, cut diagonally
1½ cups mushrooms
5-oz. can water chestnuts, drained & sliced

Directions

In skillet, toast walnuts in hot oil, stirring constantly, then remove and drain on paper towels. Place chicken in skillet and sprinkle with salt. Cook, stirring frequently, for 5 to 10 minutes, or until tender. Remove chicken.

Make sauce by combining cornstarch, soy sauce and sherry in skillet and gradually adding chicken stock. Cook for 2 to 3 minutes until sauce begins to thicken. Add chicken, onion, celery, mushrooms and water chestnuts and cook for 5 minutes, or until vegetables are slightly tender. Stir in toasted walnuts. Serve with hot rice.

Serves 4 to 6.

—*Donna Petryshyn*

Chicken Wings

Ingredients

48 chicken wings
½ cup honey
1 cup soy sauce
6 cloves garlic, minced
⅓ cup cornstarch
½ tsp. pepper
1 cup water

Directions

Cut chicken wings in half, discarding tip of wing. Mix honey, soy sauce, garlic, cornstarch and pepper and pour over wings. Marinate for minimum of 1 hour.

Drain wings, keeping marinade to one side. Fry wings in hot, shallow oil until golden brown on both sides. Place wings, marinade and water in baking dish and bake at 350°F for 15 to 20 minutes.

Serves 12.

—*Andrew Camm*

Honey Garlic Chicken

Ingredients
½ cup honey
½ cup soy sauce
2 cloves garlic, crushed
¼ cup butter
1 chicken, cut up

Directions
Combine honey, soy sauce, garlic and butter in a saucepan. Bring to a boil, reduce heat and simmer for 5 minutes.

Place chicken in a shallow pan and bake at 375°F for 15 minutes. Cover with sauce and continue baking, turning chicken occasionally, until sauce is absorbed and chicken cooked.

Serves 4.

—*Louise Olson*

Chicken Tandoori

This is an East Indian recipe traditionally served with curried rice, crisp vegetables and yogurt.

Ingredients
2 cups yogurt
2 tsp. chili powder
6 cloves garlic, crushed
¼–½ tsp. red pepper
6 tsp. vinegar
Juice of 1 lime
1 tsp. salt
1 tsp. ginger
1 tsp. coriander
1 tsp. cumin
1 tsp. cardamom
2 tsp. honey
Pepper
4–5 lbs. chicken pieces

Directions
Combine all ingredients except chicken and mix well. Marinate chicken in this mixture for about 8 hours, turning frequently. Remove from marinade and bake at 375°F for 60 to 75 minutes, basting with marinade.

Serves 4 to 6.

—*Randi Kennedy*

Chicken Talunan

This Philippine dish originally utilized the tough meat of the losing rooster (called the talunan*) in a cockfight. The sauce and lengthy stewing time serve to tenderize the meat.*

Ingredients

2 cakes tofu
1 cup vinegar
½ cup brown sugar
4 cups water
3½ lbs. chicken pieces
2 lbs. pigs' feet, or other pork bits
1 clove garlic, crushed
1 cucumber, sliced
1 bay leaf
1 Tbsp. oregano
1 whole clove
1 star anise
1 stick cinnamon

Directions

Mash tofu and mix with vinegar and sugar. Combine water, chicken, pigs' feet and tofu mixture in large saucepan. Simmer until meat is tender and remove meat.

Add garlic, cucumber, bay leaf, oregano, clove, star anise and cinnamon to stock, cover and simmer until thick. Place meat on serving dish and pour sauce over.

Serves 6.

—P.S. Reynolds

Indian Chicken Curry

Ingredients

1 chicken
Salt & pepper
Cornstarch
Oil
1 Tbsp. soy sauce
4 onions, chopped
6 cloves garlic, minced
1 green pepper, chopped
3 cups mushrooms, sliced
3 tomatoes, peeled & chopped
4 Tbsp. curry

Directions

Cut chicken into small pieces, season with salt and pepper and dust with cornstarch. Brown in hot oil and set aside.

In chicken drippings and soy sauce, brown onions and garlic. Add green pepper and mushrooms and cook for 4 minutes. Add tomatoes and cook for 2 more minutes. Return chicken to pot, sprinkle with curry and cook for 10 minutes, turning chicken frequently. Add ½ cup boiling water, cover, reduce heat and simmer for 1 hour.

Serves 4 to 6.

—Judith Goodwin

Curried Chicken with Shrimp

Ingredients

3 lbs. chicken pieces
Salt & pepper
2 Tbsp. butter
¾ cup finely chopped onion
½ cup finely chopped celery
1 tsp. finely minced garlic
2 Tbsp. curry
1 bay leaf
1 cup cubed apple
⅓ cup diced banana
2 tsp. tomato paste
1½ cups chicken stock
½ cup whipping cream
12 large shrimp

Directions

Sprinkle chicken with salt and pepper and brown in butter. Add onion, celery and garlic and cook briefly. Add curry, bay leaf, apple and banana. Cook for 5 minutes, then stir in tomato paste. Add stock and stir to blend. Cover and cook for 20 minutes longer, or until chicken is tender.

Remove chicken. Strain sauce through fine sieve. Reheat with cream. Return chicken along with shrimp to sauce and simmer until shrimp are pink.

Serves 6.

—Linda Thompson

Chicken Apple Curry

Ingredients

½ cup chopped onion
1 clove garlic, minced
3 Tbsp. butter
1 Tbsp. curry
1 cup chopped apple
½ cup chopped celery
¼ cup flour
1 cup chicken stock
¾ cup milk
½–¾ tsp. salt
2 cups cooked, diced chicken

Directions

Sauté onion and garlic in butter with curry until onion is tender. Add apple and celery and cook for about 3 minutes longer. Stir in flour, then stock, milk and salt. Stir while heating until mixture boils. Add chicken; heat and serve over rice.

Serves 4.

—Jane Lott

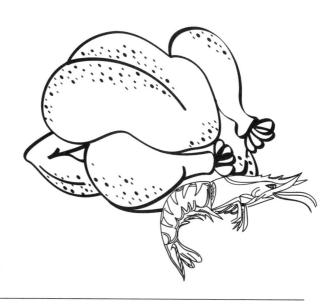

Chicken with Raisins & Almonds

Ingredients

5 lb. chicken
2 onions, chopped
¼ cup honey
1 Tbsp. butter
1 tsp. cinnamon
1 tsp. turmeric
Ginger
½ cup raisins
1 cup almonds, blanched, peeled & toasted

Directions

Place chicken in pot with water to half cover. Add remaining ingredients except raisins and almonds, bring to a boil and cook until chicken is done — about 1 hour. Add raisins and almonds and boil until liquid is about 1 to 2 inches deep. Place chicken in serving dish and pour sauce over it.

Serves 4.

—Dale Fawcett

Chicken with Lemon-Mustard Sauce

Ingredients

1 chicken, cut up
2 Tbsp. oil
2 Tbsp. flour
½ tsp. salt
⅛ tsp. pepper
1½ cups chicken stock
2 Tbsp. Dijon mustard
1 tsp. tarragon
½ lemon, thinly sliced

Directions

Brown chicken in hot oil in large skillet and move to one side. Stir in flour, salt and pepper, then stock, mustard and tarragon until well blended. Cover and simmer for 30 minutes. Add lemon slices; cover and simmer 5 minutes longer or until chicken is tender. Serve over rice or noodles.

Serves 4.

—Rosy Hale

Barbecued Chicken Burgers

Ingredients

3 lbs. chicken, skinned & deboned
1-2 strips bacon
1-2 slices dry whole wheat bread
Salt & pepper
4 slices mozzarella cheese
4 sesame seed buns

Directions

Put chicken meat through meat grinder along with bacon. When all meat has been ground, put bread through grinder and add to meat. Season with salt and pepper, mix gently and form into 4 patties. Grill over hot coals, turning when well-browned on one side. Place a slice of cheese on each patty and continue grilling until other side is browned. Serve on toasted buns with your choice of toppings.

Serves 4.

—Karen Ritchie

Hot Chinese Chicken Salad

Ingredients

8 chicken thighs, skinned, boned & cut into
   1-inch chunks
¼ cup cornstarch
¼ cup oil
⅛ tsp. garlic powder
1 large, ripe tomato, cut into chunks
4-oz. can water chestnuts, drained & sliced
   (optional)
½ cup sliced mushrooms
1 bunch green onions, coarsely chopped
1 cup celery, sliced diagonally
¼ cup soy sauce
2 cups finely shredded lettuce

Directions

Roll chicken in cornstarch. Heat oil over high heat, add chicken and brown quickly. Sprinkle with garlic powder and stir in tomato, water chestnuts, mushrooms, onions, celery and soy sauce. Cover and simmer for 5 minutes, then toss in lettuce. Serve hot with rice.

Serves 6.

—*Carol Weepers*

Chicken Salad

Either yellow summer squash or zucchini can be used successfully in this recipe. Yellow beets are advised as they do not bleed and therefore result in a more attractive presentation.

Ingredients

2 cups cooked chicken
3–4 radishes
1 cup green or yellow beans
1 cup snow peas
1 small summer squash
6 pickling-sized yellow beets, cooked until tender
1 onion
1 head lettuce
½ cup mayonnaise
4 leaves red cabbage

Directions

Chop chicken and vegetables, except cabbage, into bite-sized pieces. Toss together. Add mayonnaise and mix well. Place in serving bowl lined with cabbage.

Serves 4 to 6.

—*Cindy Majewski*

Chicken Giblet Curry

Ingredients

2 lbs. chicken giblets
2–3 onions, chopped
Butter
1–2 tsp. garlic powder
1 tsp. salt
½ tsp. crushed red pepper
1 tsp. ground coriander
12 cloves
4–5 bay leaves
1 tsp. finely chopped ginger root
2 tsp. cumin
12 peppercorns
3–4 cardamom seeds
1 tsp. turmeric
1 tsp. cinnamon
3–4 tomatoes, peeled & chopped
1 cup water

Directions

Cut giblets into small pieces. Brown onions in butter, then add giblets, garlic powder and salt. Cook for 5 minutes, add remaining spices and cook for a few minutes. Add tomatoes and water, lower heat and simmer for 45 minutes.

Serves 4 to 6.

—*Sue Griggs*

Turkey Ring

Ingredients

3 cups diced, cooked turkey
1 cup soft bread crumbs
1 Tbsp. oil
½ tsp. salt
⅛ tsp. pepper
1 cup hot milk
2 eggs, beaten
¼ cup finely chopped celery
2 Tbsp. finely chopped green pepper
2 Tbsp. finely chopped pimento

Directions

Combine all ingredients and mix thoroughly. Pour into greased ring mold and bake at 350°F for 35 to 40 minutes. Let stand for 5 minutes; remove from mold.

Serves 6.

—*Christine Curtis*

Rabbit Pie

Work on this dish must begin a day ahead as the cooked rabbit and stock need to be refrigerated overnight.

Ingredients

Pastry for double 9-inch pie
 shell
5–6 lb. rabbit
1 Tbsp. salt
½ tsp. pepper
1 cup chopped celery leaves
1 large onion, quartered
½ tsp. crumbled savory or
    thyme
1 bay leaf
6 cups boiling water
3 cups sliced carrots
2 cups diced celery
12–24 small white onions
¾ cup butter
¾ cup flour
2 cups milk
1 cup whipping cream
1 Tbsp. lemon juice
½ cup minced parsley

Directions

Place rabbit in large pot with salt, pepper, celery leaves, onion, savory or thyme, bay leaf and boiling water. Cover and simmer over low heat until rabbit is tender — 1½ to 2 hours. Leave rabbit in stock until cool enough to handle. Pull meat off bones and place in a large bowl. Put bones back in pot and boil stock, uncovered, until reduced to two-thirds its original quantity. Strain stock over rabbit, cover and refrigerate overnight.

The next day, place carrots and celery in bowl and cover with boiling water. Let stand for 1 hour. Peel onions and boil for 15 minutes.

Heat rabbit just until stock can be strained, measure out 3 cups. Melt butter, add flour and stir until blended. Add milk, cream and 3 cups stock and cook until sauce is creamy. Add drained onions, carrots, celery, rabbit, lemon juice and parsley. Place in deep pie plate lined with pastry. Top with pastry, crimp edges, make steam holes and bake at 400°F for 40 to 50 minutes, or until golden brown.

Serves 6 to 8.

—Marian Page

Cornish Game Hens Indienne

Main Ingredients

6 Cornish game hens
1½ tsp. salt
1 tsp. pepper
1 tsp. thyme
½ cup butter, melted
6 strips bacon
3 medium onions, chopped
5 Tbsp. flour
3 Tbsp. sugar
2 Tbsp. curry
2 cups apricot nectar
Juice from 1 lemon
Juice from 1 orange

Stuffing Ingredients

½ cup brown & ½ cup wild rice, cooked in
    chicken stock
½ cup chopped mushrooms
2 Tbsp. butter
⅛ cup dry red wine

Directions

Wipe hens inside and out. Combine 1 tsp. salt, pepper and thyme and sprinkle ½ tsp. inside each hen. Place hens, breast side up, in pan and brush with ¼ cup melted butter. Roast at 375°F for 50 to 60 minutes, basting with remaining ¼ cup butter and pan drippings.

Meanwhile, sauté bacon until crisp. Drain and crumble. Stir chopped onions into bacon drippings and sauté until soft. Blend in flour, sugar, curry and remaining ½ tsp. salt. Heat, stirring constantly, to boiling point. Stir in apricot nectar, lemon and orange juice, bacon and onions. Bring to a boil and simmer for 5 minutes.

Prepare stuffing by combining cooked rice, mushrooms, butter and wine. Remove hens from pan and discard drippings. Stuff hens, return to pan, pour sauce over top and roast for 10 minutes.

Serves 6.

—Mary-Lee Chase

Braised Duck

Whether made from wild or domestic duck, this dish has a deliciously delicate flavor. Of course, wild duck will result in a stronger, gamier taste.

Ingredients

4½ lb. duck, skinned & quartered
¼ cup soy sauce
¼ cup vinegar
½ cup water
1 small onion, finely chopped
1 tsp. butter
Salt & pepper
2 Tbsp. red currant jelly
2 bay leaves
1 cup chicken stock
1 tsp. ground ginger
½ cup green or red grapes

Directions

Marinate duck in soy sauce, vinegar and water for at least 2 hours or overnight. Sauté onion in butter. Add duck and brown. Add marinade plus salt and pepper, jelly, bay leaves, stock and ginger. Cover and simmer until duck is tender — approximately 1 hour.

Remove duck and reduce sauce to ¾ cup over high heat. Strain sauce over duck and add grapes.

Serves 4.

—Dianne Baker

Pheasant with Rice Stuffing

Ingredients

2 Tbsp. butter
½ cup rice
1 cup chicken stock
¼ tsp. salt
½ cup chopped onion
2 Tbsp. chopped parsley
3 Tbsp. chopped celery
2 pheasants
6 slices bacon

Directions

In heavy saucepan, melt 1 Tbsp. butter, add rice and stir constantly for 2 to 3 minutes until most of rice has turned opaque. Pour in chicken stock, add salt and bring to a boil. Cover, reduce heat and simmer for 15 minutes, or until rice has absorbed all the liquid.

Sauté onion in remaining 1 Tbsp. butter for 5 to 6 minutes. Add parsley and celery, then combine with cooked rice.

Sprinkle body cavities of pheasants with salt. Stuff and truss. Cover tops with bacon and cook at 350°F for 1 hour, remove bacon and cook until done.

Serves 2.

—Margaret Fredrickson

Shanghai Duck

Ingredients

6 green scallions
2 slices ginger root
4–6 lb. duck
1 Tbsp. sherry
¾ cup soy sauce
½ cup sugar
½ cup water
Anise seeds

Directions

Lay scallions and ginger root in bottom of large pan. Place duck on top, breast down. Pour sherry, soy sauce, sugar and water over duck and sprinkle with anise. Bring to a boil, then simmer for 45 minutes, turn duck over and simmer for another 45 minutes. Remove duck, skim fat off gravy and reduce to a thick sauce.

Serves 6.

—Anne Morrell

Partridge Pie

Ingredients

Pastry for 9-inch pie shell
3–4 bush partridges, cleaned, skinned & cut up
Salt & pepper
Flour
6 hard-boiled eggs, sliced
1 egg yolk, beaten

Directions

Cook partridges in salted water until tender. Cool enough to be handled easily and debone. Place in deep pie dish and add salt and pepper. Thicken liquid in pot with flour, then pour over meat. Cover with egg slices and top with pastry. Slash pastry to allow steam to escape and brush with beaten egg yolk. Bake at 375°F for 40 to 50 minutes, or until golden brown.

Serves 4 to 6.

—Janet Bantock

Orange Grouse

Ingredients

2 grouse, cut up
Flour, seasoned with salt & pepper
2 Tbsp. butter
2 Tbsp. oil
1½ cups white wine
½ cup orange juice
½ tsp. rosemary
½ tsp. dry mustard
Cayenne

Directions

Dredge grouse in seasoned flour and brown in butter and oil mixture in heavy skillet. Add wine, orange juice, rosemary, mustard and cayenne. Cover and simmer for 1½ hours, adding a little water if necessary. Thicken with flour and water paste and serve over hot buttered noodles.

Serves 2.

—Judy Cushman

Black Bear Stew

Ingredients

1½ lbs. lean bear meat, cubed
2 quarts water
½ cup vinegar
Salt & pepper
½ small onion, chopped
½ green pepper, chopped
2 medium potatoes, cubed
2 cups diced carrot
3 stalks celery, cut into ½-inch pieces
18-oz. can tomatoes
2 Tbsp. cornstarch

Directions

Wash meat in cold water, then soak for 15 minutes in water and vinegar. Dry meat in towel and fry with salt and pepper, onion and green pepper. When well fried, add potatoes, carrot, celery and tomatoes. Simmer for 45 minutes. While simmering, add the cornstarch dissolved in a few tablespoons of water.

Serves 2 to 4.

—Ken Laninga

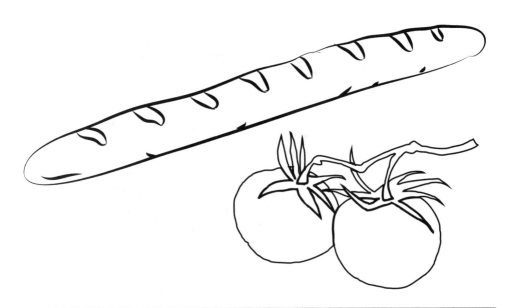

Elk Meatballs

Ingredients

1 lb. minced elk meat
½ cup cracked wheat
½ tsp. garlic powder
1 onion, minced
2 cups chicken stock
2 cups water
2 Tbsp. tamari sauce
3 Tbsp. cornstarch

Directions

Combine meat, wheat, garlic and onion and form into walnut-sized balls. Bring stock, water and tamari sauce to a boil. Simmer meat for 15 minutes. Remove and keep warm. Reduce stock to 2½ to 3 cups. Mix cornstarch and a little cold water and add to stock. Boil for 5 minutes, then pour over meatballs.

Serves 4.

—Linda Townsend

Venison Patties

Ingredients

1 lb. ground venison
½ lb. bacon, chopped
½ tsp. salt
⅛ tsp. pepper
⅛ tsp. thyme
⅛ tsp. marjoram
½ tsp. grated lemon peel
1 egg, beaten
1 cup cracker crumbs

Directions

Combine all ingredients and mix well by hand. Form into roll 2 to 3 inches diameter. Chill or freeze, then cut into slices and fry.

Serves 4.

—Taya Kwantes

Corned Bear

Served either hot with boiled potatoes, hot mustard and horseradish, or cold on a sandwich, corned bear is a delicious and unusual alternative to other corned meats.

Ingredients

4 quarts hot water
2 cups coarse salt
¼ cup sugar
2 Tbsp. mixed whole spice
5 lb. piece bear meat
3 cloves garlic, peeled

Directions

Combine hot water, salt, sugar and whole spice. When cool, pour over bear meat and garlic. Place in enameled pot, stoneware or glass jar. Weight meat to keep it submerged. Let marinate for 3 weeks in a cool place, turning every few days.

To cook, rinse meat under cold water, cover with boiling water and simmer for 4 hours, or until meat is tender.

—Kass Bennett

Wolfe Island Buttermilk Chicken

"My husband developed this recipe—it is the crispiest chicken you'll ever taste, even when reheated."

Ingredients

6 chicken breasts, halved
salt & pepper
2 cups flour
2 cups buttermilk
oil for frying

Directions

Season breasts with salt and pepper (and any other desired herbs). Coat with flour, dip in buttermilk, then coat again with flour.

Heat oil in deep skillet to 350°F, then reduce heat to keep oil at 325°. Cook chicken, a few pieces at a time, for 10 minutes, turning once.

Serves 6.

—Lorraine Smythe

Stuffed Chicken Breasts

Ingredients

2 whole chicken breasts,
halved, skinned & boned
4 slices ham
4 oz. Swiss or Gruyère cheese, grated
1 egg, beaten with ¼ cup milk
⅔ cup fine dry bread crumbs
¼ cup butter
1 clove garlic, minced
2 Tbsp. oil

Directions

Pound chicken breasts between sheets of waxed paper to ¼" thickness. In center of each chicken piece, place 1 slice ham and ½ of the cheese. Fold chicken over to make a flat rectangle and coat with flour. Dip each piece in egg-milk mixture, then roll in bread crumbs. Place pieces gently on rack and let coating set for at least 30 minutes.

Melt butter, then add garlic and oil. Add chicken and cook over medium heat for about 10 minutes on each side, or until done.

—Pamela Swainson

Down-Home Chicken & Dumplings

Exquisitely light dumplings and a flavorful sauce make this a special treat.

Main Ingredients

1 cup flour
1 tsp. paprika
1 frying chicken, cut up
3 Tbsp. oil
1 cup chicken stock
½ cup white wine
1 tsp. curry
½ tsp. tarragon

Dumpling Ingredients

1½ cups flour
1 Tbsp. baking powder
½ tsp. salt
1 cup milk

Directions

Place flour and paprika in plastic bag. Add chicken pieces and shake to coat. Heat oil in heavy pan with tight-fitting lid. Fry chicken pieces until golden, removing to platter as they brown.

To liquid in pan, add stock, wine, curry and tarragon. Add chicken and simmer, covered, until tender — about 1½ hours.

For dumplings: Sift flour and measure, then resift with baking powder and salt. Add milk and stir just until dry ingredients are dampened. Batter will be slightly lumpy. Dip a tablespoon into the hot chicken liquid to keep batter from sticking to the spoon. Drop by spoonfuls on top of chicken pieces. Cover and cook for 12 minutes, turning heat up slightly. Do not raise cover.

Put dumplings on a heated platter and surround them with chicken pieces. Serve gravy separately.

Serves 4.

—Edie Spring

Lemon Maple Chicken

The exceptional flavor belies the speed and ease of assembling this dish.

Ingredients

4 chicken legs
½ cup maple syrup
½ cup Dijon mustard
¼ cup fresh lemon juice
1 Tbsp. grated lemon rind
1 tsp. cinnamon

Directions

Cut chicken legs at the joint but do not separate. Place in casserole dish. Combine remaining ingredients and pour over chicken. Bake at 375°F for 30 minutes. Baste with pan drippings, then cook for 20 minutes longer or until done. Serve over rice using the degreased pan juices as sauce.

Serves 4.

—Gail Driscoll

Chicken & Bell Peppers

Make this with as many colors of bell peppers as are available to produce a colorful dish.

Ingredients

4 chicken breasts, skinned
&boned
2 Tbsp. seasoned flour
2 Tbsp. butter
2 Tbsp. oil
2 cloves garlic, crushed
1 onion, sliced
12 large mushrooms, sliced
1 cup sliced artichoke hearts
1½–2 cups sliced bell peppers
2 oz. white wine
2 oz. white rum
2–3 tomatoes, peeled & chopped
½ tsp. dried basil

Directions

Dredge chicken breasts in seasoned flour. Heat butter and oil in skillet and sauté chicken breasts for 2 to 3 minutes on each side. Add garlic, onion, mushrooms and artichoke hearts and cook for 5 minutes. Add peppers, wine, rum and tomatoes, simmer for 6 minutes, then sprinkle with basil and simmer for about 2 minutes more. Serve over fresh noodles or rice.

Serves 4.

—Jim & Penny Wright

Belgian Chicken

Ingredients

3–4 lbs. chicken pieces
flour
salt & pepper
3 Tbsp. butter
½ cup chopped onion
1 cup dry white wine
1 cup chopped mushrooms
½ cup golden raisins
¾ cup light cream
chopped parsley

Directions

Coat chicken pieces in flour seasoned with salt and pepper. Sauté in butter until light brown. Add onion and cook until tender. Add wine and mushrooms, cover and simmer for 30 to 35 minutes. Add raisins and cook for 5 minutes. Remove chicken pieces and place in a warmed dish. Add cream to the gravy, reheat and pour over chicken. Sprinkle chicken with chopped parsley and serve over rice or noodles.

Serves 4.

—Joanne Avelar

Orange Pecan Muffins page 11

Apple Pancakes page 15

Perfect Peanut Butter Cookies page 28

Quiche Lorraine page 32

Eggs Flourentine page 41

Minestrone Soup page 69

Miso Soup page 72

Eggplant Casserole page 110

Greek Salad page 125

Lentil Burgers page 158

Vegetarian Couscous page 174

Tuna Casserole page 181

Smoked Salmon page 186

Chicken Curry page 217

Barbequed Chicken page 218

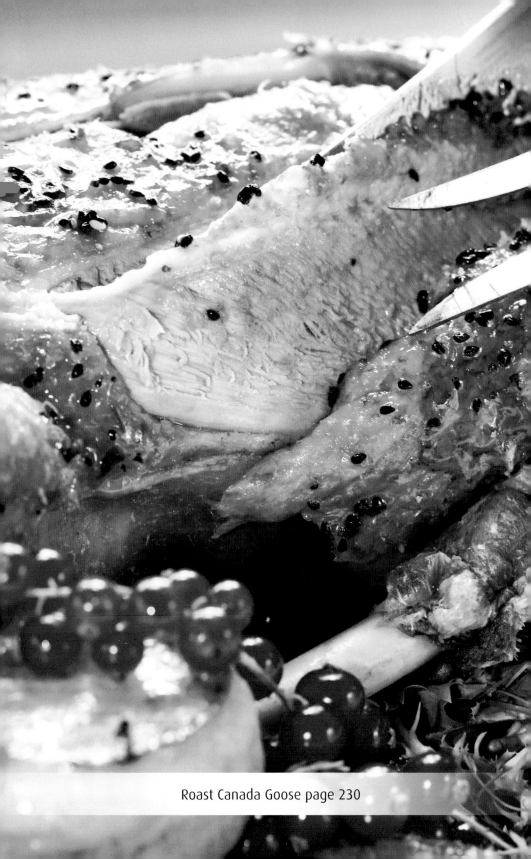

Roast Canada Goose page 230

Irish Stew page 315

Shepherd's Pie page 282

Apple Glazed Roast Pork page 306

Swedish Meatballs page 280

Savory Lamb Shanks page 333

Macaroni and Cheese page 341

Seafood Linguinie page 360

Poppyseed Lemon Bread page 366

Blueberry Oat Muffins page 398

Chocolate Chip Cookies page 390

Richard's Raisin Bread page 377

Apricot Jam Amandine page 446

Dill Pickles page 435

Blackberry Jam page 446

Pumpkin Pie page 466

Blueberry Cobbler page 476

Chicken Cacciatore

Spicy and highly flavorful, this chicken cacciatore is an interesting departure from traditional cacciatore recipes.

Ingredients

2–3 lbs. chicken pieces
28-oz. can tomatoes
7-oz. can tomato sauce
1 cup chopped onions
½ cup chopped green pepper
2 stalks celery, chopped
2 carrots, chopped
4 cloves garlic, minced
½ cup dry red wine
1 tsp. salt
½ tsp. allspice
2 bay leaves
½ tsp. thyme
pepper
cayenne

Directions

Remove skin from chicken pieces, then cut meat into serving-sized pieces. Combine remaining ingredients in large pot and bring to a boil. Add chicken, cover, reduce heat and simmer for about 2 hours, or until chicken and carrots are tender. Remove bay leaves. The cover may be removed for the last half hour of cooking to reduce and thicken sauce slightly. Serve with rice or noodles.

Serves 4.

—Judith Asbil

Chicken Fricassee

Ingredients

½ cup flour
1 tsp. salt
½ tsp. freshly ground pepper
¼ tsp. mace
¼ tsp. nutmeg
5 lb. frying chicken, cut up
⅓ cup oil
½ lb. mushrooms, sliced
1 large onion, sliced
3 cups chicken stock
¼ cup sour cream
¼ cup white wine
¼ tsp. prepared mustard
1 tsp. tomato paste

Directions

Mix flour, salt, pepper, mace and nutmeg. Roll dampened pieces of chicken in flour mixture to coat on all sides. Heat oil in large skillet over high heat. Brown chicken, then remove to a plate. Reduce heat, add mushrooms and onion and cook until soft. Add chicken and stock and bring to a boil. Reduce heat, cover, and simmer until very tender — 1 to 2 hours.

Just before serving, skim off fat and stir in a mixture of sour cream, wine, mustard and tomato paste.

Serves 4.

—Norma Somers

Chicken & Apricots

Ingredients

3 lbs. chicken pieces, skin removed
4 Tbsp. butter
2 large onions, sliced
2 Tbsp. flour
¼ tsp. nutmeg
paprika
salt & pepper
1 cup apricot juice
1 cup chicken stock
1 green pepper, sliced
1 lb. dried apricots, soaked overnight

Directions

Lightly brown chicken pieces in butter and re-move from pan. In same pan, sauté onions until soft. Add flour, nutmeg, paprika and salt and pepper. Cook for one minute. Add apricot juice and chicken stock and bring to a boil, stirring constantly. Return chicken pieces to pan. Lower heat, cover and simmer for 30 minutes. Add green pepper and apricots. Simmer for another 15 minutes. Serve over brown rice.

Serves 6 to 8.

—Patricia Daine

Baked Chicken Rosemary

The tangy barbecue-style sauce works well over pork, lamb or chicken.

Ingredients

1 frying chicken, cut up
salt & pepper
1 clove garlic, minced
1 tsp. paprika
1 Tbsp. onion, finely minced
½ cup vinegar
½ cup tomato sauce
½ cup water
1 tsp. rosemary leaves
1 Tbsp. prepared mustard
2 Tbsp. brown sugar or honey
1 tsp. soy sauce

Directions

Arrange chicken pieces one layer deep in 9" x 13" baking pan. Sprinkle with salt and pepper, garlic, paprika and onion. Combine remaining ingredients and pour over chicken. Bake at 325°F until fork-tender — about 1 hour. Serve with rice.

Serves 3 to 4.

—Mary Irwin-Gibson

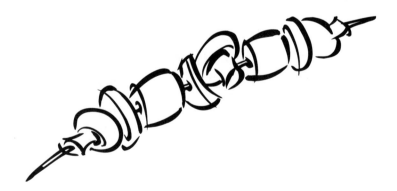

Chicken Stroganoff

Ingredients

3 Tbsp. oil
4 chicken breasts, skinned, boned & cut into thin strips
½ tsp. salt
1 tsp. pepper
1 clove garlic, minced
3 onions, sliced
1 cup sliced mushrooms
3 Tbsp. flour
6 Tbsp. white wine
2 cups chicken stock, heated
⅔ cup sour cream
1 Tbsp. tomato paste

Directions

Heat oil in heavy pan. Sear chicken pieces, season with salt and pepper and remove. Mix chicken with garlic and keep warm. Cook onions and mushrooms in pan until onions are transparent. Add extra oil if needed. Stir in flour to make a roux. Add wine, hot stock, sour cream and tomato paste, stirring it into a smooth mixture. Add chicken and garlic. Simmer gently for 20 minutes, or until chicken is tender. Serve in a ring of hot buttered noodles.

Serves 4.

—Ann Coyle

Lemon Chicken

Ingredients

4 chicken breasts, skinned & boned
1 egg
flour
2 Tbsp. peanut oil
2½ Tbsp. cornstarch
¼ cup lemon juice
grated rind of 1 lemon
⅓ cup sugar
¼ tsp. ginger
rind of ½ lemon, cut into thin strips

Directions

Cut chicken into 1-inch strips. Beat egg with 2 Tbsp. water. Dip chicken in this, then dredge in flour. Heat peanut oil in skillet or wok and fry chicken, removing pieces once they are cooked. Mix remaining ingredients except strips of lemon rind. Bring to a boil in skillet. Add chicken and lemon rind to the mixture and heat for 5 minutes.

Serves 4.

—Mary-Lee Judah

Oven-Crisp Chicken

Our Vermont tester says, "Hurrah! This chicken has an unusual and flavorful coating; it is very tender and moist and not at all greasy."

Ingredients

¾ cup cracker crumbs
½ cup Parmesan cheese
½ cup ground pecans
2 eggs
1 cup buttermilk
3–4 lb. broiler chicken, cut up
melted butter

Directions

Combine cracker crumbs, cheese and pecans. Beat together eggs and buttermilk. Roll chicken pieces in crumb mixture until evenly coated, dip in egg mixture, then roll in crumbs again. Place a single layer in lightly oiled 9" x 13" baking dish. Brush lightly with melted butter.

Bake, brushing occasionally with more butter, at 400°F for 1 hour.

Serves 4.

—Nancy R. Franklin

Cashew Chicken

This dish, often with almonds replacing the cashews, is a standard in Cantonese Chinese restaurants. It is quick and simple to prepare at home.

Ingredients

2 Tbsp. plus 2 tsp. cornstarch
1 cup chicken stock
5 Tbsp. soy sauce
2 lbs. chicken breasts, skinned & boned
4 Tbsp. oil
4 stalks celery, sliced
2 cups sliced mushrooms
½ lb. snow peas
1 onion, sliced
1 clove garlic, minced
1 cup cashews
cooked rice

Directions

Combine 2 tsp. cornstarch with chicken stock and 1 Tbsp. soy sauce. Set aside.

Slice chicken into strips. Blend remaining 2 Tbsp. cornstarch with remaining 4 Tbsp. soy sauce in a bowl and stir in chicken. Heat 2 Tbsp. oil in large frying pan or wok, add chicken and stir over medium head for 3 minutes. Remove chicken. Add remaining 2 Tbsp. oil and reheat pan. Add remaining ingredients, except cashews and rice, cover and cook over medium heat for 1 minute, shaking the pan several times. Uncover and cook for another 2 to 4 minutes, stirring occasionally. Add chicken-cornstarch mixture, and stir over medium heat until the sauce thickens — about 3 minutes. Stir in most of the cashews just before serving, reserving a few for garnish. Serve over rice.

Serves 6.

— Diane Milan

A Simple Chicken Curry

"When I was living in Bombay, I was part of a culture-sharing organization comprising American, Canadian, British and Indian women. This is one of the many interesting recipes that were exchanged." Either buy commercial canned coconut milk, or make it by pouring 2 cups hot milk over 2 cups dried coconut. Let stand for 1 hour, then strain, pressing the coconut hard to release all the milk. Feed the coconut to the birds and use the milk.

Ingredients

2 Tbsp. butter
1 onion, chopped
2 cloves garlic, chopped
1 Tbsp. ground coriander
1 tsp. mustard seed
1 tsp. cumin seed
1 tsp. turmeric
½ tsp. ground ginger
½ tsp. dry crushed chilies
1 frying chicken, cut up
2 cups coconut milk
2 tsp. lime juice

Directions

Melt butter, then saute onion and garlic until golden. Add coriander, mustard, cumin, turmeric, ginger and chilies and cook gently, stirring, for 3 minutes. Add chicken and cook until lightly browned. Add coconut milk and simmer until chicken is cooked through. Season with a little salt and lime juice and serve over rice.

Serves 4 to 5.

—*Ethel Hunter*

Chicken Curry

Not a curry you would find in a small, rural Indian village, this is a very rich dish. Serve the delicately flavored curry with an assortment of condiments — roasted cashews, diced green pepper and celery, mandarin oranges, bananas, coconut, raisins and plain yogurt.

Ingredients

5–6 lb. chicken
1 onion
3 celery tops
1 Tbsp. salt
1 bay leaf
4 cloves
2½ cups hot milk
3 cups coconut
½ cup butter
2 cloves garlic, chopped
1½ cups chopped onion
¼ tsp. ginger
1½–3 Tbsp. curry
½ cup flour
1 tsp. salt
1 Tbsp. lemon juice
1 cup light cream

Directions

Place chicken, whole onion, celery tops, salt, bay leaf and cloves in large stockpot with 12 cups water. Bring to a boil, reduce heat and simmer, covered, for 2 hours. Remove chicken and set aside to cool, then remove meat from bones and chop. Strain stock and reserve 2 cups for use in curry.

Pour hot milk over coconut and let stand for 45 minutes. Melt ¼ cup butter in heavy skillet, then sauté garlic, chopped onion, ginger and curry for 3 to 5 minutes. Stir in 2 cups stock, then coconut and milk. Reduce heat and simmer for 1 hour, stirring occasionally Strain and press, reserving liquid and discarding coconut.

Melt remaining ¼ cup butter, stir in flour, salt and lemon juice. Gradually stir in cream and simmer for 5 minutes. Add chicken and curry sauce and gently heat through.

Serves 8.

Sweet & Sour Chicken Wings

When we tested these wings in our Vermont kitchen, they were very popular. The meat was falling-off-the-bone tender, and the sauce adhered well to the wings.

Ingredients
16–20 chicken wings
2 cups brown sugar
2 Tbsp. vinegar
4 Tbsp. soy sauce
1 tsp. chopped garlic

Directions
Cut tips off wings. (Freeze tips and add to soup stock the next time you make it.) Place wings in large shallow baking dish. Mix remaining ingredients together and pour over wings. Cover and bake at 350°F for 1 hour, remove cover, turn wings and bake for 40 to 60 minutes more.

Serves 4 to 6.

—Jan Higenbottam

Sesame Chicken Wings

Good, crunchy wings. Serve with dips for a delicious snack to have with drinks on a summer afternoon or evening.

Ingredients
3-4 lbs. chicken wings
2 cups flour
½ cup sesame seeds
1 tsp. ginger
1–1½ cups melted butter

Directions
Wash and dry wings and cut off tips. Combine flour, sesame seeds and ginger and mix well. Dip wings in butter and shake off excess, then roll in flour mixture. Place on cookie sheet and bake for 45 to 60 minutes at 350°F. Place under broiler briefly to brown.

Serves 12 as an appetizer.

—Gail Driscoll

Creamed Horseradish Sauce

Ingredients
2 Tbsp. butter
2 Tbsp. flour
1¼ cups light cream
salt
white pepper
3 Tbsp. vinegar
2 Tbsp. sugar
2-3 Tbsp. freshly shredded horseradish

Directions
Melt butter in small saucepan. Add flour and stir for a few minutes. Add cream, a little at a time, while stirring. Add salt, white pepper, vinegar, sugar and horseradish. Stir until thickened.

Serve over boiled, boned chicken meat.

—Erik Panum

Spicy Wing Sauce

This recipe and the two that follow make good dips for chicken wings. They can also be used as basting sauces.

Ingredients

1 onion, finely chopped
2 Tbsp. olive oil
2 tsp. coriander
1 tsp. cumin
1 tsp. cinnamon
1 tsp. ground cardamom
¼ tsp. cloves
¼ tsp. cayenne
2 Tbsp. white wine vinegar
1 Tbsp. tomato paste
1 tsp. salt
¼ cup water

Directions

Sauté onion in olive oil until transparent. Add remaining ingredients and stir well.

Satay Sauce

Ingredients

½ cup smooth peanut butter
⅓ cup soy sauce
⅓ cup lemon juice
⅓ cup sherry
2 Tbsp. brown sugar
1 tsp. Tabasco sauce
2 cloves garlic, finely minced

Directions

Combine all ingredients and mix well. Serve warm or at room temperature.

Curried Lemon Dip

Ingredients

2 Tbsp. butter
4 cloves garlic, minced
½ tsp. salt
½ tsp. pepper
1 tsp. hot curry
2 Tbsp. freshly grated lemon peel
½ cup lemon juice

Directions

Melt butter and sauté garlic for 3 minutes. Stir in all other ingredients and simmer for 5 minutes.

Best Ever Barbecue Sauce

"We use this sauce on almost everything: beef, pork, poultry. It's great on chicken wings."

Ingredients

2 Tbsp. butter
1 onion, finely chopped
2 cloves garlic, minced
juice of 1 orange
1 Tbsp. raisins
2 Tbsp. cider vinegar
2 Tbsp. oil
grated zest of 1 orange
1 cup molasses
1 cup tomato sauce
2 tsp. chili powder
⅛ tsp. allspice
1 tsp. prepared mustard
1 tsp. Worcestershire sauce
2 tsp. crushed hot red pepper
½ tsp. salt

Directions

Melt butter and add onion and garlic. Cook for 5 minutes. Combine orange juice, raisins, vinegar and oil in food processor or blender until smooth. Add processed ingredients and remaining ingredients to onion-garlic mixture. Heat until boiling, reduce heat and simmer uncovered, for 15 minutes.

Makes enough sauce for 36 wings.

—Mary-Eileen Clear

Chicken Broccoli Salad

Perfect picnic fare, this salad can be adapted to make use of a variety of green vegetables — use whatever is in season. Homemade mayonnaise could be spiced up with garlic or blue cheese to give more zest to the dressing.

Ingredients

1 whole chicken breast,
    cooked & chopped
1 head broccoli, cut into florets & steamed
1 avocado, chopped
3 green onions, chopped
2 cups dry macaroni shells, cooked & cooled
1 tsp. lemon juice
1 cup mayonnaise
½ tsp. dry mustard
1 tsp. basil
Salt & pepper

Directions

Combine chicken, broccoli, avocado, onions and macaroni. Sprinkle with lemon juice. Add mayonnaise, mustard, basil and salt and pepper, and toss lightly. Chill.

Serves 6.

Paté à l'Orange

A delicious paté, this recipe eliminates the need for eggs, pork fat and a long cooking time but retains the rich, luxurious taste.

Ingredients

1 lb. poultry livers
1 lb. lean ground pork
1 onion, chopped
1½ cups butter
1 tsp. coriander
¼ cup Cointreau or orange liqueur
½ tsp. pepper
grated orange peel

Directions

Sauté livers, pork and onion in ¾ cup butter until cooked through. Put meat mixture, remaining butter, coriander, Cointreau and pepper in blender or food processor. Chop until mixture is smooth. (It may be slightly soupy but will become firm when chilled.) Place in mold and chill for at least 4 hours.

To serve, cut into thin slices and garnish with grated orange peel.

Serves 12 to 16.

—J.R. Galen

Butter-Braised Pheasant

Ingredients

2 pheasants, 2–3 lb. each
2 cups red wine
2 bay leaves
¼ cup oil
1 Tbsp. juniper berries
¼ tsp. peppercorns
3 Tbsp. butter

Directions

Clean and quarter pheasants, then rinse well in cold water. Combine wine, bay leaves and oil. Coarsely crush juniper berries and peppercorns and add to marinade. Place pheasant in shallow dish, pour marinade over, cover, and refrigerate for 3 days, turning several times.

In Dutch oven, brown pheasants in butter. Remove from heat, add marinade and bake, covered, at 400°F for 1 to 1½ hours, or until tender.

Serves 6 to 8.

—J.R. Galen

Turkey Dressing

Ingredients

2 cups dry brown & white rice
½ lb. bacon
1½ cups dried fruit (peaches, pears, apples)
¾ cup butter
2 cups diced celery
1 cup diced leeks
1½ tsp. salt
2 Tbsp. tarragon
1 Tbsp. mint
½–1 cup sliced mushrooms

Directions

Cook rice in 4½ cups water for 45 minutes. Fry bacon and crumble. Soak dried fruit in ⅔ cup boiling water. Melt butter in large heavy pan, and sauté celery and leeks. Add salt. Remove from heat and stir in rice, bacon, fruit, seasonings and mushrooms. Stuff bird and cook as usual.

Enough stuffing for a 12 lb. bird.

—*Diane Ladouceur*

Wild Rice, Sausage & Almond Stuffing

This is a wonderfully crunchy stuffing for chicken, goose, duck or even pork. It can be baked in a greased casserole dish by itself, if you wish, to accompany pork chops or baked chicken breasts.

Ingredients

½ cup dry wild rice
½ lb. sausage meat
1 small onion, chopped
½ cup chopped celery
½ cup sliced mushrooms
½ cup coarsely chopped almonds
3 slices dry whole wheat bread, cubed
½ tsp. salt
½ tsp. pepper
¼ tsp. sage
savory
thyme

Directions

Place wild rice in strainer and rinse thoroughly under cold water. Drain well. Place in saucepan and pour 1½ cups boiling water over. Return to boil. Reduce heat and simmer for 45 minutes, or until tender but not mushy. Drain well and transfer to a large bowl.

In large skillet, cook sausage meat over medium heat until no longer pink, breaking it up as it cooks. Stir in onion, celery and mushrooms, and cook until tender — about 5 minutes.

With slotted spoon, transfer sausage-vegetable mixture to wild rice. Add remaining ingredients, stirring gently. Taste and adjust seasoning. Pack loosely into the cavity of a 10 lb. bird, or place in greased casserole dish and bake, covered, at 350°F for 45 minutes.

—*Sandy Robertson*

Canard à l'Orange

Main Ingredients

2 ducks
2 tsp. salt
2 tsp. grated orange peel
½ tsp. thyme
½ tsp. pepper
2 Tbsp. finely chopped onion
¼ tsp. sage

Sauce Ingredients

wing tips & giblets
2 Tbsp. butter
2 Tbsp. finely chopped onion
1 tsp. dried parsley
1 bay leaf
3 Tbsp. sugar
¼ cup vinegar
1 tsp. grated orange peel
2 Tbsp. cornstarch
½ cup port wine

Directions

Remove giblets, wash and dry ducks and cut off wing tips at the first joint. Reserve, with giblets, for sauce. Combine salt, orange peel, thyme, pepper, onion and sage. Rub mixture on skin and inside the cavity of each duck. Tie legs together, then place ducks on rack in roasting pan. Roast at 350°F for 2½ to 3 hours, or until drumstick moves and skin is crisp and golden.

Meanwhile, prepare sauce. Brown wing tips and giblets in butter. Add onion and cook until lightly browned. Add parsley, bay leaf and 3 cups water. Cover and simmer for 1 hour. Strain and cook liquid until reduced to 2 cups. Combine sugar and vinegar and cook until sugar caramelizes to a dark brown. Add stock, orange peel and cornstarch mixed with ¼ cup of port wine. Cook, stirring, until thickened.

About half an hour before ducks are done, remove them from pan. Drain off the fat and add ¼ cup port to pan. Heat and scrape browned particles into liquid. Add this to basting sauce. Replace ducks and baste until done. Serve extra sauce over sliced duck.

Serves 4 to 6.

—Laurie Noblet

Venison Stroganoff

"Wondering how to prepare the piece of venison you've been presented with need never be a problem again. This simple recipe does not require the extensive marinating often called for when cooking game. Venison should be well trimmed of all fat and strong membrane before use."

Ingredients

1 lb venison steak
flour
4 Tbsp. butter
½ cup chopped onion
1 clove garlic, minced
½ lb. mushrooms, sliced
3 Tbsp. flour
1 Tbsp. tomato paste
1½ cups beef stock
2 Tbsp. white wine
1 cup sour cream
cooked noodles

Directions

Cut meat into ¼-inch strips, against the grain, and dust with flour. Heat 2 Tbsp. butter in large skillet. When foam dies down, add meat and brown quickly. Add onion, garlic and mushrooms, adding more butter if necessary. Sauté for 3 to 5 minutes, or until onion and mushrooms are tender. Remove meat mixture and add 2 Tbsp. butter to pan. Blend in flour and tomato paste. Stir in stock and cook, stirring, until thickened. Return meat mixture to skillet. Stir in wine and sour cream. Heat gently but do not boil. Serve over hot buttered noodles.

Serves 4.

—Susan Baker

Breaded Venison Steaks

Ingredients

1½ lbs. boneless venison
steak
½ cup flour
½ tsp. salt
⅛ tsp. pepper
¾ tsp. paprika
1 egg, lightly beaten
1 Tbsp. milk
1 cup fine dry bread crumbs
2 Tbsp. grated onion
1 clove garlic, crushed
½ tsp. basil
½ tsp. thyme
½ cup oil

Directions

Pound steaks to tenderize. Combine flour, salt, pepper and ¼ tsp. paprika in one bowl, egg and milk in a second and bread crumbs, onion, garlic, basil, thyme and remaining ½ tsp. paprika in a third.

Dip meat first in flour, then egg, then bread crumb mixtures. Be sure entire surface of meat is covered. Sauté steak in oil to desired doneness.

Serves 2.

—Dorothy Cage

Yogurt Fried Rabbit

Ingredients

¼ cup whole wheat flour
1 tsp. thyme
salt & pepper
1 rabbit, cut up
3 Tbsp. oil
½ cup yogurt
1 egg, beaten
1 tsp. basil
⅛ cup heavy cream

Directions

Combine flour, thyme, salt and pepper. Dust rabbit with flour mixture. Heat oil and fry rabbit until golden. Cover pan tightly and simmer for 30 minutes or until meat is tender. Remove meat and keep warm.

Combine yogurt and egg, then stir into pan juices to blend. Add basil, then cream. Pour over rabbit and serve.

Serves 4.

—Helen Campbell

Michigan Dutch-Style Rabbit

Despite its simplicity, this dish is full of flavor.
Serve over mashed potatoes.

Ingredients

1 cup flour
salt & pepper
1 rabbit, cut into serving-sized pieces
¼ cup butter
½ tsp. thyme
1 cup heavy cream

Directions

Combine flour and salt and pepper in paper bag. Place one piece of rabbit in bag at a time and shake to coat completely. Melt butter in deep, heavy skillet that has a lid, and brown meat on both sides. Sprinkle with thyme and add cream. Cover and simmer over very low heat for about 1½ hours or until tender. If cream gets too thick, stir in a little water.

Serves 4.

—Teresa Carel

Beer-Braised Rabbit

Ingredients

1½–2 lbs. rabbit, cut up
salt & pepper
3 Tbsp. oil
3 potatoes, peeled & halved
2 cups carrots, cut into 1" pieces
1 onion, sliced
1 cup beer
¼ cup chili sauce
1 Tbsp. brown sugar
½ tsp. salt
1 clove garlic, minced
⅓ cup water
3 Tbsp. flour

Directions

Generously season rabbit with salt and pepper. Heat oil in 10-inch skillet and brown rabbit. Add potatoes, carrots and onion. Combine beer, chili sauce, brown sugar, salt and garlic and pour over rabbit. Bring to a boil; cover, reduce heat and simmer for 45 minutes or until tender. Remove rabbit and vegetables to a serving platter and keep warm.

Measure pan juices, adding additional beer or water if needed to make 1½ cups liquid. Return pan juices to skillet. Blend ⅓ cup water into flour and stir into juices. Cook, stirring, until thickened and bubbly. Continue cooking for 1 to 2 minutes more. Serve with rabbit.

Serves 4.

—Kristine Mattila

Meat

Sauté of Veal with Herbs

Ingredients

2 lbs. veal, cut into 1½" cubes
Salt & pepper
2 Tbsp. butter
2 Tbsp. oil
½ lb. mushrooms, sliced
1 medium onion, chopped
¾ cup chopped celery
1 clove garlic, minced
½ cup dry white wine
¼ cup flour
1½ cups chicken stock
1 cup crushed tomatoes
½ tsp. dried rosemary
2 sprigs parsley
1 bay leaf
2 medium onions, quartered

Directions

Sprinkle meat with salt and pepper, heat butter and oil in skillet and brown meat, a few pieces at a time. Set aside.

Add mushrooms, chopped onion, celery and garlic to skillet and cook until onion is soft. Add wine, and cook to evaporate.

Return meat to skillet and sprinkle with flour. Gradually add the stock, stirring to blend. Add the tomatoes, rosemary, parsley and bay leaf and cover. Cook over low heat for about 1 hour. Add the quartered onions and cook 45 minutes longer. Serve sprinkled with parsley.

Serves 4 to 6.

—Shirley Hill

Veal Parmesan

Ingredients

3 Tbsp. butter
½ cup fine bread crumbs
¼ cup grated Parmesan cheese
½ tsp. salt
Dash pepper
1 lb. veal cutlets
1 egg, slightly beaten
1 cup tomato sauce, page 339
1 cup grated mozzarella cheese

Directions

Melt butter in 8-inch square baking dish. Combine crumbs, Parmesan cheese, salt and pepper. Cut veal into serving-sized pieces. Dip first into egg and then into crumb mixture. Place in baking dish and bake at 400°F for 20 minutes, turn and bake for another 15 minutes.

Pour tomato sauce over meat and top with mozzarella cheese. Return to oven to melt cheese — about 3 minutes.

Serves 4.

—Mrs. W. Atkins

Beef Wellington

Ingredients
5 lb. fillet of beef
1 tsp. dry mustard
Fat back to cover beef
4 chicken livers
½ lb. mushrooms
¼ lb. cooked ham
1 small clove garlic
2 Tbsp. butter
⅓ cup sherry
1 Tbsp. meat extract
1 Tbsp. tomato purée
Puff pastry

Directions

Sprinkle beef with mustard and cover with fat back. Roast at 400°F for 25 minutes. Cool and remove fat. Sauté chicken livers, chop finely and set aside. Finely mince mushrooms, ham and garlic and sauté for 5 minutes in butter. Add chicken livers, sherry, meat extract and tomato purée. Mix well and remove from heat. Roll out puff pastry in a large enough sheet to enclose the fillet. Lay the fillet in center of pastry and spoon mushroom mixture over and around it. Carefully wrap pastry around fillet, turning in the ends and pressing all the seams together firmly. Lay fillet seam-side down in a baking dish. Bake at 350°F for 30 to 35 minutes, until crust is lightly browned.

Serves 8 to 10.

—*Cary Elizabeth Marshall*

Lazy Man's Roast

This recipe is also easily adapted to a slow cooker — simply allow 2 hours more cooking time.

Ingredients
3–4 lb. rump roast
1 cup red wine
1½ tsp. salt
10 whole peppercorns
1½ Tbsp. brown sugar
2 bay leaves
½ tsp. dried sage

Directions

Trim most of fat from roast and place meat in a casserole dish. Add wine, salt, peppercorns, sugar and herbs. Cover tightly and cook for 4 hours at 275°F. Remove pan from heat and let meat sit in its liquid for 1 hour before serving.

Serves 6.

—*Kathleen Fitzgerald*

Yorkshire Pudding

This traditional British accompaniment to roast beef can be prepared as the roast cooks and baked while the roast rests before carving.

Ingredients

¼ cup hot drippings from roast
1 egg, well beaten
½ cup milk
½ cup flour
¼ tsp. salt

Directions

Divide drippings among 6 large muffin tins.

Beat egg and milk together until light. Gradually beat in flour and salt, and continue beating until batter is smooth.

Pour into muffin tins and let stand for 30 minutes. Bake at 450°F for 15 to 20 minutes.

Serves 6.

—Mrs. W. Atkins

Corned Beef

Ingredients

4 lb. rump roast
8 cups water
4 Tbsp. sugar
2 bay leaves
10 peppercorns
4 tsp. mixed pickling spice
2 cloves garlic, minced
1 cup salt

Directions

Place meat in a crock. Combine the remaining ingredients and pour over meat. Weight the meat down in the brine and cover. Let stand in a cool place for 5 to 7 days. Remove meat from brine and place in cold water. Bring to a boil. Remove scum from the surface. Cover and simmer for 5 hours.

Serves 6.

—Pam McFeeters

Marinated Beef

Ingredients

½ cup soy sauce
½ cup lemon juice
2 cloves garlic, crushed
1 lb. chuck, blade or round steak cut into thin strips

Directions

Mix soy sauce, lemon juice and garlic. Pour over beef and marinate for 4 hours, turning once. Drain and dry beef, reserving marinade. Fry or broil beef at a high temperature, so that it cooks quickly.

Serve with rice, using marinade as a sauce.

Serves 3 to 4.

—Judy Wuest

Stir-Fried Meat & Vegetables

Ingredients

1 green pepper, cut in strips
2 stalks celery, cut in strips
1 cup thinly sliced onions
1 cup sliced mushrooms
4 Tbsp. butter
2 cups green beans, cut in pieces
½ cup leftover gravy
⅛ tsp. pepper
3 cups cooked meat, cut in 1-inch pieces
3 Tbsp. soy sauce
2 cups fresh bean sprouts

Directions

Brown green pepper, celery, onions and mushrooms in butter. Add green beans and stir gently. Then add remaining ingredients except for the bean sprouts and stir. Heat thoroughly. Stir in bean sprouts when ready to serve.

Serves 6.

—Ruth Anne Laverty

Wine Beef Stew

The flavor of beef simmered slowly in red wine is difficult to surpass. This recipe adds potatoes and carrots to provide a complete meal in one dish.

Ingredients

6 Tbsp. oil
3 lbs. beef chuck, cut into ½-inch cubes
1 cup chopped onion
1 cup sliced celery
2 Tbsp. parsley
1 clove garlic, finely chopped
1½ Tbsp. salt
¼ tsp. pepper
⅛ tsp. thyme
1 bay leaf
1 cup tomato sauce, page 339
2 cups beef stock
1 cup dry red wine
6 medium potatoes, diced
6 medium carrots, sliced
1–2 Tbsp. flour
2 Tbsp. cold water

Directions

In hot oil, brown beef well on all sides. Remove and set aside. Add onion and celery and sauté until tender — about 8 minutes. Return beef to pan. Add parsley, garlic, salt, pepper, thyme, bay leaf, tomato sauce, beef stock and wine. Bring to a boil. Reduce heat and simmer, covered, for 1¼ hours. Add potatoes and carrots. Simmer, covered, 1 hour longer, or until tender. Remove from heat and skim off fat. Mix flour with cold water and stir into beef mixture. Return to stove and simmer, covered, for 10 minutes.

Serves 6.

—Myrna Henderson

Steak & Kidney Pie

For an unusual version of this traditional dish, add a pint of fresh oysters and a bay leaf.

Ingredients

Pastry for double 9-inch pie crust
1½ lbs. sirloin or round steak
1 lb. kidneys
2 tsp. salt
1 tsp. pepper
¼ cup flour
3 Tbsp. butter & 1 Tbsp. oil
1 cup sliced mushrooms
½ cup chopped onion
1½ cups water
¼ cup dry red wine
1 Tbsp. chopped parsley
¼ tsp. thyme
¼ tsp. Worcestershire sauce

Directions

Cut steak and kidney into cubes and dry with paper towels. Sprinkle with 1 tsp. salt and ½ tsp. pepper. Toss in a bowl with the flour.

Melt the butter and oil in a pan. Brown a few of the meat cubes at a time and transfer to a large casserole dish.

Stir the mushrooms and onion in the same pan for 2 to 3 minutes, then add to the meat.

Pour the water into the frying pan, bring to a boil, stirring to pick up the residues, and pour into casserole dish. Add wine, parsley, thyme, Worcestershire sauce and the rest of the salt and pepper. Stir gently.

Cover with pastry. Brush with water and bake at 425°F for 30 minutes, reduce heat to 350° and bake for 30 minutes longer.

—Carolyn Hills

Barbecued Beef Braising Ribs

Ingredients

3½ lbs. beef braising ribs
3 Tbsp. oil
1 clove garlic, minced
¼ cup white vinegar
1 cup tomato paste
1 cup water
1 Tbsp. Worcestershire sauce
¼ cup brown sugar
½ cup minced onion
½ tsp. salt
¼ tsp. pepper
1 Tbsp. butter

Directions

Brown ribs in oil with garlic. Transfer ribs and drippings to roasting pan.

Combine remaining ingredients in a saucepan and simmer for 15 minutes. Pour over ribs and bake, covered, at 350°F for 1½ to 2 hours, stirring after 1 hour.

Serves 6.

—Diane Cane

Beef Curry

Ingredients

3 lbs. stewing beef, in 1-inch cubes
1 cup chopped onion
1 cup chopped apple
3 cloves garlic, minced
½ cup butter
1 Tbsp. turmeric
2 bay leaves, crumbled
1 inch fresh ginger, minced
2 tsp. coriander
2 tsp. cumin
½ tsp. cardamom
½ tsp. ground mustard seed
½ tsp. cinnamon
½ tsp. ground fenugreek
4 hot chilies, crushed
Salt & pepper
3 cups coconut milk

Directions

Sauté meat, onion, apple and garlic in the butter. Combine spices and add to meat when well browned. Cook briefly, stirring.

Add coconut milk and simmer until meat is very tender — 3 to 6 hours.

Serve over rice with any or all of: fresh fruit, nuts, chopped celery, green peppers, coconut, raisins and yogurt.

Serves 8 to 10.

—*Ingrid Birker*

Red Eye Stew

Ingredients

3 lbs. stewing beef, cut into 1-inch pieces
¼ cup flour
2 Tbsp. salt
1 tsp. pepper
¼ cup oil
4 large onions, sliced
1 clove garlic
12 oz. beer
1 Tbsp. soy sauce
1 Tbsp. Worcestershire sauce
1 Tbsp. tomato paste
½ tsp. thyme
2 bay leaves
2–3 cups tomato juice
3 potatoes, peeled & diced
2 cups peas

Directions

Dredge meat in flour mixed with salt and pepper. Brown in hot oil.

Add onions and garlic and cook until onions are transparent. Add beer, soy sauce, Worcestershire sauce, tomato paste, thyme and bay leaves. Bring to a boil, then reduce heat and simmer for 1 hour.

Add tomato juice and simmer for 30 minutes. Add potatoes, cook 20 minutes, then peas, and cook until tender. Remove bay leaves and serve.

Serves 10 to 12.

—*Barbara Smith*

Hungarian Goulash

Almost any meat can be used in goulash; vegetables or red wine may be added. The one constant is sweet paprika, available from specialty stores.

Ingredients

2 lbs. round steak
¼ cup butter
1½ cups chopped onion
1 cup boiling tomato juice
1 tsp. salt
½ tsp. Hungarian paprika
Cornstarch
6 cups cooked noodles

Directions

Cut beef into 1-inch cubes. Melt butter and brown meat on both sides. Add onion and sauté. Add tomato juice, salt and paprika. Cover and simmer for 1½ to 2 hours. Remove meat from pot and keep warm. To thicken gravy, mix cornstarch with a small amount of cold water and stir rapidly into hot gravy. Bring to a boil and cook until desired consistency is reached. Place meat on noodles and pour thickened gravy over all.

Serves 6.

Italian Steak

Ingredients

2 lbs. round steak
1 cup bread crumbs
1 cup Parmesan cheese
2 eggs, beaten
4 Tbsp. cooking oil
¾ cup chopped onion
2 cups tomato sauce, page 339
¼ cup water
¼ tsp. salt
⅛ tsp. pepper
1 tsp. oregano
¼ lb. mozzarella cheese, grated

Directions

Trim fat from meat and cut into serving-sized pieces. Combine bread crumbs and Parmesan cheese. Dip meat in egg and then in cheese mixture. Brown on both sides in 2 Tbsp. oil.

Sauté onion in remaining oil until tender — about 3 minutes. Stir in tomato sauce, water, seasonings and bring to a boil. Reduce heat and simmer for 10 minutes, stirring occasionally.

Arrange meat in a shallow baking dish, cover with three-quarters of sauce, spread with mozzarella and add remaining sauce.

Bake at 300°F for 30 to 45 minutes, until meat is tender.

Serves 6.

—John & Leone Lackey

Beef Stroganoff

Ingredients

1½ lbs. round steak, cut in narrow strips
¼ cup flour
4 Tbsp. butter
1 onion, diced
½ cup dry red wine
½ lb. mushrooms, sliced
2 green onions, chopped
1 tsp. salt
¼ tsp. chervil
1 cup sour cream

Directions

Dredge meat in flour and brown in butter. Add onion and cook until translucent. Add wine and simmer, covered, for 30 minutes. Add mushrooms, green onions, salt and chervil. Cook 2 to 3 minutes. Stir in sour cream and heat through but do not boil.

Serves 4.

Meat Loaf

Ingredients

2 eggs, slightly beaten
¼ cup milk
¼ cup ketchup
¾ cup onion, minced
¾ tsp. dry mustard
2 tsp. salt
2 cups soft bread crumbs
2 lbs. ground beef

Directions

Combine eggs, milk, ketchup, onion, mustard, salt and bread crumbs. Let stand for 10 minutes. Add beef and mix well. Place in loaf pan.

Bake at 350°F for 35 minutes, then lower heat to 325° and bake 1 hour longer.

Serves 8.

—Joanne Ramsy

Chili for Twenty

Ingredients

3–3½ lbs. lean ground beef
2 medium onions, chopped
2 medium green peppers, chopped
5 stalks celery, chopped
Salt & pepper
Crushed chilies to taste
15 cups cooked kidney beans
2 28-oz. cans tomatoes

Directions

Brown meat, onions, green peppers and celery. Add salt, pepper and chilies and cook for a few minutes. Add kidney beans and tomatoes and simmer for 3 hours. The flavor of this dish improves with 1 or 2 days of aging.

Serves 20.

—Janice Touesnard

Beef & Potato Pie

Ingredients

1 partially baked pie shell
1 large onion, chopped
1 clove garlic, minced
1 stalk celery, chopped
½ cup minced celery leaves
4 Tbsp. oil
2 lbs. ground beef
1½ cups beef stock
2 Tbsp. cornstarch
1 tsp. salt
Dash pepper
Dash Worcestershire sauce
Dash Tabasco sauce
½ tsp. chili powder
1½ cups grated Cheddar cheese
8 potatoes, boiled
1 egg, beaten
½ cup milk
⅛ tsp. salt
1 tsp. butter

Directions

Cook onion, garlic, celery and leaves in oil until tender. Remove from pan. Cook ground beef until browned and drain. Combine beef, vegetables, stock, cornstarch, salt, pepper, Worcestershire sauce, Tabasco sauce, chili powder and cheese. Simmer until thick, then place in pie shell. Whip potatoes until fluffy. Add remaining ingredients and spread over pie. Bake at 350°F for 30 minutes.

Serves 4 to 6.

—Jaine Fraser

Swedish Meatballs

Ingredients

1 lb. ground beef
1 cup soft bread crumbs
½ cup milk
1 egg, well beaten
2 medium onions, finely chopped
2 tsp. salt
⅛ tsp. pepper
½ tsp. nutmeg
Oil
1 cup hot water
1 Tbsp. flour
2 Tbsp. cold water

Directions

Mix beef, bread crumbs, milk, egg, onions, salt, pepper and nutmeg. Form into 1-inch balls. Heat a little oil in skillet and brown balls on all sides. Remove and keep warm.

Add hot water to meat drippings and stir. Mix flour and cold water well and add to drippings. Bring to a boil, stirring until thick. Return meatballs to skillet, cover and cook for 30 minutes, adding more water if necessary.

Serves 4 as a main course, 12 as hors d'oeuvres.

—Peter Suffel

Tomato Meat Loaf

Ingredients
1½ lbs. ground beef
1 egg, beaten
1 cup fresh bread crumbs or wheat germ
1 medium onion, chopped
1¼ tsp. salt
¼ tsp. pepper
1 cup tomato sauce, page 339
2 Tbsp. vinegar
1 cup water
2 Tbsp. brown sugar

Directions

Combine beef, egg, bread crumbs, onion, salt, pepper and ½ cup tomato sauce and mix well. Place in loaf pan and bake at 350°F.

Meanwhile, combine remaining tomato sauce, vinegar, water and brown sugar. Pour over meat loaf after it has cooked for 30 minutes, then bake 1 hour more.

Serves 6.

—Laura Poitras

Pita Tacos

Ingredients
Pita bread for 4
½ lb. ground beef
1 small onion, chopped
½ cup kidney or pinto beans, mashed
½ tsp. ground pepper
Salt
2–3 Tbsp. chili powder
Dash Tabasco sauce
6-oz. can tomato paste
½ lb. grated Cheddar cheese
Lettuce & tomato

Directions

Slit bread to form a pocket and warm in oven. Sauté beef and onion until brown. Drain. Add remaining ingredients except lettuce and tomato. Stuff into bread. Garnish with lettuce and tomato.

Serves 4.

—Melody Scott

New England Boiled Dinner

Ingredients
4 lbs. corned beef brisket
Salt to taste
6 medium-sized carrots, diced
1 turnip, halved
1 small cabbage, quartered
6 medium potatoes, diced

Directions

Cover meat with cold water, bring to a boil, then lower heat and simmer gently for 2 hours.

Skim off fat. Add salt, carrots, turnip, cabbage and potatoes. Continue to cook for 1 more hour.

Serves 6 to 8.

—Shirley Morrish

Beef Enchiladas

Ingredients

Olive oil
1 lb. ground beef
1 onion, chopped
1 green pepper, chopped
1 tsp. parsley flakes
2 cloves garlic, crushed
¾ tsp. chili powder
½ tsp. cumin
½ tsp. dried chilies
Salt & pepper
½ cup kernel corn
1 tomato, chopped
2–4 Tbsp. sour cream
3½ cups tomato sauce, page 339
1 Tbsp. white vinegar
½ tsp. oregano
½ tsp. basil
½ tsp. rosemary
½ tsp. garlic powder
1 tsp. brown sugar
6 tortillas
2 cups grated Cheddar cheese

Directions

In olive oil, fry ground beef, onion and green pepper. Season with ½ tsp. parsley, garlic, ½ tsp. chili powder, ¼ tsp. cumin, chilies and salt and pepper. Add corn, tomato, sour cream and ½ cup tomato sauce. Cook for 15 minutes. Combine remaining ingredients, except for tortillas, to make sauce. Fill tortillas with beef mixture. Cover with sauce and top with cheese. Bake, covered, at 350°F for 45 minutes.

Serves 6.

—*Diane Schoemperlen*

Shepherd's Pie

Ingredients

1 lb. ground beef or 3 cups leftover meat
¼ cup chopped green pepper
¼ cup chopped onion
1 Tbsp. shortening
1 Tbsp. flour
1 tsp. salt
½ tsp. chili powder
Dash pepper
½ cup tomato sauce, page 339
1 cup water
½ cup cooked carrots
½ cup peas
½ cup cooked celery
½ cup chopped mushrooms
3 cups seasoned hot mashed potatoes
Paprika

Directions

Sauté ground beef, green pepper and onion in shortening until meat is browned and pepper tender. Drain off any excess fat. Sprinkle next four ingredients in. Stir in tomato sauce, water, carrots, peas, celery and mushrooms. Combine well and cook until mixture thickens.

Place mixture in 2-quart casserole dish. Top with potatoes and sprinkle with paprika. Place under broiler to brown, or bake at 425°F for 15 minutes.

Serves 6.

—*Mrs. W. Atkins*

Cabbage Rolls with Sour Cream

Ingredients

1 large cabbage
1 cup raw rice
1 lb. ground beef
1 large onion, chopped
8 oz. can stewed tomatoes
1 pint sour cream

Directions

Peel leaves from cabbage and place in boiling water until limp. Drain and remove center vein.

Mix together rice, ground beef and chopped onion. Place about 2 Tbsp. of mixture on each cabbage leaf and roll up, envelope fashion. Line baking dish with remaining leaves. Place cabbage rolls in layers and pour the stewed tomatoes over them. Add tomato juice, if necessary, to cover.

Bake at 350°F for approximately 2 hours. Remove from oven and spread sour cream over rolls. Return dish to oven for 5 minutes, then serve.

Serves 4 to 6.

—Paula Gustafson

Chinese Meatballs

Ingredients

1½ lbs. ground beef
½ cup chopped onion
Salt & pepper
3 Tbsp. soy sauce
2 Tbsp. cornstarch
½ cup pineapple juice
2 Tbsp. brown sugar
1 tsp. soy sauce
2 Tbsp. vinegar
1 Tbsp. cornstarch dissolved in ⅔ cup water
1 cup pineapple chunks

Directions

Combine beef, onion, salt, pepper, 3 Tbsp. soy sauce and 2 Tbsp. cornstarch and shape into balls.

Fry until brown, remove from pan and set aside. Discard all but 2 Tbsp. of drippings.

To drippings add pineapple juice, brown sugar, 1 tsp. soy sauce and vinegar. Thicken with cornstarch mixture. Add pineapple and meatballs and cook until heated through.

Serves 4.

—Velma Hughes

Beef Noodle Bake

Ingredients

1 lb. ground beef
¼ cup butter
2 onions, thinly sliced
1 stalk celery, chopped
1 clove garlic
1½ tsp. salt
⅛ tsp. pepper
1½ tsp. chili powder
6-oz. can tomato paste
1 cup tomato sauce, page 339
2 cups water
2 cups uncooked noodles
1½ cups shredded Cheddar cheese

Directions

Brown meat in butter, then add onions, celery and garlic. Fry until onions are translucent. Add remaining ingredients except for noodles and cheese. Cover and simmer for 30 minutes. Remove garlic.

In a greased 2-quart casserole dish, layer the ingredients: first, half the noodles, then half the meat mixture, and finally one-third of the cheese. Repeat.

Bake at 325°F for 30 to 35 minutes. Sprinkle with remaining cheese and brown under broiler.

Serves 4 to 6.

—Maud Doerksen

Crustless Pizza

Ingredients

1 lb. minced beef
¼ cup bread crumbs
½ tsp. garlic salt
¼ tsp. pepper
⅔ cup milk
⅓ cup minced onion
1½ cups tomato sauce, page 339
¼ tsp. oregano
¾ cup sliced mushrooms
1½ cups grated cheese

Directions

Combine minced beef, bread crumbs, garlic salt, pepper, milk and onion. Flatten mixture into a greased 9-inch square pan. Cover with tomato sauce. Sprinkle with oregano. Distribute mushrooms evenly over sauce, then top with grated cheese.

Bake at 400°F for 30 to 45 minutes.

—Heather Rochon

Cheese Stuffed Meatballs

Ingredients

1½ lbs. medium ground beef
¾ cup fine bread crumbs
1 egg, lightly beaten
1 tsp. salt
1 small onion, minced
4 tsp. Worcestershire sauce
¼ lb. Cheddar cheese, cubed
12 slices bacon, cut in half

Directions

Combine beef, bread crumbs, egg, salt, onion and Worcestershire sauce. Roll into 24 small balls and push a cube of cheese into the center of each one. Wrap a bacon slice around each meatball.

Place on a broiler pan and bake at 375°F for 20 to 25 minutes.

—Margaret Bezanson

Baked Liver

Ingredients

1 lb. liver, sliced
⅓ cup flour
Salt & pepper
½ tsp. dry mustard
1 large onion, sliced
8–10 slices bacon
1½ cups tomato juice
1 Tbsp. ketchup

Directions

Coat liver slices in flour mixed with salt, pepper and mustard. Place in baking dish and cover with sliced onion and bacon. Mix together tomato juice and ketchup and pour over meat. Bake at 300°F for 1 hour.

Serves 3 to 4.

—Albert Sauer

Venetian Liver

Ingredients

1 Tbsp. flour
1 tsp. salt
¼ tsp. pepper
1 tsp. paprika
1 lb. beef liver, cut in strips
1 Tbsp. vegetable oil
2 medium onions, sliced
1 stalk celery, chopped
1 green pepper, cut in strips
1 tomato, cut in wedges
¾ cup beef stock
¼ tsp. basil

Directions

Put flour, salt, pepper and paprika in a bag and coat liver strips by shaking them in the flour mixture. Sauté liver in oil in a large frying pan, about 3 minutes on each side. Remove to serving platter and keep warm in oven.

Sauté onions, celery and green pepper until soft and golden. Add tomato and cook for another 2 minutes. Arrange vegetables on top of liver.

In the frying pan, combine stock and basil, and bring to a boil. Simmer, uncovered, for about 2 minutes. Pour over liver and serve at once.

Serves 4.

—Diane Wilson-Meyer

Orange Pork

Ingredients

2 lbs. pork tenderloin, cut into 6 pieces
½ cup flour
¼ cup oil or bacon drippings
Salt & pepper
2 large onions, chopped
½ lb. mushrooms, sliced
3 Tbsp. flour
2 cups orange juice

Directions

Coat pork with ½ cup flour, then brown in oil.
Sprinkle with salt and lots of pepper. Remove to
shallow casserole dish, reserving pan drippings.
To pan drippings, add onions and cook lightly.
Add mushrooms and stir briefly. Sprinkle with 3
Tbsp. flour and mix. Gradually add orange juice,
stirring constantly, to make a smooth sauce. Taste
and adjust seasoning. Pour sauce over pork and
cover with foil. Bake at 350°F for 1 hour, check-
ing occasionally. Add more juice if necessary.
Serve, garnished with orange segments, strips of
orange rind or fresh mint.

Serves 6.

—Nita Hunton

Jager Schnitzel

*This pork in mushroom and cream sauce dish can
also make use of veal.*

Ingredients

2 10-oz. pork fillets
1 Tbsp. seasoned flour
3 Tbsp. oil
½ cup butter
½ lb. mushrooms, sliced
1 Tbsp. flour
4 Tbsp. chicken stock
4 Tbsp. dry white wine
Pinch grated nutmeg
Salt & pepper
4 Tbsp. whipping cream

Directions

Halve each fillet lengthwise, leaving attached at
one side. Open out and pound until flat and thin.

Toss in seasoned flour, then fry gently in 2
Tbsp. oil and ¼ cup butter until golden brown.

Meanwhile, gently fry mushrooms in remaining butter and oil. Add flour and cook for 2 minutes. Gradually add stock, wine and seasonings,
stirring all the time. Bring to a boil, and cook
gently for 2 to 3 minutes, stirring. Remove from
heat and stir in cream.

Pour sauce over meat.

Serves 4.

—Sheila Bear

Pork Chop & Potato Casserole

Ingredients

4 shoulder pork chops
3 cups sliced potatoes
½ onion, sliced
4 tsp. flour
1 tsp. salt
¼ tsp. pepper
1¼ cups milk

Directions

Brown chops in frying pan. Arrange potatoes and onion in layers in greased casserole dish. Sprinkle with flour and seasonings. Top with chops, add milk and cover.

Bake at 350°F for 45 minutes, or until tender. Uncover and continue baking until brown.

Serves 4.

—Maureen Johnson

Italian Pork Chops

Ingredients

1 egg
3 Tbsp. cold water
3 Tbsp. fine bread crumbs
3 Tbsp. grated Parmesan cheese
4 pork chops
Flour, seasoned with salt & pepper

Directions

Beat egg with cold water. Combine bread crumbs and cheese. Coat chops with flour. Dip them into the egg mixture, then into bread crumbs and cheese. Place on wax paper and let stand for 1 hour. Cook in oil, 10 minutes on each side.

Serves 2 to 4.

—Helen Potts

Curried Pork with Peaches

Ingredients

4–6 lean loin chops
¼ cup butter
1 medium onion, minced
¼ cup flour
1 tsp. salt
1 tsp. curry powder
2 cups milk
1 cup button mushrooms
3 peaches, halved

Directions

Brown chops in small amount of butter. Remove from pan, add remaining butter and sauté onion. Add flour, salt and curry powder to butter and onions to form a paste. Slowly add milk and stir until smooth. Add mushrooms and simmer 2 minutes over low heat. Arrange pork in large shallow pan which has a tightly fitting lid. Place half a peach on each chop and pour curried sauce over. Bake at 350°F, covered, for 45 minutes, then for 15 minutes, uncovered.

Serves 4 to 6.

—Judy Parfitt

Pork Stew with Apples & Potatoes

Ingredients

1 lb. lean pork, cut into 1-inch cubes
2 Tbsp. butter
½ tsp. paprika
¼ tsp. pepper
2 tsp. salt
Dash sage
1 clove garlic, crushed
2 Tbsp. flour
3 onions, sliced
4 large potatoes, cubed
2 apples, cored & cut up
2 Tbsp. dry sherry
1½ cups chicken stock

Directions

Brown pork in heavy pot with butter. Add paprika, pepper, salt, sage and garlic and stir well. Sprinkle with flour and add onions, potatoes, apples, sherry and stock.

Cover and simmer 40 minutes.

Serves 4.

—*Bryanna Clark*

Stuffed Pork Chops

Home butchered pork chops are ideal for this recipe — slice them thick enough to allow for stuffing.

Ingredients

4 thick loin pork chops
1 cup dry bread crumbs
¾ cup finely chopped apple
½ tsp. salt
2 Tbsp. minced onion
¼ tsp. sage
2 Tbsp. melted butter
Salt & pepper

Directions

Combine all ingredients except chops and moisten slightly with a little water. With a sharp knife, cut pockets in the pork chops. Fill loosely with stuffing, then fasten with toothpicks.

Flour the chops and brown well in hot fat in a skillet. Sprinkle each side with salt and pepper. Add ¼ cup water, cover the pan tightly and simmer over low heat until very tender, about 1½ hours.

Serves 4.

—*Sherrie Dick*

Quebec Tourtière

In French Canadian families, this traditional meat pie is eaten hot after midnight mass on Christmas Eve.

Ingredients

Lard pastry for double-crust 9-inch pie
1 lb. lean ground pork
1 medium onion, chopped
Salt & pepper
½ tsp. savory
Pinch ground cloves
¼ cup boiling water

Directions

Mix meat, onions and spices in a saucepan. Add boiling water. Simmer, uncovered, for 20 minutes, stirring occasionally. Skim off any fat.

Roll out half the pastry and line a 9-inch pie plate. Place filling in pie plate and cover with the remaining pastry. Prick with a fork. Bake at 375°F for 30 minutes or until golden.

Serve piping hot topped with homemade tomato ketchup or chili sauce.

Serves 4 to 6.

—*Nicole Chartrand*

Terrine of Pork

Terrine originally meant the dish in which patés were cooked; it has come to mean the paté itself.

Ingredients

3–4 strips bacon
1 lb. lean pork, minced
8 oz. pork sausage meat
4 oz. rolled oats
Zest & juice of 1 lemon
Salt & pepper
½ Tbsp. sage
1 grated onion
1 egg, beaten

Directions

Stretch bacon to line a loaf pan. Combine remaining ingredients. Press meat mixture into pan and level the top.

Cover with foil, set in a large shallow baking dish containing 1 inch of water and cook 1½ hours at 350°F.

Remove from oven and pour off grease but leave loaf in pan. Weight down the top and leave overnight before removing from pan.

Serve cold, sliced.

—*Wendy Wallace*

Sweet & Sour Spareribs

Ingredients
2 lbs. spareribs
⅓ cup flour
1 tsp. dry mustard
⅓ cup soy sauce
1 tsp. vegetable oil
1 clove garlic, crushed
1 inch fresh ginger
⅓ cup vinegar
1½ cups water
½ cup brown sugar
1 tsp. salt
1 small onion, diced

Directions
Chop ribs into small pieces. Mix flour, mustard and soy sauce and marinate ribs in this mixture for 30 minutes to 1 hour.

Heat oil. Add crushed garlic and ginger. Brown ribs, add vinegar, water, sugar, salt and onion. Simmer for 1 hour.

Serves 4 to 6.

—Pieter Timmermans

Stuffed Peppers

There are many ways of preparing stuffed peppers. The fillings can contain everything from pork, as in this recipe, to beef, lamb or seafood. Methods of preparation also vary — these peppers are cooked on top of the stove, but they may also be baked.

Ingredients
2 Tbsp. shortening
¼ cup flour
8-oz. can tomato paste
2 cups stock
Salt
2 small onions, chopped
Celery leaves
¼ cup raw rice
8 green peppers
1 lb. minced pork
Small bunch fresh parsley
1 egg
Salt & pepper
Marjoram

Directions
Heat 1 Tbsp. shortening in a deep saucepan and stir in flour until light brown. Add tomato paste and stir until smooth. Add stock, salt, 1 onion and celery leaves, and bring to a boil. Cook over medium heat, stirring occasionally to keep from burning.

In the meantime, cook rice in boiling water until half done, and cool. Seed and core peppers and wash them thoroughly. Sauté remaining onion in the rest of the shortening. Combine meat, onion, parsley, rice and egg in a bowl. Add salt, pepper and marjoram to taste. Mix well and stuff into peppers.

Place peppers in a large saucepan and pour sauce over them. Bring to a boil, cover and cook over medium heat until done — 25 to 30 minutes.

Serves 4.

—Anton Gross

Tangy Pork

Ingredients
2 medium onions, finely chopped
2 cups cooked pork, cut in cubes
2 medium carrots, cubed
2 cups tomato juice
½ cup chopped cabbage
2 apples, peeled & chopped
¼ cup brown sugar
¼ cup vinegar
½ tsp. salt
½ tsp. pepper
1 tsp. Worcestershire sauce
1 Tbsp. soy sauce

Directions
Fry onions in a small amount of oil until golden. Place in a heavy pot with remaining ingredients. Simmer for 45 minutes on top of stove.

Serves 4.

—Louise R. Taylor

Baked Cottage Roll

Ingredients
4 slices cottage roll
4 Tbsp. brown sugar
1 Tbsp. dry mustard
½ cup orange juice

Directions
Place slices of meat in baking dish. Combine remaining ingredients and pour over meat. Bake at 350°F for 1 hour, basting once or twice.

Serves 4.

—Paula Gustafson

Ham & Rice Skillet

Ingredients
1 cup cooked ham
1 cup sliced mushrooms
½ onion, finely chopped
2 cloves garlic, crushed
⅓ cup chopped raisins
Butter
½ tsp. paprika
½ tsp. Worcestershire sauce
½ tsp. basil
½ tsp. dry mustard
½ tsp. curry powder
Salt & pepper
1 cup cooked rice
2 eggs, slightly beaten

Directions
Sauté ham, mushrooms, onion, garlic and raisins in butter until mushrooms are nearly cooked. Add seasonings and rice. Cook over low heat about 10 minutes. Turn up heat, add eggs and stir-fry until eggs are done.

Serves 2.

—Kynda Fenton

Sausage, Bacon & Tomato Pie

Ingredients

1 lb. sausages
4 slices bacon
1 medium onion, chopped
4 tomatoes
2 Tbsp. flour
Salt & pepper
2 lbs. potatoes, cooked
Butter & milk

Directions

Fry sausages, bacon and onion. Place in greased casserole dish. Fry tomatoes and arrange on top of sausage mixture.

Add flour to remaining fat in pan and cook for a minute or two. Make a thick gravy by adding about 1 cup water. Pour on top of meat and tomatoes.

Mash potatoes, adding milk and butter to taste. Spread on top of casserole and dot with more butter. Bake at 400°F for 20 to 30 minutes until golden brown on top.

Serves 4.

—Sheila Bear

Ham & Potato Casserole

Ingredients

4 or 5 boiled potatoes
¼ cup butter
¼ cup flour
½ tsp. salt
2 cups milk
½ tsp. Worcestershire sauce
2 cups cubed cooked ham
½ cup grated Cheddar cheese

Directions

Slice or dice the potatoes and set aside. In a saucepan, melt the butter and add the flour and salt. Stir until blended. Slowly add the milk, stirring constantly, until smooth and thickened. Stir in Worcestershire sauce, potatoes and ham.

Spoon into 1½-quart baking dish. Sprinkle with cheese. Bake at 350°F for 30 to 40 minutes.

Serves 4 to 5.

—Dianne Orlowski

Chinese Hot Sausages

Ingredients

1 lb. pork sausage links
1 Tbsp. vegetable oil
7½-oz. can tomato sauce
¼ cup brown sugar
1 Tbsp. soy sauce
1 tsp. Worcestershire sauce
¼ tsp. garlic powder
Generous pinch of salt

Directions

Prick sausage skin in several places. Heat oil in a frying pan just large enough to hold the sausages. Add sausages and brown evenly. Pour off fat.

Stir remaining ingredients together and pour into frying pan. Roll sausages until coated with sauce. Cover, reduce heat to medium-low and simmer for 20 minutes. Stir occasionally. Serve in crusty rolls, or with rice or baked potatoes.

Serves 4.

—Diane Wilson-Meyer

Couscous

This is a traditional North African stew (making use of North American vegetables).

Ingredients

3 cups couscous (semolina)
1½ tsp. salt dissolved in 1½ cups cold water
1 Tbsp. oil
½ cup oil
2 lbs. lamb, cut into 2" chunks
3 cups finely chopped onion
1½ Tbsp. salt
1 Tbsp. black pepper
¼ tsp. allspice
2 cinnamon sticks
¾ tsp. turmeric
1 tsp. chopped parsley
4-5 tomatoes, quartered
1 cup raw chickpeas, cooked
1 lb. carrots
1 lb. turnips
1 lb. zucchini
½ lb. pumpkin
4 potatoes, peeled & quartered
1 chili pepper
Handful raisins

Directions

Spread couscous evenly in large, shallow pan. Sprinkle with salted water and 1 Tbsp. oil, then rub grains between fingers, dropping back into pan until water and oil are completely absorbed. Cover with plastic wrap and set aside for 15 minutes.

Meanwhile, in a deep pot, heat ½ cup oil until light haze forms above it. Add meat, onions, salt and pepper. Fry over high heat for 6 to 8 minutes, until browned. Add spices, parsley, tomatoes, chickpeas and 3 cups cold water, and stir until mixture boils. Reduce heat to low and simmer, covered, for 1 hour.

Steam couscous in a large sieve over rapidly boiling water for 20 minutes. Do not cover pot, or couscous will get sticky.

Prepare vegetables: scrape carrots and turnips and cut into 1½-inch lengths. Cut zucchini into quarters. Peel and cut pumpkin into 2-inch pieces. After meat broth has cooked for 1 hour, add carrots and turnips and cook 30 minutes more, adding more water if necessary.

Half an hour before serving time, add potatoes, zucchini, pumpkin, chili and raisins to lamb broth, bring to a boil and simmer. Steam couscous another 30 minutes. Serve lamb mixture over couscous.

Serves 6.

—Ann Simpson

Lamb with Green Peppers

Ingredients
2 lbs. lamb
Salt & pepper
Flour
3 Tbsp. olive oil
2 cloves garlic
1¼ cups white wine
6 green peppers
½ lb. tomatoes
1 bay leaf

Directions

Cut meat into 1-inch pieces, sprinkle with salt and pepper and dust with flour.

Heat oil in wide-mouthed casserole dish, crush in peeled garlic, add meat and fry until lightly browned, stirring frequently. Add wine, and boil rapidly until reduced by a third.

Cut peppers lengthwise into quarters, discard seeds and pith and rinse in cold water. Peel and quarter tomatoes. Add peppers, tomatoes and bay leaf to lamb. Cover and simmer gently for about 45 minutes. Check seasoning and serve.

Serves 4.

—Sheila Bear

Veal Rolls Divan

Ingredients
3 slices bacon
1½ cups dry herbed dressing
¼ cup butter
6 thin veal steaks, pounded
Salt
1 Tbsp. oil
2 heads broccoli, chopped & parboiled
½ cup chicken stock
1 cup cream of mushroom sauce (page 129)
½ cup cooked shrimp

Directions

Cook bacon until crisp and drain. Combine dressing and butter and crumble bacon into mixture.

Sprinkle veal with salt. Place ⅓ cup dressing on each steak, roll and tie securely. Heat oil in skillet and brown veal. Arrange veal and broccoli in greased, shallow baking dish.

Pour chicken stock over casserole, cover and bake at 350°F for 1 hour. Combine mushroom sauce with shrimp in saucepan and heat through. To serve, remove ties from meat and pour sauce over casserole.

Serves 6.

—Tracy Cane

Barbecue Sauce

Ingredients

5½-oz. can tomato paste
½ cup vinegar
1½ Tbsp. dry mustard
3 Tbsp. corn syrup
½ tsp. garlic powder
1 tsp. onion powder
½ tsp. celery salt
⅛ tsp. cayenne pepper
½ tsp. salt
1 Tbsp. brown sugar

Directions

Mix all ingredients and store in covered container in refrigerator.

—Angela Denholm

Meat Coating

This recipe provides a healthy, homemade alternative to commercial Shake 'n' Bake.

Ingredients

½ cup wheat germ
½ cup corn meal
1 cup triticale flour
Salt & pepper

Directions

Mix until well blended and store in covered container until ready to use.

—Angela Denholm

Brown Sugar Mustard

Ingredients

½ cup lemon juice
¼ cup corn oil
⅛ tsp. Tabasco sauce
½ tsp. coarse salt
¼ tsp. black pepper
¼ tsp. marjoram, crushed
1½ cups well-packed brown sugar
4 oz. dry mustard

Directions

Combine lemon juice, oil, Tabasco sauce, salt, pepper, marjoram and brown sugar in blender. Cover and blend at high speed for about 12 seconds, or until the ingredients are thoroughly mixed.

Add about half of the mustard, cover and blend at medium speed for 10 seconds, or until smooth. Repeat with remaining mustard, adding it in 3 parts.

Spoon mustard into jars and seal with plastic wrap.

—V. Alice Hughes

Steak Sauce

Ingredients

6 qts. tomatoes, cooked & strained
2 lbs. brown sugar
1 lb. granulated sugar
1 cup flour
2 tsp. ginger
2 tsp. cinnamon
Cayenne pepper
2 tsp. ground cloves
2 Tbsp. dry mustard
¼ cup salt

Directions

Combine all ingredients and mix well. Boil 20 minutes, stirring constantly. Pack in hot sterilized jars and seal. Serve with hot or cold meats or as a barbecue marinade.

—Marilyn Fuller

Wiener Schnitzel

Ingredients

6 veal scallops
Salt & pepper
2 eggs, slightly beaten
Flour
3 Tbsp. bacon drippings
Juice of 1 lemon
1 Tbsp. flour
1 cup sour cream
Lemon slices

Directions

Sprinkle veal with salt and pepper. Dip into beaten eggs then into flour. Brown on both sides in hot bacon drippings, then cover and cook slowly until chops are tender — about 1 hour. Sprinkle with lemon juice and arrange on hot platter.

Blend 1 Tbsp. flour with fat in pan, add sour cream and cook for 3 minutes, stirring constantly. Season with salt and pepper and serve with chops. Garnish with lemon slices.

Serves 6.

—Lorraine Murphy

Korean Vegetables & Beef

Ingredients

3–4 Tbsp. soy sauce
1 Tbsp. oil
1 tsp. honey
1 clove garlic, crushed
½ lb. beef, thinly sliced
Sesame oil
1 onion, chopped
2½ cups chopped assorted vegetables (green beans, zucchini, cauliflower, broccoli)
3 Tbsp. crushed sesame seeds

Directions

Combine soy sauce, oil, honey and garlic. Marinate beef in this for 15 minutes.

Heat oil in wok. Stir-fry drained beef and onion. Add vegetables and fry until bright in color. Add sesame seeds and leftover marinade. Heat through and serve with rice.

Serves 3 to 4.

—Gwen Miller

Steak with Green Peppers

Ingredients

1½ cups raw rice, cooked
1 lb. lean steak
1 Tbsp. paprika
2 Tbsp. butter
2 cloves garlic, crushed
⅛ tsp. cayenne
½ tsp. salt
1½ cups beef stock
1 cup sliced green onions
2 green peppers, cut into strips
2 Tbsp. cornstarch
¼ cup water
½ cup soy sauce
2 large tomatoes, cut into eighths

Directions

While rice is cooking, thinly slice steak across grain. Sprinkle meat with paprika and let sit for a few minutes. Brown in butter in large skillet. Add garlic, cayenne, salt and beef stock. Cover and simmer for 30 minutes. Add green onions and green peppers, cover and cook for 5 more minutes. Blend together cornstarch, water and soy sauce and stir into meat. Cook, stirring, until stock is clear and thickened — about 2 minutes. Add tomatoes and serve over rice.

Serves 3.

—Janice Hyatt

Greek Slipper Steak

Ingredients

4½ lb. steaks
8 Tbsp. chopped, lightly toasted almonds
4 Tbsp. chopped stuffed olives
2 tsp. minced hot Greek pickled pepper
1 tsp. minced garlic
½ tsp. cinnamon
Salt & pepper
Butter
Red wine
Onion slices

Directions

Slice a pocket in one side of each steak, cutting to within ¼ inch of the edges. Combine remaining ingredients, except butter, wine and onion slices, and stuff steaks. Stitch opening shut.

Sear steaks in butter in frying pan. When cooked, place on warm platter in oven. Deglaze pan with a little red wine. Add onion slices and sauté briefly. Garnish steaks with onion and spoon pan juices over them.

Serves 4.

—Elizabeth Ballantyne

Bulkoki

Ingredients

5 tsp. soy sauce
7 Tbsp. oil
3 Tbsp. sherry
3 cloves garlic, crushed
½ cup chopped onion
1 Tbsp. sugar
2 Tbsp. peppercorns, coarsely ground
¼ cup chopped scallions
2 tsp. dill seed
1-1½ lbs. beef, cut into thin strips

Directions

Combine soy sauce, 5 Tbsp. oil, sherry, garlic, onion, sugar, peppercorns, scallions and dill seed and marinate beef in this, covered, for 2 to 3 hours. Sauté in remaining 2 Tbsp. oil over high heat for 3 to 4 minutes.

Serves 4.

—Sheila Livingston

Steak Teriyaki

Ingredients

¾ cup oil
¼ cup soy sauce
¼ cup honey
2 Tbsp. cider vinegar
2 Tbsp. finely chopped green onion
1 large clove garlic, chopped
1½ tsp. ground ginger
2 lbs. flank steak

Directions

Mix together oil, soy sauce, honey, vinegar, onion, garlic and ginger and pour over meat. Let marinate, turning occasionally, for several hours.

Broil or cook over coals, basting with marinade.

Serves 4.

—Michèle Raymond

Beef and Pork Curry

Ingredients

4 Tbsp. oil
1½ lbs. round steak, cubed
1½ lbs. pork butt or shoulder, cubed
2 onions, peeled & chopped
3 cloves garlic, crushed
2 potatoes, peeled & cubed
4 Tbsp. curry
2 tsp. salt

Directions

Sauté beef and pork in oil until browned.

Add onions and garlic and cook until soft. Add curry powder and salt and continue cooking, stirring frequently, for one minute. Add potatoes and cover with water. Let simmer on low heat with lid slightly ajar for 1½ to 2 hours. Serve on bed of rice.

Serves 6.

—Terry Pereira

Italian Steak

Ingredients

3 lbs. steaks
¾ cup bread crumbs
1 Tbsp. oregano
1 egg, beaten
Seasoned flour
Oil
28-oz. can tomatoes
1 green pepper, chopped
1 clove garlic, minced
1 large onion, thinly sliced
1 cup sliced green olives
1 cup sliced black olives
1 lb. mushrooms, sliced
Chopped capers

Directions

Cut steak into serving-sized pieces. Combine bread crumbs and oregano. Dip meat in egg, flour, egg again, then bread crumbs. Brown in oil in heavy skillet.

Blend remaining ingredients together. Place meat and sauce in alternating layers in greased casserole dish. Bake at 350°F for 1 hour.

Serves 6.

—*Marni Olson*

Asian-Style Beef Pot Roast

Ingredients

4 lb. roast of beef
1 tsp. garlic powder
½ tsp. dry mustard
¼ tsp. pepper
2 Tbsp. oil
¾ cup water
3 Tbsp. honey
2 Tbsp. soy sauce
1 Tbsp. vinegar
1½ tsp. celery seed
½ tsp. ginger
1 Tbsp. cornstarch, dissolved in 2 Tbsp. water

Directions

Rub roast with mixture of garlic powder, mustard and pepper. Heat a 6-quart roasting pan, add oil and brown roast well on all sides. Combine water, honey, soy sauce, vinegar, celery seed and ginger and pour over meat. Cover and roast at 325°F for 2½ hours. Transfer roast to heated platter and thicken gravy with cornstarch-water mixture.

Serves 8.

—*Midge Denault*

Crab Apple Pot Roast

Ingredients

3 Tbsp. flour
1½ tsp. salt
¼ tsp. pepper
¼ tsp. allspice
4 lb. beef pot roast
2 Tbsp. butter
14-oz. jar spiced crab apples
2 Tbsp. lemon juice
¼ cup raisins

Directions

Combine 1 Tbsp. flour, salt, pepper and allspice. Dredge meat in mixture. In heavy saucepan, heat butter and brown meat on all sides.

Drain crab apples, reserving juice. Add enough water to juice to make 1 cup, then add to meat along with lemon juice. Cover and simmer for 3 hours or until tender. About 15 minutes before meat is done, add crab apples and raisins.

To serve, place meat and crab apples on platter. Blend remaining 2 Tbsp. flour with ½ cup cold water and stir into liquid. Let boil for a few minutes to thicken and serve with meat.

Serves 8.

—Mary Hewson

African Beef

Ingredients

2 lbs. stewing beef
2 large onions, sliced
1½ cups chopped celery
10-oz. can tomato paste
19-oz. can tomatoes
¼ tsp. pepper
⅓ cup brown sugar
1 tsp. ginger
1 tsp. Worcestershire sauce
¼ cup vinegar
Garlic, mushrooms & green peppers to taste

Directions

Brown meat. Add remaining ingredients. Cover and bake for 3 hours at 325°F. Serve with rice.

Serves 6.

—Valerie Moore

Texas Chili

Ingredients

2 Tbsp. oil
3 lbs. boneless chuck, cut into 1-inch cubes
2–3 cloves garlic, chopped
4–6 Tbsp. chili powder
2 tsp. cumin
3 Tbsp. flour
1 Tbsp. oregano
3 cups beef stock
Salt & pepper
Sour cream
Lime wedges

Directions

Heat oil in 4-quart pot over medium heat. Add beef and cook, stirring frequently, until meat changes color but is not browned. Lower heat and stir in garlic. Combine chili powder, cumin and flour and sprinkle over meat, stirring until meat is evenly coated. Crumble oregano over meat. Add 2 cups stock and stir until liquid is well blended. Add salt and pepper and bring to a boil, stirring occasionally.

Reduce heat and simmer, partially covered, for 1½ to 2 hours, stirring from time to time. Add remaining 1 cup stock and cook for 30 minutes longer. Cool thoroughly, cover and refrigerate overnight. Reheat and serve with sour cream and lime wedges.

Serves 8.

—Joan Hampton

Beef and Mushroom Ragoût

This French-style ragoût is as easy to make as an everyday beef stew, but is impressive enough for an elegant dinner. Serve with a tossed salad of mixed greens topped with finely chopped hard-boiled eggs, warm French bread, and complete the meal with a crème caramel.

Ingredients

3 Tbsp. oil
2 lbs. stewing beef
2 large onions, chopped
1 cup sherry or red wine
1 cup water
2 large carrots, finely sliced
1 bay leaf
2 cloves garlic, whole & unpeeled
1 lb. mushrooms, finely sliced
Salt & pepper
4 cups cooked rice

Directions

In a large, deep pan, heat oil and cook meat over medium-high heat, removing pieces as they become well-browned. In same pan, brown onion. Return meat to pan, add sherry or red wine and boil gently until alcohol has evaporated. Add water, carrots, bay leaf and garlic. Cover and simmer for 2 to 3 hours until meat is tender. Add mushrooms and simmer for 15 more minutes. To thicken, uncover and bring to a boil. Remove garlic and bay leaf and adjust seasoning with salt and pepper.

To serve, place cooked rice around the outside of a large platter. Remove the meat and vegetables from the pot with a slotted spoon and place in the center of the platter. Serve the sauce in a gravy boat.

Serves 4.

—Sandra James-Mitchell

Sicilian Meat Roll

Ingredients

2 eggs, beaten
½ cup tomato juice
¾ cup soft bread crumbs
2 Tbsp. chopped parsley
½ tsp. oregano
¼ tsp. salt
¼ tsp. pepper
¼ tsp. garlic powder
2 lbs. ground beef
4-6 oz. thinly sliced ham
6 oz. sliced mozzarella cheese

Directions

In a bowl, combine eggs and tomato juice. Stir in bread crumbs, parsley, oregano, salt, pepper and garlic. Add ground beef and mix well. On wax paper, pat meat into an 8" x 10" rectangle. Arrange ham slices on top of meat, leaving a small margin around edges.

Reserve 1 slice of cheese. Tear up remaining cheese and sprinkle over ham. Starting from short end, carefully roll up meat, using paper to lift. Seal edges and ends. Place roll, seam side down, in a 9" x 13" baking pan.

Bake at 350°F for about 1¼ hours. Center of roll will be pink due to ham. Cut reserved cheese slice into 4 triangles, overlap atop meat and return to oven until cheese melts.

Serves 8.

—Patricia A. Leahy

Roast Pork Stuffed with Apples & Prunes

Ingredients

1 onion, chopped
1 apple, chopped
½ cup chopped, pitted prunes
3 Tbsp. apple butter
1 clove garlic, chopped
½ tsp. thyme
½ tsp. rosemary
Pepper
4 lb. pork loin roast, deboned

Directions

Mix together onion, apple, prunes, apple butter, garlic and seasonings. Stuff the roast with this mixture, place in roasting pan and bake at 325°F for 2 hours.

Serves 6 to 8.

—Lynn Biscott

Stuffed Ham

Ingredients

12 lb. ham
2 heads cabbage
2 lbs. kale
2 large onions
1½ small red peppers
Salt & pepper

Directions

Wash ham. Cut up vegetables, mix and season to taste. Parboil, saving water for cooking ham.

Make deep slits across top and down sides of ham with sharp knife. Stuff vegetables into slits, piling any leftover mixture on top of the ham.

Sew ham in cheesecloth to hold dressing in place and cook slowly in vegetable water until meat is tender.

—Judy Lord

Apple Meat Loaf

This is a very moist meat loaf with an excellent flavor — a good standby for a cold winter night's supper.

Loaf Ingredients

2 cooking apples
1½ lbs. ground beef
1½ cups soft bread crumbs
1 onion, finely chopped
Salt & pepper
1 tsp. Worcestershire sauce
2 eggs

Topping Ingredients

⅓ cup ketchup
2 Tbsp. maple syrup

Directions

Peel, core and grate apples and combine with ground beef, onion, bread crumbs and seasonings. Beat eggs and add to meat mixture. Press into loaf pan. Combine topping ingredients and spoon over the meat loaf. Bake at 325°F for 1¼ hours.

Serves 4 to 6.

—Linda Plant

East Indian Meatballs

Ingredients

1 large onion, chopped (reserve 2 Tbsp. for meat)
2 Tbsp. butter
½ tsp. cinnamon
½ tsp. mace
¾ tsp. curry
1 tsp. whole peppers in cheesecloth bag
⅓ cup seedless raisins
¼ cup slivered blanched almonds
1½ cups water
1 tsp. salt
½ cup soft bread crumbs
¼ cup milk
1 lb. ground beef
2 Tbsp. chopped parsley
1 egg
1 tsp. Worcestershire sauce
¼ tsp. pepper

Directions

In a large skillet, cook onion in butter until lightly browned. Add cinnamon, mace, curry, peppers, raisins, almonds and water and simmer for 15 minutes. Remove pepper bag.

Mix remaining ingredients and shape into 1-inch balls. Brown on all sides in a skillet, using a small amount of fat. Pour off excess fat and add sauce to meatballs. Cover and simmer for 20 minutes.

Serves 4.

—Anita Cunningham

Ground Beef & Squash

Ingredients

3 acorn squash, cut in half & cleaned
2 lbs. ground beef
2 eggs
2 tsp. lemon juice
Salt & pepper
2 Tbsp. grated onion
1½ cups cooked rice
6 Tbsp. chili sauce

Directions

Bake squash at 250°F for 30 minutes. Combine remaining ingredients, spoon into squash and bake for another 40 minutes.

Serves 6.

—Susan Boehm

Boboti

Ingredients

1 medium onion, minced
2 Tbsp. oil
½ tsp. nutmeg
½ tsp. cinnamon
1 tsp. coriander
1 tsp. cumin
1 tsp. garam masala
1 tsp. turmeric
1½ lbs. ground beef
¼–½ cup water
¼ cup raisins
Dash nutmeg

Directions

Sauté onion in oil. Add spices and stir into onions. Add ground beef and cook until browned, stirring frequently. Stir in water and raisins. Turn into greased casserole dish. Smooth surface and sprinkle with nutmeg.

Bake at 350°F for 15 to 20 minutes.

Serves 6.

—Pamela Morninglight

Egg Dumplings

These dumplings can be added in the last few minutes of cooking in almost any stew.

Ingredients

1⅔ cups flour
3 tsp. baking powder
½ tsp. salt
1 Tbsp. butter
½ cup milk
1 egg, beaten

Directions

Blend dry ingredients. Rub in butter with fingers, then stir in milk and egg and drop by large spoonfuls into stewpot, cover and simmer for 12 to 15 minutes. Makes 8 dumplings.

—Robert Brandon

Pepper Steak Patties

Ingredients

1 lb. lean ground beef
1 Tbsp. cracked peppercorns
½ tsp. salt
1 cup sliced mushrooms
½ cup chopped onion
2 Tbsp. butter
1 tsp. Worcestershire sauce
2 Tbsp. lemon juice
2 Tbsp. Cognac

Directions

Shape beef into 4 patties. Spread peppercorns on wax paper, then press patties into pepper until both sides are coated. Sprinkle salt over bottom of heavy skillet. Set over medium-high heat and add mushrooms and onions. Cook patties to suit individual preference.

In a separate pan, heat butter, Worcestershire sauce and lemon juice. Pour off drippings from meat, pour butter mixture over meat and flambé with Cognac. Serve.

Serves 4.

—Nan & Phil Millette

Roast Pork & Red Cabbage

Ingredients

¼ lb. bacon, cut into strips 1½ inches long
   & ¼ inch across
½ cup thinly sliced carrots
1 cup sliced onion
3 Tbsp. butter
3 cups red cabbage, cut into ½-inch slices
2 cups dry red wine or beer
2 cups beef stock
2 apples, diced
2 cloves garlic, crushed
Salt & pepper
3 lbs. deboned & rolled pork loin, tenderloin
   or shoulder end

Directions

Place bacon in saucepan and cover with cold water. Bring to a boil, simmer for 10 minutes and drain. Sauté carrots, onion, bacon and butter in covered pot for 10 minutes. Add cabbage, wine or beer, stock, apples, garlic and salt and pepper and blend; cover and bake at 325°F for 3 hours, stirring occasionally.

After 3 hours, brown the pork loin in small amount of fat and place on cabbage. Cover and return to oven for 2 hours. Remove pork and let sit, covered with foil, for 15 to 20 minutes. Place cabbage on a warm platter, slice pork and arrange on cabbage. Serve with cooking juices in a gravy boat.

Serves 6.

—Jeff Greenberg

Pork and Apple Pie

Ingredients

Pastry for double 9-inch pie shell
3 cups diced, cooked pork
5 tart apples, peeled, cored & thinly sliced
1-2 medium onions, thinly sliced
3 Tbsp. flour
¼ tsp. salt
2 Tbsp. brown sugar
½ tsp. cinnamon
½ tsp. nutmeg
1 Tbsp. lemon juice
Milk

Directions

Line pie plate with one-half of pastry.

Combine pork, apples and onions in a large bowl. Mix flour, sugar, salt, cinnamon and nutmeg. Toss together pork and flour mixtures with lemon juice. Spoon into shell. Cover with second half of pastry, flute edges and cut slits in top for steam. Brush with milk.

Bake at 425°F for 45 to 60 minutes.

Serves 4 to 6.

—Janie Zwicker

Apple Glazed Roast Pork

Ingredients

4–5 lbs. pork roast
1 Tbsp. butter
1 small onion, grated
1 Tbsp. cornstarch
1 Tbsp. brown sugar
1 Tbsp. soy sauce
½ tsp. ginger
1 cup apple juice

Directions

Place pork fat side up on rack in shallow roasting pan. Score fat layer in diamonds and roast, uncovered, at 325°F for 1 hour.

While roast is in oven, prepare glaze. Melt butter in saucepan and sauté onion until soft. Thoroughly mix together cornstarch, brown sugar, soy sauce, ginger and juice. Pour into pan with sautéed onions and cook over low heat, stirring constantly, until thick. Brush part of glaze over meat, then continue brushing every 15 minutes for the next hour, or until meat is done.

Serves 8.

—Donna Sopha

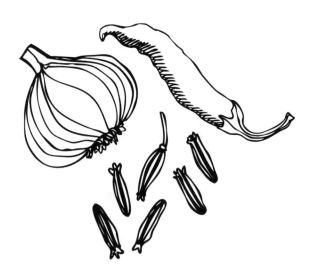

Pork Cubes in Apple Cider

Ingredients

¼ cup flour
½ tsp. salt
¼ tsp. pepper
¼ tsp. paprika
Garlic powder
2 lbs. pork, cubed
¼ cup butter
2 cups chopped onion
2 cups unsweetened apple cider

Directions

Mix flour and seasonings in paper bag. Add pork a few cubes at a time and shake to coat. Melt butter in skillet and brown cubes a single layer at a time, placing in an ovenproof casserole dish as they brown. Cook onions until limp but not brown and add to pork cubes. Pour cider over all, cover and bake at 350°F until pork is tender — 1 to 1½ hours.

Serves 4.

—Mary Lennox

Mediterranean Pork Chops

Ingredients

6 large pork butt chops
6 Tbsp. flour
½ tsp. salt
¼ tsp. coarsely ground pepper
¼ tsp. oregano
2 oz. tomato paste
12 leaves fresh sage
2 oz. dry white wine
3 cloves garlic, minced

Directions

Remove fat from chops and set aside. Mix together flour, salt, pepper and oregano and coat chops with this mixture. Let sit on a rack for 1 hour to help flour adhere.

Place scraps of fat in large shallow pan which can be tightly covered and heat them until bottom of pan is covered with a thin film of liquid fat. Discard scraps.

Put chops in pan and brown lightly on both sides. Spread tomato paste evenly on top of each chop. Add water to cover bottom of pan and simmer meat for 45 minutes with the lid on the pan. Remove lid, place 2 sage leaves on each chop, add wine and place garlic on bottom of pan. Bring to a boil, then cover, decrease heat, and simmer for an additional 5 minutes. Discard sage and garlic and serve immediately.

Serves 6.

—Glenn McMichael

Pork Chops with Peaches

Ingredients

4 pork chops
¼ cup brown sugar
1 tsp. ginger
1 large onion, sliced
1 cup water
2 Tbsp. soy sauce
¼ cup cider vinegar
1 Tbsp. cornstarch, dissolved in cold water
2 fresh peaches, peeled & sliced

Directions

Brown pork chops in hot pan. Sprinkle sugar and ginger over chops, top with onion slices and cover with water, soy sauce and vinegar. Cover tightly and simmer for 35 minutes, turning chops once. Thicken sauce with cornstarch mixture, add peaches and heat until warm.

Serves 4.

—Judy Wuest

Leeks with Ham and Cheese

Ingredients

12 small leeks, cleaned
½ lb. cooked ham, chopped
½ cup grated Swiss cheese
¾ cup whipping cream
Salt & pepper

Directions

Simmer leeks in water for 15 minutes and drain. Arrange in greased baking dish. Sprinkle with salt and pepper and cover with chopped ham. Sprinkle with cheese and pour cream over all.

Bake at 400°F for 10 to 15 minutes.

Serves 4.

—Denyse Fournier

Steamed Spareribs with Black Bean Sauce

Ingredients

½ lbs. spareribs, cut into
2"–3" pieces
4–5 Tbsp. cooked black beans
6–10 cloves garlic
1 tsp. salt
3 Tbsp. sherry
3 Tbsp. water
3 Tbsp. vinegar
2 Tbsp. oil
4 Tbsp. sugar
6 spring onions, chopped into 1-inch pieces

Directions

Boil ribs for 5 minutes and drain. Blend remaining ingredients except onions and pour over ribs. Marinate for 4 hours.

Place ribs in steamer, add onions and steam for 45 minutes.

Serves 6 as an appetizer or 3 to 4 as a meal.

—Harvey Griggs

Favorite Pork Spareribs

The contributor of this recipe says, "This has been a favorite in our family for 30 years. In fact, each of my married children has sent home for the recipe."

Ingredients

4 lbs. pork spareribs, cut up
1 large onion, minced
1 clove garlic, crushed
3 Tbsp. butter
2 Tbsp. cider vinegar
2 Tbsp. orange juice
6 Tbsp. brown sugar
3 tsp. salt
1 Tbsp. mustard
1 tsp. cinnamon
4 Tbsp. Worcestershire sauce
2 cups ketchup
1½ cups diced celery
1 cup water
8-oz. can crushed pineapple

Directions

Cover ribs with water, boil for 15 minutes and drain. In another pan, simmer onion and garlic in butter until tender. Add remaining ingredients and cook for 5 to 10 minutes. Add ribs and cook gently until meat is tender — about 1 hour.

Place ribs in broiling pan, cover with sauce and broil until brown.

Serves 4 to 6.

—Ritta Wright

Spareribs Cantonese

Ingredients

4 lbs. pork spareribs
1 cup orange marmalade
½ cup soy sauce
½ tsp. garlic powder
½ tsp. ginger
Orange slices

Directions

Cut ribs into serving-sized pieces. Arrange in a rectangular casserole dish. Brown at 400°F for 15 minutes. Drain off fat.

In a bowl, combine marmalade, soy sauce, garlic powder, ginger and ¾ cup water. Mix well. Pour over ribs, cover casserole dish and bake at 350°For 1 hour, or until the ribs are done to your liking, basting occasionally.

Place ribs on serving dish and garnish with orange slices.

Serves 4 to 6.

—Irene Louden

Zucchini Pork Bake

Ingredients

1 lb. ground pork
½ tsp. garlic powder
3 Tbsp. Parmesan cheese
½ cup yogurt
4 small zucchini, sliced
½ lb. mozzarella cheese, grated

Directions

Fry pork until browned, drain. Add garlic, Parmesan cheese and yogurt.

Place half of zucchini in shallow greased pan, cover with meat and top with remaining zucchini. Cover with grated mozzarella cheese. Bake at 375°F for 20 to 25 minutes.

Serves 4.

—Linda Townsend

Sausage & Spinach Pie

Ingredients

Pastry for 9-inch pie shell
1 lb. sausage meat, cooked
3 large eggs
1 lb. spinach, cooked, drained & chopped
½ lb. mozzarella cheese, grated
¼ cup cottage cheese
¼ tsp. salt
⅛ tsp. pepper
¼ tsp. garlic powder
½ tsp. oregano

Directions

Combine all ingredients and mix well. Pour into unbaked pie shell and bake at 375°F for 1 hour.

Serves 4 to 6.

—J. Kristine MacDonald

Lecho

This is a Czechoslovakian meal in itself and is delicious served with a hearty rye bread.

Ingredients

2 lbs. onions, finely chopped
Oil
2 lbs. green peppers, finely chopped
2 lbs. tomatoes, chopped
Salt & pepper
1½ lbs. Ukrainian sausage
1 egg, beaten

Directions

Place onions in large pot with enough oil to prevent sticking and cook until transparent. Add green peppers and cook until color changes. Add tomatoes and cook for 1 hour. Season with salt and pepper. Cut sausage into ¼-inch rounds and add. Cook 30 minutes longer. Just before serving time, stir in the beaten egg to thicken.

Serves 6.

—Faye Hugar

Orange Glazed Ham

Ingredients

4–5 lbs. ham
1 Tbsp. grated orange rind
1 cup orange juice
¼ cup brown sugar
1½ Tbsp. soy sauce
½ tsp. ginger
1 Tbsp. cornstarch

Directions

Bake ham on rack in roasting pan at 325°F for 45 minutes. Remove excess fat and any rind with a sharp knife, leaving ¼ inch fat layer. Score fat in a diamond pattern. Combine orange rind, juice, sugar, soy sauce and ginger in small bowl. Remove and reserve ⅔ cup for orange sauce.

Brush ham with remaining glaze. Continue roasting, brushing with glaze every 15 minutes for an hour longer. Remove roast from oven to a heated platter.

For orange sauce, combine reserved glaze with ⅔ cup water and the cornstarch in a small saucepan. Heat, stirring constantly, until mixture thickens and bubbles. Cook for 1 minute. Slice ham and serve with sauce.

Serves 6 to 8.

—Valerie Gillis

Bacon Wrapped Chutney Bananas

Ingredients

2 bananas
1 lb. bacon
Lemon juice
1 cup mango chutney

Directions

Slice bananas into halves lengthwise, then into quarters crosswise. Dip bacon in lemon juice, roll around a piece of banana and secure with toothpick. Repeat until all banana pieces are used up.

Place on cookie sheet and bake at 375°F for 20 minutes. Remove from oven, dip into chutney and bake for another 10 to 15 minutes.

Serves 4 as an appetizer.

—Joanne McInveen

Danish Liver Paste

Ingredients

1½ lbs. pork liver
2–3 large onions
1 lb. bacon fat
½ cup butter
½ cup flour
Milk
Salt & pepper
2 eggs

Directions

Grind liver, then onions, then bacon fat to desired smoothness. Melt butter, add flour and stir until smooth. Add milk to make a thick gravy. Add salt and pepper and eggs. Stir in meat, mix well and bake in a loaf pan at 325°F for 1¼ hours.

Makes 3 to 4 cups.

—Mary Alice Self

Roast Mustard Lamb

Ingredients

4 lb. leg of lamb
12 Tbsp. oil
1 Tbsp. soy sauce
4 Tbsp. mustard
¼ tsp. garlic powder
½ tsp. rosemary

Directions

Trim away most of the fat from the leg of lamb and place the lamb in a shallow roasting pan. Mix together remaining ingredients and spread over the surface of the leg. Leave at room temperature for about an hour, then roast at 325°F for 20 to 30 minutes a pound, or until an internal temperature of 175° is reached.

Serves 6.

—Adele Dueck

Honey Soy Leg of Lamb

Ingredients

6 lb. leg of lamb
Salt & pepper
5–6 Tbsp. liquid honey
4–6 Tbsp. soy sauce

Directions

Remove fat and membrane from lamb. Liberally salt and pepper the meat, rubbing in well. Place leg of lamb on a rack in roasting pan and apply honey as a glaze. Add 1 inch of water to pan and roast, uncovered, at 425°F for 30 minutes. Reduce heat to 350° and pour 2 Tbsp. soy sauce over lamb. Repeat every 45 minutes. Total roasting time is 2½ hours. Remove lamb to platter and keep warm.

Remove any fat from sauce in roasting pan and serve sauce with lamb.

Serves 8.

—Lynne Zahariuk

Pineapple Soy Lamb Chops

Ingredients

1 small onion, chopped
2 cloves garlic, chopped
⅓ cup oil
½ cup soy sauce
⅓ cup pineapple juice
Pineapple rings
2 Tbsp. brown sugar
6 2-inch lamb chops

Directions

Combine onion, garlic, oil, soy sauce, pineapple juice, pineapple and sugar and marinate meat for at least 4 hours, turning once. Broil for 12 minutes on each side. Serve topped with pineapple rings.

Serves 2 to 3.

—Barbara Littlejohn

Herb Marinade for Lamb

Ingredients

2 Tbsp. oil
1 Tbsp. lemon juice
1 clove garlic, crushed
½ tsp. marjoram
½ tsp. rosemary
½ tsp. thyme
½ tsp. sage
½ tsp. mint
½ tsp. pepper
½ tsp. salt

Directions

Combine all ingredients and mix thoroughly. This can be brushed on a leg of lamb or added to a marinade for cubed lamb. Let sit at room temperature for at least 30 minutes.

—Trudi Keillor

Mutton Curry

This dish is particularly tasty served over rice, with side dishes of yogurt, almonds, coconut and sliced bananas.

Ingredients

3 Tbsp. oil
2 onions, chopped
2 cloves garlic, chopped
1½ lbs. mutton, cut into small pieces
Flour
2 cups boiling water
¼ cup stewed tomatoes
2 tsp. salt
2 tsp. curry
1½ tsp. cumin
1 tsp. ginger
Pepper
1 apple, peeled & diced
½ cup raisins

Directions

Heat oil in heavy pot and brown onions and garlic. Dredge meat in flour and brown. Add boiling water, tomato, salt, curry, cumin, ginger, pepper, apple and raisins. Simmer for 2 hours.

Serves 4.

—Jeannie Rosenberg

Tenderloin with Oyster Sauce

Ingredients

½ cup beer
½ cup oil
2 cloves garlic, chopped
1 medium onion, chopped
½ tsp. dry mustard
1 large bay leaf
Pepper
2 small lamb tenderloins
Oil for cooking
2 stalks celery, diagonally sliced
½ cup sliced mushrooms
½ cup sliced green pepper
2 scallions, chopped
2 Tbsp. oyster sauce
3 Tbsp. water
1 Tbsp. cornstarch
Pepper

Directions

Combine beer, oil, garlic, onion, mustard, bay leaf and pepper. Cut meat in ¼-inch slices and marinate for 1 hour in above mixture, then drain.

Heat oil in skillet and add meat. Fry until browned, then add vegetables and fry until celery is softened. Combine last 4 items and add to meat, bring back to boil and serve over brown rice.

Serves 3 to 4.

—Charlene Skidmore

Moussaka

Of Greek origin, the delicate flavor of the eggplant mingling with the succulence of the spring lamb makes this dish well worth the work.

Ingredients

1½ lbs. potatoes
2 medium eggplants
Olive oil
4 large tomatoes, peeled & thinly sliced
Basil
1 large white onion, thinly sliced
1 lb. ground spring lamb
Mint
Garlic powder
2 Tbsp. butter
2 Tbsp. flour
1 cup milk, heated
½ cup grated Emmenthal cheese

Directions

Peel potatoes, slice ¼-inch thick and parboil for 10 minutes. Drain and place half in bottom of greased casserole dish.

Trim eggplant and slice ½-inch thick. Fry a few at a time in oil until lightly browned on both sides. Place half the eggplant over the potatoes. Place half the sliced tomatoes over top of eggplant and sprinkle lightly with basil.

Sauté onion in same skillet as eggplant in small amount of oil until transparent, and top tomatoes with half the onions.

In same skillet, adding more oil if necessary, brown lamb and season lightly with mint and garlic. If meat seems dry, add a few tablespoons water or stock. Spread meat evenly over onions. Add remaining layers in this order: onions, tomatoes sprinkled with basil, eggplant and potatoes.

Melt butter in small saucepan, add flour and stir roux for a minute or so over medium-low heat. Whisk in heated milk over medium heat until thick, then stir in cheese and cook until melted. Pour over casserole and bake at 375°F for 30 to 35 minutes, or until top is lightly browned. Remove from oven and cool for 10 minutes before serving.

Serves 6.

—Veronica Green

Apple Mint Lamb Shanks

These are easy, delicious and economical. The glaze can be used as a marinade, a roasting sauce or a barbecuing glaze and can be used on any cut of lamb with good results.

Ingredients

1 cup boiling water
3 Tbsp. dried or 1 cup fresh mint leaves
6-oz. can frozen apple juice concentrate, thawed
3 Tbsp. honey
4 lbs. lamb shanks

Directions

Combine water and mint leaves in a saucepan and let steep for 15 minutes to make a strong tea. Add apple juice and honey and heat gently to blend.

Marinate shanks in this for at least I hour and as long as 24 hours. Remove shanks from marinade and roast, uncovered, at 325°F for 1 to 1½ hours, turning and basting frequently.

Serves 4.

—*Randi Kennedy*

Irish Stew

Ingredients

3–4 Tbsp. shortening
1 medium onion, chopped
1 clove garlic, minced
1–1½ lbs. stewing lamb
1¼ cup flour
1 tsp. salt
¼ tsp. pepper
8–10 medium potatoes, chopped
3 large carrots, cut in strips
¼ large cabbage, chopped

Directions

Melt 1 Tbsp. shortening in large pot. Brown onion and garlic and set aside. Melt another tablespoon of shortening. Coat meat with flour, salt and pepper and brown, adding shortening as needed. Combine meat and onion mixture, add water to cover and simmer, covered, for 2 to 3 hours or until tender. Add potatoes and carrots and cook for 30 minutes. Add cabbage and cook until tender. Thicken with a little flour and water mixture if desired.

Serves 4.

—*Lucille Kalyniak*

Lamb & Apple Stew

Ingredients

4 Tbsp. oil
1 onion, finely chopped
1½ lbs. lean stewing lamb, cubed
1 tsp. salt
White pepper
Cinnamon
1½ cups water
4 small cooking apples

Directions

Heat half the oil in a heavy pot and sauté onion until wilted. Add lamb and brown on all sides. Add seasonings and water and bring to a boil. Reduce heat, then cover and simmer for 1 hour. Heat remaining oil in a skillet and sauté apples gently for 2 minutes. Add apples to stew and continue to simmer for 15 minutes.

Serves 4.

—Margaret Babcock

Chevon Stew

Ingredients

2 lbs. goat meat, cubed
6 Tbsp. olive oil
6 Tbsp. flour
2 tsp. salt
¼ tsp. pepper
2 cloves garlic, crushed
1 bay leaf
2 Tbsp. parsley
2 cups beef stock
2 cups water
1 cup dry red wine
1 cup sliced carrots
1 cup diced potatoes
½ cup diced turnip
½ cup diced parsnip
1 cup peas
6 medium onions, chopped

Directions

Brown meat in oil in large pot, then remove and set aside. Stir flour and spices into oil in pot. Gradually stir in beef stock, water and wine, stirring until smooth. Return meat to pot, add onions and simmer for 1 hour. Add remaining ingredients and cook over low heat for 3 to 4 hours.

Serves 4.

—Maria Nisbett

Hot Stir-Fried Beef

Ingredients

1 lb. lean beef
2 stalks celery
1 chili pepper
1 Tbsp. cornstarch
1 egg white
oil
1 Tbsp. soy sauce
½ tsp. sugar
1 tsp. hot pepper oil
3 cloves garlic
2 Tbsp. sweet rice wine
1 Tbsp. black bean sauce
½ tsp. minced gingerroot

Directions

Cut beef into very thin strips, slice celery and crush chili pepper. Blend cornstarch and egg white, add beef and toss. Heat oil and deep-fry beef for 3 minutes. Remove meat from oil. Heat 1 Tbsp. oil in another skillet. Sauté celery for 2 minutes, stir in beef and remaining ingredients and stir-fry until heated through.

Serves 2.

—*Mary-Lee Judah*

Anglo-Irish Stew

"My mother used wartime rationing as an excuse for not teaching me to cook when I was growing up in England. However, I watched her make Irish Stew so often that I discovered I could make it years later. My recipe has never let me down and has been passed on to sons, daughters-in-law and countless friends."

Ingredients

¾ cup flour
salt & pepper
1–1½ lbs. stewing beef or lamb
3 Tbsp. shortening
beef stock
2 bay leaves
3 large carrots
1 leek (optional)
3 onions
4 large potatoes
small turnip (optional)
thyme
1 tsp. curry powder
2 tsp. Worcestershire sauce

Directions

Put flour and salt and pepper into paper bag and shake to combine. Cut meat into cubes approximately 1½ inches square. Toss a few at a time into the bag and shake until coated. Melt shortening in large skillet and brown meat well.

Fill a large heavy pot about two-thirds full with stock or water and bring to a full boil. Add bay leaves and browned meat, including any drippings from the skillet. Bring back to full boil, then simmer for approximately 1 hour.

Slice carrots and leek and chop onions, potatoes and turnip. Add all vegetables to pot. Add remaining ingredients, using at least a teaspoon of whole thyme, more if you like its flavor. Stir well, return to boil and then lower heat until the stew is just bubbling gently. Taste and correct seasoning. Cook for 20 minutes. Serve with dumplings if desired.

Serves 6.

—*Barbara Brennan*

French Pot Roast

"This fills the house with a wonderful smell and produces tender meat with lots of rich sauce."

Ingredients

4–5 lb. rump or round roast
salt & pepper
2 Tbsp. shortening, lard or suet
2 Tbsp. butter
12–16 small white onions
12–16 small carrots
1 cup dry red wine
2 cups beef stock
2 cloves garlic, crushed
1 small bay leaf
thyme
chopped parsley
4 Tbsp. cornstarch, mixed with 1 cup water

Directions

Rub roast with salt and pepper. In large pot, brown roast on all sides in hot shortening. Remove roast and set aside.

Add butter to pot and brown onions and carrots lightly. Remove vegetables and set aside. Return meat to pot, add wine, stock, garlic, bay leaf, thyme and parsley. Cover and cook slowly for about 1½ hours. Add onions and carrots, cover and cook slowly for about 1 hour longer, or until meat is tender. Remove bay leaf and discard.

Transfer meat to warm platter and surround with vegetables. Add cornstarch mixture to liquid in pot and boil until sauce is slightly thickened. Spoon a little sauce over the roast and serve remainder in a gravy boat.

Serves 6.

—*Mrs. D.J. Zurbrigg*

Beer Stew

Ingredients

4 slices bacon
2 lbs. stewing beef, cut into 1" cubes
2½ cups chopped onions
2 cloves garlic, minced
salt & pepper
12 oz. beer
1 cup beef stock
1 Tbsp. vinegar
¼ tsp. thyme
2 Tbsp. flour

Directions

Fry bacon until crisp, remove from pan and set aside. Brown meat in bacon drippings with onions, garlic and salt and pepper. Add beer, stock, vinegar, thyme and reserved bacon and simmer for 2½ hours.

Stir a little of the hot juice into the flour until smooth, then stir back into stew, cooking until gravy is slightly thickened.

Serves 4.

—*Reo Belhumeur*

Sauerbraten

A very popular German dish, this is similar in concept to corned beef. The beef needs to marinate for 4 days. Serve with potato pancakes.

Ingredients

4 lb. blade roast
1 large onion, sliced
8–10 peppercorns
3 cloves
2 bay leaves
¼ cup sugar
2 cups vinegar
2 tsp. salt
1 lemon, sliced
2 Tbsp. plus ¼ cup butter
¼ cup flour
½ cup sour cream

Directions

Wipe meat and place in deep crock with cover. In stainless-steel or enamel pot, combine 2 cups water, onion, peppercorns, cloves, bay leaves, sugar, vinegar and salt. Heat but do not boil, then pour over meat and cool. Add lemon slices, cover and refrigerate for 4 days, turning daily. Remove meat from marinade and drain well. Strain marinade and reserve.

Heat 2 Tbsp. butter in deep Dutch oven over low heat. Add meat and brown slowly. Gradually add 2 cups marinade and bring to a boil. Reduce heat, cover and simmer for 2½ to 3 hours, or until meat is tender. Add liquid if necessary. Remove meat, set aside and keep warm. Set aside cooking liquid as well.

In same pot, melt ¼ cup butter and blend in flour, cooking until golden. Remove from heat and slowly add 3 cups liquid (cooking liquid, more marinade and hot water if needed). Bring to a rapid boil, stirring constantly, until gravy thickens. Reduce heat and slowly stir in sour cream, making certain it does not curdle. Serve with meat.

Serves 6 to 8.

—Anton Gross

Orange Marinated Beef

"This roast is delicious served on a warm platter with buttered yams. But it just might be even better the next day, sliced very thinly and served cold."

Ingredients

4 lb. boneless round or rump roast
½ cup red wine vinegar
2 cups orange juice
2 onions, chopped
1 Tbsp. pickling spice
12 peppercorns
1 bay leaf
2 Tbsp. oil

Directions

Pierce roast all over with fork. Combine vinegar, juice, onions, pickling spice, peppercorns and bay leaf and bring to a boil. Simmer for 5 minutes, then cool. Pour marinade over roast. Refrigerate for 48 hours, turning roast frequently.

Remove from marinade and brown in oil in Dutch oven. Pour marinade over beef, cover and cook over low heat for 3 to 3½ hours, turning occasionally.

Serves 6 to 8.

—Kathryn MacDonald

London Broil with Lime & Ginger Marinade

Lime and ginger bring an unexpected but delicious flavor to this steak dish.

Ingredients

3 cloves garlic, minced
2–3 pieces gingerroot, minced
½ cup soy sauce
4 tsp. sugar
2 tsp. sesame oil
juice of 1 lime
2 Tbsp. sherry
½ tsp. pepper
2–3 lbs. flank steak

Directions

Combine all ingredients except steak and mix well. Pour over meat and marinate for at least 6 hours but preferably overnight. Broil in oven or on grill, about 10 minutes per side.

Serves 4 to 6.

—*Kathy Lempert*

German Meatloaf

The applesauce glaze on top of this meat loaf makes it really attractive—a good combination of apple, beer and meat.

Ingredients

2 lbs. ground beef
1 lb. ground pork
1 egg
1 small onion, finely chopped
½ cup fine dry bread crumbs
1 medium apple, peeled, cored & chopped
1 tsp. savory
1 tsp. salt
¼ tsp. pepper
1 cup beer
1 cup thick applesauce

Directions

Combine all ingredients but applesauce and mix well. Turn into greased shallow baking pan and shape into a loaf. Bake for 45 minutes at 350°F, then spread with applesauce. Bake, uncovered, for another 30 to 45 minutes. Serve hot or cold.

Serves 6 to 8.

—*Louise Poole*

Swedish Meatballs

Ingredients

¾ cup milk
4 slices bread, crumbled
1 lb. ground steak
½ lb. ground veal
½ lb. ground pork
1 onion, grated
2 tsp. salt
⅛ tsp. nutmeg
⅛ tsp. allspice
1 clove garlic, crushed
¼ tsp. pepper
oil
1½ cups beef stock

Directions

Pour milk over bread and beat until consistency of paste. Add remaining ingredients except oil and stock and mix well. Form into meatballs, 1 inch in diameter. Fry in a little oil until browned on all sides. Place in casserole dish, pour stock over and bake, uncovered, at 350°F for 30 minutes.

Makes approximately 36 meatballs.

Italian Meatballs

Ingredients

4 slices stale bread
2 eggs, beaten
1 lb. ground beef
¼ cup Parmesan cheese
2 Tbsp. snipped parsley
1 tsp. salt
¼ tsp. oregano
pepper
2 Tbsp. oil

Directions

Trim crusts from bread and soak bread in ½ cup water for 2 to 3 minutes. Wring out bread and discard excess water. Tear bread up into large bowl. Add eggs and mix well with egg beater. Combine with beef, cheese, parsley, salt, oregano and pepper. With wet hands, form into small balls. Brown slowly in hot oil, turning often so they don't stick to the bottom. Add meatballs to your favorite sauce and simmer for 30 minutes. Serve over hot spaghetti. Pass extra Parmesan cheese.

Makes 20 meatballs.

—*Joyce M. Holland*

Sweet & Sour Meatballs with Prunes

Ingredients

2 lbs. ground beef
2 eggs
1 cup bread crumbs
1 onion, chopped
1 tsp. salt
6 prunes
3 tsp. raisins
8–10 peppercorns
2–3 bay leaves
20 oz. tomato juice
¼ cup sugar
juice of 2–3 lemons
½ cabbage, coarsely chopped

Directions

Combine beef, eggs and bread crumbs, mix well and form into meatballs. Bring 4 cups water to a boil, then add onion, salt, prunes, raisins, peppercorns, bay leaves and meatballs. Cook for 20 minutes, then add tomato juice, sugar, lemon juice and cabbage. Simmer, covered, for 1 hour.

Serves 6 to 8.

—Lynn Andersen

Liver with Mushrooms & Bacon

Ingredients

1 lb. calf's liver
8 slices bacon, chopped
10–12 mushrooms, sliced
1 large onion, chopped
1 clove garlic, minced
1–2 tsp. flour
½–1 cup beef stock
salt & pepper
parsley

Directions

Slice liver into thin strips and set aside. Sauté bacon, mushrooms, onion and garlic until bacon is quite crisp. Remove from skillet with slotted spoon. Add flour to a very small amount of heated stock. Blend well and continue adding stock until you have ½ cup. Set aside.

Cook liver over medium-high heat in bacon fat until lightly colored. Add bacon mixture and stock. Cook until thickened, adding salt and pepper and parsley.

Serves 3 to 4.

—Colleen Suche

Bacon & Liver Bake

Ingredients

6 slices bacon, chopped
1 cup chopped onion
½ cup flour
1 tsp. salt
pepper
1 lb. calf's liver, cut into serving-sized pieces
1½ cups milk
¼ cup fine bread crumbs
1 Tbsp. butter, melted

Directions

Combine bacon and onion in skillet and cook until bacon is crisp and onion is tender.

Remove and set aside, reserving drippings in skillet. Combine flour, salt and pepper, and coat liver with this. Reserve leftover flour mixture. Brown liver in skillet, then remove to baking dish. Blend reserved flour with pan drippings until smooth and bubbly, then add milk. Cook, stirring, until thickened and bubbly. Pour sauce over liver and sprinkle with bacon and onion pieces. Combine bread crumbs with melted butter and sprinkle over all. Bake, uncovered, at 350°F for 25 minutes.

Serves 4.

—*LaRae DuFresne Bergo*

Pork with Port & Garlic

Ingredients

several cloves garlic
2½ lb. rolled loin of pork
1 Tbsp. oil
1 cup port wine
1 tsp. rosemary
½ tsp. salt
1 Tbsp. butter
1 Tbsp. flour

Directions

Cut garlic into slivers and stick into folds of pork loin. In Dutch oven, brown pork on all sides in oil. Pour off fat and add port, rosemary and salt. Bring to a boil. Bake, tightly covered, at 325°F for about 2 hours, adding water if necessary. Soften butter and mix with flour. When pork is tender, remove to a platter and mix butter-flour mixture into pan juices a little at a time, just until sauce begins to thicken. Add salt to taste.

Serves 4 to 6.

—*Ruth Ellis Haworth*

Pork in Red Wine with Apple Rings

Start this the evening before you plan to serve it by soaking the dried apple rings in water overnight.

Ingredients

2 Tbsp. oil
2 onions chopped
2 lbs. pork tenderloin, cubed
1¼ cups red wine
⅔ cup chicken stock
2" cinnamon stick
2 slivers lemon rind
salt & pepper
2–3 Tbsp. tomato paste
2 Tbsp. chopped parsley
½ cup dried apple rings, soaked overnight
2 Tbsp. cornstarch

Directions

Heat oil and sauté onions until soft. Add pork and cook until browned. Add wine, stock, cinnamon, lemon rind, salt and pepper and tomato paste. Cover and simmer for 1 hour. Stir in parsley and apple rings and cook for 30 minutes more. Discard cinnamon and lemon rind. Dissolve cornstarch in a bit of the hot liquid, then stir into pot and cook, stirring, until gravy is thickened.

Serves 6.

—Ellen Wicklum

Pepper Pork en Brochette

Ingredients

2 large cloves garlic, crushed
3 Tbsp. soy sauce
2 Tbsp. sherry
1 Tbsp. cracked pepper
1 tsp. coriander
1 tsp. brown sugar
½ tsp. cumin
2 green peppers, diced
2 onions, quartered
2 lbs. lean pork roast, cubed
⅓ cup oil

Directions

Combine all ingredients except oil and marinate for 1 to 2 hours. Thread pork and vegetables on skewers and barbecue. Add oil to marinade and baste meat and vegetables. Serve with rice or pita bread.

Serves 4.

—Colleen Bruning Fann

Buttermilk Pork Roast

Ingredients

3–4 lb. boned pork shoulder
salt
2 Tbsp. oil
2 cups buttermilk
2 Tbsp. cider vinegar
1 onion, sliced
1 bay leaf
3 peppercorns, crushed
6 carrots, sliced
2 large potatoes, quartered
6 small white onions
cornstarch

Directions

Sprinkle meat with salt. Heat oil in Dutch oven, brown meat well on all sides, and remove excess fat. Add buttermilk, 1 cup water, vinegar, onion, bay leaf and peppercorns. Bring to a boil, cover and simmer for 2½ hours, or until meat is tender. Add carrots, potatoes and onions and cook for another 30 minutes. Thicken gravy with cornstarch dissolved in water.

Serves 6 to 8.

—Anna J. Lee

Mustard Marinade for Pork

Ingredients

2–3 Tbsp. Dijon mustard
2 cloves garlic, crushed
2 Tbsp. dry white wine
2 Tbsp. olive oil
½ tsp. pepper

Directions

Combine all ingredients and mix well. Brush on meat and let sit at room temperature for at least 30 minutes before proceeding with preparation.

—Trudi Keillor

Stuffed Pork Chops

Ingredients

4 pork chops, 1" thick
2 Tbsp. butter
2 Tbsp. chopped onion
1 clove garlic, crushed
1 cup bread crumbs
¼ tsp. savory
¼ tsp. salt
pepper
2–4 Tbsp. orange juice

Directions

Trim fat from chops. Melt butter in frying pan and brown chops on both sides. Remove chops and add onion and garlic to pan. Cook until onion is tender, stirring frequently. Add bread crumbs and seasonings and stir together. Remove from heat. Stir in enough juice to make mixture crumbly but not soggy. Scrape pan to remove all drippings. Cut meat to bone to form a pocket, being careful not to tear meat. Pack each chop with ¼ cup stuffing. Wrap in foil and seal tightly.

Bake at 350°F for 1 hour, opening foil for last 15 minutes to brown.

—M. Raven

Pork & Beans

This meal is rich and hearty and the marmalade adds a pleasant, sweet tang.

Ingredients

1 lb. dried lima beans
2 lbs. lean boneless pork, cubed
3 Tbsp. oil
2 tsp. celery salt
2 bay leaves
1 tsp. rosemary
2 cups tomato sauce
1 cup sliced mushrooms
1 onion, chopped
⅓ cup orange marmalade
2 Tbsp. cider vinegar
1 Tbsp. Worcestershire sauce
2 tsp. dry mustard

Directions

Rinse beans, cover with 6 cups water and boil for 2 minutes. Remove from heat, cover and let stand for 1 hour.

Brown pork in oil in heavy skillet. Add beans and cooking liquid, celery salt, bay leaves and rosemary. Cover, bring to a boil, reduce heat and simmer for 2 hours. Remove bay leaves. Stir in remaining ingredients and place in casserole dish. Bake, covered, at 350°F for 1 hour. Uncover, stir well, re-cover and bake for 30 minutes more.

Serves 12.

—Midge Denault

Maple Pork Chops

"I serve this with a creamy squash soup first. Accompany the chops with carrots, oven-browned potatoes and a crunchy green vegetable. End the meal with crème caramel." Made with home-grown pork and thick, fresh maple syrup, this dish turns plain pork chops into company fare.

Ingredients

4 pork chops, 1" thick
¼ cup apricot brandy
½ tsp. dry mustard
2 slices gingerroot
1½ tsp. cornstarch
3 Tbsp. maple syrup
salt & pepper

Directions

Brown chops in large frying pan and drain off fat. Pour 2 Tbsp. brandy over top, then add ¼ cup water, mustard and ginger. Cover tightly and simmer, turning occasionally, until tender — about 1 hour.

Remove chops to warm platter. Blend cornstarch with 1 Tbsp. water and stir into remaining sauce in pan along with 2 Tbsp. brandy, maple syrup and salt and pepper. Boil, stirring constantly, until thickened and clear. Pour sauce over chops.

Serves 4.

—Linda Russell

Vietnamese Sweet & Sour Pork

The traditional way to serve this dish is to line a large platter with romaine lettuce, add a layer of peeled, sliced cucumber and a layer of sliced tomato. Place pork on top of tomato, garnish with chopped cilantro, and serve sauce in a separate bowl.

Ingredients
⅓ cup sugar
4 tsp. cornstarch
½ cup rice vinegar
1¼ cups chicken stock
½ cup slivered red or green pepper
2 lbs. pork spareribs
1 egg, lightly beaten
1 Tbsp. flour
2 Tbsp. cornstarch
1 tsp. pepper
¼ cup oil
4 or more cloves garlic, chopped
⅓ cup fish sauce

Directions
Make sauce by mixing sugar and cornstarch in saucepan. Add remaining sauce ingredients and simmer until thickened, stirring, then cook over low heat for a few minutes. Set aside, but keep at room temperature.

Cut ribs into small pieces. Combine egg, 3 Tbsp. water, flour, cornstarch and pepper and mix well. Place ribs in this and turn to coat.

Heat oil in skillet. Fry ribs until batter is crisp. Pour out oil, but do not wipe out pan. Cook garlic briefly — 10 seconds — then add fish sauce. Return ribs and turn to coat with garlic and fish sauce. Stir in sauce and heat through.

Serves 3 to 4.

—Donna J. Torres

Spareribs Barbecue

"This is a recipe I received from a favorite aunt who is an excellent cook. I often substitute pork chops for spareribs, and it is still delicious."

Ingredients
4–6 lbs. spareribs
2 onions
2 stalks celery
1 cup sliced mushrooms
1 green pepper
2 Tbsp. brown sugar
3 Tbsp. vinegar
4 Tbsp. lemon juice
1 Tbsp. Worcestershire sauce
1 tsp. prepared mustard
1 cup tomato sauce
½ cup hot water
1 tsp. salt

Directions
Cut ribs into pieces of 2 to 3 ribs each and place in roasting pan. Chop onions, celery, mushrooms and green pepper and add to ribs. Combine remaining ingredients and pour over ribs and vegetables. Cover and bake at 350°F for 1½ hours, basting several times.

Serves 4 to 6.

—Lorraine Guilfoyle

Baked Ham with Beer

This recipe produces a dark-skinned ham with a flavor similar to that of Black Forest ham. Save the cooking juice to add to baked beans.

Ingredients

1 large ham
1 cup brown sugar
1 Tbsp. dry mustard
1 pint beer

Directions

Place ham in roasting pan with lid. Sprinkle ham with sugar and mustard, then pour the beer over, along with 4 cups water. Bake, uncovered, at 350°F for 2 hours, basting every 30 minutes and adding water if necessary. Cool, covered, before slicing.

—Linda Palaisy

Sparky's Sweet & Sour Ribs

Ingredients

3–4 lbs. pork spareribs
¼ cup vinegar
3 Tbsp. soy sauce
1 tsp. sugar
½ tsp. pepper
4 Tbsp. flour
3 Tbsp. oil
½ cup vinegar
1½ cups brown sugar
1 Tbsp. cornstarch

Directions

Parboil ribs in ¼ cup vinegar and water to cover for 1 hour. Drain, leaving ribs in pot. Pour soy sauce, sugar, pepper and flour over ribs, turning to cover each piece.

Heat oil in skillet and brown ribs, then place in large casserole dish.

Combine ½ cup vinegar, brown sugar, 1 cup water and cornstarch dissolved in a bit of water in saucepan. Cook over medium heat until slightly thickened. Pour over ribs and bake, uncovered, at 350°F for 30 to 60 minutes.

Serves 4.

—Pat de la Ronde

Sausage Spinach Stuffed Brioche

The flavor of this spectacular-looking brioche depends very much on the type of sausage used. We recommend a garlic or even hotter sausage, but for a milder brioche, use a regular sausage.

Filling Ingredients

½ lb. garlic sausage, crumbled
1 onion, minced
1 clove garlic, crushed
1 pkg. spinach, chopped
½ tsp. pepper
¼ tsp. salt
¼ tsp. thyme
¼ tsp. hot pepper sauce
1 egg

Brioche Ingredients

¼ cup milk
⅓ cup butter, cut up
3 Tbsp. sugar
¼ tsp. salt
1 Tbsp. yeast
¼ cup warm water
2¼–2¾ cups flour
2 eggs

Directions

Brown sausage well in large skillet. Remove and set aside. In drippings, sauté onion and garlic until tender, stirring occasionally. Stir in sausage, spinach, pepper, salt, thyme and pepper sauce. Cook, stirring, for 5 minutes. Cool slightly.

Beat egg and set aside 1 tsp. of it. Stir remaining egg into sausage mixture and mix well. Combine 1 tsp. egg with ¼ tsp. water and reserve for glaze.

To make brioche: Scald milk in small saucepan. Add butter and stir until melted. Stir in sugar and salt and cool to lukewarm. In large bowl, dissolve yeast in ¼ cup warm water. Stir in milk mixture and 1 cup flour. Beat well. Add eggs and 1 cup flour, or enough to make thick batter. Beat until well blended. Cover and let rise until doubled — about 1 hour. Stir down.

Place large tablespoonful of dough on heavily floured surface and form into smooth ball with well-floured hands. Set aside.

Place half remaining dough in greased, deep 1½-quart casserole dish. Press some dough evenly against sides of dish to form hollow. Fill with sausage-spinach mixture. Place remaining dough over filling and pat to cover filling evenly. Press edges to seal. Make small indentation in center and press in dough ball. Cover and let rise until almost doubled — 30 minutes. Brush with egg-water glaze. Bake at 400°F for 25 minutes, covering with foil after 10 to 15 minutes. Loosen sides with spatula and turn out. Serve warm.

Serves 4 to 6.

—*Christine Taylor*

Sausage-Stuffed Apples

Ingredients

8 baking apples
8 mushrooms
1 lb. garlic sausage meat

Directions

Wash, dry and core apples. Place in 9" x 13" baking dish. Stem mushrooms, chop stems and mix with sausage meat. Brown over medium heat, then drain fat. Stuff apples with sausage and top with mushroom caps. Bake, uncovered, at 350°F for 30 minutes.

Serves 6.

—Laurie Bradley

Maple Barbecued Spareribs

Tasty and unusual, this is not at all like traditional barbecue or sweet and sour recipes.

Ingredients

3 lbs. spareribs
1 cup maple syrup
1 Tbsp. chili sauce
1 Tbsp. vinegar
1 Tbsp. Worcestershire sauce
1 onion, finely chopped
½ tsp. salt
¼ tsp. dry mustard
⅛ tsp. pepper

Directions

Roast ribs on rack in roasting pan at 425°F for 30 minutes. Drain fat from pan and cut ribs into serving-sized pieces. Place in 9" x 13" pan.

Combine remaining ingredients in saucepan and boil for 5 minutes. Pour over ribs and bake, uncovered, at 375°F for 1 hour, basting occasionally and turning ribs after 30 minutes.

Serves 4.

—Donna Jubb

Apples, Yams & Sausage

The flavors of the sausage, yams and apples combine in a very tasty fashion in this simple dish.

Ingredients

1 lb. bulk sausage
2 yams, peeled & cut into 1" chunks
3 medium apples
1 Tbsp. flour
1 Tbsp. brown sugar
½ tsp. cinnamon
salt & pepper

Directions

Brown sausage in skillet, cutting into large chunks. Drain off excess fat and place in 2-quart casserole. Add yams. Peel, core and slice apples, then add to casserole and mix gently.

Combine dry ingredients and add to meat, yams and apples, mixing well. Add ½ cup water, cover, and bake for 50 to 60 minutes at 375°F, or until apples and yams are tender.

Serves 3.

—Judith Almond-Best

Baked Ham with Port Wine Sauce

Main Ingredients
1½ cups firmly packed brown sugar
1 Tbsp. wine vinegar
1 Tbsp. prepared mustard
2–3 lb. ham
1 cup white wine

Sauce Ingredients
1 cup currant jelly
1 cup port
1 Tbsp. butter

Directions

Make a paste of the brown sugar, vinegar and mustard. Remove skin from ham and spread with paste. Let stand overnight.

Place in roasting pan with wine. Cover and bake at 350°F for 1½ hours, uncover and bake for 30 minutes longer at 400°F. Remove from oven and let stand for 30 minutes.

Meanwhile, prepare sauce. Heat together currant jelly, port and butter, but do not allow to boil. Slice ham and serve with sauce.

Serves 4 to 6.

—Dolores De Rosario

Chili Verde Mexican Salsa

Hot and spicy, this is a wonderful salsa recipe. Serve it on tortillas, potatoes, eggs, whatever. It makes a good dip too. We suggest you start with the smaller quantities of peppers, then add more if you want a hotter taste.

Ingredients
1 Tbsp. shortening
1 lb. pork, diced
2 onions, chopped
2 28-oz. cans tomatoes, chopped
10–12 oz. canned green chilies, seeded & diced
4–8 oz. jalapeño peppers, seeded & diced
2 tsp. salt
½ tsp. pepper
2 cloves garlic, minced
2 Tbsp. oil
2 Tbsp. flour

Directions

Melt shortening and brown pork. Add onions and cook until they are translucent. Add tomatoes, chilies, jalapeños, salt, pepper and garlic and simmer. Heat oil in another skillet and stir in flour, cooking until browned. Add to other ingredients, cover and simmer for 3 hours, stirring occasionally.

—Rosemary Huffman

Riverslea Lamb Shanks

"Lamb shanks are often boned and used for stew, but the meat is perhaps the most tasty cut of lamb. This delicious recipe makes great use of an inexpensive cut."

Ingredients

4 lamb shanks
flour
oil
1 cup pitted prunes
½ cup brown sugar
½ tsp. cinnamon
½ tsp. allspice
3 Tbsp. vinegar

Directions

Dust shanks with flour and brown all over in a little hot oil. Mix remaining ingredients and 1 cup water and pour over shanks. Cover and bake at 350°F for 2 hours, turning shanks over occasionally.

Serves 4.

—Jean Rivers

Green Peppers Stuffed with Pork & Veal

Serve these stuffed peppers with a lightly flavored tomato sauce if desired—the pepper filling is delicate, so be sure not to overpower it with sauce.

Ingredients

2 Tbsp. plus 1 tsp. butter
4 large green peppers
1 large onion, chopped
½ lb. pork sausage
½ lb. ground veal
1 cup dry bread crumbs
2 Tbsp. milk
1 tsp. salt
½ tsp. pepper
⅛ tsp. nutmeg
½ tsp. thyme

Directions

With 1 tsp. butter, grease baking dish large enough to hold peppers. Set aside.

Wash peppers, then slice off and discard 1 inch from tops of peppers. Remove and discard pith and seeds. Melt remaining butter over medium heat. When foam subsides, add onion and cook for 5 to 7 minutes, stirring occasionally, until onion is soft and translucent. Add sausage and veal and stir to break up. Cook, stirring, until meat has lost its pink color.

Stir in remaining ingredients and cook for another 5 minutes. Spoon filling into peppers, then place peppers in baking dish. Bake, uncovered, at 375°F for 40 to 50 minutes, or until peppers are cooked.

Serves 4.

—Dolores De Rosario

Savory Lamb Shanks

Ingredients

4 lamb shanks
3 large cloves garlic, slivered
salt & pepper
1 tsp. rosemary
2 Tbsp. chopped parsley
1 tsp. oregano
2 onions, thinly sliced
1 lb. fresh Italian plum tomatoes, peeled,
    seeded & coarsely chopped or 2 cups canned
Italian plum tomatoes
¾ cup dry white wine
¾ cup olive oil

Directions

Remove excess fat and tendons from shanks. Insert garlic into meat in 2 or 3 crevices, then sprinkle remainder on top. Season with salt and pepper. Arrange shanks in baking dish and roast, uncovered, at 425°F for 20 minutes. Reduce heat to 350°F and sprinkle rosemary, parsley, oregano and onions over meat. Spoon tomatoes over meat and pour wine over all. Drizzle olive oil on top.

Return to oven and cook for 1 to 1½ hours, or until tender. Remove shanks to serving dish. Reduce liquid slightly and season with salt and pepper.

Serves 4.

—Ann L. Combs

Lamb with Fennel & Tomatoes

Also known as finocchio, fennel is an anise-flavored vegetable. The root looks much like a celery heart, and the stalks end in dill-like, feathery leaves. It can be eaten raw, made into soup, braised or added to casseroles. If using the leaves for seasoning, be discreet, as the anise flavor is very strong.

Ingredients

5 Tbsp. olive oil
2 lb. boned leg of lamb, cubed
1 onion, chopped
2 cups peeled, seeded & mashed tomatoes
salt & pepper
1½ lbs. fennel, quartered

Directions

Heat oil in heavy casserole dish, then brown meat on all sides. Stir in onion and sauté for 5 minutes more, then add tomatoes and salt and pepper. Reduce heat, cover and simmer for 40 minutes, adding water if necessary.

Cook fennel in boiling salted water for 20 minutes. Drain, reserving 1 cup liquid. Add fennel and 1 cup liquid to lamb and cook for 20 minutes more.

Serves 4.

—Carroll MacDonald

Sweet & Sour Meatloaf

Serve this hot or cold—it makes excellent sand-wiches on thick slices of rye bread with mustard.

Meatloaf Ingredients

1½ lbs. ground beef
1 onion, chopped
½ cup tomato sauce
1 cup bread crumbs
¼ tsp. salt
1 egg, beaten

Sauce Ingredients

½ cup tomato sauce
2 Tbsp. vinegar
2 Tbsp. brown sugar
2 Tbsp. Dijon mustard

Directions

Combine meat loaf ingredients and mix well. Press into greased loaf pan, leaving 1-inch space on all sides.

Combine sauce ingredients with 1 cup water and mix well. Pour over meat loaf. Bake, uncovered, at 350°F for 1½ hours, basting frequently.

Serves 6.

—Bette Warkentin

Saturday Night Pie

A variation of Shepherd's Pie, this recipe bases its crust on cornmeal rather than on mashed potatoes.

Filling Ingredients

1 lb. ground beef
1 cup chopped onion
1 cup chopped green pepper
2 cups tomato sauce
1–2 Tbsp. chili powder
1 tsp. salt
1 tsp. pepper
1 cup corn

Topping Ingredients

2 eggs
½ cup buttermilk
1 Tbsp. butter
1 Tbsp. flour
1 tsp. baking soda
¼ tsp. salt
¾ cup cornmeal

Directions

Brown beef and onion in skillet. Add remaining filling ingredients, bring to a boil, reduce heat, cover and simmer for 15 minutes. Pour into ungreased deep 10" pie plate.

For topping: Beat together eggs, buttermilk and butter. Beat in remaining ingredients until smooth. Spread evenly over filling and bake, uncovered, at 350°F for 20 minutes.

Serves 6.

—Carroll MacDonald

Steak & Kidney Pie

Prepare the filling for this pie a day ahead to allow the flavors to blend together properly. Use beef, veal or lamb kidneys.

Filling Ingredients

1 lb. kidneys
2½ lbs. round steak
½ cup flour
6 Tbsp. oil
1 cup thinly sliced onions
½ lb. mushrooms, sliced
½ tsp. salt
½ tsp. pepper
½ tsp. rosemary
½ tsp. tarragon
1 Tbsp. tomato paste
2 tsp. Worcestershire sauce
1 cup red wine
1 cup beef stock

Pastry Ingredients

1½ cups flour
½ tsp. salt
½ cup shortening
1 egg yolk, beaten

Directions

To make filling: Clean kidneys, split, remove fat and soak in salted water for 1 hour. Dry and cube. Cut steak into cubes. Toss steak and kidneys with flour to coat. Heat oil and brown meat, removing it as it browns. Add onions and mushrooms to drippings, adding oil if necessary. Sauté for 5 minutes, until onions and mushrooms are lightly browned, stirring frequently. Return meat to skillet, add remaining filling ingredients and simmer for 2 hours or until meat is tender. Cool, then refrigerate overnight.

To prepare crust: Sift flour and salt into bowl, then cut in shortening until mixture resembles coarse cornmeal. Mix egg yolk with 3 Tbsp. ice water and add to flour, tossing with a fork until particles cling together. Form into a ball and refrigerate overnight.

To assemble: After removing any congealed fat from the surface of the filling, place filling in greased 2-quart casserole dish. Roll out pastry until it is 2 inches larger around than the top of the casserole dish. Place dough on top of filling, turning it under at the edges. Cut steam vents and bake at 400°F for 30 minutes, reduce heat to 350°F and bake for another 15 to 20 minutes.

Serves 4 to 6.

—Shirley Mullen Hooper

Pasta

Egg Noodles

Ingredients
Flour
3 large eggs
Olive oil

Directions

Mound flour on large, clean working surface. Make a well in the center of the flour and break eggs into it.

Take ½ eggshell and measure 3 shellfuls of water and 3 of olive oil into the well.

Using a fork, gently beat the liquids to blend and gradually flick flour from the edges into the center. Keep beating until mixture becomes very stiff. Sprinkle dough with flour and roll it out, adding flour as necessary to make a very stiff, thin dough. When dough has been rolled as thin as possible, let rest for 10 minutes.

Divide dough into strips 8 inches to 10 inches wide and cut into ¼-inch strips for noodles. Hang over broom handle to dry — 15 to 30 minutes.

To cook, place in boiling water and cook 3 to 7 minutes — until tender. To store, bag and refrigerate for up to 3 days, or freeze.

—Noni Fidler

Pizza

Ingredients
2 Tbsp. yeast
1¼ cups warm water
1 tsp. honey
¼ cup olive oil
1 tsp. salt
3½ cups whole wheat flour
6-8 cups tomato sauce, page 339
3 cups sliced mushrooms
1½ cups chopped green olives
2 green peppers, chopped
1 lb. chopped bacon, cooked to eliminate fat but not until crisp
6 cups grated Swiss cheese
6 cups grated mozzarella cheese
3 cups grated Parmesan cheese

Directions

To make dough, dissolve yeast and honey in water. Add oil, salt and flour and mix well. Knead until smooth and elastic. Let rise in a warm place until doubled in size – about 1½ hours. Punch down and knead again briefly.

Divide dough into 3 equal portions. Roll each portion out to a 10-inch circle, ⅛ inch thick. Place crust in pizza pan.

Top each crust with about 2 to 2½ cups tomato sauce, then sprinkle vegetables, olives and bacon over this. Top with grated cheeses.

Bake at 425°F for 15 to 20 minutes, until cheese has melted and crust is golden brown.

Makes 3 10-inch pizzas.

German Pizza Dough

Ingredients

1 cup cottage cheese
2¼ cups flour
2 tsp. baking powder
4 Tbsp. milk
4 Tbsp. oil
1 egg, beaten

Directions

Mix cottage cheese, flour and baking powder with pastry blender until crumbly. Combine milk, oil and beaten egg and add to dry ingredients. Stir until well combined and roll out on floured surface to fit pizza pan. Makes two 12-inch pizza crusts. Bake with favorite toppings at 400°F for 35 to 40 minutes.

—Joann Hudson

Basic Tomato Sauce

This sauce can be used as a basis for spaghetti, lasagne, canneloni, manicotti or pizza, with or without the addition of ground beef and other vegetables.

Ingredients

¼ cup olive oil
1 clove garlic, minced
2 onions, diced
1 qt. canned tomatoes
½ cup tomato paste
½ cup water
1½ tsp. salt
¼ tsp. pepper
1 tsp. basil
1 tsp. oregano
1 Tbsp. parsley
1 bay leaf
½ cup mushrooms, sliced

Directions

Heat olive oil in heavy saucepan. Add other ingredients in order listed. Simmer, uncovered, for 1 to 6 hours.

Add sliced mushrooms for the last 15 minutes.

—Helen Shepherd

Macaroni Salad

Ingredients

2 cups uncooked macaroni
1 cup sliced celery
½ cup chopped green onions
¼ cup sliced radishes
1 cup cubed Cheddar cheese
¾ cup mayonnaise
1 Tbsp. vinegar
1 tsp. mustard
1 tsp. salt
Pepper to taste

Directions

Cook the macaroni. Drain and rinse with cold water until cool. Toss together the cooked macaroni, vegetables and cheese.

Mix together the mayonnaise, vinegar, mustard, salt and pepper. Toss dressing together with salad. Refrigerate.

Serves 6 to 8.

—*Bertha Geddert*

Noodle Casserole

Ingredients

3 Tbsp. butter
2 Tbsp. flour
1 cup milk
¼ cup soy grits, soaked in ¼ cup water
¼ cup vegetable flakes
½ tsp. salt
½ cup chopped parsley
½ cup grated Cheddar cheese
3-4 cups cooked & drained broad egg noodles

Directions

Melt butter in heavy saucepan and stir in flour. Cook for 1 minute, then add milk slowly, stirring constantly. Add remaining ingredients except cheese and noodles and simmer for 10 minutes. Mix in cheese, then noodles and place in greased loaf pan.

Bake at 350°F for 30 minutes.

Serves 4 to 6.

—*Shiela Alexandrovich*

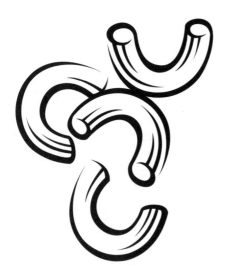

Macaroni & Cheese

The addition of tomato sauce to this traditional macaroni and cheese casserole can provide an interesting variation.

Ingredients

3 Tbsp. butter
3 Tbsp. flour
2 cups milk
½ tsp. salt
Pepper to taste
2 cups grated old Cheddar cheese
2 cups cooked macaroni
¾ cup fine bread crumbs

Directions

Melt butter, blend in flour and add milk. Cook and stir over low heat until thick. Add seasonings and 1½ cups cheese. Stir and heat until melted.

Put macaroni in greased baking dish. Pour in sauce and mix well. Mix bread crumbs with remaining ½ cup cheese and sprinkle over top of casserole. Bake at 350°F for 30 to 40 minutes.

Serves 4.

—*Mrs. Bruce Bowden*

Cottage Cheese & Noodle Bake

Ingredients

½ cup chopped onion
2 Tbsp. butter
2 Tbsp. flour
1 tsp. salt
Pepper
1 cup milk
1 tsp. mustard
1 cup cottage cheese
½ cup Cheddar cheese, grated
2 Tbsp. lemon juice
8 oz. noodles, cooked
Parsley

Directions

Sauté onion in butter until tender. Stir in flour, salt and pepper until smooth. Gradually stir in milk and mustard. Cook until thickened. Stir in cheeses, lemon juice, then noodles. Pour into a greased casserole dish. Bake at 350°F for 40 to 45 minutes. Sprinkle with fresh parsley to serve.

Serves 4.

White Sauce for Spaghetti

Ingredients

2 Tbsp. fresh parsley
2 Tbsp. fresh basil
1 cup butter, melted
⅓ cup grated Parmesan cheese
¼ cup olive oil
2 cloves garlic, mashed
8 oz. cream cheese
⅔ cup boiling water

Directions

Mix together parsley, basil and butter. Add cheese, then mix in remaining ingredients. Simmer until well blended. Serve over cooked noodles.

Makes 2½ cups.

—Ken Parejko

Vegetable Lasagne

Zucchini and olives provide another interesting variation on the standard lasagne flavor. This recipe, like the others, can be frozen with no detraction from the original flavor.

Ingredients

2 Tbsp. oil
1 large clove garlic, minced
1 large onion, chopped
1 green pepper, chopped
2 stalks celery, chopped
½ tsp. oregano
½ tsp. basil
½ tsp. thyme
1 medium zucchini, coarsely grated
1½ cups sliced mushrooms
1½ cups tomato sauce, page 339
5½-oz. can tomato paste
¼ cup grated Parmesan cheese
2 cups cottage cheese, mixed with 1 egg
½ cup chopped black olives
2 cups grated mozzarella cheese
8 oz. lasagne noodles, cooked
10 oz. spinach, torn into 1-inch pieces

Directions

Sauté garlic in oil for 1 minute. Add onion, green pepper, celery and herbs and cook for 5 minutes. Add zucchini and cook another 5 minutes. Add mushrooms, tomato sauce and tomato paste. Simmer 20 minutes, remove from heat, add Parmesan cheese and mix well.

Spread a small amount of the sauce in the bottom of a greased, 2-qt. casserole dish. Layer in half of each of the ingredients: noodles, sauce, cottage cheese, spinach, mozzarella and olives. Repeat.

Cover and bake for 1 hour at 350°F. Allow to sit for 10 minutes before serving.

Serves 6 to 8.

—Shan Simpson

Lasagne

Ingredients

6 oz. lasagne noodles
2 Tbsp. cooking oil
2 cloves garlic, minced
2 onions, chopped
1 lb. ground beef
½ lb. mushrooms, sliced
2 stalks celery, diced
1 green pepper, diced
12 oz. tomato paste
3 cups stewed tomatoes
1 tsp. salt
¼ tsp. pepper
1 tsp. oregano
1 tsp. basil
2 tsp. parsley
1 bay leaf
1 lb. ricotta cheese
5 oz. spinach
¾ cup Parmesan cheese
1 lb. mozzarella cheese, grated

Directions

Cook noodles in boiling water until tender. Drain and set aside.

Heat oil in large heavy frying pan. Add garlic and onions and sauté until onion is soft. Add ground beef and continue to sauté, stirring frequently, until beef begins to lose pink color. Add mushrooms, celery and green pepper. Continue cooking until meat is well browned. Stir in tomato paste, tomatoes and seasonings. Simmer for at least 1 hour or all day. The longer the sauce simmers, the richer the flavor.

To assemble, mix together ricotta cheese, washed and torn spinach and ½ cup Parmesan cheese.

Pour a very thin layer of meat sauce into a 9" x 13" baking dish. This will prevent the casserole from sticking to the dish. Arrange a layer of cooked noodles over sauce. Top with half of meat sauce, half ricotta-spinach mixture and half grated mozzarella cheese. Repeat layers. Sprinkle remaining ¼ cup of Parmesan cheese over top layer.

Bake at 350°F for 35 to 45 minutes.

Serves 8.

—Wanda Mary Murdock

Rotini & Sauce

Ingredients

¾ lb. rotini noodles
¾ lb. ground beef
Olive oil
⅔ cup sliced carrots
⅔ cup sliced celery
⅔ cup sliced onion
1½ cups tomato sauce, page 339
Salt & pepper
1 tsp. oregano
Cayenne pepper
1 clove garlic, minced

Directions

Cook rotini noodles in boiling, salted water for about 20 minutes, until tender. Meanwhile, brown beef in a skillet, draining off excess fat. Sauté carrots, celery and onion in oil on low heat for 5 minutes. Add tomato sauce, seasonings and cooked beef. Simmer, covered, for 10 minutes. Drain and rinse rotini and top with sauce and Parmesan cheese.

Serves 4.

—Glenn F. McMichael

Szechuan Noodles

Ingredients

1 lb. spaghetti or Chinese noodles
2 Tbsp. oil
4 green onions, chopped
½ cup minced cooked ham
¼ cup chopped peanuts
⅓ cup sesame seeds
⅓ cup soy sauce
1 Tbsp. cider vinegar
1 tsp. honey
Tabasco sauce
2 Tbsp. ketchup
⅔ cup chopped cucumber or celery

Directions

Cook noodles, drain and toss with 1 Tbsp. oil. Set aside.

Stir-fry green onions in remaining oil for 1 minute. Add ham, peanuts, sesame seeds, soy sauce, vinegar, honey, Tabasco and ketchup. Simmer 2 to 3 minutes, add cucumber or celery and cook a few minutes longer.

Add noodles, toss and heat through.

Serves 4.

—Bryanna Clark

Manicotti

Manicotti can be made with homemade crêpes, as this recipe indicates, or with commercial pasta. Canneloni noodles may also be used with either of these fillings and do not need to be pre-boiled.

Ingredients

6 eggs
1½ cups flour
¼ tsp. salt
2 lbs. ricotta cheese
½ lb. mozzarella cheese
⅓ cup grated Parmesan cheese
2 eggs
1 tsp. salt
¼ tsp. pepper
1 Tbsp. chopped parsley
¼ cup grated Parmesan cheese
2–3 cups tomato sauce, page 339

Directions

Combine 6 eggs, flour, salt and 1½ cups water in blender. After blending, let stand 30 minutes or longer.

Grease and heat an 8-inch skillet. Pour in 3 Tbsp. of batter, rotating skillet quickly to spread batter evenly. Cook over medium heat until top is dry. Cool on wire rack, then stack with wax paper between them.

For filling, combine all remaining ingredients except the ¼ cup of Parmesan cheese. Beat with a wooden spoon to blend well. Spread about ¼ cup filling down the center of each manicotti and roll up. Place completed rolls, seam-side down, in a shallow casserole dish, making 2 layers if necessary. Top with homemade tomato sauce and remaining Parmesan cheese.

Bake at 350°F for 30 minutes.

Serves 8.

—Hazel R. Baker

Basil Butter Balls

Simple it is, but seasoned, buttered pasta is one of the most delicious treats possible. These butter balls can be assembled and stored in the freezer, removed at the last minute and served with cooked fresh pasta for a quick and easy supper. All else that is needed is a tossed salad.

Ingredients

½ cup unsalted butter
10 basil leaves
1 clove garlic
¼ tsp. black pepper

Directions

In blender or food processor, purée ingredients. Shape into small balls, place on cookie sheet and freeze. When balls are well frozen, remove from cookie sheet and store in covered container in freezer.

—Louise McDonald

Pesto

Ingredients
2 cups fresh basil
2 cloves garlic
½ cup parsley
½ tsp. salt
⅓–½ cup olive oil
¼ cup Parmesan cheese

Directions

Place basil, garlic, parsley, salt and ⅓ cup oil in blender. Process, adding more oil if necessary to make a smooth paste. Add cheese and blend for a few seconds. Serve over cooked, buttered spaghetti.

Serves 4.

Spaghetti with Garlic & Oil

Quick and simple, this dish allows the diner to really appreciate the flavors of the pasta and the garlic.

Ingredients

4 oz. spaghetti
½ cup olive oil
4 cloves garlic, peeled & crushed
Black pepper

Directions

Cook spaghetti in boiling, salted water. When almost cooked, heat oil in heavy pot. Add garlic and cook until browned. Drain and rinse spaghetti. Mix with garlic-oil mixture and serve topped with black pepper.

Serves 2.

Noodle Salad

An excellent and easy way to use up leftover pasta, this dish can even utilize pasta with sauce on it — just rinse thoroughly in cold water before mixing with dressing.

Ingredients

½ cup yogurt
½ cup mayonnaise
1 Tbsp. Dijon mustard
1 Tbsp. dill
3–4 cups cooked pasta

Directions

Combine yogurt, mayonnaise, mustard and dill. Mix with rinsed pasta and chill well.

Serves 4.

Clam Sauce for Spaghetti

Ingredients

¼ cup butter
5 cloves garlic, peeled & halved
2 Tbsp. whole wheat flour
2 Tbsp. powdered milk
2 5-oz. cans whole baby butter clams
Oregano

Directions

Melt butter and slowly sauté garlic for 3 minutes. Do not let butter brown. Remove garlic and add flour and milk. Blend well and remove from heat.

Drain clams and add liquid to flour slowly, beating well with a whisk. Return sauce to medium heat and cook until thick (about 4 minutes). Add clams and oregano and pour over spaghetti.

Serves 2.

—Linda Townsend

Fettucini Alfredo

This rich pasta dish is particularly delicious served with veal cooked in a cream sauce or with stuffed zucchini. If spinach noodles are used, the dish will be an attractive green.

Ingredients

½ lb. fettucini noodles
¼ lb. butter
1 cup whipping cream
½ cup grated Parmesan cheese
½ cup chopped parsley
Salt & pepper

Directions

Cook noodles in boiling salted water. Drain. Return to pot. Over low heat, stir in butter, cream and cheese and cook, mixing well, until butter is melted and mixture is hot. Stir in parsley and salt and pepper.

Serves 2 as a main dish, 4 as a side dish.

Pork Meatballs and Spaghetti Sauce

A variation of the traditional beef meatballs, pork meatballs provide a flavorful addition to this spaghetti sauce, which is also enhanced by the addition of zucchini.

Meatball Ingredients

1 lb. ground pork
¼ cup Parmesan cheese
¼ cup oatmeal
½ cup chopped onion
3 Tbsp. chopped parsley
1 tsp. oregano
½ tsp. salt
¼ tsp. pepper
2 drops Tabasco sauce
1 Tbsp. oil

Sauce Ingredients

28-oz. can tomatoes
6-oz. can tomato paste
¾ cup chopped celery
½ cup chopped green pepper
½ cup chopped green olives
1 tsp. oregano
1 tsp. basil
2 drops Tabasco sauce
¾ cup grated zucchini
1 cup chopped mushrooms

Directions

To make meatballs, combine pork, cheese, oatmeal, onion, parsley, oregano, salt, pepper and Tabasco sauce. Mix well and form into small balls. Refrigerate for 1 hour to allow to set. Heat oil in skillet and brown meatballs on all sides. Drain on paper towels.

For sauce, combine tomatoes and tomato paste in large saucepan. Stir in celery, green pepper, olives, oregano, basil and Tabasco sauce. Bring to a boil, then drop in meatballs, zucchini and mushrooms. Simmer for 10 minutes and serve over cooked spaghetti.

Serves 6 to 8.

Chicken & Vegetable Sauce for Macaroni

Ingredients

1 Tbsp. cornstarch
½ tsp. salt
Pepper
2 Tbsp. soy sauce
½ cup chicken stock
2 Tbsp. vegetable oil
1 clove garlic, peeled
½ lb. raw chicken meat, cut into strips
1 medium onion, sliced
1 cup sliced celery
1 cup sliced mushrooms
2 cups broccoli, cut into florets & steamed until
    tender-crisp
1 tomato, cut into 8 pieces
2 green onions, chopped

Directions

Combine cornstarch, salt, pepper, soy sauce and chicken stock and set aside.

Heat oil in wok or heavy skillet. Sauté garlic until golden, then discard. Add chicken and sauté for 3 or 4 minutes, stirring constantly. Remove and set aside. Add onion, celery, mushrooms and broccoli and sauté until celery is tender — 4 minutes. Add chicken, tomato, green onions and cornstarch mixture. Cook until thickened, stirring constantly. Serve over cooked macaroni.

Serves 4.

Chicken & Sausage Spaghetti Sauce

Ingredients

3 Tbsp. olive oil
4 cloves garlic, peeled & crushed
2 medium onions, chopped
1 lb. hot Italian sausage, cut into ½-inch slices
3 stalks celery, chopped
1 green pepper, chopped
6 leaves basil
1–2 tsp. oregano
Salt & pepper
Bay leaf
½ lb. mushrooms, sliced
28-oz. can tomatoes
13-oz. can tomato paste
1 chicken, boiled, removed from bones &
    chopped

Directions

Heat oil and fry garlic and onions until onions are limp. Add sausage and cook, stirring occasionally, until browned. Stir in celery, green pepper, basil, oregano, salt and pepper and bay leaf. Cook for 5 to 10 minutes. Add mushrooms and cook for 5 more minutes. Add tomatoes, tomato paste and chicken and mix well.

Lower heat to simmer, cover and cook for at least 1 hour, adding water if sauce becomes too thick. Serve over cooked pasta and top with Parmesan cheese.

Serves 8 to 10.

Fettuccine Primavera

This recipe makes use of early spring vegetables — they must be fresh — in a white sauce. Additions or changes may be made according to personal taste. Green beans and cauliflower are good, as is the addition of shrimp. Because so many vegetables appear in the sauce, it is best to use unflavored fettuccine noodles.

Ingredients

½ large head broccoli, cut into florets
1 zucchini, thinly sliced
½ cup sliced mushrooms
10 snow peas
1 medium onion, sliced
1 carrot, sliced
8 oz. fettuccine
¼ cup butter
2 cloves garlic, minced
2 Tbsp. basil
¼ cup cream
¼ cup white wine
2 Tbsp. parsley
½ cup Parmesan cheese

Directions

Steam broccoli, zucchini, mushrooms, snow peas, onion and carrot for 10 minutes. Cook fettuccine in boiling, salted water for 10 minutes.

Meanwhile, prepare sauce. Melt butter and brown garlic. Add remaining ingredients, mix thoroughly and heat through. Remove from heat, and toss with vegetables and fettuccine.

Serves 4.

—Janis Scattergood

Pasta e Piselli

This is a southern Italian recipe for pasta with peas, which has been in the contributor's family for four generations.

Ingredients

2 cloves garlic
⅓ cup olive oil
1 medium onion, sliced
1 lb. tomatoes, coarsely chopped
½ lb. fresh peas
½ tsp. oregano
Salt & pepper
Chili pepper flakes
1 lb. bite-sized pasta
2 eggs
½ cup Parmesan or Romano cheese
2 Tbsp. milk

Directions

Peel garlic and brown in oil in large skillet, then remove garlic and discard. Sauté onion in oil until tender. Add tomatoes, peas, oregano, salt and pepper and chili pepper. Cover and simmer slowly as pasta cooks.

Cook pasta in boiling, salted water. While pasta is cooking, beat eggs in bowl and mix in cheese and milk.

Drain cooked pasta and return to pot. Add vegetable mixture, then egg-cheese mixture and heat slowly, stirring constantly, until eggs are cooked.

Serves 6.

—Anthony Balzano

Linguini with Zucchini al Pesto

Ingredients

2 small zucchini,
   cut into strips
2 Tbsp. butter
½ cup fresh basil
½ cup snipped parsley
3 cloves garlic, crushed
4 Tbsp. pine nuts, lightly roasted
Handful Parmesan cheese
1 cup olive oil
6 Tbsp. butter, softened
Salt & pepper
8 oz. linguini

Directions

Fry zucchini in oil until limp and golden. Whir in blender basil, parsley, garlic, pine nuts and Parmesan cheese, adding oil and butter a little at a time to keep the sauce thick.

Cook linguini until just tender. Combine linguini, zucchini and sauce. Add salt and pepper to taste.

Serves 4 to 6.

—*Cary Elizabeth Marshall*

Spaghetti alla Carbonara

Ingredients

1 lb. ham, cubed
2 Tbsp. butter
8 oz. spaghetti
¼ cup butter
1 Tbsp. flour
1 cup whipping cream
4 eggs, beaten
1 cup Parmesan cheese
Freshly ground pepper

Directions

Fry ham in 2 Tbsp. butter until crispy and set aside. Cook spaghetti in boiling, salted water.

While spaghetti is cooking, make sauce. Melt ¼ cup butter and stir in flour. Gradually blend in whipping cream and bring almost to a boil. Add eggs and ham and simmer for 2 minutes, stirring constantly. Add Parmesan cheese and pepper, pour over cooked, drained spaghetti and serve.

Serves 4.

—*Fern Acton*

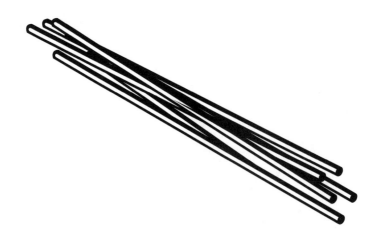

Zucchini and Spaghetti Casserole

Ingredients

4 medium zucchini, sliced
1 large onion, chopped
4 tomatoes, peeled & chopped
½ cup butter
½ cup grated Parmesan cheese
Salt & pepper
1 lb. spaghetti, cooked
1 lb. mozzarella cheese, grated

Directions

Sauté vegetables in butter until tender. In casserole dish, toss with Parmesan cheese, salt and pepper and spaghetti. Top with mozzarella cheese.

Bake at 350°F for 30 minutes, or until cheese is melted and bubbling.

Serves 6 to 8.

—*Glenda McCawder*

Macaroni with Sausage

Ingredients

1 lb. sausage meat
1 onion, finely chopped
1 clove garlic, chopped
¼ cup sliced mushrooms
1 Tbsp. butter
¼ tsp. savory
¼ tsp. celery seed
¼ tsp. oregano
¼ tsp. chili powder
¼ tsp. pepper
¼ tsp. dry mustard
6-oz. can tomato paste
¼ cup water
3 cups cooked macaroni
1 cup cottage cheese

Directions

Sauté sausage meat until lightly browned. Drain off fat, separate meat with fork and set aside. Sauté onion, garlic and mushrooms in butter. Add sausage meat, savory, celery seed, oregano, chili powder, pepper and dry mustard. Stir in tomato paste and water and mix well. Add macaroni and stir.

Arrange alternate layers of macaroni-meat mixture and cottage cheese in greased casserole dish, ending with meat on top. Bake at 350°F for 25 to 30 minutes.

Serves 8.

—*Ruth Anne Laverty*

Savory Noodle Bake

Ingredients

2 Tbsp. oil
4 Tbsp. butter
2 onions, finely chopped
1 clove garlic, minced
2 cups canned tomatoes
⅛ tsp. salt
Pepper
¼ tsp. oregano or basil
1 bay leaf
8 oz. egg noodles
3 cups grated Cheddar cheese

Directions

Combine oil and 2 Tbsp. butter, place over low heat and, when butter has melted, add onions and garlic. Cook over low heat until soft.

Combine tomatoes, salt and spices. Add to onion mixture; simmer for 15 minutes and discard bay leaf.

Cook noodles until tender; rinse with hot water and drain. Add remaining 2 Tbsp. butter and 2 cups cheese. Add tomato sauce. Turn mixture into greased baking dish and top with remaining 1 cup cheese.

Bake at 350°F for 30 minutes.

—Georgina Mitchell

Lasagne Ham Roll-Ups

Ingredients

8 lasagne noodles
8 thin slices ham
2 Tbsp. prepared mustard
1 cup grated Cheddar cheese
Salt & pepper
2 cups tomato or mushroom sauce, pages 339 & 129
2 large tomatoes, sliced
Parsley sprigs

Directions

Cook noodles until tender. Drain, rinse and lay on sheet of greased foil. Lay slice of ham on each noodle, trimming to fit. Spread with mustard and sprinkle with cheese and seasonings. Roll up each noodle, enclosing the filling. Place in greased shallow baking dish. Pour sauce over top and arrange tomato slices over this. Bake at 375°F for 30 minutes. Garnish with parsley and serve.

Serves 4.

—Anne Budge

Baked Rigatoni

Ingredients

16 oz. rigatoni noodles
3 Tbsp. butter
8 oz. mozzarella cheese, diced
4 cups spaghetti sauce
1 cup sliced mushrooms
¾ cup Parmesan cheese

Directions

Cook rigatoni in boiling, salted water and place in greased casserole dish. Add 2 Tbsp. butter, cheese, spaghetti sauce and mushrooms and mix well. Sprinkle with Parmesan cheese and dot with remaining butter. Bake at 350°F for 20 to 30 minutes, or until heated through.

Serves 4 to 6.

—Debbie Anne McCully

Lokshen Kugel

Kugel is a traditional Sabbath dish. This noodle pudding was prepared the day before and slow cooked over a fire until the Sabbath, when fires could not be started. It can also be made as a sweet dish by the addition of raisins and cinnamon.

Ingredients

1 pkg. wide egg noodles
1 sleeve soda crackers
Salt & pepper
3–6 eggs

Directions

Cook noodles in boiling, salted water until tender. Drain but do not rinse. Crush crackers and add to noodles. Add salt and pepper to taste. Add eggs one at a time until creamy. Bake in greased, deep baking dish at 400°F for 50 to 60 minutes or until golden brown.

Serves 6.

—Lisa Mann

Creamy Pasta Sauce with Fresh Herbs

Ingredients

1½ cups heavy cream
4 Tbsp. butter
½ tsp. salt
⅛ tsp. nutmeg
cayenne
¼ cup Parmesan cheese
¼ cup chopped mixed herbs (basil, mint, parsley, chives)
1 lb. angel hair pasta, cooked, drained & rinsed

Directions

Combine cream, butter, salt, nutmeg and cayenne in heavy saucepan. Simmer for 15 minutes, or until slightly reduced and thickened. Whisk in cheese and herbs and simmer for 5 minutes. Serve over cooked pasta.

Serves 4.

—*Barb McDonald*

Pork & Mushroom Spaghetti Sauce

Ingredients

4 lbs. coarsely ground pork
2 lbs. mushrooms, sliced
1½ cups chopped celery
1 cup chopped onion
1½ cups chopped green pepper
2 Tbsp. salt
3 Tbsp. oregano
3 Tbsp. paprika
1 tsp. pepper
13-oz. can tomato paste
28-oz. can tomatoes

Directions

Brown pork in heavy saucepan. Add mushrooms, celery, onion, green pepper, salt, oregano, paprika, pepper and 1 cup water. Bring to a boil. Add tomato paste and tomatoes. Simmer for 1½ hours. Serve over cooked pasta.

Serves 10 to 12.

—*Fran Pytko*

Pasta

Ingredients

2 cups flour
3 eggs
2 tsp. oil
2 Tbsp. water

Directions

To make dough by hand, mound flour on work surface, and make a well in the center. Combine eggs, oil and water, and pour into well. Mix together, using a fork at first and then working by hand. Knead dough for 5 to 8 minutes, or until smooth and elastic. Cover and let stand for 10 minutes.

If using a food processor, place all ingredients in machine and process until a ball forms. Knead for 2 to 4 minutes, or until smooth and elastic. Cover and let stand for 2 minutes.

In either case, if dough is too wet, add flour; if too dry, add an egg.

To roll pasta by hand, divide dough into thirds, and roll on floured board until it reaches desired thinness. Cut as desired. If using a pasta machine, divide dough into thirds, and begin with rollers at first setting, rolling twice through each setting, until desired thinness is attained. Cut by machine or by hand.

Smooth Spaghetti Sauce

This recipe is for those who prefer a smooth sauce for spaghetti, lasagne or manicotti. Quick to assemble, it can be left to simmer for hours. The vinegar adds an unusual taste.

Ingredients

2 Tbsp. olive oil
½ cup chopped onion
1 large clove garlic, minced
⅓ cup red wine vinegar
¼ tsp. thyme
½ tsp. basil
½ tsp. oregano
1½ tsp. salt
2 Tbsp. parsley
½ tsp. Worcestershire sauce
¼ tsp. pepper
2 Tbsp. honey
28-oz. can tomatoes
3 6½-oz. cans tomato paste

Directions

Heat oil and sauté onion and garlic until onion is translucent. Add remaining ingredients and simmer for 1 hour.

Makes 7 cups.

—Susan O'Neill

Olivade

Ingredients

2 lbs. large Kalamata olives, pitted
½ cup olive oil
1¼ cups chopped walnuts
2 cloves garlic, minced
2 tsp. chopped basil
½ tsp. pepper
1 cup Parmesan cheese
2–4 tsp. red wine vinegar

Directions

Combine olives, oil, walnuts, garlic, basil and pepper. Mix well. Add cheese and vinegar to taste. This mixture may be stored, refrigerated, for up to 2 months.

—Sandra K. Bennett

Spinach Sauce

Ingredients

¼ cup butter
10 oz. spinach, finely chopped
1 tsp. salt
1 cup cottage cheese
¼ cup Parmesan cheese
¼ cup milk
⅛ tsp. nutmeg

Directions

Melt butter, add spinach and salt and cook until spinach is limp — about 5 minutes. Lower heat to simmer, stir in cottage and Parmesan cheeses, milk and nutmeg, and cook, stirring, until mixture is heated through. Serve with cooked spaghetti.

Serves 6.

Pasta Carbonara

We offer here two carbonara recipes. Although both retain the basic concept of a carbonara, they differ considerably from each other.

Ingredients

1 lb. thickly sliced bacon, diced
1 lb. linguine
3 eggs
⅓ cup chopped Italian parsley
½ cup Parmesan cheese
pepper

Directions

Fry bacon until crisp. Drain well on paper towels. Cook linguine until just tender. While this is cooking, beat eggs, then stir in parsley and cheese. Drain and rinse linguine, then mix with egg mixture. Add bacon and pepper and toss again.

Serves 4 to 6.

—Barb McDonald

Spaghetti alla Carbonara

Ingredients

1 lb. spaghetti
1 clove garlic, minced
2 Tbsp. olive oil
½ lb. mushrooms, sliced
2 cups diced ham
4 eggs
¼ cup minced parsley
¾ cup Parmesan cheese

Directions

Cook spaghetti until just tender. Drain and rinse. Meanwhile, sauté garlic in olive oil for 2 minutes. Add mushrooms and ham and sauté until ham is slightly crisp. Beat eggs lightly, add parsley and cheese and mix with spaghetti. Pour ham mixture over and mix well.

Serves 4 to 6.

—Diane Pearse

Creamy Garlic Sauce

The creaminess of this sauce complements its tangy garlic flavor — cottage cheese may be substituted if ricotta is unavailable.

Ingredients

½ cup milk
2 Tbsp. butter
3-4 cloves garlic, crushed
1 lb. ricotta cheese
pasta of your choice, cooked, drained & rinsed
½ cup Parmesan cheese
pepper

Directions

Heat milk and butter in heavy pot. Add garlic and simmer for 5 minutes, then remove garlic. Add ricotta cheese and cook, stirring, over low heat until ricotta has melted. Remove from heat and cover. Toss pasta with ricotta mixture, and sprinkle with Parmesan cheese and pepper.

Serves 2 to 3.

—Irene Louden

Hungarian Stew & Noodles

"I developed this recipe for my daughter's first birthday party, when I was still an inexperienced cook. I wanted something that was tasty but would appeal to people from 1 year old to 80 years old, something I could make ahead of time and something that could be made easily in a large quantity. This was the result, and I've used it for many family gatherings since."

Ingredients

½ cup oil
1 clove garlic, crushed
5 lbs. stewing beef, cut into 1" cubes
4 onions, sliced
18-oz. can tomato paste
2½ cups water
1 Tbsp. paprika
2 tsp. salt
1 tsp. pepper
1 bay leaf
16 oz. noodles
2 Tbsp. butter
1 Tbsp. parsley

Directions

Heat oil. Cook garlic for 1 minute, then discard. Add beef and onions, and cook over medium-high heat until meat is lightly browned. Stir in tomato paste, water, paprika, salt, pepper and bay leaf. Bring to a boil, reduce heat to low, cover and simmer for 3 hours.

When stew is nearly done, cook noodles. Toss with butter and parsley. To serve, heap noodles in middle of serving plate and surround with stew.

Serves 10.

Basiled Noodles

Ingredients

1 lb. curly noodles
4 Tbsp. butter
¾ cup chopped walnuts
⅓ cup chopped basil
salt & pepper

Directions

Cook noodles in boiling water. Meanwhile, melt butter in small saucepan over medium heat and add nuts. Cook for 3 to 4 minutes. Add basil and cook for 1 minute to soften and to release flavor. Mix with drained noodles and add salt and pepper to taste.

Serves 8 as a side dish.

—*Diane M. Johnson*

Spaghetti Balls & Sauce

Delicious nonmeat "meatballs," these are based on cream cheese and walnuts. The spaghetti balls are simmered in the tomato sauce and then poured over cooked pasta.

Cheese Ball Ingredients

2 eggs
¾ cup cracker crumbs
¼ cup wheat germ
½ cup ground walnuts
4 oz. cream cheese
1 clove garlic, chopped
oil or butter

Sauce Ingredients

3 Tbsp. oil
¼ green pepper, chopped
¼ lb. mushrooms, sliced
1 onion, chopped
salt
¼ tsp. sage
½ tsp. oregano
½ bay leaf
28-oz. can tomatoes
6½-oz. can tomato sauce

Directions

Lightly beat eggs, then combine with cracker crumbs, wheat germ, walnuts, cream cheese and garlic. Mix well. Shape into small balls. Chill for 1 hour, then brown in oil or butter.

Meanwhile, make sauce. Heat oil and sauté green pepper, mushrooms and onion. Add salt, herbs, tomatoes and tomato sauce. Add browned spaghetti balls, and simmer for 1 hour.

Serve over spaghetti.

Serves 6.

—*Vicky Chandler*

Ravioli

If you make ravioli often, you may wish to invest in a ravioli cutter. This looks like a wooden rolling pin with small square indentations. The serrated edges on the squares cut easily through the dough. If you use this, roll the dough out in sheets and then fill, rather than rolling out in strips.

Ingredients

Pasta recipe (page 355)
1 egg, lightly beaten
1½ lbs. ground beef
¼ cup Parmesan cheese
1¼ cups chopped raw spinach
2 Tbsp. chopped parsley
½ cup bread crumbs
¼ lb. dry Italian salami, chopped
2 eggs, lightly beaten
salt & pepper

Directions

Make pasta dough using basic pasta recipe (page 355); set aside.

Cook beef until well browned. Drain off fat, then mix with remaining filling ingredients. Cool.

Flour a large work surface. Roll out dough until it is very thin. Brush with lightly beaten egg. Cut dough into ½-inch strips. Place filling on alternate strips of dough by teaspoonfuls, about 2 inches apart. Place empty dough strips on top of filled ones. Pinch down sides well with a fork, cut between hills of filling and pinch edges closed.

Cook a few at a time in boiling water for 15 minutes, remove and drain. Serve with tomato sauce, if desired.

Makes approximately 4 dozen.

—*Diane Capelazo*

Curried Pasta Salad

Salad Ingredients

16 oz. dry spiral pasta
¼ cup olive oil
1 green pepper, sliced
1 red pepper, sliced
3-4 stalks celery, chopped
2 cups broccoli florets
1 13-oz. can pitted black olives, drained
1 4-oz. can water chestnuts, drained & sliced
2 cups chopped purple cabbage

Dressing Ingredients

⅔ cup olive oil
3 Tbsp. wine vinegar
1 large clove garlic, crushed
1-1½ Tbsp. curry powder
1 tsp. coriander
⅓ cup Parmesan cheese

Directions

Cook pasta in boiling water until soft but not soggy. Rinse in cold water and then toss with olive oil. Add remaining salad ingredients and set aside.

Combine dressing ingredients, except Parmesan cheese. Toss with salad, then allow to sit for 5 to 10 minutes. Add Parmesan cheese, toss and serve.

Serves 8 to 10.

—Colleen Suche

Seafood Linguine

Ingredients

2 cups sliced mushrooms
4 shallots or green onions, finely chopped
½ cup butter
1½ cups Madeira
1 Tbsp. tomato paste
1 Tbsp. snipped tarragon
¼ tsp. salt
pepper
10 oz. linguine
1½ lbs. shrimp, shelled
1½ cups heavy cream
4 egg yolks, beaten
salt & pepper

Directions

Cook mushrooms and shallots in butter, uncovered, over medium-high heat for 4 to 5 minutes, or until vegetables are tender. Remove with slotted spoon and set aside.

Stir Madeira, tomato paste, tarragon, ¼ tsp. salt and pepper into butter in skillet. Bring to a boil, and cook vigorously for 10 minutes, or until mixture is reduced to cup.

Meanwhile, cook pasta. Drain and keep warm. Drop shrimp into boiling water and cook for 1 to 3 minutes, or until shrimp turn pink. Drain and keep warm.

In small bowl, stir together cream and egg yolks. Add Madeira mixture. Return to skillet. Cook and stir until thickened. Stir in shrimp and mushroom mixture and heat through. Season with salt and pepper. Toss with pasta.

Serves 6.

—Kristine Mattila

Macaroni & Cheese Casserole

Tomatoes give this macaroni and cheese casserole an added zing. It was developed by the adopted grandmother of the contributor and can be frozen successfully.

Ingredients

3 cups dry elbow macaroni, cooked & drained
1 lb. sharp Cheddar cheese, grated
28-oz. can tomatoes, including juice
pepper
1 cup chopped onion, sautéed in butter
Parmesan cheese

Directions

Combine all ingredients except Parmesan cheese and mix well. Top with Parmesan cheese. Bake, uncovered, at 350°F for 1 hour.

Serves 8.

—Anna J. Lee

Noodle Casserole Deluxe

Available for order online, dried tree ears have a distinctive taste and texture. They are somewhat similar to black Chinese mushrooms, which can be substituted if tree ears are not available.

Ingredients

1 oz. tree ears
1 oz. black Chinese mushrooms
1 lb. mushrooms, quartered
2 Tbsp. lemon juice
3 Tbsp. butter
1 onion, finely chopped
1 bunch parsley, chopped
salt & pepper
¼ tsp. thyme
3 eggs, beaten
1 cup heavy cream
½ cup milk
nutmeg
3 cups dry egg noodles, cooked
5 Tbsp. Parmesan cheese
1 cup buttered bread crumbs

Directions

Soak tree ears in warm water for 30 minutes and the Chinese mushrooms for 15 minutes. Drain, then chop. Mix regular mushrooms with lemon juice.

Melt butter and sauté onion for 5 minutes. Add all mushrooms and sauté for 2 minutes longer. Add parsley, salt and pepper and thyme and sauté for 10 minutes.

Mix together eggs, cream, milk, nutmeg and salt and pepper. Place cooked noodles and mushroom mixture in greased 9" x 9" casserole dish. Pour egg mixture over and mix well. Sprinkle with cheese and bread crumbs.

Bake, uncovered, at 400°F for 25 to 30 minutes.

Serves 4.

—Inge Benda

Cheesy Broccoli Casserole

This is a rich, tasty casserole. It feeds a crowd and can be prepared and assembled a day ahead.

Ingredients

3 eggs
2½ cups ricotta cheese
¾ cup sour cream
¼ cup butter
1 lb. mushrooms, sliced
2 heads broccoli, cut into florets
2 onions, chopped
salt & pepper
1 lb. dry egg noodles, cooked, drained & rinsed
2 Tbsp. yeast
½ cup bread crumbs
1 cup grated Swiss cheese

Directions

Combine eggs, ricotta cheese and sour cream; mix well. Set aside.

Melt butter in heavy skillet. Sauté mushrooms, broccoli and onions until onions are transparent – 5 to 10 minutes. Sprinkle with salt and pepper.

In greased 9" x 13" pan, combine cooked noodles, egg mixture and vegetables. Add yeast and mix well. Sprinkle with bread crumbs and grated cheese.

Bake, covered, at 350°F for 30 minutes, then uncovered for 15 minutes.

Serves 8.

Turkey-Stuffed Pasta Shells

Ingredients

1 lb. ground raw turkey
1 onion, chopped
2 Tbsp. butter
1 egg, slightly beaten
2 cups cottage cheese
1½ cups grated Cheddar cheese
½ tsp. oregano
½ tsp. sage
¼ tsp. pepper
1 lb. spinach, chopped & steamed
1 lb. large pasta shells
2–3 cups rich tomato sauce
Parmesan cheese

Directions

Brown turkey and onion in butter. Combine egg with cottage cheese, Cheddar cheese, oregano, sage and pepper. Squeeze excess liquid from spinach and stir into cheese mixture along with turkey and onion. Mix well.

Stuff pasta shells with filling. Place 3 to 4 Tbsp. tomato sauce in bottom of greased 9" x 13" baking pan. Arrange shells in pan, then pour tomato sauce over. Sprinkle with Parmesan cheese and bake at 350°F for 50 to 60 minutes.

Serves 6 to 8.

—Lois B. Demerich

Lasagne Stuffed with Tiny Meatballs

A lot of work but well worth the effort, this recipe makes enough lasagne to serve 16 people. It can also be frozen and used for a last-minute meal.

Main Ingredients

1 lb. lasagne noodles
2 cups cottage or ricotta cheese, puréed
2 eggs, lightly beaten
1 lb. mozzarella cheese, grated
½ cup Parmesan cheese

Sauce Ingredients

3 Tbsp. oil
2 onions, chopped
½ green pepper, diced
10 mushrooms, sliced
1–2 cloves garlic, minced
3 28-oz. cans tomato sauce
1 Tbsp. chopped parsley
1 tsp. basil
½ tsp. oregano

Meatball Ingredients

1½ lbs. ground meat
(beef, veal or pork)
¼ cup Parmesan cheese
1 clove garlic, minced
1½ Tbsp. chopped parsley
⅛ tsp. nutmeg
1 tsp. basil
½ tsp. grated lemon rind
¼ tsp. salt
¼ tsp. pepper
⅔ cup dry bread crumbs
1 Tbsp. milk
1 egg

Directions

Cook noodles in boiling water, drain, rinse and set aside.

Prepare sauce. Heat oil in large pot. Add onions and sauté until soft. Add green pepper, mushrooms and garlic and cook, stirring, for 3 minutes. Stir in tomato sauce and herbs. Bring to a boil, reduce heat, and simmer while preparing rest of dish.

Combine meat, cheese, garlic, parsley, nutmeg, basil, lemon rind, salt and pepper and mix well. In another bowl, combine bread crumbs, milk and egg. Work this into meat, then chill mixture for 1 hour. Shape into tiny meatballs, keeping your hands damp with cold water. Cook meatballs by steaming over low heat in enough water to prevent sticking. Drop cooked meatballs into tomato sauce, setting aside a small amount of sauce to spread on bottom of lasagne pans.

Combine cottage or ricotta cheese with eggs and mozzarella cheese.

To assemble, grease two 9" x 13" pans. Spread bottom of pans with very thin layer of tomato sauce. On top of this, place a layer of noodles, then half the cheese mixture, then one third the meatballs and tomato sauce. Sprinkle with Parmesan cheese. Repeat. Top with layer of noodles, remaining meatballs and sauce and Parmesan cheese.

Bake, uncovered, at 375°F for 30 minutes, or until bubbling and golden. Let stand for 10 minutes before serving.

Serves 16.

—Lynne Roe

Baking

Poppy Seed Lemon Bread

Ingredients

4 eggs
1½ cups oil
1½ cups light cream
1 tsp. vanilla
½ cup poppy seeds
3 cups flour
2¼ cups sugar
1 tsp. salt
1½ tsp. baking soda
2 tsp. baking powder
Rind & juice of 1 lemon

Directions

Combine eggs, oil, cream, vanilla and poppy seeds. Mix together flour, 2 cups sugar, salt, baking soda, baking powder and lemon rind.

Add dry ingredients to egg-cream mixture and blend well. Pour into 2 greased loaf pans and bake at 325°F for 70 minutes.

Meanwhile, mix lemon juice and rind with remaining ¼ cup sugar. Pour over bread while hot and still in pan.

Makes 2 loaves.

—Audrey Moroso

Orange Date Nut Bread

Ingredients

1 cup boiling water
¼ cup orange juice
1 cup chopped dates
1½ cups flour
¼ tsp. cinnamon
¼ tsp. nutmeg
Ground cloves
1½ tsp. baking soda
½ tsp. salt
¼ cup shortening
¾ cup brown sugar
1 egg
1 cup chopped walnuts
2 tsp. grated orange peel

Directions

Mix together boiling water, orange juice and chopped dates. Set aside until cooled to room temperature.

Sift together flour, cinnamon, nutmeg, cloves, baking soda and salt and set aside.

Cream together shortening and brown sugar. Add egg, beat well and stir in date mixture. Add dry ingredients and stir batter until moistened. Fold in walnuts and orange peel.

Pour into a greased loaf pan and bake at 325°F for 65 to 70 minutes. Cool bread in pan for 10 minutes, remove and cool completely before slicing.

Makes 1 loaf.

—Kathy & Rhett Hagerty

Blueberry Quick Bread

Ingredients

2½ cups flour
¾ cup sugar
1 Tbsp. baking powder
½ tsp. salt
6 Tbsp. butter
¾ cup chopped walnuts
2 eggs
1 cup milk
1 tsp. vanilla
1½ cups blueberries

Directions

In large bowl, mix flour, sugar, baking powder and salt. Cut in butter until fine. Stir in walnuts.

In small bowl, beat eggs lightly and stir in milk and vanilla. Stir into flour just until flour is moistened. Gently stir blueberries into batter.

Spoon batter into greased and floured loaf pan. Bake at 350°F for 1 hour and 20 minutes or until toothpick inserted into center of loaf comes out clean.

Makes 1 loaf.

Pumpkin Bread

Ingredients

4 eggs
2 cups granulated sugar
1¼ cups oil
2 cups cooked & mashed pumpkin
1 tsp. salt
3 cups flour
2 tsp. baking powder
2 tsp. baking soda
2 tsp. cinnamon
½ cup chopped walnuts
1 cup seedless raisins

Directions

Beat eggs and add sugar, oil and pumpkin. Mix dry ingredients together and add to egg mixture. Stir in nuts and raisins. Bake at 350°F for one hour.

Makes 2 large loaves.

—*Irene P. Simonson*

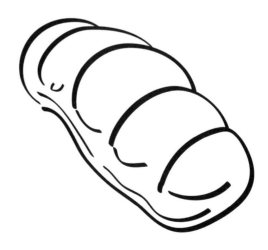

Banana Nut Bread

Ingredients

2 cups flour
2 tsp. baking powder
1 tsp. baking soda
¾ tsp. salt
½ cup shortening
1 cup sugar
2 eggs, well beaten
1 cup mashed bananas
1 cup chopped walnuts

Directions

Sift together flour, baking powder, baking soda and salt. Cream together shortening, sugar and eggs.

Add bananas to creamed mixture alternately with dry ingredients, combining well after each addition. Stir in walnuts.

Spoon into greased loaf pan and bake at 350°F for 1 to 1¼ hours or until straw inserted into center comes out clean.

Makes 1 loaf.

—Janice Clynick

Cinnamon Bread

Ingredients

2 Tbsp. brown sugar
1 Tbsp. cinnamon
½ cup butter
1 cup granulated sugar
2 eggs
2 cups flour
2 tsp. baking powder
½ tsp. salt
1 cup milk
1 tsp. vanilla

Directions

Mix together brown sugar and cinnamon and set aside. Cream butter, granulated sugar and eggs. Combine dry ingredients and add to creamed mixture alternately with milk. Stir in vanilla. Layer batter and brown sugar-cinnamon mixture in a greased loaf pan, ending with batter. Bake at 350°F for 1 hour.

Makes 1 loaf.

—Karen Carter

Orange Raisin Bread

Ingredients

1 large orange, unpeeled
¾ cup boiling water
1 egg
¼ cup vegetable oil
2 cups flour
2 tsp. baking powder
1 tsp. baking soda
½ tsp. salt
¾ cup lightly packed brown sugar
¾ cup raisins
½ cup chopped nuts

Directions

Cut orange into pieces and remove seeds. Combine in blender with boiling water and blend until almost smooth. Add egg and oil and blend for a few seconds.

Combine remaining ingredients. Add orange mixture and stir just until well blended. Pour into greased loaf pan. Bake at 350°F for 45 to 55 minutes.

Makes 1 loaf.

—Margaret Butler

Date & Nut Loaf

Ingredients

1 cup walnuts
1 cup chopped dates
1½ tsp. baking soda
½ tsp. salt
3 Tbsp. shortening
¾ cup boiling water
2 eggs
1 tsp. vanilla
1 cup granulated sugar
1½ cups flour

Directions

Combine walnuts, dates, baking soda, salt, shortening and boiling water. Set aside for 20 minutes. Beat eggs with a fork and add vanilla, sugar and flour. Add to date mixture and blend. Pour into a greased bread pan and bake at 350°F for 1 hour.

Makes 1 loaf.

—Joyce Marshall

Carrot Bread

Ingredients

½ cup oil
1 cup sugar
2 eggs, beaten
1 cup shredded carrots
1½ cups flour
1 tsp. baking powder
1 tsp. baking soda
¼ tsp. salt
1 tsp. cinnamon
½ cup milk

Directions

Mix oil and sugar. Add beaten eggs and stir in carrots. Sift flour, baking powder, baking soda, salt and cinnamon.

Add small amounts of dry ingredients to sugar mixture alternately with milk. Bake in greased loaf pan for 55 minutes at 350°F.

Makes 1 loaf.

—Patricia A. Leahy

Zucchini Loaf

Ingredients

2 eggs
1 cup sugar
½ cup oil
1½ cups flour
½ tsp. salt
1 tsp. baking powder
½ tsp. baking soda
1 tsp. cinnamon
1 tsp. vanilla
1 cup finely grated raw zucchini
½ cup chopped walnuts

Directions

Beat eggs until light and add sugar and oil. Stir together flour, salt, baking powder, baking soda and cinnamon. Add to egg mixture, beating until blended. Mix in vanilla, zucchini and nuts.

Turn into a greased loaf pan and bake at 350°F for 1 hour or until a toothpick inserted in center comes out clean.

Makes 1 loaf.

—Carolyn Hills

Dutch Pumpernickel Bread

Ingredients

2 Tbsp. molasses
3 cups hot water
3 cups Red River cereal
1 cup whole wheat flour
2 tsp. baking soda
1 tsp. salt

Directions

In large mixing bowl, combine water and molasses. Add remaining ingredients. Beat at high speed for 2 minutes. Cover with cloth towel and let stand overnight, then pour into greased loaf pan and smooth top.

Bake at 275°F for 1 hour, reduce heat to 250° and bake 1 hour longer. Store in refrigerator for one day before slicing.

Makes 1 loaf.

—Sandra Binnington

Bran Bread

Ingredients

½ cup brown sugar
2 cups bran
1 cup whole wheat flour
1 cup unbleached white flour
2 Tbsp. wheat germ
1 tsp. salt
2 tsp. baking soda
2 cups buttermilk

Directions

Combine dry ingredients. Stir in buttermilk. Spoon into a greased pan and bake at 350°F for 1 hour.

Makes 1 loaf.

—Johanna Genge

Lemon Bread

Ingredients

1 cup butter
1½ cups sugar
3 eggs
1½ cups flour
1 tsp. baking powder
Salt
½ cup milk
½ cup chopped walnuts
Grated rind & juice of 1 lemon

Directions

Cream together butter and 1 cup sugar. Beat in eggs. Combine flour, baking powder and salt. Add to creamed mixture alternately with milk and mix well. Stir in walnuts and lemon rind.

Pour into greased loaf pan and bake at 350°F for 1 hour or until firm on top.

Meanwhile, combine remaining ½ cup sugar with lemon juice. When loaf is baked, spoon lemon sugar over top.

Makes 1 loaf.

—Lily Andrews

Apple Honey Muffins

Ingredients

¼ cup honey
1 egg
¼ cup oil
1 cup apple sauce
⅓ cup orange juice
¾ cup rolled oats
1 cup flour
1 Tbsp. baking powder
½ tsp. cinnamon

Directions

In a small bowl, mix honey, egg, oil, apple sauce and orange juice until well combined.

Mix dry ingredients in a large bowl. Make a well in the center and pour in liquid ingredients, then stir just to moisten.

Spoon into greased muffin tins and bake at 400°F for 25 to 30 minutes.

Makes 12 muffins.

—*Carol A. Frost*

Orange Oatmeal Muffins

Ingredients

1 whole orange, unpeeled
1 cup rolled oats
½ cup boiling water
½ cup orange juice
½ cup butter
½ cup brown sugar
½ cup granulated sugar
2 eggs, beaten
1 cup flour
1 tsp. baking powder
1 tsp. baking soda
½ tsp. salt
1 tsp. vanilla
½ cup raisins

Directions

Place whole orange in blender and purée. Mix with oats, water and orange juice and set aside.

Cream together butter and sugars and add eggs. Combine dry ingredients and add to creamed mixture. Add rolled oat/orange mixture, vanilla and raisins, and stir well.

Bake in greased muffin tins at 350°F for 15 to 20 minutes.

Makes 18 muffins.

—*M. Heggison*

Poppy Seed Muffins

Ingredients

2 eggs
2 Tbsp. soft butter
¾ cup sugar
½ cup poppy seeds
1 cup sour cream
2 cups flour
½ tsp. baking soda
2 tsp. baking powder

Directions

Cream together eggs, butter and sugar. Add poppy seeds and sour cream. Sift together dry ingredients and stir into creamed mixture until just blended.

Pour into greased muffin tins, filling each two-thirds full. Bake at 425°F for 20 minutes.

Makes 12 large muffins.

—Sheri Israels

Blueberry Muffins

Ingredients

1 cup fresh blueberries
1¾ cups flour
¾ tsp. salt
3 tsp. baking powder
2 eggs, well beaten
3 Tbsp. melted butter
¾ cup milk
¼ cup granulated sugar

Directions

Mix blueberries and 1 Tbsp. flour. Sift together remaining flour, salt and baking powder. Combine beaten eggs, melted butter, milk and sugar. Beat until foamy. Add dry ingredients all at once and stir quickly.

Fill greased muffin tins one-third full with batter. Put blueberries on top and cover with remaining batter until tins are two-thirds full. Bake at 400°F for 15 to 20 minutes. Makes 12 large muffins.

—Janet Young

Banana Muffins

Ingredients

½ cup shortening
1 cup granulated sugar
1 egg, slightly beaten
1 cup mashed ripe bananas
1 tsp. baking soda
2 Tbsp. hot water
½ tsp. salt
1½ cups flour

Directions

Cream shortening and sugar together, blend in egg and mashed bananas. Dissolve soda in hot water and add to creamed mixture.

Combine dry ingredients and stir into creamed mixture until just blended. Pour into greased muffin tins and bake at 375°F for 20 minutes.

Makes 12 muffins.

—Helen Potts

Apple Muffins

Ingredients

4 eggs
2 cups milk
4 Tbsp. melted butter
1⅓ cups sugar
4 cups flour
1 tsp. salt
8 tsp. baking powder
1 tsp. cinnamon
½ tsp. nutmeg
4 medium apples, peeled, cored & chopped

Directions

Beat together eggs, milk, butter and ⅔ cup sugar. Combine flour, salt, baking powder, ½ tsp. cinnamon and nutmeg. Add to egg mixture and fold in apples.

Spoon into greased muffin tins until two-thirds full. Combine remaining ⅔ cup sugar and ½ tsp. cinnamon and sprinkle over muffins. Bake at 375°F for 30 minutes.

Makes 24 large muffins.

Buttermilk Bran Muffins

Ingredients

1 cup bran
1 cup wheat germ
2 cups boiling water
1 cup oil
2 cups granulated or brown sugar
4 eggs, beaten
5 cups flour
5 tsp. baking soda
1½ Tbsp. salt
4 cups milk
4 cups bran flakes
1–1½ cups raisins

Directions

Stir together bran, wheat germ and boiling water. Set aside to cool.

Combine remaining ingredients and mix well. Stir in bran mixture. Let sit for 24 hours before using.

Spoon into well greased muffin tins and bake at 400°F for 15 to 20 minutes. Batter will keep up to a week in the refrigerator.

Makes 4 to 5 dozen muffins.

—Dawn Livingstone

Quick Muffins

Ingredients

4 eggs
1½ cups milk
¾ cup oil
1 tsp. orange juice
2 cups white flour
2 cups rye flour
1 cup sugar
2 Tbsp. baking powder
Salt
Cinnamon & nutmeg

Directions

Combine liquid ingredients well, add flours, sugar, baking powder, salt and spices and mix until just moist.

Bake in greased muffin tins at 400°F for 20 minutes.

Makes 18 muffins.

—C. Majewski

Corn Muffins

Ingredients

1 cup milk
1 egg
3 Tbsp. oil
¾ cup flour
1 Tbsp. baking powder
3 Tbsp. sugar
1¼ cups corn meal

Directions

Beat together milk, egg and oil. Sift together dry ingredients and stir into milk mixture until moist.

Pour into greased muffin tins and bake at 425°F for 20 minutes.

Makes 12 muffins.

—Sheri Israels

Wheat Germ Muffins

Ingredients

1 Tbsp. butter
¾ cup granulated sugar
1 egg
1 cup wheat germ
¾ cup whole wheat flour
¼ cup unbleached white flour
1 tsp. baking soda
1 cup buttermilk

Directions

Cream butter and sugar and add egg. Mix dry ingredients and add alternately with buttermilk to creamed mixture.

Pour into greased muffin tins and bake at 350°F for 15 to 20 minutes.

Makes 12 muffins.

—Audrey Moroso

Oatmeal Muffins

Ingredients

1 cup oatmeal
1 cup buttermilk
1 egg
½ cup brown sugar
½ cup oil
1 cup flour
½ tsp. salt
1 tsp. baking powder
½ tsp. soda

Directions

Soak oatmeal in buttermilk for 1 hour. Add egg, sugar and oil, and beat well. Combine dry ingredients and stir into oatmeal mixture.

Fill greased muffin tins and bake at 400°F for 15 to 20 minutes.

Makes 12 large muffins.

—Kass Bennett

Flaky Biscuits

Ingredients

1 cup whole wheat flour
1 cup unbleached white flour
1 Tbsp. baking powder
½ tsp. salt
½ cup butter
2 eggs, beaten
½ cup milk

Directions

Sift dry ingredients together. Cut in butter until mixture is the texture of small peas. Combine eggs and milk and add to the flour mixture, stirring until moistened.

Turn dough onto a floured board. Roll out to ½-inch thickness. Fold in thirds and roll out again. Repeat 5 times.

Cut into 2-inch rounds. Place on a lightly greased cookie sheet and bake at 400°F for 8 to 10 minutes.

Makes 12 to 15 biscuits.

—Jan Post

Scotch Soda Scones

These sweet scones are cooked on top of the stove rather than in the oven. Quickly assembled, they are especially delicious served warm with butter, fresh strawberries and whipped cream.

Ingredients

1½ cups flour
½ tsp. baking soda
½ tsp. cream of tartar
¼ cup granulated sugar
Salt
¼ cup lard
½ cup sour milk

Directions

Combine flour, baking soda, cream of tartar, sugar and a pinch of salt. Cut in lard until mixture resembles coarse meal. Add milk and mix with a fork until dough forms a ball.

Divide dough in half. Form each half into a ball, pat down and divide into quarters. Pat into biscuit shape.

Wipe heavy frying pan gently with lard. Fry biscuits on very low heat approximately 15 to 20 minutes per side, turning once.

Makes 8 biscuits.

—Donna Gordon

Herb Loaf

Ingredients

2 Tbsp. sugar
2 pkgs. dry yeast
2 cups warm water
2 tsp. salt
2 Tbsp. butter
½ cup & 1 Tbsp. grated Parmesan cheese
4½ cups flour
1½ Tbsp. dried oregano

Directions

Dissolve sugar and yeast in warm water in a large bowl. Add salt, butter, ½ cup cheese, 3 cups flour and oregano. Beat on low speed of electric mixer until blended, then on medium speed for 2 minutes. Add balance of flour by hand until well blended.

Cover and let rise for 45 minutes. Stir down and beat for 30 seconds. Turn into greased 1½-quart casserole dish, sprinkle with 1 Tbsp. Parmesan cheese and bake at 375°F for 55 minutes.

Makes 1 loaf.

—Shirley Hill

Old-Fashioned Honey Wheatbread

Ingredients

1½ cups water
1 cup cream-style cottage cheese
½ cup honey
¼ cup butter
2 cups unbleached white flour
2 Tbsp. brown sugar
3 tsp. salt
2 pkgs. yeast
1 egg, beaten
5½-6 cups whole wheat flour

Directions

Heat water, cottage cheese, honey and butter until very warm — 120 to 130°F. Combine with white flour, sugar, salt, yeast and egg and beat for 2 minutes with electric mixer at medium speed. Stir in remaining flour by hand to make a stiff dough.

Knead well and place in a greased bowl. Cover and let rise 45 to 60 minutes — until double in size.

Punch down dough, divide into 2 pieces, shape and place in greased loaf pans. Let rise again for 45 to 60 minutes. Bake at 350°F for 40 to 50 minutes.

Makes 2 loaves.

—Laura Poitras

Challah

This traditional Jewish egg bread can make a beautiful gift.

Ingredients

1½ cups milk
¼ cup sugar
3 tsp. salt
⅓ cup butter
3 eggs
2 pkgs. dry yeast
½ cup warm water
7½ cups flour
Poppy seeds

Directions

Combine milk, sugar, salt and butter. Heat until butter melts, then cool to lukewarm.

Beat eggs and reserve 3 Tbsp. for glazing. Soften yeast in the warm water in a large bowl. Stir in the eggs and milk mixture. Beat in 4 cups of the flour until smooth. Beat in enough of the remaining flour to make a smooth dough. Turn out and knead on floured surface until smooth and elastic — 15 minutes.

Place in a bowl, cover and let rise for 1½ hours. Punch down and let rise for another 30 minutes. Punch down and turn out onto board. Divide the dough into six equal portions. Form two braids and place them on two greased cookie sheets.

Let rise for one hour. Brush with the reserved egg, to which a tablespoon of water has been added. Sprinkle with poppy seeds.

Bake at 350°F for 30 minutes.

Makes 2 braids.

—Ruth E. Geddes

Richard's Raisin Bread

Ingredients

1 cup warm water
3 Tbsp. yeast
1 tsp. sugar
4 cups sour milk
⅔ cup oil
4 eggs, beaten
2 cups sugar
2 tsp. salt
3½ cups raisins
1 cup cracked wheat
1 cup soy flour
9 cups whole wheat flour
4½ cups unbleached white flour

Directions

In large bowl, combine water, yeast and 1 tsp. sugar and let stand for 5 minutes. Add sour milk, oil, eggs, sugar and salt to yeast mixture and stir gently. Add raisins. Gradually add flour, beating well after each addition.

When dough is thick enough to knead, turn onto lightly floured board. Keep adding flour, kneading well after each addition, until smooth and elastic.

Place in bowl, cover and let rise in a warm place for 30 minutes or until almost doubled. Punch down, divide into 4 equal parts and place in greased loaf pans. Let rise until double — about 1 hour. Bake at 350°F for 45 to 55 minutes.

Makes 4 loaves.

—Richard Domsy

Cracked Wheat Bread

Ingredients

1 tsp. sugar
1 cup warm water
2 pkgs. yeast
2 cups scalded milk
¼ cup butter
¼ cup sugar
1 Tbsp. salt
2 cups cracked wheat
2 cups cold water
9–10 cups flour

Directions

Dissolve 1 tsp. sugar in warm water and add yeast. Let stand for 10 minutes.

To hot milk, add butter, ¼ cup sugar, salt, cracked wheat and cold water. Stir yeast liquid and add milk mixture to it. Add approximately 4 cups flour and beat in. Mix in additional flour until dough leaves sides of bowl — about 5 cups.

Turn dough onto floured counter and knead. Place in greased bowl, cover and let rise until doubled. Punch down, turn out onto floured counter and cut into 4 equal pieces. Round each piece, cover and let rest for 10 minutes.

Shape into 4 loaves and place in greased loaf pans. Brush with melted butter, cover and let rise until dough is higher than pan edge. Bake at 400°F for 35 to 40 minutes.

Makes 4 loaves.

—Cecilia Roy

Finnish Coffee Braid

This moist coffee bread, rich enough to serve without butter, was invented by the contributor's grandmother.

Ingredients

2 Tbsp. yeast
½ cup warm water
½ tsp. sugar
1 cup warm milk
1 cup warm water
1 tsp. crushed cardamom
8 cups flour
1½ cups sugar
1 tsp. salt
3 eggs
¼ cup melted butter

Directions

Combine yeast, water and ½ tsp. sugar. Let stand for 10 minutes. Stir in warm milk, warm water, cardamom and 2½ cups flour. Let stand until foamy — 2 to 2½ hours.

In another dish, combine 1½ cups sugar, salt, eggs and melted butter. Add to yeast-flour mixture and mix well. Add 5½ cups flour. Let rise until double in bulk and punch down.

Form dough into 12 round strips, 2 inches in diameter. Work into 4 braids and place in loaf pans. Let rise until double. Brush tops with a mixture of egg and milk and sprinkle with sugar.

Bake at 350°F for 35 minutes, or until golden brown.

Makes 4 loaves.

—A.E. Koivu

Orange Bread

Ingredients

2 tsp. yeast
¼ cup water
Grated rind of 1 orange
¾ cup orange juice
3 Tbsp. honey
½ cup cooked soy grits
½ cup tofu
2 Tbsp. oil
2 cups flour

Directions

Dissolve yeast in water. Heat together orange rind, orange juice and 1 Tbsp. honey and simmer for 5 minutes. Stir in soy grits and remove from heat.

Cream tofu and 2 Tbsp. honey until well blended. Add orange juice mixture and yeast and mix well. Stir in oil and flour. Pour into a greased loaf pan and let rise for 1 hour. Bake at 350°F for 45 to 60 minutes.

—Sheri Nelson

Rosemary Bread

Ingredients
7⅓ cups unbleached white flour
2 Tbsp. rosemary leaves
1 Tbsp. salt
4 tsp. dry yeast
1 Tbsp. soft butter
2½ cups hot water

Directions
Mix together 2⅓ cups flour, rosemary, salt and yeast. Add butter and hot water. Beat for 2 minutes on medium speed of electric mixer. Mix in 1 cup flour by hand, then beat with electric mixer on high speed for 2 minutes. Add 3 to 4 cups flour, mixing with a spoon. Let rise for 1 hour in bowl.

Divide dough into 6 pieces. Roll into 6 ropes of equal length and make 2 braids. Let rise for 1 hour on a greased cookie sheet. Bake at 450°F for 25 minutes.

Makes 2 braids.

—Lynne Hawkes

Yogurt Granola Bread

Ingredients
2 tsp. honey
2 cups warm water
2 Tbsp. yeast
¾ cup plain yogurt
¼ cup honey
¼ cup oil
1 Tbsp. salt
4½–6 cups unbleached flour
2 cups granola

Directions
Dissolve 2 tsp. honey in warm water. Sprinkle yeast into water and let stand for 10 minutes. Add yogurt, ¼ cup honey, oil, salt and 3 cups of flour and beat with an electric mixer for 2 minutes. Add granola and mix well. Gradually add the rest of the flour.

Cover and let rise for 1 hour until doubled. Punch down and divide into 2 greased loaf pans. Let rise for 45 minutes, then bake at 375°F for 45 minutes.

—Mary Giesz

Whole Wheat Bread

Ingredients

3 Tbsp. yeast
1 Tbsp. honey
1½ cups warm water
7½ cups hot water
1–2 cups powdered milk
½ cup vegetable oil
½ cup molasses
1½ Tbsp. salt
3 cups rolled oats
10 cups whole wheat flour
10–12 cups unbleached white flour

Directions

Dissolve yeast and honey in 1½ cups water and let sit for 10 minutes.

Combine 7½ cups water and milk powder in bowl and stir to dissolve. Add oil, molasses and salt and stir to dissolve. Stir in oats, then stir mixture into yeast combination. Add whole wheat flour 3 cups at a time, stirring well after each addition. Add white flour until dough is stiff enough to turn onto a lightly floured bread board.

Knead flour into dough until it is bouncy and no longer sticky. Place in a large bowl, cover and let rise in a warm spot for 1 hour, or until doubled. Punch down, let rest 10 minutes and divide into 6 parts.

Knead each piece lightly, roll out to form an 8" x 11" rectangle and roll up like a jelly roll. Pinch seam closed. With seam-side down, tuck ends under and place in an oiled loaf pan.

Cover and let rise in a warm spot until double. Bake at 375°F for 30 minutes, or until pans sound hollow when rapped on the bottom. Remove from pans to cool.

Makes 6 loaves.

—*Susan Burke*

Sweet Dough Cinnamon Rolls

Ingredients

1½ cups milk
½ cup butter
1 pkg. yeast
1 tsp. sugar
3 eggs
1 cup sugar
½ cup sour cream
½ tsp. salt
4–5 cups flour
Oil
Brown sugar
Raisins
Nuts
Cinnamon

Directions

Warm milk, add butter and dissolve yeast and 1 tsp. sugar in it. Beat eggs, add remaining sugar, sour cream and yeast-milk mixture and blend well. Add salt and enough flour to make a manageable dough.

Knead well, place in a large bowl and let rise until double.

Roll out to a ¼-inch thick circle and spread with oil and desired fillings. Cut circle into pie-shaped pieces and roll up from wide end to form crescents. Place on cookie sheets and let rise. Bake at 325°F for 15 to 25 minutes.

Makes 12 rolls.

—*Irene Simonson*

Ukrainian Easter Bread

Ingredients

2 pkgs. yeast
2 cups milk, scalded & cooled to lukewarm
8 cups flour
5 egg yolks, beaten
1 cup sugar
½ cup melted butter
1 cup currants
1 Tbsp. vanilla

Directions

Dissolve yeast in milk, add 3 cups flour and let stand in a warm place overnight.

In the morning, add egg yolks, sugar, butter, currants, vanilla and enough flour to make a light dough. Let rise until doubled.

Turn onto a floured board and knead well, adding flour if necessary. Shape into 2 loaves and place in greased loaf pans. Let rise until doubled. Bake at 400°F for 10 minutes, reduce heat to 350°F and bake for 50 minutes.

Makes 2 loaves.

—Donna Petryshyn

Vienna Coffee Cake

Ingredients

¼ cup lukewarm water
1 pkg. dry yeast
½ tsp. granulated sugar
1 cup milk
½ cup white sugar
¼ cup butter
Salt
1 egg
3 cups flour
⅓ cup sugar
¼ tsp. cinnamon
¼ cup chopped walnuts

Directions

Combine water, yeast and ½ tsp. sugar and let sit for 10 minutes. Scald milk and add ½ cup sugar, butter and pinch of salt. Cool to lukewarm and add to yeast mixture. Mix well. Add egg and 1 cup flour and beat well. Add remaining flour and beat for 3 minutes. Place in a greased tube pan.

Combine ⅓ cup sugar, cinnamon and nuts and sprinkle over cake. Let rise in a warm place until doubled in bulk. Bake at 375°F for 35 minutes.

—Dorothy Hett

Pita Bread

This Middle Eastern bread forms a pocket in the center as it bakes, which can be split open and filled for sandwiches.

Ingredients
2¼–2¾ cups lukewarm water
2 pkgs. dry yeast
Pinch sugar
8 cups flour
2 tsp. salt
¼ cup olive oil
1 cup corn meal or flour

Directions

Pour ¼ cup of water into a small bowl and sprinkle with yeast and sugar. Let rest 2 to 3 minutes, then stir to dissolve completely. Set bowl in warm place for 5 minutes or until mixture has doubled in volume.

Combine flour and salt, make a well in the center and pour in the yeast mixture, oil and 2 cups of lukewarm water.

Gently stir until well combined. Add up to ½ cup more water until dough forms a ball. Knead for 20 minutes, then let rise 45 minutes or until doubled.

Punch down and divide into 8 pieces. Roll into balls and let rest for 30 minutes.

Sprinkle 2 cookie sheets with corn meal or flour. Roll balls into round, flat loaves about 8 inches in diameter and ⅛-inch thick. Arrange 2 to 3 inches apart on sheets and let rise 30 minutes longer.

Bake at 500°F for about 10 minutes until they are brown and puffy in the center.

Makes 8.

—Nina Kenzie

Dinner Rolls

Ingredients
2 Tbsp. yeast
½ cup warm water
1 tsp. sugar
3 eggs
½ cup oil
2 tsp. salt
2-3 cups warm water
7½–8 cups flour

Directions

Dissolve yeast and sugar in ½ cup warm water. Mix together eggs, oil, salt and warm water, Add yeast and enough flour to make dough soft.

Allow dough to double, punch down and allow to rise again. Shape into rolls and let rise until doubled. Bake at 375°F for 15 minutes.

—Delia Schlesinger

Fresh Raspberry Cake

Ingredients

½ cup butter
¾ cup honey
2 eggs, well beaten
2 cups unbleached flour
¼ tsp. salt
2 tsp. baking powder
2 Tbsp. milk or cream
1 cup fresh raspberries

Directions

Cream butter and honey. Add eggs and mix until light and fluffy. Sift together dry ingredients and add to creamed mixture alternately with milk. Fold in berries.

Bake in a greased and floured 8-inch square pan at 350°F for 40 to 50 minutes. Serve with whipped cream or ice cream.

—Mary Giesz

Rhubarb Cake

Ingredients

2½ cups flour
¼ tsp. salt
1 tsp. baking powder
½ cup butter
1 egg
1½ cups sugar
4 cups cooked chopped rhubarb
½ cup melted butter
2 eggs, beaten

Directions

Combine 2 cups flour, salt and baking powder. Cut in butter until mixture is crumbly, then stir in 1 egg. Reserve 1 cup of mixture for topping and flatten remainder in greased 8-inch square pan.

Mix together remaining ½ cup flour, sugar, rhubarb, butter and beaten eggs. Pour into pan and top with reserved pastry.

Bake at 350°F for 1 hour.

—Marie Sadoway

Carrot Cake

Ingredients

3 cups flour
2 tsp. baking soda
1½ tsp. baking powder
2 tsp. cinnamon
1 cup honey
1 cup oil
4 eggs
2 cups grated carrot
1 cup raisins or chopped nuts

Directions

Measure flour, baking soda, baking powder and cinnamon into bowl. Stir and add honey, oil and eggs. Beat hard by hand for 1 minute. Add carrot and nuts or raisins and beat to mix.

Pour into greased 9" x 13" pan and bake at 350°F for 35 minutes.

—Lynn Hill

Coffee Cake

Ingredients

½ cup butter
1¼ cups sugar
2 eggs
1 tsp. baking soda
1 cup sour cream
1½ cups flour (half whole wheat)
½ tsp. salt
1½ tsp. baking powder
1 tsp. vanilla
1 Tbsp. cinnamon
2 Tbsp. chopped nuts

Directions

Cream butter. Add 1 cup sugar gradually, creaming well. Add eggs one at a time, beating until light after each. Stir baking soda into the sour cream. Sift together flour, salt and baking powder. Add sour cream and flour mixtures alternately to the creamed mixture, beating well. Stir in vanilla.

For topping, mix together the ¼ cup sugar, cinnamon and nuts. Spoon half the batter into an 8-inch square pan. Sprinkle with half the topping. Smooth on the remaining batter, then sprinkle on the rest of the topping. Bake at 350°F for 45 minutes. Serve warm.

—Merilyn Mohr

Apple Spice Cake

Ingredients

3 cups flour
1½ cups sugar
1½ tsp. baking soda
½ tsp. salt
1 tsp. cinnamon
½ tsp. allspice
½ tsp. cloves
¾ cup shortening
1½ cups apple sauce
2 eggs
1 tsp. vanilla
1 cup raisins
½ cup chopped walnuts

Directions

Sift flour, sugar, baking soda, salt, cinnamon, allspice and cloves into a large bowl. Add shortening and apple sauce. Beat with electric mixer on medium speed for 2 minutes. Add eggs and vanilla and beat for 1 more minute. Stir in raisins and nuts and blend well.

Pour into greased and floured tube pan. Bake at 350°F for 70 minutes. Cool in pan for 10 minutes, loosen with a knife and turn onto wire rack to finish cooling.

Pumpkin Spice Cake

Ingredients

1¾ cups ground pumpkin flesh
2 cups flour
6 tsp. baking powder
1½ tsp. salt
2 tsp. cinnamon
1 tsp. ginger
½ tsp. nutmeg
¼ tsp. cloves
⅔ cup shortening
1½ cups honey
4 eggs
2 tsp. vanilla

Directions

Combine pumpkin, flour, baking powder, salt, cinnamon, ginger, nutmeg and cloves and mix well.

Cream shortening, honey, eggs and vanilla. Add flour mixture and mix well.

Bake at 350°F in a 9" x 13" pan for 50 to 60 minutes.

—Wayne Gochee

Date Oatmeal Cake

This spicy snacking cake is so rich and moist that there is no need for icing.

Ingredients

½ cup flour
1 tsp. baking soda
1 tsp. cinnamon
1 tsp. cloves
1 cup boiling water
2 cups rolled oats
¾ cup butter
2 cups brown sugar
2 eggs
1½ cups finely chopped dates
1 cup chopped walnuts

Directions

Sift together flour, baking soda, cinnamon and cloves into a large bowl.

Pour boiling water over oats, mix well, cool slightly and blend in remaining ingredients.

Pour oatmeal mixture into dry ingredients and mix well. Bake in an 8-inch square pan at 350°F for 45 minutes.

—Margaret Butler

Chocolate Buttermilk Cake

Ingredients

1⅔ cups flour
1 cup sugar
½ cup cocoa
1 tsp. baking soda
½ tsp. salt
1 cup buttermilk
½ cup melted shortening
1½ tsp. vanilla

Directions

Mix together flour, sugar, cocoa, baking soda and salt. Beat in buttermilk, shortening and vanilla. Stir until smooth.

Spread into a greased 9" x 13" pan and bake at 375°F for 30 minutes.

—Ruby McDonald

White Cake

Ingredients

2¼ cups flour
4 tsp. baking powder
¾ tsp. salt
1½ cups granulated sugar
½ cup shortening
1 cup milk
1 tsp. salt
3 eggs

Directions

Sift together flour, baking powder, salt and sugar. Add shortening, ¼ cup milk and salt. Beat for 1 minute, then add ¼ cup milk and eggs. Beat for 2 more minutes.

Pour into 2 greased 8-inch round pans and bake at 350°F for 35 to 40 minutes or until cake springs back when lightly touched.

—Shirley Morrish

Grandma's Pound Cake

Ingredients

2 cups flour
1 cup butter
1⅔ cups granulated sugar
5 large eggs
1 tsp. almond extract

Directions

Sift flour, measure and then sift 5 times. Cream butter until frothy and pale, then add sugar gradually and mix until fluffy. Add eggs, one at a time, beating after each addition until well blended. After last egg is added, beat for 5 minutes. Fold in flour slowly by hand. Add almond extract and pour into a well greased tube pan.

Bake at 300°F for 1½ hours.

—Mrs. R.F. Kempf

Princess Elizabeth Cake

Ingredients

1 cup boiling water
1 cup chopped dates
1 cup brown sugar
½ cup butter
1 egg
1½ cups flour
1 tsp. baking powder
1 tsp. baking soda
Salt
1 tsp. vanilla
5 Tbsp. brown sugar
1 Tbsp. butter
3 Tbsp. cream
½ cup coconut
¾ cup chopped walnuts

Directions

Pour boiling water over dates. Add 1 cup brown sugar, ½ cup butter and egg. Mix well and let cool. Add flour, baking powders baking soda, salt and vanilla. Mix well, place in greased 8-inch square pan and bake at 350°F for 5 minutes.

Meanwhile, combine remaining ingredients in a saucepan and bring to a boil. Spread topping over cake, return to oven and bake for 30 to 40 minutes.

—Eileen Caldwell

Chocolate Zucchini Cake

Ingredients

2½ cups flour
½ cup cocoa
2½ tsp. baking powder
1½ tsp. baking soda
1 tsp. salt
1 tsp. cinnamon
¾ cup butter
2 cups sugar
3 eggs
2½ tsp. grated orange rind
2 tsp. vanilla
2 cups grated zucchini
½ cup milk
1 cup ground nuts
¾ cup icing sugar, sifted
1 Tbsp. orange juice

Directions

Combine flour, cocoa, baking powder, baking soda, salt and cinnamon. In a large bowl, combine butter and sugars then beat in eggs. Stir in 2 tsp. orange rind, vanilla and zucchini.

Stir in dry ingredients, alternating with milk and nuts. Pour into greased bundt pan and bake at 350°F for 1 hour.

Combine icing sugar with orange juice and ½ tsp. orange rind and spread over warm cake.

—Elizabeth Eder

Marmorkuchen

This German marble cake makes an eye-catching dessert. For added appeal, cocoa icing, page 389, may be dribbled over the top while the cake is still warm.

Ingredients

1½ cups granulated sugar
1 cup unsalted butter
6 eggs, separated
1½ cups flour
1½ tsp. baking powder
Grated rind & juice of 1 lemon
¾ cup cocoa powder

Directions

Cream butter and sugar until smooth. Beat in egg yolks.

Mix flour and baking powder and add slowly to creamed mixture. Add lemon rind and juice. Beat egg whites until stiff. Fold into cake mixture until just blended.

Divide dough in half. Add cocoa to one half and leave the other half white.

In the bottom of a greased bundt pan, place blobs of some of the chocolate batter then fill in the gaps with white batter. Continue alternating chocolate and white until all the batter Is used up.

Bake at 350°F for 45 minutes.

—Kris Brown

Chocolate Icing

Ingredients

½ cup sugar
1½ Tbsp. cornstarch
2–3 Tbsp. cocoa
Dash salt
½ cup boiling water
1½ Tbsp. butter
½ tsp. vanilla

Directions

Mix sugar and cornstarch together. Add cocoa and salt. Add water and cook until thick. Remove from heat and stir in butter and vanilla. Spread while hot.

—*Barbara Davis*

White-White Icing

The amount of icing sugar in this recipe may be varied to make a soft icing for spreading or a stiffer icing for decorating.

Ingredients

1 lb. shortening
½ tsp. peppermint flavoring
¼ tsp. salt
1 lb. icing sugar
7 Tbsp. milk

Directions

Cream softened shortening with electric mixer. Add flavoring and salt. Beat in sugar one cup at a time with a little milk, blending well after each addition. Beat at high speed until light and fluffy.

—*Sharon Cooper*

Butter Icing

Ingredients

½ cup soft butter
1 cup less 2 Tbsp. sifted icing sugar
¼ cup cold milk
¼ cup boiling water
1 tsp. vanilla

Directions

Cream butter and add sugar. Beat until thick and creamy. Add milk and blend. Gradually beat in hot water, then add vanilla.

—*Catherine Rupke*

Lemon Honey Frosting

Ingredients

½ cup butter
½ cup honey
8 oz. cream cheese
1 tsp. vanilla
2 Tbsp. lemon juice
2 cups instant milk powder

Directions

Cream the butter and add honey and cream cheese. Beat until smooth. Stir in the vanilla and lemon juice and work in the milk powder, mixing until thick and creamy.

—*Cary Elizabeth Marshall*

Cocoa Icing

Ingredients

⅓ cup cocoa
2 cups icing sugar
2 Tbsp. butter
1 tsp. vanilla
Hot water

Directions

Melt cocoa and add sugar, butter and vanilla. Blend in hot water until mixture will spread smoothly.

—Roxanne Kistler

Cream Cheese Icing

Ingredients

8 oz. cream cheese
4 Tbsp. butter
3½ cups icing sugar
Salt
2 tsp. vanilla

Directions

Cream cheese with a fork, blend in butter, add sugar and salt, mix until smooth and spread.

—Cary Elizabeth Marshall

Dad's Cookies

Ingredients

1 cup butter
1 cup granulated sugar
½ cup brown sugar
1 egg
1 cup flour
1 tsp. baking powder
1 tsp. baking soda
1 cup bran flakes
1 cup rolled oats
1 cup fine coconut

Directions

Cream butter, add sugars and then the egg. Beat until light and creamy.

Sift together flour, baking powder and baking soda. Add bran flakes, oats and coconut. Stir into creamed mixture and mix well.

Drop by teaspoonfuls onto greased cookie sheets. Press down with a fork and bake at 350°F for 10 minutes or until cookies are light brown.

Makes 6 to 8 dozen cookies.

—Christine Davidson

Oatmeal Chocolate Chip Cookies

Ingredients

1 cup butter
1½ cups brown sugar
2 eggs
1 tsp. vanilla
1½ cups flour
2⅓ cups rolled oats
2 tsp. baking soda
1 tsp. salt
12-oz. pkg. chocolate chips
1½ cups chopped nuts

Directions

Cream butter and sugar. Beat in eggs and vanilla. Add flour, oats, baking soda and salt. Mix well and stir in chips and nuts. Drop by spoonfuls onto greased cookie sheets and bake at 350°F for 12 to 15 minutes.

Makes 6 to 8 dozen cookies.

—Sandra Lloyd

Chocolate Chip Cookies

Ingredients

1 cup butter
1 cup brown sugar
1 cup granulated sugar
2 eggs
1 tsp. vanilla
2¼ cups flour
3 tsp. baking powder
1 tsp. salt
1 cup chopped walnuts
12-oz. pkg. chocolate chips

Directions

Cream butter, sugars, eggs and vanilla. Add remaining ingredients in order listed. Mix well.

Drop by spoonfuls onto greased cookie sheet with 2 inches between cookies. Bake at 375°F for 8 to 10 minutes.

Makes 6 dozen cookies.

—Shirley Morrish

Oatmeal Cookies

Ingredients

1 cup butter
½ cup granulated sugar
1 cup brown sugar
1 egg
1 tsp. vanilla
3 Tbsp. milk
1½ cups flour
1½ cups rolled oats
¾ cup coconut
1 tsp. baking powder
1 tsp. baking soda
⅛ tsp. salt

Directions

Cream together butter and sugar, then beat in egg, vanilla and milk. Combine dry ingredients and add to creamed mixture.

Drop by spoonfuls onto greased cookie sheets and bake at 375°F for 15 to 20 minutes or until golden brown.

Makes 5 to 6 dozen cookies.

—Andrea Stuart

Hermits

Ingredients

2 cups flour
½ tsp. baking soda
½ tsp. salt
½ tsp. cinnamon
½ tsp. nutmeg
¾ cup shortening
1 cup brown sugar
1 egg
¼ cup cold strong coffee
½ cup raisins
½ cup chopped walnuts

Directions

Combine flour, baking soda, salt, cinnamon and nutmeg. Cream shortening and sugar and add egg. Add dry ingredients to creamed mixture alternately with coffee. Stir in raisins and nuts.

Drop by teaspoonfuls onto greased cookie sheet and bake at 400°F for 6 to 8 minutes.

Makes 3 to 4 dozen cookies.

—Audrey Moroso

Auntie Susie's Peanut Butter Cookies

Ingredients

½ cup shortening
1 cup peanut butter
½ cup white sugar
½ cup brown sugar
1 egg
1½ cups flour
1 tsp. baking soda
½ tsp. baking powder
½ tsp. vanilla

Directions

Cream shortening and peanut butter. Gradually add sugars. Add egg and beat well. Sift dry ingredients together. Gradually add to creamed mixture. Stir in vanilla.

Roll batter into small balls, place on ungreased cookie sheet and flatten with a fork. Bake at 375°F for 10 to 15 minutes. Cool on a rack.

Makes 4 dozen cookies.

—Patricia Forrest

Sugar Cookies

Ingredients

¾ cup butter
1 cup sugar
1 egg
1 tsp. baking soda
1 tsp. cream of tartar
2 cups flour
Salt
½ cup milk
½ tsp. vanilla

Directions

Cream butter and sugar together. Stir in egg. Combine dry ingredients and add to creamed mixture alternately with milk. Stir in vanilla.

Roll out dough and cut into shapes. Bake on greased cookie sheets at 375°F for 10 to 12 minutes.

Makes 3 to 4 dozen cookies.

—Goldie Connell

Shortbread

Ingredients

½ lb. butter
½ cup cornstarch
½ cup icing sugar
1 cup flour

Directions

Beat butter until light and add remaining ingredients one at a time, beating well after each addition. Roll into small balls and flatten with fork.

Bake at 300°F for 30 minutes.

Makes 3 dozen.

—Shirley Hill

Digestive Cookies

Ingredients

½ cup whole wheat flour
½ cup unbleached white flour
½ cup wheat germ
¼ cup sugar
¼ cup sesame seeds
½ tsp. salt
½ tsp. baking powder
1 cup rolled oats
½ cup butter
½ cup cold water
1 tsp. vanilla

Directions

Mix together dry ingredients. Cut in butter, then add water mixed with vanilla to form an easily handled dough.

Roll to ¼-inch thickness. Cut out cookies with floured glass. Place on greased cookie sheets and bake at 350°F for 10 to 12 minutes.

Makes 3 to 4 dozen cookies.

—Brigitte Wolf

Butterscotch Cookies

Ingredients

1 cup butter
2 cups brown sugar
2 eggs
1 cup walnuts
1 tsp. vanilla
1 tsp. cream of tartar
4 cups flour

Directions

Cream butter and sugar and add eggs, walnuts and vanilla. Mix cream of tartar and flour and combine with creamed mixture.

Pack into loaf pan or wrap in rolls in wax paper and chill overnight. Remove from pan and cut into thin slices. Bake at 350°F for 10 to 15 minutes.

Makes 8 dozen cookies.

—Pat McCormack

Cardamom Cookies

Ingredients

2½ cups flour
2 tsp. ground cardamom
3½ tsp. cinnamon
1¼ cups butter, softened
½ cup white sugar

Directions

Combine flour, cardamom and cinnamon in a bowl. In another bowl, cream together sugar and butter. Gradually add flour and spices, mixing until texture resembles coarse sand.

Form dough into ¾-inch-diameter rolls and chill until stiff — at least 1 hour. Cut into ¾-inch-thick slices and place on lightly greased cookie sheets. Bake at 350°F for 12 to 15 minutes — until very lightly browned.

Makes 4 dozen.

—Janet Jokinen

Cream Cheese Cookies

Ingredients

½ lb. butter
8-oz. pkg. cream cheese
2 cups flour
3 Tbsp. sugar
2 tsp. salt
Grape jelly

Directions

Cream butter and cheese and add flour, sugar and salt. Chill thoroughly in refrigerator. Roll out dough, using plenty of flour, and cut half into circles and half into strips. Place 1 tsp. grape jelly in center of each circle and top with strips in the shape of an X. Press edges together.

Bake at 350°F until golden.

—Shirley Hill

Butterhorn Cookies

Ingredients

1 cup butter
1 egg yolk
¾ cup sour cream
2 cups flour
¾ cup sugar
1 tsp. cinnamon
¾ cup raisins

Directions

Cream the butter and yolk and add the sour cream and flour. Blend well and chill for 1 hour.

Roll out dough to ¼-inch thickness. Combine the sugar, cinnamon and raisins and sprinkle evenly over dough.

Cut dough into triangles. Roll triangles up from large end and curve to form a semi-circle. Place on ungreased cookie sheets. Bake at 375°F for 30 minutes.

Makes 2 to 3 dozen.

—Sheri Israels

Banana Date Cookies

Ingredients

3 ripe bananas
1 cup chopped dates
⅓ cup oil
2 cups oatmeal
½ cup sunflower seeds
1 tsp. vanilla

Directions

Mash the bananas and combine with chopped dates and oil. Add remaining ingredients and mix well.

Drop by spoonfuls onto a greased cookie sheet and flatten with a fork. Bake at 375°F for about 15 minutes.

Makes 24.

—Heather Struckett

Raisin Cookies

Ingredients

1 cup water
2 cups raisins
1 cup shortening
2 cups sugar
3 eggs
1 tsp. vanilla
1 cup chopped walnuts
4 cups flour
1 tsp. baking powder
1 tsp. baking soda
2 tsp. salt
1½ tsp. cinnamon
¼ tsp. nutmeg
¼ tsp. allspice

Directions

Combine water and raisins, boil for 5 minutes and cool. Cream shortening and add sugar, eggs, vanilla, cooled raisins and walnuts. Combine remaining ingredients, add to creamed mixture and blend well. Drop by teaspoonfuls onto greased cookie sheets and bake at 350°F for 12 to 15 minutes. Makes 10 dozen cookies.

—Mrs. Jack Stacey

Apple Sauce Oatmeal Cookies

Ingredients

½ cup shortening
1 cup sugar
1 egg
1 cup unsweetened apple sauce
1 tsp. baking soda
1¾ cups flour
½ tsp. salt
1 tsp. cinnamon
½ tsp. nutmeg
1 cup raisins
1 cup oatmeal

Directions

Cream together shortening, sugar and egg. Mix apple sauce and baking soda, and sift together the flour, salt and spices. Add apple sauce and dry ingredients to creamed mixture. Mix in raisins and oatmeal.

Drop by spoonfuls onto greased cookie sheet. Bake at 350°F for 10 minutes.

Makes 3 dozen.

—Audrey Moroso

Banana Oat Bars

Ingredients

¾ cup butter
1 cup packed brown sugar
1 egg
½ tsp. salt
1½ cups mashed ripe bananas (4–5 medium)
4 cups uncooked oats
½ cup coconut
1 cup chocolate chips

Directions

Cream butter and sugar until fluffy. Beat in egg, salt and bananas. Stir in remaining ingredients. Turn into greased 9" x 13" pan.

Bake at 350°F for 1 hour or until golden brown and toothpick comes clean.

Cool and cut into 2-inch bars. Store in refrigerator until needed.

—Jan Gibbs

Poppy Seed Cookies

Ingredients

½ cup butter
⅓ cup sugar
1 egg
1 cup flour
⅓ tsp. salt
½ tsp. vanilla
¼ tsp. grated lemon rind
2 Tbsp. poppy seeds

Directions

Cream butter and mix in sugar and egg. Combine flour and salt and add to butter along with vanilla, lemon rind and poppy seeds. Mix well.

Roll into balls and flatten on greased baking sheets. Bake at 350°F for 10 to 12 minutes.

Makes 2 dozen cookies.

—Shirley Morrish

Kislings

These are rich Christmas-time cookies.

Ingredients

1 cup butter
¼ cup granulated sugar
2 cups sifted flour
¼ tsp. salt
½ cup well drained, sliced maraschino cherries
½ cup chopped walnuts
Confectioners' sugar

Directions

Cream butter, add sugar and mix until fluffy. Add remaining ingredients and mix well. Form dough into small balls and place on ungreased cookie sheet.

Bake at 300°F for 30 to 40 minutes or until bottoms are golden.

Roll in confectioners' sugar.

Makes 3 dozen cookies.

—Bonnie Byrnes

Ginger Snaps

These cookies have been served to guests of the renowned historic Marshlands Inn, New Brunswick, Canada, every evening since the inn opened in 1935.

Ingredients

1 cup melted shortening
½ cup granulated sugar
1½ cups molasses
2 heaping tsp. baking soda
2 heaping tsp. ginger
2 heaping tsp. salt
4½ cups flour

Directions

Combine shortening, sugar and molasses. Sift baking soda, ginger and salt with flour, and stir into creamed mixture.

Shape into rectangular logs and chill overnight. Slice very thinly and bake at 350°F for 7 to 8 minutes.

Makes 10 dozen cookies.

—Marshlands Inn

Lemon Squares

Ingredients

1 cup butter
½ cup icing sugar
2 cups flour
4 eggs
1½ cups sugar
Pinch salt
4 Tbsp. flour
1 tsp. baking powder
8 Tbsp. lemon juice

Directions

Stir butter, icing sugar and flour together and press into a 9" x 13" pan. Bake at 350°F for 10 minutes.

Beat eggs and add remaining ingredients. Pour over cookie base and bake 25 minutes longer.

Cut into bars while hot, and sprinkle with icing sugar when cool.

—Mrs. W. Atkins

Jam Bars

Ingredients

½ cup shortening
½ cup sugar
½ tsp. vanilla
½ tsp. almond extract
1 egg
1½ cups flour
1 tsp. baking powder
½ tsp. cinnamon
¼ tsp. ground cloves
½ tsp. salt
Jam or marmalade

Directions

Cream together shortening, sugar, vanilla and almond extract. Stir in egg. Sift together dry ingredients, add to creamed mixture and blend well.

Spread half the dough in a greased 8-inch square pan, cover with jam or marmalade and top with remaining dough.

Bake at 400°F for 25 minutes. Cool, then cut into bars.

Makes 20 bars.

—Donna Jubb

Maple Sugar Cookies

Ingredients

½ cup butter
½ cup maple sugar
1 egg
½ cup milk
1 cup whole wheat flour
¾ cup unbleached white flour
½ tsp. salt
½ cup raisins

Directions

Cream together butter and maple sugar. Add egg and milk and beat. Mix in flours, salt and raisins.

Drop by teaspoonfuls onto greased cookie sheets. Bake at 325°F for 10 minutes or until browned around edges.

Makes 40 cookies.

—Andra Hughes

Soft Molasses Cookies

Ingredients

1 cup granulated sugar
1 cup molasses
1 cup shortening, melted
4 cups flour
2 tsp. baking soda
1 egg
1 cup cold water
1 tsp. cinnamon
½ tsp. ground cloves
1 tsp. salt

Directions

Cream together sugar, molasses and shortening. Stir in 1 cup flour, baking soda, egg and water.

Sift together remaining 3 cups flour, cinnamon, cloves and salt. Stir into creamed mixture.

Refrigerate for 1 hour, then drop by teaspoonfuls onto cookie sheet. Bake at 375°F for 12 to 15 minutes.

Makes 8 dozen cookies.

—Janice Touesnard

Date Squares

Ingredients

1 lb. dates
¾ cup hot water
Salt
1 tsp. vanilla
1½ cups flour
½ tsp. baking soda
1½ cups rolled oats
1½ cups brown sugar
1 cup butter

Directions

Combine dates, hot water and salt in a saucepan. Cook over medium heat until dates are soft and water is absorbed. Add vanilla and let cool.

Stir flour and baking soda together. Add oats and brown sugar and mix well. Work in butter with fork until mixture is crumbly.

Spread half the mixture in the bottom of a 9-inch square pan and pat down. Cover with date filling and pat remaining mixture on top.

Bake at 350°F for 20 to 25 minutes.

—Mrs. Fred Smith

Anna Lieb's Brownies

My grandmother, who lived with us until I was 17 years old, was an excellent cook with a pronounced Old-World style. In order to preserve her recipes, I tried following her around the kitchen making notes on quantities used and steps followed. This worked for a few uncomplicated treats, but was unsuccessful for her more intricate creations. One recipe which we have managed to duplicate is her brownies. Always moist and rich, they are my idea of what brownies should be.

Ingredients

1 cup butter
2 cups sugar
4 eggs
4 squares unsweetened chocolate, melted
2 cups flour
1 Tbsp. baking powder
1 tsp. salt
2 tsp. vanilla
1 cup chopped walnuts or slivered almonds

Directions

Cream together butter and sugar until light. Beat in eggs. Add melted chocolate and beat again. Mix in flour, baking powder, salt and vanilla.

Spread mixture in a greased 9" x 13" baking pan and sprinkle liberally with nuts. Bake at 350°F for 35 minutes. When cool, cut in squares.

Makes 2 dozen brownies.

—Alice O'Connell

Lynn's Granola Bars

Ingredients

1 cup butter
1 cup brown sugar
2 eggs
¼ cup molasses
1 tsp. vanilla
1¾ cups flour
½ tsp. baking soda
½ tsp. salt
½ cup powdered milk
1½ cups rolled oats
¾ cup wheat germ
¾ cup coconut
¾ cup sunflower seeds
¾ cup chopped dried fruit
⅓ cup sesame seeds

Directions

Cream together butter, brown sugar, eggs, molasses and vanilla. Sift together flour, baking soda, salt and powdered milk, add to creamed mixture and blend well. Add remaining ingredients and mix well.

Spread in a 9" x 13" pan and bake at 350°F for 20 to 25 minutes or until golden.

—Judy Wuest

Banana Oat Muffins

Ingredients

1 cup unbleached flour
½ cup brown sugar
2½ tsp. baking powder
½ tsp. salt
¼ tsp. baking soda
¾ cup oats
1 egg, beaten
3 Tbsp. oil
½ cup milk
½ cup mashed banana
⅓ cup chopped nuts

Directions

Combine flour, sugar, baking powder, salt and baking soda. Stir well to blend. Stir in oats. Add remaining ingredients and stir with a fork until dry ingredients are just moistened.

Fill well-greased muffin tins two-thirds full. Bake at 400°F for 18 to 20 minutes.

Makes 12 muffins.

—Nan & Phil Millette

Blueberry Oat Muffins

Ingredients

1 cup rolled oats
1 cup buttermilk
1 cup flour
1 tsp. baking powder
½ tsp baking soda
½ tsp. salt
¼ cup brown sugar
1 egg, beaten
4 Tbsp. melted shortening
1 cup blueberries

Directions

Combine oats and buttermilk and let stand for 1 hour. Stir together flour, baking powder, baking soda, salt and sugar.

Add egg and shortening to oat mixture. Stir this into dry ingredients until just mixed. Fold in blueberries. Fill greased muffin tins two-thirds full. Bake at 400°F for 20 minutes.

Makes 12 large muffins.

—Eva Whitmore

Banana Bran Muffins

Ingredients

1 cup sour milk
2 Tbsp. molasses
1 egg
2 Tbsp. butter
⅔ cup raisins
½ cup walnuts
1½ cups bran
1 cup whole wheat flour
½ cup brown sugar
½ tsp. salt
½ tsp. baking soda
2 tsp. baking powder
1 cup mashed bananas

Directions

Combine milk, molasses, egg, butter, raisins, walnuts and bran in a bowl and stir to blend. Sift together dry ingredients and add to moist mixture. Add bananas and stir only enough to moisten.

Fill greased muffin tins three-quarters full and bake at 375°F for 20 to 25 minutes.

Makes 24 muffins.

—Kathy Crawley

Raspberry Bars

Ingredients

1 cup butter, softened
⅓ cup sugar
2 egg yolks
2 cups flour
1 cup raspberry jam
4 Tbsp. confectioners' sugar
½ cup chopped walnuts

Directions

Cream butter and sugar. Beat in egg yolks, then stir in flour, half a cup at a time. Press half the dough into a 9-inch square baking pan. Spread with jam and top with remaining dough. Sprinkle with confectioners' sugar and walnuts.

Bake at 375°F for 35 minutes. When cool, cut into bars.

Makes 27 bars.

Cranberry Oatmeal Muffins

Ingredients

¾ cup unbleached flour
¾ cup whole wheat flour
1 cup rolled oats
½ cup brown sugar
1 Tbsp. baking powder
1 tsp. salt
1 tsp. cinnamon
1 cup fresh or frozen cranberries
¼ cup butter
1 cup milk
1 egg

Directions

Combine dry ingredients. Toss the cranberries with 1 Tbsp. of dry ingredients and set aside. Melt butter and combine with milk and egg. Stir butter mixture into dry ingredients and then add cranberries.

Fill muffin tins two-thirds full and bake at 425°F for 15 to 20 minutes. Let stand 5 minutes before removing from pans.

Makes 12 muffins.

—Kathleen Walker

Cranberry Muffins

Ingredients

¾ cup halved,
 raw cranberries
½ cup icing sugar
1 egg
1 cup milk
¼ cup oil
1 cup whole wheat flour
1 cup unbleached flour
3 tsp. baking powder
½ tsp. salt
¼ cup sugar

Directions

Mix cranberries and icing sugar well and set aside.

Beat egg, milk and oil together. Add whole wheat flour, then sift together and add remaining ingredients. Stir just to blend. Fold in cranberries with as few strokes as possible.

Fill greased muffin tins two-thirds full. Bake at 350°F for 20 minutes.

Makes 18 muffins.

—Ann Fraser

Orange Raisin Muffins

Ingredients

½ cup shortening
1 cup brown sugar
1 egg
¾ tsp. baking soda
Rind of ½ orange, grated
1 cup sour cream
2 cups flour
1 tsp. baking powder
¼ tsp. salt
1 tsp. cinnamon
1 cup chopped raisins
½ cup chopped nuts

Directions

Cream shortening and add sugar and egg. Mix baking soda, orange rind and sour cream. Combine dry ingredients and add to creamed mixture alternately with sour cream. Add raisins and nuts, mixing to just combine.

Fill greased muffin tins two-thirds full. Bake at 350°F for 15 to 20 minutes.

Makes 24 muffins.

—Sally Ireland

Raspberry Oatmeal Muffins

Ingredients

1 cup flour
3 tsp. baking powder
½ tsp. salt
¾ cup rolled oats
¼ cup brown sugar
1 egg
¼ cup melted butter
⅓ cup milk
1 cup mashed, fresh or frozen raspberries

Directions

Measure dry ingredients into a large mixing bowl. Stir with a fork until well blended.

Whisk or beat egg, butter and milk. Stir in dry ingredients and mix briefly. Add raspberries and mix until evenly blended. Fill greased muffin tins two-thirds full. Bake at 400°F for 20 minutes, or until done.

Makes 12 large muffins.

—Linda Palaisy

Apple Honey Deluxe Granola Muffins

Ingredients

½ cup whole wheat flour
½ cup raw bran
⅓ cup wheat germ
½ cup rolled oats
½ cup ground walnuts
¼ cup soy flour
2½ tsp. baking powder
½ tsp. cinnamon
½ cup milk
1 egg, beaten
⅓ cup honey
2 Tbsp. safflower oil
1 cup finely grated cooking apple

Directions

Mix together in a large bowl whole wheat flour, bran, wheat germ, oats, walnuts, soy flour, baking powder and cinnamon. Combine milk, egg, honey, oil and apple and stir into dry ingredients to just moisten.

Fill greased muffin tins two-thirds full and bake at 375°F for 20 minutes.

Makes 12 large muffins.

—Carolyn Cronk

Lemon Muffins

Ingredients

2 cups flour
½ cup & 2 Tbsp. sugar
1 Tbsp. baking powder
1 tsp. salt
½ cup butter
½ cup fresh lemon juice
Rind of 1 or 2 lemons, grated
2 eggs

Directions

Combine flour, ½ cup sugar, baking powder and salt. Blend well.

Melt butter, remove from heat and stir in lemon juice, rind and eggs. Stir into dry ingredients until well moistened.

Fill greased muffin tins. Sprinkle tops with sugar. Bake at 400°F for 15 minutes.

Makes 12 large muffins.

—Linda Charron

Delicious Muffins

Ingredients

¼ cup butter
½ cup brown sugar
¼ tsp. salt
¼ cup molasses
2 eggs
1 cup milk
½ tsp. baking soda
1 tsp. vanilla
1 cup flour
2 tsp. baking powder
1½ cups bran
2-3 Tbsp. wheat germ

Directions

Cream together butter, sugar, salt and molasses. Beat in eggs. Add milk, baking soda and vanilla. Mix slightly. Sift flour and baking powder into creamed mixture, stirring only a little. Add bran and wheat germ. Mix only until all ingredients are moist. Fill greased muffin tins three-quarters full. Bake at 325 to 350°F for 20 to 25 minutes.

Makes 12 large muffins.

—Donna Wallis

Pumpkin Muffins

Ingredients

1 cup sugar
⅔ cup oil
2 eggs
1½ cups whole wheat flour
1 tsp. baking powder
1 tsp. baking soda
Cloves
1 tsp. cinnamon
¼ tsp. mace
½ tsp. nutmeg
¼ tsp. ginger
½ tsp. salt
1 cup pumpkin
1 cup raisins

Directions

Cream together sugar and oil. Add eggs and mix thoroughly. Combine dry ingredients.

Add pumpkin to moist ingredients, followed by dry mixture. Stir in raisins.

Fill greased muffin tins two-thirds full and bake at 350°F for 25 minutes.

Makes 18 muffins.

—Karen Bowcott

Rhubarb Muffins

Ingredients

1 cup brown sugar
¼ cup salad oil
1 egg
2 tsp. vanilla
1 cup buttermilk
1½ cups finely diced rhubarb
½ cup walnut pieces
2½ cups flour
1 tsp. baking powder
1 tsp. baking soda
½ tsp. salt

Directions

Combine brown sugar, oil, egg and vanilla. Beat until well blended. Stir in buttermilk, rhubarb and nuts.

Sift flour with baking powder, baking soda and salt. Add all at once to the rhubarb mixture and stir until just moistened.

Fill greased muffin tins two-thirds full. Bake at 400°F for 15 to 20 minutes.

Makes 24 muffins.

—*Ann Fraser*

Date Nut Muffins

Ingredients

1 cup pitted, chopped dates
¾ cup boiling water
1 egg
½ cup sugar
¼ cup butter
¾ tsp. salt
1 tsp. vanilla
½ cup chopped walnuts
1¼ cups flour
¼ cup wheat germ
1 tsp. baking powder
1 tsp. cinnamon
¼ tsp. allspice
¼ tsp. nutmeg
1 tsp. baking soda

Directions

Soften dates in boiling water and allow to cool. Beat egg and gradually add sugar, butter, salt and vanilla. Add nuts.

Combine dry ingredients, except baking soda. Stir baking soda into dates and add to egg mixture. Stir in dry ingredients, mixing until just blended.

Spoon into lightly greased muffin tins. Bake at 375°F for 15 to 20 minutes.

Makes 12 muffins.

—*Maxine Farr-Jones*

Honey Walnut Bread

Ingredients

1 cup milk
1 cup honey
½ cup sugar
¼ cup oil
2 egg yolks
1½ cups unbleached flour
1 tsp. salt
1 tsp. baking soda
1 cup whole wheat flour
1 cup chopped walnuts

Directions

Scald milk and stir in honey and sugar until sugar dissolves. Cool. Beat in oil and egg yolks. Sift together unbleached flour, salt and baking soda. Stir in whole wheat flour. Add nuts, then milk mixture. Stir to just blend. Spoon into 2 greased loaf pans.

Bake at 325°F for 1 hour, or until toothpick inserted in loaf comes out clean. Cool in pans for 15 minutes, then turn out onto rack.

Makes 2 loaves.

—Ingrid Birker

Blueberry Banana Bread

Ingredients

1 cup blueberries
1¾ cups flour
2 tsp. baking powder
¼ tsp. baking soda
½ tsp. salt
⅓ cup butter
⅔ cup sugar
2 eggs
1 cup mashed bananas

Directions

Toss berries with 2 Tbsp. flour. Sift remaining flour, baking powder, baking soda and salt.

Cream butter and beat in sugar until light and fluffy. Beat in eggs one at a time. Add flour mixture and bananas alternately in 3 parts to butter mixture. Stir in berries.

Spoon into greased loaf pan and bake at 350°F for 50 minutes.

—Gillian Richardson

Nuts & Seeds Bread

Ingredients

2 cups flour
1 tsp. baking powder
1 tsp. baking soda
½ tsp. salt
1 cup brown sugar
½ cup chopped nuts
2 Tbsp. sesame seeds
2 Tbsp. poppy seeds
1 egg, beaten
1 cup milk
¼ cup oil

Directions

Mix dry ingredients together. Combine egg, milk and oil, then add to dry mixture.

Pour batter into greased loaf pan and bake at 350°F for 45 minutes.

—Linda Purvis

Peanut Butter Bread

This recipe produces a very dense, moist loaf with a pleasant peanut butter taste. It could be eaten plain or could serve as the basis for a sandwich.

Ingredients

¾ cup sugar
½ cup peanut butter
1 tsp. vanilla
1¾ cups milk
2¼ cups flour
4 tsp. baking powder
½ tsp. salt

Directions

Cream together sugar, peanut butter and vanilla. Add milk and mix well. Combine flour, baking powder and salt. Add to creamed mixture and beat well.

Place in greased loaf pan and bake at 350°F for 45 to 50 minutes, or until golden brown. Allow to cool for 10 minutes before removing from pan.

Lemon Sesame Bread

Bread Ingredients

¼ cup oil
½ cup honey
3 eggs
Juice of 1 lemon
Rind of 2 lemons, grated
½ cup sesame seeds
¼ cup soy flour
1 cup whole wheat flour
1½ Tbsp. milk powder
½ tsp. salt
2 tsp. baking powder

Topping Ingredients
Juice of 1 lemon
3 Tbsp. honey

Directions

Beat oil and honey together until blended, then beat in eggs, lemon juice and rind. Stir the dry ingredients together, then stir into the liquid mixture.

Bake in greased loaf pan at 350°F for 45 minutes.

To make topping, combine lemon juice and honey, heating if necessary. Poke holes in the warm loaf with a toothpick and pour topping over it. Cool for 10 minutes before serving.

—Norah Ashmore

Coconut Orange Loaf

Ingredients

2½ cups flour
1 cup sugar
¼ tsp. mace
3½ tsp. baking powder
¾ tsp. salt
3 tsp. grated orange rind
½ cup orange juice
¾ cup milk
2 eggs, beaten
2 Tbsp. oil
½ cup coconut
1 cup raisins

Directions

Mix together flour, sugar, mace, baking powder, salt and orange rind. Make a well in the center.

Combine orange juice, milk, eggs and oil and pour into well. Blend well. Add coconut and raisins.

Pour into greased loaf pan and bake at 350°F for 1 hour.

—Jacqueline Dysart

Savory Cheddar Bread

Ingredients

2 cups flour
4 tsp. baking powder
1 Tbsp. sugar
½ tsp. garlic powder
½ tsp. oregano
¼ tsp. dry mustard
1¼ cups grated Cheddar cheese
1 egg, beaten
1 cup milk
1 Tbsp. butter, melted

Directions

Stir together the flour, baking powder, sugar, garlic powder, oregano, dry mustard and cheese. Combine egg, milk and butter and add all at once to dry ingredients, stirring until just moistened.

Spread batter in a greased loaf pan and bake at 350°F for 45 minutes. Cool 10 minutes on a wire rack before removing from pan.

—Nan & Phil Millette

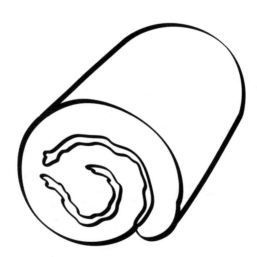

Cranberry-Filled Braid

Braid Ingredients

2 Tbsp. sugar
1 pkg. yeast
⅓ cup warm water
3–3½ cups flour
¼ cup sugar
1 tsp. salt
1 tsp. shredded orange peel
⅓ cup orange juice
⅓ cup milk
¼ cup butter
1 egg

Filling Ingredients

⅔ cup cranberries
¼ orange, unpeeled
⅓ apple, unpeeled
⅓ cup sugar
1 Tbsp. cornstarch

Icing Ingredients

½ cup icing sugar
2 tsp. orange juice
Toasted, sliced almonds

Directions

Combine 2 Tbsp. sugar, yeast and warm water. Let sit for 10 minutes. Combine 1 cup flour, sugar, salt and orange peel. Heat together orange juice, milk and butter until warm and add to flour mixture. Add yeast mixture and stir in egg. Add remaining flour to make a soft dough. Knead for 5 to 10 minutes. Place dough in greased bowl, cover and let rise until doubled in bulk — 1 to 1½ hours.

Meanwhile, prepare the filling. Chop all fruit together until fine. Add sugar and stir until dissolved. Add cornstarch and cook until thick and bubbly. Cool.

Punch down dough and let sit for 10 minutes. On lightly floured surface, roll dough into a 9-by-12-inch rectangle. Cut into three 12-by-3-inch strips. Spread cranberry mixture down center of each strip, bring long edges together and pinch to seal. Place strips side by side, seam down, on a greased baking sheet. Braid and secure ends. Cover and let rise until doubled. Bake at 350°F for 20 minutes, or until golden.

To make icing, combine icing sugar and orange juice. Drizzle over warm braid and sprinkle with toasted almonds.

Makes 1 braid.

—Karen Quinney

Potica

This is a traditional recipe for Yugoslavian Christmas bread.

Bread Ingredients

3½ cups flour
1 pkg. yeast
1 cup milk
2 Tbsp. sugar
2 Tbsp. butter
1 tsp. salt
1 egg

Filling Ingredients

2 cups finely ground walnuts
1 egg, beaten
¼ cup brown sugar
2 Tbsp. honey
2 Tbsp. milk
1 Tbsp. melted butter
1 tsp. cinnamon
½ tsp. vanilla

Directions

Stir together 1½ cups flour and the yeast. Heat milk, sugar, butter and salt until just warm. Add to flour-yeast mixture. Add egg and beat with electric mixer at low setting. Scrape bowl. Beat for 3 minutes at high speed. Stir in remaining flour to make a moderately stiff dough. Turn out and knead until smooth and elastic. Place in greased bowl and let rise until doubled — about 1½ hours.

Combine filling ingredients and set aside.

Punch dough down and let sit for 10 minutes. Roll out until very thin and approximately 20 by 30 inches. Spread with nut filling and roll up along longer side. Pinch edge to seal. Place in U-shape on greased baking sheet and let rise until doubled. Bake at 350°F for 30 to 35 minutes.

—*Marie Yelich*

Cracked Rye Bread

Ingredients

4 cups hot water
1½ Tbsp. salt
¾ cup brown sugar
⅜ cup shortening
1 Tbsp. yeast
⅜ cup warm water
2 cups rye flour
2 cups cracked rye
8 cups unbleached flour

Directions

Mix together hot water, salt, sugar and shortening. Let cool to lukewarm. Combine yeast and warm water and let sit for 10 minutes. Pour into hot-water mixture. Add flours until dough cannot be mixed any longer. Knead, adding flour as required, until dough is smooth and satiny. Cover and let rise for 1½ hours.

Punch down and let sit for 10 minutes. Place in greased loaf pans and let rise for 1¼ hours. Bake at 375°F for 45 minutes.

Makes 3 to 4 loaves.

—*Lynne Hawkes*

Dark Rye Bread

Ingredients

3 Tbsp. yeast
1 tsp. brown sugar
1 cup warm water
½ cup dark molasses
½ cup boiling water
2 Tbsp. butter
2 Tbsp. caraway seeds
2 tsp. salt
½ cup wheat germ
2¾ cups dark rye flour
2½–2¾ cups unbleached flour

Directions

Dissolve yeast and brown sugar in warm water. In large bowl, combine molasses, boiling water, butter, caraway seeds and salt, stirring until butter melts. Cool to lukewarm. Stir in yeast mixture and wheat germ. Stir in all of rye flour and as much unbleached flour as you can mix in with a spoon. Turn onto floured board. Knead in enough of remaining flour to make a medium-stiff dough that is smooth and elastic. Place in greased bowl, turning once to grease surface. Cover and let rise until doubled — about 1½ hours.

Punch down dough and divide in half. Cover and let sit for 10 minutes. Shape into 2 loaves and place in pans. Cover and let rise again until doubled — about 1 hour. Brush tops of loaves with water. With sharp knife, gently score tops of loaves diagonally at 2-inch intervals. Bake at 350°F for 45 minutes.

Makes 2 loaves.

—Janet Ueberschlag

Greek Easter Bread

Ingredients

1 pkg. yeast
½ cup warm water
2 cups warm milk
2 cups & 1 Tbsp. sugar
6–8 cups flour
5 eggs
1 orange peel, grated
1 lemon peel, grated
½ tsp. crushed cardamom seeds
½ lb. butter, melted
1 egg white, beaten

Directions

Dissolve yeast in water. Add 1 cup warm milk, 1 Tbsp. sugar and 1½ cups flour to make a pudding-like batter. Cover and let stand in warm place for 1 hour.

Meanwhile, combine 2 cups sugar and eggs. Place 5 cups flour in large pan and add orange and lemon peel, cardamom, remaining 1 cup milk and melted butter. Stir in yeast mixture and then sugar-egg mixture. Add flour as needed to make a kneadable dough. Knead gently.

Place dough in clean, oiled pan, cover and let rise for about 8 hours. Punch down, knead lightly again and divide into 9 balls.

Shape each ball into a long strip — 18 to 24 inches — then braid 3 strips together. Place the 3 loaves on a greased cookie sheet, cover and let rise for 2 hours. Brush the top of the loaves with lightly beaten egg white and bake at 325°F for 30 minutes.

Makes 3 loaves.

—Patrick A. Thrasher

Sesame Wheat Bread

This recipe results in a somewhat heavy bread, which is particularly delicious toasted and spread with honey for breakfast.

Ingredients

4 cups milk, scalded
½ cup packed brown sugar
½ cup honey
5 tsp. salt
¾ cup butter
4 pkgs. yeast
1¼ cups warm water
1 cup sesame seeds,
   lightly toasted
¾ cup wheat germ
6 cups whole wheat flour
6 cups unbleached flour

Directions

Combine scalded milk, sugar, honey, salt and butter and cool to lukewarm. Dissolve yeast in warm water and add to cooled milk mixture. Stir in sesame seeds, wheat germ and whole wheat flour. Add unbleached flour. Knead until dough is smooth and satiny. Cover and let rise until doubled — about 1 hour.

Punch down and let sit for 15 minutes. Divide into 4 loaves and place in greased loaf pans. Let rise until doubled — about 1 hour. Bake at 425°F for 45 to 55 minutes.

Makes 4 loaves.

—Heidi Magnuson-Ford

Honey Whole Wheat Buns

Ingredients

1 tsp. honey
2 pkgs. yeast
½ cup warm water
2 eggs, beaten
½ cup melted shortening
¾ cup honey
¼ cup sugar
1 Tbsp. salt
2 cups milk, scalded & cooled
4 cups unbleached flour
3 cups whole wheat flour

Directions

Combine honey, yeast and water and let sit for 10 minutes. Mix together eggs, shortening, honey, sugar, salt, milk, 2 cups unbleached flour and whole wheat flour. Add yeast mixture. Knead dough with remaining 2 cups unbleached flour. Let rise until doubled in size — 1½ hours.

Punch down. Shape into rolls and place on greased cookie sheet. Let rise for another hour. Bake at 400°F for 10 to 15 minutes.

Makes 24 rolls.

—Laine Roddick

English Muffins

Ingredients

1 cup milk
2 Tbsp. sugar
1 tsp. salt
¼ cup butter
1 pkg. yeast
1 cup warm water
5½ cups flour
Cornmeal

Directions

Scald milk and stir in sugar, salt and butter. Cool to lukewarm. Sprinkle yeast in warm water in large bowl and stir until dissolved. Add milk mixture and 3 cups of flour and beat until smooth. Add enough flour to make soft dough. On floured board, knead 10 minutes, adding flour as necessary. Place in greased bowl, turning to grease top. Cover and let rise for 1 hour.

Punch down and divide in half. On board, roll out dough to ½-inch thickness. Cut with 4inch round cutter. Roll in cornmeal and let stand for 30 minutes. Cook on medium-hot griddle for 15 minutes. Turn and cook for another 15 minutes.

Makes 24 muffins.

—Reo Belhumeur

Bread Pretzels

Ingredients

2 cups warm water
1 Tbsp. dry yeast
½ tsp. sugar
4½ cups whole wheat flour
1 egg yolk, beaten
Coarse salt

Directions

Dissolve yeast and sugar in warm water. Stir in the flour and knead for 8 to 10 minutes. Cover and let rise in a warm place until doubled in bulk.

Punch down and form into 12 small balls. Roll each out into a sausage shape, then form into pretzel shape. If desired, brush with beaten egg yolk and sprinkle with coarse salt. Allow to rise until not quite doubled. Bake at 475°F for about 10 minutes.

Makes 12 pretzels.

—Mary Flegel

Orange Chocolate Cookies

Ingredients

½ cup butter
½ cup sugar
1 egg
2 tsp. grated orange rind
2¼ cups flour
½ tsp. salt
1½ tsp. baking powder
Melted semisweet chocolate
Finely chopped nuts

Directions

Cream butter and add sugar, egg and orange rind. Mix flour, salt and baking powder and add to butter mixture.

Roll out on floured surface to about ⅛ inch and cut into desired shapes. Bake at 350°F for 10 minutes. Spread melted chocolate on cooled cookies and top with chopped nuts.

Makes 4 dozen cookies.

—Barbara & Dana Leahey

Peanut Butter Chocolate Chip Cookies

Ingredients

½ cup shortening
½ cup brown sugar
½ cup white sugar
½ cup peanut butter
1 egg, beaten
½ tsp. vanilla
1½ cups flour
½ tsp. salt
½ tsp. baking soda
⅔ cup chocolate chips
¼ cup chopped peanuts

Directions

Cream together shortening and sugars. Add peanut butter and blend. Stir in egg and vanilla.

Mix together remaining ingredients in a separate bowl, and then combine with creamed mixture.

Place by teaspoonful on greased cookie sheets and flatten with a fork. Bake at 350°F for 12 to 15 minutes.

Makes 3 to 3½ dozen cookies.

—Jane Lott

Italian Anise Cookies

Ingredients

2½ cups flour
½ cup sugar
3 tsp. baking powder
1 tsp. ground anise
⅓ cup soft butter
3 eggs

Directions

Sift together dry ingredients and cut in butter. Beat in eggs with fork until dough is smooth. Mix well with hands.

Wrap in plastic and refrigerate overnight. Roll to ¼-inch thickness and cut into circles.

Bake on greased cookie sheet at 350°F for 8 to 10 minutes, until lightly browned.

Makes 3 to 4 dozen cookies.

—Linda Townsend

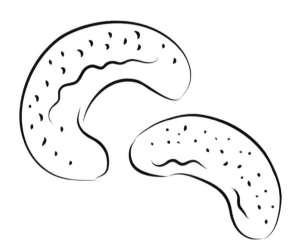

German Springerle Cookies

Ingredients

6 eggs
3 cups sugar
6 cups flour
¾ cup whole anise seed

Directions

Beat eggs and sugar together with electric mix-master on high until thick and creamy — about 4 minutes. Reduce speed to low and slowly add flour, scraping down and mixing thoroughly. Dough will be stiff.

Liberally flour a pastry board and scoop dough out onto it. Knead dough until it has a smooth surface, incorporating as much flour as necessary to keep it from sticking.

Clean off board and reflour. Using a regular rolling pin, roll dough into ¾-inch-thick rectangle. Flour springerle rolling pin and evenly press down design into dough. Cut cookies apart and place on greased cookie sheet that has been sprinkled with anise seed. Set aside overnight to dry.

Bake at 300°F for 10 minutes, or until bottoms are golden brown.

—Edith Cumming Coe

Italian Jam & Nut Cookies

Ingredients

4 eggs
1 cup oil
1¼ cups sugar
2 Tbsp. lemon juice
Flour
4 tsp. baking powder
Plum jam
1 cup raisins
1½ cups coarsely chopped walnuts

Directions

Beat together eggs, oil, sugar and lemon juice. Add enough flour to form soft dough. Add baking powder. Continue adding flour until a soft, but not sticky, dough is formed. Knead dough a little, then cut into 4 pieces.

Roll each piece of dough out ¼-inch thick. Spread jam on the dough, then sprinkle with raisins and nuts. Roll up like a jelly roll and seal the edges. Bake on a cookie sheet for 20 minutes at 350°F. Remove from oven and cut 1-inch thick at an angle. Turn off oven and return cookies to it until oven has completely cooled.

Makes 4 dozen cookies.

—Mary Andrasi

Banana Cookies

Ingredients

2¼ cups flour
2 tsp. baking powder
½ tsp. salt
¼ tsp. baking soda
⅔ cup butter
1 cup sugar
2 eggs
1 tsp. vanilla
6 oz. chocolate chips
1 cup mashed ripe banana

Directions

Sift together flour, baking powder, salt and baking soda. Cream together butter, sugar, eggs and vanilla. Add dry ingredients and blend well. Stir in chocolate chips and banana. Drop by teaspoonful onto greased cookie sheets. Bake at 400°F for 12 to 15 minutes.

Makes 4 dozen cookies.

—Linda Charron

Cranberry Cookies

This recipe results in a flavorful and colorful Christmas cookie which is not overly rich or sweet.

Ingredients

½ cup butter
¾ cup white sugar
¾ cup brown sugar
1 egg, beaten
¼ cup milk
3 cups flour
1 tsp. baking powder
¼ tsp. baking soda
½ tsp. salt
1 tsp. lemon juice
3 cups chopped cranberries
1 cup chopped nuts

Directions

Cream together butter and sugars. Add egg and milk. Sift together flour, baking powder, baking soda and salt and add to creamed ingredients, mixing well. Add lemon juice, cranberries and nuts.

Drop by teaspoonful onto greased cookie sheets and bake at 375°F for 15 minutes.

Makes 8 dozen cookies.

—Helen Hawkes

Banana Bars

Ingredients

½ cup butter
1 cup sugar
2 eggs
1 tsp. almond extract
2 cups sliced ripe bananas
2 cups flour
1 tsp. baking powder
¼ tsp. salt
¼ tsp. baking soda
½ cup chopped almonds
1 cup chopped dates
Icing sugar

Directions

Cream butter and sugar. Beat in eggs one at a time until fluffy. Add almond extract and bananas. Sift together dry ingredients and stir into batter. Add almonds and dates.

Spread in greased 9" x 13" baking pan and bake at 350°F for 30 minutes. While still warm, sprinkle lightly with icing sugar.

Makes 4 to 5 dozen bars.

—*Ann Budge*

Mom's Chocolate Shortbread

Bread Ingredients

¾ cup flour
2 Tbsp. cocoa
½ cup butter
2 Tbsp. white sugar
1½ tsp. salt
2 eggs
1¼ cups brown sugar
1 Tbsp. flour
½ tsp. baking powder
½ cup coconut
¾ cup chopped nuts
1 tsp. vanilla

Icing Ingredients

1 cup icing sugar
2 Tbsp. butter
1 heaping Tbsp. cocoa
Boiling water

Directions

Combine flour, cocoa, butter, white sugar and 1 tsp. salt. Press into a greased 8-inch-square cake pan. Bake at 300°F for 20 minutes.

Cream together eggs, remaining ½ tsp. salt, brown sugar, flour and baking powder. Add coconut, nuts and vanilla and mix well. Pour over shortbread base. Raise oven temperature to 350°F and bake for 20 minutes.

To make icing, combine icing sugar, butter, cocoa and enough boiling water to make a creamy mixture. Pour over baked shortbread. Cut into squares.

Makes 2 to 3 dozen squares.

—*Dianne Radcliffe*

Nanaimo Bars

Ingredients

¾ cup & 1 Tbsp. butter
5 Tbsp. sugar
5 Tbsp. cocoa
1 tsp. peppermint extract
1 egg
2 cups finely crushed graham crackers
½ cup vanilla pudding
2 cups icing sugar
2 oz. unsweetened chocolate

Directions

Heat ½ cup butter, the sugar, cocoa and peppermint in saucepan. Beat in egg and stir until consistency of custard. Remove from heat and stir in crushed graham crackers. Press mixture into a greased 8-inch square pan.

Cream together ¼ cup of remaining butter, the pudding and icing sugar. Spread over graham cracker layer.

Melt chocolate with remaining 1 Tbsp. butter, then pour over second layer. Let sit for a few minutes, then refrigerate for an hour before cutting.

Makes 3 dozen squares.

—*Margie Hancock*

Chocolate Chip Bars

Ingredients

½ cup butter
1¼ cups brown sugar
¼ cup white sugar
2 eggs, separated
½ tsp. vanilla
1 cup flour
1 tsp. baking powder
⅛ tsp. salt
Chocolate chips
1 cup coconut

Directions

Cream together butter, ¼ cup brown sugar, white sugar and egg yolks. Add vanilla. Sift together flour, baking powder and salt and add to creamed mixture. Spread in greased 9" x 13" pan. Sprinkle with chocolate chips.

Beat egg whites and remaining 1 cup brown sugar until stiff. Fold in coconut. Spread evenly over mixture in pan. Bake at 350°F for 20 to 30 minutes. Cut into bars while still warm, then cool in pan.

Makes 3 dozen bars.

—*Pauline Longmore*

Chocolate Cheese Brownies

Ingredients

8 oz. cream cheese
⅓ cup white sugar
3 eggs
½ tsp. vanilla
2 oz. unsweetened chocolate
½ cup butter
1 cup brown sugar
¾ cup flour
¾ tsp. baking powder
¼ cup chopped nuts

Directions

Blend cream cheese, white sugar, 1 egg and vanilla until smooth. Melt chocolate and butter and cool. Cream together remaining 2 eggs and brown sugar and beat in chocolate mixture. Sift together flour and baking powder and mix into chocolate.

Pour half the batter into a greased 9-inch cake pan. Spoon cream cheese mixture on top, spread out carefully and pour remaining batter over all. Sprinkle with nuts. Bake at 350°F for 45 to 50 minutes.

Makes 1 to 2 dozen brownies.

—*Linda Townsend*

Scottish Currant Slices

Ingredients

Pastry for 2 double 9-inch pie shells
1½ cups currants
½ tsp. cinnamon
¼ tsp. allspice
1 Tbsp. butter
1 Tbsp. lemon juice
½ cup sugar
2 tsp. cornstarch
½ cup water
3½ cups thinly sliced apples
Milk
Sugar

Directions

Combine currants, cinnamon, allspice, butter, lemon juice and sugar in saucepan. Stir together cornstarch and water until smooth. Add to currant mixture and bring to a boil stirring constantly, then simmer for 5 minutes until very thick. Cool.

Divide pastry in half. Roll out one half and line a jelly roll pan with it, pressing the dough part way up the sides. Spread with cooled currant mixture and top with sliced apples. Roll out remaining pastry and lay on top, sealing edges so that the filling is enclosed.

Brush top with milk and sprinkle with sugar. Bake at 450°F for 10 minutes, reduce heat to 375° and continue baking for 20 minutes. Cut into squares when cool.

Makes 6 dozen squares.

—*Elma MacLachlin*

Orange Squares

Ingredients

½ cup shortening
1 cup sugar
1 egg
Juice & grated rind of 1 large orange
2 cups flour
1 tsp. baking soda
1 tsp. baking powder
½ tsp. salt
1 cup sour milk
1 cup raisins

Directions

Cream together shortening and sugar. Add egg and orange juice and rind. Sift flour, baking soda, baking powder and salt and add to creamed mixture alternately with sour milk. Stir in raisins. Place in greased 9" x 13" baking pan and bake at 350°F for 35 minutes. Let cool before cutting and removing from pan.

Makes 3 to 4 dozen squares.

—*Orian Steele*

Coconut Squares

Ingredients

3 eggs
2 cups brown sugar
1 tsp. vanilla
2 cups coconut
½ cup chocolate chips
½ cup currants or raisins
½ cup chopped walnuts
½ cup wheat germ
½ cup flour

Directions

Beat eggs until foamy. Add remaining ingredients and mix well. Spread in greased 9" x 13" pan and bake at 350°F for 30 minutes.

Makes 4 dozen squares.

Boterkoek

This is a well known and much loved traditional Dutch recipe.

Ingredients

1 cup butter
1 cup sugar
1 egg
1 tsp. almond extract
2 cups flour
Milk
Slivered almonds

Directions

Cream together butter and sugar. Add egg, almond extract and then flour, mixing well by hand. Press evenly onto cookie sheet, making a ½-inch-thick layer. Wet the surface lightly with milk and press in almond slivers. Bake at 375°F for 30 minutes. Cut into squares while still warm.

Makes 20 squares.

—*Wilma Zomer*

Rhubarb Sour Cream Coffee Cake

Cake Ingredients

½ cup butter
1½ cups brown sugar
1 egg
1 cup whole wheat flour
1 cup unbleached flour
1 tsp. baking soda
½ tsp. salt
1 cup sour cream
1½ cups rhubarb, cut into ½-inch pieces
½ cup chopped walnuts or pecans

Topping Ingredients

½ cup butter
1 cup sugar
½ cup light cream
1 tsp. vanilla

Directions

Cream together butter, brown sugar and egg until light and fluffy. Combine flours, baking soda and salt. Add to creamed mixture alternately with sour cream, mixing well after each addition. Stir in rhubarb and nuts.

Spoon into well-greased 9" x 13" cake pan. Bake at 350°F for 35 to 40 minutes.

To make topping, combine butter, sugar, cream and vanilla in small saucepan. Heat until butter melts, then pour over cooled cake.

—*Valerie Gillis*

Apple Gingerbread

Ingredients

4 apples, peeled & sliced
2 cups flour
1½ tsp. baking soda
½ tsp. salt
½ cup sugar
1 tsp. ginger
1 tsp. cinnamon
½ cup butter
¾ cup molasses
1 egg
1 cup boiling water

Directions

Place apples in greased 9" x 9" cake pan. Sift together flour, baking soda, salt, sugar, ginger and cinnamon. Add butter, molasses and egg and mix well. Add boiling water and beat well. Pour mixture over apples and bake at 350°F for 30 minutes.

—*Judy Wuest*

Orange Sponge Cake

Cake Ingredients

3 eggs, separated
¼ tsp. cream of tartar
1 cup sugar
2 tsp. grated orange rind
⅓ cup orange juice
1¼ cups flour
1½ tsp. baking powder
¼ tsp. salt

Glaze Ingredients

Juice of 1 orange
¼ cup sugar

Directions

Beat egg whites with cream of tartar until stiff. Add yolks one
at a time, beating well after each addition. Add sugar gradually, beating well. Add rind and juice.

Sift together flour, baking powder and salt and fold into liquid ingredients. Place batter in greased tube pan and bake
at 325°F for 18 to 20 minutes.

Combine orange juice and sugar to make glaze and pour over warm cake.

—Lee Robinson

Coconut Pound Cake

Ingredients

1 cup butter
2 cups sugar
5 eggs
3 cups flour
¼ tsp. salt
1 cup milk
1½ cups coconut
1 tsp. lemon juice
½ tsp. vanilla

Directions

Cream butter and sugar together until fluffy. Add eggs one at a time, beating well after each addition. Sift flour with salt and add alternately with milk to creamed mixture, beating after each addition. Add coconut, lemon juice and vanilla. Turn into greased and floured tube pan. Bake at 325°F for 90 minutes. Cool for 10 minutes, then remove from pan and cool on rack.

—Sheila Couture

Sour Cream Spice Cake

Ingredients

1 cup shortening
½ cup brown sugar
2 eggs, beaten
1 cup molasses
1 cup sour cream
1 tsp. salt
½ tsp. nutmeg
½ tsp. ginger
1 tsp. cloves
1 tsp. baking soda
1 tsp. cream of tartar
3 cups flour
1 cup raisins
½ cup chopped nuts

Directions

Cream together shortening and sugar. Add eggs, then molasses and sour cream. Combine salt, nutmeg, ginger, cloves, baking soda and cream of tartar with flour and add to creamed ingredients. Mix well, then stir in raisins and nuts. Place in greased 9-inch cake pan and bake at 350°F for 1 hour.

—Jan Johnson

Great Aunt Bessie's Maple Cake

This recipe was developed by the contributor's Great Aunt Bessie. It became such a favorite of the young members of the family that she continued to bake it on her birthday each year, when the family gathered for a reunion.

Cake Ingredients

½ cup butter
½ cup sugar
½ cup maple syrup
1 tsp. vanilla
2 eggs, well beaten
1¾ cups flour
½ tsp. salt
2½ tsp. baking powder
¼ cup milk
½ cup chopped walnuts

Frosting Ingredients

1 cup maple syrup
2 egg whites
Salt

Directions

Cream together butter and sugar. Gradually add maple syrup and vanilla and cream well again. Add eggs and mix well. Sift together dry ingredients and add to creamed mixture alternately with milk. Stir in chopped nuts.

Pour into 2 greased and floured 8-inch cake pans. Bake at 375°F for 25 to 30 minutes.

To make frosting, cook maple syrup to soft ball stage. Beat egg whites with pinch of salt until peaks form. Add cooled syrup in fine stream, beating constantly. Frost cooled cake.

—Joyce Barton

Banana Yogurt Cupcakes

Ingredients

½ cup butter
1 cup honey
2 eggs
2 ripe bananas, mashed
2 tsp. lemon juice
1 tsp. grated lemon rind
1 cup whole wheat flour
1 cup & 2 Tbsp. unbleached flour
1 tsp. baking soda
½ tsp. salt
½ cup yogurt

Directions

Cream butter, then add honey and mix. Add eggs one at a time, beating well after each addition, then bananas. Stir in lemon juice and rind.

Sift together flours, baking soda and salt and add to creamed mixture alternately with yogurt. Spoon into prepared muffin tins and bake at 350°F for 15 to 20 minutes.

Makes 24 cupcakes.

—Linda Ewert

Carrot Walnut Cupcakes

Ingredients

1 cup oil
¾ cup brown sugar
2 eggs
1 tsp. vanilla
1½ cups flour
1½ tsp. baking soda
½ tsp. salt
1 tsp. cinnamon
½ tsp. nutmeg
2 cups finely shredded carrots
1 cup finely chopped walnuts

Directions

Combine oil, sugar, eggs and vanilla in large bowl. Beat until thick. Sift together flour, baking soda, salt, cinnamon and nutmeg and add to creamed ingredients. Stir in carrots and walnuts. Place in prepared muffin tins and bake at 350°F for 20 minutes.

Makes 18 to 20 cupcakes.

—Anne Sanderson

Coconut Black Walnut Pound Cake

This is a delicious, moist, heavy cake, equally successful with black or regular walnuts.

Ingredients

2 cups sugar
1 cup oil
4 eggs, beaten
3 cups flour
½ tsp. baking soda
½ tsp. salt
½ tsp. baking powder
1 cup buttermilk
1 cup chopped black walnuts
1 cup flaked coconut
2 tsp. coconut extract

Directions

Combine sugar, oil and eggs and beat well. Mix together flour, baking soda, salt and baking powder. Add to sugar mixture alternately with buttermilk, beating well after each addition. Stir in walnuts, coconut and extract. Pour into greased and floured 10-inch bundt pan and bake at 325°F for 65 minutes.

—Dorothy Hollis

Greek Walnut Cake

The honey syrup for this cake can also be used for baklava.

Cake Ingredients

¾ cup oil
½ cup honey
3 eggs
2 tsp. grated orange rind
1 cup flour
1½ tsp. baking powder
½ tsp. cinnamon
¼ tsp. salt
⅛ tsp. nutmeg
⅓ cup milk powder
1½ cups finely chopped walnuts

Syrup Ingredients

1 lemon
1 cup sugar
2" stick cinnamon
2 whole cloves
1 cup honey
1 Tbsp. brandy

Directions

To make cake: Beat oil and honey until light — about 5 minutes. Beat in eggs, one at a time. Add orange rind. Sift together all dry ingredients except walnuts. Add to liquid mixture alternately with ¼ cup water. Stir in walnuts. Bake in a greased 9" x 9" pan at 350°F for 35 minutes, or until a toothpick inserted in the center comes out clean.

To make honey syrup: Juice the lemon, reserving 1½ tsp. of juice. Place the lemon rind in a heavy saucepan with 1 cup water, sugar, cinnamon stick and cloves. Bring to a boil, lower heat and cook without stirring for about 25 minutes, or until 230°F is reached on a candy thermometer. Pick out rind and spices. Stir in lemon juice, honey and brandy. Cool. Makes 2 cups.

—Susan O'Neill

Traditional Lithuanian Honey Cake

Ingredients

4 eggs
¾ cup sugar
¾ cup honey
½ cup oil
1 cup milk
3 tsp. baking powder
½ tsp. baking soda
2½ cups flour
1 Tbsp. mixed spices (cinnamon, cloves, ginger, cardamom)

Directions

Beat eggs, then add sugar, honey, oil and milk. Sift together baking powder, baking soda, flour and spices, and add to liquid ingredients. Stir to blend. Pour into greased bundt pan, and bake at 350°F for 1 hour.

—Linda Barsauskas

Russian Poppy Seed Cake

Loaded with poppy seeds, this is an irresistible cake. All the tasters in Vermont ate more of this cake than they needed and still came back for more.

Ingredients

2 cups poppy seeds
2 cups milk
1 cup honey
1½ cups butter
1 cup sugar
5 eggs, separated
1 tsp. almond extract
1½ cups whole wheat flour
1½ cups white flour
2 tsp. baking powder
½ tsp. salt

Directions

Heat poppy seeds, milk and honey to boiling point, then set aside to cool.

Cream together butter and sugar, then add egg yolks and almond extract. Sift together flours, baking powder and salt. Add flour mixture and poppy seed mixture alternately to creamed mixture, beating well. Gently fold in stiffly beaten egg whites. Pour into greased and floured bundt pan. Bake at 350°F for 40 to 50 minutes.

—Christine A. Lichatz

Cream Cheese Pound Cake with Cranberries

For orange rind rich with flavor, dry orange peels (preferably from Mandarin oranges), then grind them. They can be stored in a tightly capped jar or in the freezer.

Ingredients

1 cup butter
½ lb. cream cheese
4 eggs
2 cups brown sugar
1 tsp. vanilla
1 Tbsp. dried orange rind soaked in 1½ Tbsp. lemon juice
2¼ cups flour
1½ tsp. baking powder
1 cup cranberries with ¾ tsp. orange rind

Directions

Beat butter and cream cheese until fluffy. Add eggs one at a time, beating until fluffy after each addition. Add sugar and beat well, then add vanilla and orange rind-lemon juice mixture. Sift flour and baking powder together, then fold into creamed mixture. Drop half the batter into bundt pan that has been greased and dusted with brown sugar. Sprinkle liberally with cranberries and top with remaining batter. Bake at 350°F for 60 to 70 minutes.

—Helen P. Slama

Double Chocolate Zucchini Cake

A great way to get zucchini into zucchini haters, this cake improves in flavor if allowed to sit for a day before it is eaten.

Ingredients

3 cups flour
1½ tsp. baking powder
1½ tsp. cinnamon
1¼ tsp. salt
1 tsp. baking soda
⅛ tsp. cloves
1½ cups oil
2⅓ cups packed brown sugar
4 eggs
2 oz. unsweetened chocolate, melted
3 zucchini, grated
1 cup chocolate chips
1 cup chopped nuts

Directions

Combine flour, baking powder, cinnamon, salt, baking soda and cloves and set aside. Beat together oil and sugar, then add eggs, one at a time, beating well after each addition. Gradually beat in melted chocolate, then dry ingredients. Beat until smooth. Fold in zucchini, chocolate chips and nuts. Pour into greased and floured bundt pan and bake at 350°F for 1 hour 20 minutes. Frost with Chocolate Cake Glaze (page 430).

—Debra J. Eddy

Tiger Cake

This cake combines with great success the flavors of chocolate and orange. It is a cake that can be made in a hurry and served simply sprinkled with confectioners' sugar.

Ingredients
½ cup butter
1 tsp. salt
½ tsp. vanilla
1¼ cups sugar
2 eggs
2½ tsp. baking powder
2 cups flour
⅔ cup milk
1 oz. unsweetened chocolate or 3 Tbsp. cocoa
2 Tbsp. grated orange rind

Directions
Cream together butter, salt, vanilla and sugar, then add eggs, one at a time, beating well. Sift together dry ingredients and add to creamed mixture alternately with milk. Divide batter in half.

Melt chocolate (or dissolve cocoa in 2 Tbsp. water) and add to half of batter. Add orange rind to other half. Pour orange batter into greased 9" x 9" pan. Pour chocolate batter on top and cut through with a knife, just enough to create a marbled effect. Bake at 350°F for 30 minutes. Frost with Orange Frosting (page 430).

—Donna Parker

Pumpkin Bundt Cake

Our tester says, "This cake will become a family favorite in our house. It mixes up fast and is a moist, lightly spiced cake."

Ingredients
3 cups flour
2 tsp. baking soda
2 tsp. baking powder
3 tsp. cinnamon
1 tsp. salt
4 eggs, beaten
2 cups sugar
1¼ cups oil
2 cups cooked, mashed pumpkin
½ cup chopped pecans
½ cup chocolate chips

Directions
Sift flour, baking soda, baking powder, cinnamon and salt together twice. Beat eggs and sugar together. Add oil and pumpkin, then blend in flour mixture. Fold in pecans and chocolate chips. Bake in greased and floured bundt pan at 350°F for 60 minutes. Let cool in pan for 10 minutes, then turn out onto cooling rack.

—Gladys Sykes

Sweet Potato Cake

Ingredients

½ cup shortening
1 cup sugar
2 eggs
1 cup cooked, mashed sweet potato
2 cups flour
½ tsp. salt
2 tsp. baking powder
¼ tsp. baking soda
¼ tsp. cloves
½ tsp. cinnamon
½ tsp. nutmeg
½ cup milk
½ cup chopped nuts

Directions

Cream together shortening and sugar, then add eggs, beating after each addition. Add sweet potato. Sift together flour, salt, baking powder, baking soda, cloves, cinnamon and nutmeg. Add to creamed mixture alternately with milk. Fold in nuts. Bake in greased bundt pan at 350°F for 45 to 50 minutes.

—Betty Hay

Chocolate Brownie Cake

"A friend, knowing my love of chocolate, created this cake for my birthday a few years ago — it's a chocolate-lover's dream come true."

Ingredients

6 oz. unsweetened chocolate
¾ cup butter, softened
2¼ cups sugar
4 eggs
1 tsp. vanilla
2 cups flour
1½ tsp. baking powder
¼ tsp. salt
1½ cups milk

Directions

Melt chocolate and set aside to cool. Cream together butter and sugar until light and fluffy. Beat in eggs, one at a time, then beat in chocolate and vanilla. Sift flour, baking powder and salt together, then add to creamed mixture alternately with milk. Grease and flour three 9-inch cake pans and divide batter among them. Bake at 350°F for 25 to 30 minutes.

—Bobbie Nelson

Applesauce Cake

"This is my grandmother's recipe — it takes me back to my visits to her house, where the kitchen was filled with the smell of cinnamon and cloves."

Ingredients

1 cup sugar
½ cup butter
1 egg
1 cup applesauce
1 tsp. baking soda
1 cup flour
salt
1 tsp. cinnamon
1 tsp. allspice
1 cup raisins
1 cup chopped walnuts

Directions

Cream together sugar and butter, then beat in egg. Mix together applesauce and baking soda. Sift together flour, salt, cinnamon and allspice. Add applesauce and dry ingredients alternately, in thirds, to creamed mixture. Fold in raisins and nuts. Pour into greased loaf pan and bake at 375°For 50 to 60 minutes.

—Jeanne Reitz

Upside-Down Macaroon Cake

Ingredients

⅓ cup butter
2 cups sugar
3 eggs, separated
1¼ cups milk
1 cup flour
1 tsp. baking powder
coconut
2 Tbsp. cornstarch
salt
1 tsp. vanilla

Directions

Cream together butter and ½ cup sugar. Add 2 egg yolks, ½ cup milk, flour and baking powder and mix well. Place in two 8-inch cake pans lined with waxed paper. Beat 3 egg whites with 1 cup sugar until stiff and glossy. Spread over cakes and sprinkle with coconut. Bake at 350°F for 20 to 30 minutes, or until golden brown.

Meanwhile, prepare filling: Combine remaining ½ cup sugar, cornstarch, salt, remaining egg yolk and vanilla in heavy pot. Add remaining milk slowly while cooking over medium heat. Cook until thickened. Spread as filling between cooled cake layers.

—Jane Matthews

Gâteau Marguerite

"This recipe originated in a Belgian convent. It is dense and rich — just dust with icing sugar to serve." Our tester says this is one of the three best cakes he has ever eaten.

Ingredients

1 cup butter
1¼ cups sugar
¼ tsp. salt
juice of 1 lemon
4-5 eggs, separated
3 cups flour
1 Tbsp. baking powder
8 oz. semisweet chocolate, chopped
2 cups ground hazelnuts

Directions

Beat together butter, sugar, salt, lemon juice and egg yolks until creamy. Stir in flour, baking powder, chocolate and nuts. Beat egg whites until stiff, then gently fold into batter. Pour into well-greased and floured 9½-inch springform pan. Bake at 350°F for 1 to 1½ hours, or until toothpick inserted in middle comes out clean.

—*Trudi Keillor*

Mama's Johnny Cake

"My grandmother lived in a grand house in Toronto and entertained a great deal. This recipe was served often, even to the likes of Mrs. Timothy Eaton Senior, who summoned my grand-mother's cook for the recipe."

Ingredients

¼ cup butter
1 cup sugar
2 eggs, beaten
1 cup flour
3 tsp. baking powder
1 cup cornmeal
2 Tbsp. beef or chicken stock
1 cup milk

Directions

Cream butter then blend in sugar and eggs. In another bowl, sift together flour and baking powder, then stir in cornmeal. Add stock to milk. Mix dry ingredients and milk mixture alternately into butter-sugar mixture.

Pour into a 9" x 9" pan and bake at 375°F for 30 to 40 minutes. Serve warm as an alternative to rolls or bread.

—*Mary Matear*

Coconut Cream Frosting

Ingredients

1 cup coconut
3 oz. cream cheese
¼ cup butter
3 cups icing sugar
1 Tbsp. milk
½ tsp. vanilla

Directions

Toast coconut and cool. Cream cheese with butter, then add sugar, milk and vanilla. Beat until smooth, then stir in half the coconut. Frost cake and top with remaining coconut.

Frosts a 9" x 13" cake.

—Paddi Caldwell

Chocolate Cake Glaze

Ingredients

1 cup icing sugar
1 Tbsp. butter, melted
salt
2 Tbsp. corn syrup
½ tsp. vanilla
1 oz. semisweet chocolate curls

Directions

Beat together sugar, butter and salt, then add corn syrup, 2 Tbsp. water and vanilla, stirring until smooth. Garnish cake with chocolate curls after spreading with glaze.

Frosts a bundt cake.

—Debra J. Eddy

Chocolate Cream Frosting

Ingredients

5 oz. semisweet chocolate
½ cup sugar
3 eggs
2 Tbsp. coffee liqueur
1 cup softened butter

Directions

Melt chocolate and let cool. Mix sugar and eggs in top of double boiler and cook, stirring constantly, until thickened. Remove from heat and pour into glass or metal bowl. Fold in chocolate and coffee liqueur, then beat in butter in chunks until smooth. Chill.

Frosts a 2-layer cake.

—Bobbi Hobbs

Orange Frosting

Ingredients

1 egg yolk, beaten
3 Tbsp. butter
2 cups icing sugar
3 Tbsp. orange juice
1 tsp. grated orange rind
salt

Directions

Combine all ingredients and beat well.

Frosts a 9" x 9" cake.

—Donna Parker

Vanilla Butter Frosting

Ingredients

4 Tbsp. softened butter
2 Tbsp. yogurt
1 tsp. vanilla
2 cups icing sugar

Directions

Beat butter until light and fluffy, then add remaining ingredients. Beat well.

Frosts a 2-layer cake.

—Marcia D. Powers

Old-Fashioned Raisin Cake

Ingredients

1 cup brown sugar
1 cup & 3 Tbsp. water
2 cups raisins
½ tsp. salt
1 tsp. cinnamon
½ tsp. ground cloves
¼ tsp. mace
¼ tsp. nutmeg
⅓ cup shortening
2 cups flour
1 tsp. baking soda
½ tsp. baking powder

Directions

Place sugar, water, raisins, salt and spices in a pan and bring to a boil. Cool. Stir in shortening and remaining ingredients.

Pour batter into greased and floured 9-inch square pan. Bake at 325°F for 1 hour or until top springs back when touched.

—Patty Robinson

Honey Nut Bread

The cottage cheese adds an interesting dimension to this exceptionally moist and flavorful bread.

Ingredients

3 cups white flour
2 Tbsp. yeast
1 tsp. salt
1 cup cottage cheese
4 Tbsp. butter
½ cup honey
2 eggs
2–2½ cups whole wheat flour
½ cup rolled oats
⅔ cup chopped walnuts

Directions

In a large bowl, mix 2 cups white flour, yeast and salt. Heat 1 cup water, cottage cheese, butter and honey in a saucepan until just warm. Add to flour mixture. Beat in eggs. Stir in whole wheat flour, oats and nuts. Add remaining white flour. On a floured surface, knead dough until smooth and elastic, adding more white flour if dough is sticky. Let dough rise in a warm place until it has doubled in size — about 1 hour.

Punch down dough and divide into thirds. Shape loaves and place in greased bread pans. Let rise until doubled — about half an hour. Bake at 350°F for 45 minutes, or until the loaf sounds hollow when tapped.

Makes 3 loaves.

—Shirley Miller

Preserves

Chunky Mustard Pickles

Ingredients

1 medium cauliflower
1 qt. large cucumbers
3 sweet red peppers
3 green peppers
1 qt. small cucumbers
1 qt. onions, chopped
1 qt. pickling onions
1 cup pickling salt
3 qts. water
5 cups sugar
½ cup water
4½ cups vinegar
¼ oz. celery seed
¼ oz. mustard seed
¼ cup dry mustard
¾ cup flour
1 Tbsp. turmeric

Directions

Chop cauliflower, large cucumbers and peppers into chunks. Add small cucumbers, onions and pickling onions. Cover with a brine made of the pickling salt and 3 quarts water and leave overnight. In the morning, rinse and drain well.

Combine with sugar, ½ cup water, vinegar, celery seed and mustard seed and bring to a boil. When boiling, take some of the liquid and mix to a smooth paste with dry mustard, flour and turmeric. Stir back into pickles and cook for 5 minutes. Bottle and seal.

Makes 6 to 8 quarts.

—Beth Hopkins

Dilled Green Tomatoes

Ingredients

15 medium-sized green tomatoes
Fresh dill
5 cloves garlic
5 whole cloves
2½ tsp. cayenne pepper
1 qt. vinegar
1 qt. water
⅓ cup pickling salt

Directions

Wash tomatoes and slice if necessary. Pack into 5 quart jars. Add 3 heads dill, 1 clove garlic, 1 whole clove and ½ tsp. cayenne to each jar.

Boil vinegar, water and salt for 5 minutes. Pour over tomatoes and process for 20 minutes in a boiling water bath.

Makes 5 quarts.

—E. V. Estey

Dilled Bean Pickles

Ingredients

3 lbs. fresh green beans
½ cup chopped fresh dill
2 cloves garlic, peeled & halved
2 cups water
4 Tbsp. salt
2 cups white vinegar
4 tsp. sugar
½ tsp. cayenne pepper

Directions

Parboil beans in unsalted water until tender — 5 to 10 minutes. Pack upright in sterile jars and add dill and garlic.

Heat water, salt, vinegar, sugar and cayenne to a boil. Pour over beans. Seal jars and let stand for 6 weeks.

Makes 4 to 5 pints.

—E. Evans

Dill Pickles

Ingredients

4 lbs. small cucumbers
Fresh dill
8 cloves garlic
3 cups water
3 cups white vinegar
5 Tbsp. pickling salt

Directions

Scrub cucumbers and soak overnight in ice water. Drain and pack into 4 hot, sterilized quart jars. Place sprays of dill and garlic cloves on top of cucumbers.

Combine remaining ingredients and bring to a boil. Pour over cucumbers and seal jars. Store for 1 month before eating.

Makes 4 quarts.

—Sheila Couture

Dilled Zucchini

Ingredients

6 lbs. zucchini, trimmed & thinly sliced
2 cups thinly sliced celery
2 large onions, chopped
⅓ cup salt
Ice cubes
2 cups sugar
2 Tbsp. dill seeds
2 cups white vinegar
6 cloves garlic, halved

Directions

Combine zucchini, celery, onions and salt in large bowl, place a layer of ice on top, cover and let stand for 3 hours. Drain well.

Combine sugar, dill seeds and vinegar in a saucepan and bring to a boil, stirring constantly. Stir in vegetables, and heat, stirring several times, just to a full boil. Ladle into hot, sterilized jars, place 1 to 2 pieces of garlic in each and seal.

Makes 8 to 10 pints.

—Laura Poitras

Swiss Chard Pickles

Ingredients

4 qts. Swiss chard, cut into 1-inch pieces
8 medium onions, sliced
Pickling salt
White vinegar
4 cups white sugar
2 Tbsp. celery seed
3 Tbsp. mustard seed
½ cup cornstarch
2 Tbsp. dry mustard
1 Tbsp. curry powder
2 tsp. turmeric

Directions

Layer Swiss chard and onions in large pickling kettle and sprinkle with salt. Let stand for 1 hour. Drain and add vinegar to cover.

Stir in sugar, celery seed and mustard seed and cook until tender. Add cornstarch, mustard, curry powder and turmeric.

Seal in sterilized jars.

Makes 12 pints.

— Dorothy Hall

Dilled Carrots

Ingredients

6 cups cold water
2 cups white vinegar
½ cup pickling salt
¼ tsp. cream of tartar
6 lbs. baby carrots
6–7 cloves garlic, slivered
6–7 large sprigs fresh dill

Directions

Combine water, vinegar, salt and cream of tartar, stirring until salt is dissolved. Scrape and trim carrots. Put a slivered clove of garlic in each of 6 or 7 pint jars. Add a dill sprig to each, then pack in carrots upright. Pour vinegar mixture over carrots to fill jars.

Process for 10 minutes in a boiling water bath and store in a cool place for 3 weeks.

Makes 6 to 7 pints.

—Kathee Roy

Pickled Carrots Rosemary

Ingredients

2 hot peppers
4 cloves garlic
1 tsp. rosemary
2 lbs. carrots, peeled & cut into 4-inch long strips
2 cups water
2 cups white vinegar
3 Tbsp. pickling salt
3 Tbsp. sugar

Directions

Cut peppers into quarters lengthwise. Place 2 strips pepper and 1 clove garlic into each of 4 pint jars. Add ¼ tsp. rosemary to each jar. Pack tightly with carrot sticks.

Bring water, vinegar, salt and sugar to a boil, reduce heat and simmer, uncovered, for 5 minutes. Pour over carrots, seal and process for 10 minutes in boiling water bath.

Let pickles age for 1 month before eating.

Makes 4 pints.

—Lynn Hill

Sweet Pickles

Ingredients

6 qts. cucumbers
¾ cup pickling salt
Boiling water
1 plum
3 pints white vinegar
4 Tbsp. white sugar
4 Tbsp. pickling salt
4 Tbsp. mustard seed &
½ cup mixed pickling
   spice tied in a bag
11–12 cups white sugar

Directions

Cut cucumbers into chunks and place in a large crock with ¾ cup pickling salt. Cover with boiling water and let sit overnight. In the morning, drain and wipe each piece dry. Return to crock with plum.

Heat vinegar, 4 Tbsp. sugar, 4 Tbsp. pickling salt, mustard seed and pickling spice together and add to cucumber. Cover with a plate.

Add 1 cup sugar each day for 11 to 12 days. Mix with a wooden spoon.

After 12 days, drain cucumbers and heat syrup. Place cucumbers in jars, pour syrup over and seal.

Makes 6 quarts.

—Hilda Jackson

Pickled Mushrooms

This traditional Russian recipe can be used with both domestic and wild mushrooms and is especially suited to shaggy manes and the honey mushroom.

Ingredients

1 cup red wine vinegar
2 whole cloves
½ cup cold water
5 whole peppercorns
1 bay leaf
2 tsp. salt
2 cloves garlic, crushed
1 lb. mushrooms
1 Tbsp. vegetable oil

Directions

Combine vinegar, cloves, water, peppercorns, bay leaf, salt and garlic in a 2-quart enameled saucepan. Bring to a boil, add mushrooms and reduce heat. Simmer, uncovered, for 10 minutes, stirring occasionally.

Cool to room temperature. Pour into 1-quart jar and slowly pour oil on top. Secure top with plastic wrap, cover tightly and let sit for at least 1 week.

Makes 1 quart.

—Sandra Kapral

Piccalilli

Ingredients

6 green peppers
6 red peppers
8 cucumbers
8 cups chopped green tomatoes
6 large onions
1 cup pickling salt
5 cups vinegar
2 lbs. brown sugar
2 tsp. dry mustard
2 Tbsp. mixed pickling spice, tied in cheese cloth

Directions

Wash peppers, cut in half and remove seeds. Peel cucumbers, cut stem ends from tomatoes and peel onions.

Put peppers, onions and cucumbers through coarse setting of meat grinder. Score tomatoes and cut into small cubes.

Measure 8 cups of tomatoes into bowl. Put ground and chopped vegetables in layers in large pot, sprinkling each layer with salt, using 1 cup salt in all. Let stand overnight.

Strain vegetables through fine-holed colander. Remove as much liquid as possible and replace vegetables in pot. Add vinegar, brown sugar, mustard and pickling spice. Cook until sauce becomes clear — about 35 minutes — stirring occasionally.

Remove pickling spice and place piccalilli in hot, sterilized jars and seal.

Makes 8 to 10 pints.

—Mrs. W. Atkins

Peter Piper's Pickled Peppers

Ingredients

10 lbs. sweet green peppers
Pickling salt
24 ice cubes
3 cloves garlic, sliced
3 cups vinegar
5 cups sugar
½ tsp. celery seed
½ tsp. turmeric
2 Tbsp. mustard seed

Directions

Slice peppers and sprinkle lightly with pickling salt. Mix in ice cubes and garlic and chill for 3 hours.

Remove garlic and drain peppers. Combine remaining ingredients in a heavy saucepan and add peppers. Bring to a boil, then place in hot jars and seal.

Makes 6 to 8 quarts.

—Dee Lowe

Honey Pickled Beets

Ingredients

2 qts. beets
1½ cups white vinegar
1 cup honey
1 cup water
1 tsp. salt
1 tsp. allspice
2 cups onion rings
2 tsp. each whole cloves, mustard seed & 2
   cinnamon sticks placed in a spice bag

Directions

Cook the beets and slip off the skins. Combine the vinegar, honey and water in a large saucepan and add to this the salt and allspice. Drop the spice bag in and simmer for 5 minutes.

Add the beets and onion rings and simmer gently for 20 minutes.

Pack into hot sterile jars, cover with liquid and seal.

Makes 4 pints.

—*Ruth E. Geddes*

Curry Pickle

Ingredients

Zucchini & onions to fill 4 or 5 quart jars,
   thinly sliced
Salt brine to cover zucchini & onion
6 cups vinegar
6 cups sugar
2 Tbsp. celery seed
2 Tbsp. dry mustard
4 Tbsp. hot curry powder
2 Tbsp. turmeric
6 whole cloves
8–10 slices ginger root
1 tsp. Tabasco sauce

Directions

Soak zucchini and onion slices in salt brine overnight. Drain and pack in jars.

Combine remaining ingredients, bring to a boil and pour over vegetables. Seal jars and let stand a few weeks before eating.

Makes 4 to 5 quarts.

—*Brigitte Wolf*

Horseradish

Ingredients

2 cups grated horseradish
1 cup white vinegar
½ tsp. salt

Directions

Place horseradish in sterilized 1-quart jar. Combine vinegar and salt and pour over horseradish. Seal jar and store in a cool place.

Makes 1 quart.

—Shirley Morrish

Sauerkraut

Ingredients

2 lbs. cabbage
4 tsp. pickling salt

Directions

Remove loose outer leaves of cabbage. Wash and drain inner head, cut into quarters and remove core. Shred or cut into ⅛-inch strips. Mix thoroughly with 3 tsp. salt by hand.

Tightly pack cabbage into clean, hot jars. Press down with fingers and cover with a piece of clean cheesecloth. Cross 2 wooden sticks on top of the cheesecloth below the neck of the jar, place lid on loosely and set in a shallow pan to catch any overflow of brine.

Store for 2 to 3 weeks at 70°F. When fermentation has stopped, wipe jars clean and remove sticks and cheesecloth. Press cabbage down firmly to release the last of the air bubbles. Combine 1 quart water with remaining 1 tsp. salt and pour over cabbage. Place lid on jar and process for 10 minutes in boiling water bath.

Makes 1 quart.

—Mary Dzielak

Chili Sauce

Ingredients

30 ripe tomatoes, peeled & diced
8 onions, diced
3 sweet red peppers, diced
3 green peppers, diced
2 cups diced celery
2½ cups brown sugar
3 cups vinegar
3 Tbsp. pickling salt

Directions

Combine all ingredients in a large pot and mix well. Simmer, uncovered, until thick — 4½ hours. Seal into jars while hot.

Makes 5 pints.

—Karen Herder

Watermelon Pickle

Ingredients

4 qts. watermelon rind
4 Tbsp. salt
3 Tbsp. alum
11 cups sugar
2 cups white vinegar
1½ tsp. whole cloves
3 sticks cinnamon

Directions

Cut rind into 1-inch cubes, place in pot and add salt. Cover with water and add alum. Bring to a boil, reduce heat and simmer for 30 minutes. Drain and rinse.

Simmer in 4 more quarts of water (or enough to cover) until tender. Add sugar and cook until transparent. Add vinegar and cook another 25 minutes. Toss in cloves and cinnamon and cook 5 minutes. Pack in 6 jars, with syrup and spices. Seal. Let sit for 2 weeks before eating.

Makes 6 pints.

—Cary Elizabeth Marshall

Hot Tamale Sauce

This sauce is delicious with Mexican cooking and almost any bean or meat dish.

Ingredients

15 large ripe tomatoes
4 large peaches
3 large tart apples
4 pears
6 medium onions
3 cups diced celery
3 Tbsp. mixed pickling spice
4 tsp. salt
1½ cups cider vinegar
1 cup honey
12 small chili peppers

Directions

Blanch, peel and slice tomatoes and peaches. Core and slice apples and pears. Peel and thinly slice onions. Cut celery into small pieces. Tie pickling spice in a cheesecloth bag.

Combine all ingredients in a large pot and cook slowly until honey is dissolved and fruit is well mixed. Boil steadily, stirring occasionally, until sauce is thickened — about 40 minutes.

Turn into hot, sterile jars and seal.

Makes 3 to 4 quarts.

—Betty Ternier Daniels

Ketchup

Ingredients

1½ tsp. whole cloves
1 stick cinnamon
1 tsp. celery seed
1 tsp. allspice
1 cup white vinegar
8 lbs. ripe tomatoes
2 medium onions, chopped
¼ tsp. red pepper
6 apples, cut in eighths (optional)
1 cup sugar
4 tsp. salt

Directions

Add spices to vinegar and bring to a boil. Cover, turn off heat and let stand.

Mash tomatoes in a pot, add onion, pepper and apples. Heat to a boil and cook for 15 minutes. Put through a sieve. Add sugar to tomato juice and reheat to a boil. Skim. Cook down to half the original volume.

Strain vinegar mixture and add to juice with salt. Simmer, stirring frequently, for 30 minutes.

Fill hot, sterilized jars and seal.

Makes 4 to 5 pints.

—Kathy MacRow

Pickled Onions

Ingredients

Boiling water
4 lbs. pickling onions
2½ cups pickling salt
3 qts. cold water
3 cups white vinegar
1 cup water
3 cups sugar
2 Tbsp. mixed pickling spice, tied in a bag

Directions

Pour boiling water over onions and let stand 5 minutes. Drain and plunge into ice water. Drain and peel off skins.

Dissolve pickling salt in 3 quarts cold water and pour over onions. Let stand overnight. Drain and rinse several times under cold running water.

Bring vinegar, 1 cup water, sugar and spices to a boil. Reduce heat and simmer for 15 minutes. Remove spices, add onions and bring back to a boil.

Ladle into sterilized jars and fill with vinegar syrup. Seal.

Makes 5 pints.

—Linda Forsyth

Zucchini Relish

Ingredients

10 cups zucchini
4 cups onions
5 Tbsp. pickling salt
1 red pepper
1 green pepper
2¼ cups vinegar
3 cups sugar
1 tsp. nutmeg
1 tsp. dry mustard
1 tsp. turmeric
1 tsp. cornstarch
2 Tbsp. celery seed
½ tsp. pepper

Directions

Grind zucchini, onions and salt and let stand overnight. Drain and rinse twice in cold water to remove salt.

Grind red and green peppers together. Add to zucchini with remaining ingredients. Cook for 30 minutes.

Ladle while hot into sterile jars and seal.

Makes 5 to 6 pints.

—Gail Berg

Rhubarb Relish

Ingredients

2 qts. rhubarb, chopped into 1-inch lengths
1 qt. onions, thinly sliced
2 cups vinegar
2 cups sugar
1 Tbsp. salt
1 tsp. cloves
1 tsp. allspice
1 tsp. cinnamon
1 tsp. pepper

Directions

Place all ingredients in a large pot and mix well. Cook slowly until rhubarb is soft, then boil for 1 hour.

Seal in sterilized jars.

Makes 4 pints.

—Shirley Gilbert

Tomato Juice

Ingredients

12 very large ripe tomatoes,
  cut in thin wedges
1 large green pepper, diced
3 medium onions, chopped
1 celery stalk, diced
⅓ cup sugar
1 Tbsp. salt

Directions

Place all ingredients in a large heavy pot. Bring to a boil, lower heat, cover and simmer for 35 minutes, stirring occasionally.

Put mixture through a food mill, strain, return juice to pot and bring to a boil. Pour into 3 hot sterilized quart jars, leaving ¼-inch head room. Screw lids on, then process in a boiling water bath for 15 minutes.

Makes 3 quarts.

—Gwen Steinbusch

Patty's Mint Relish

Ingredients

1 cup packed mint leaves
6 medium onions
2 green peppers
2 lbs. apples
3 pears
¾ lb. raisins
1 oz. mustard seed
2 Tbsp. salt
2½ lbs. white sugar
1 qt. cider vinegar

Directions

Put mint, onions, green peppers, apples, pears and raisins through a meat chopper, then place in a crock.

Boil together remaining ingredients and pour over mint mixture. Let stand 1 week, bottle in sterile jars and seal.

Makes about 4 pints.

—Mary Reid

Corn Relish

Ingredients

6 cups corn
4 onions
½ large cabbage
2½ cups vinegar
1 Tbsp. salt
2½ cups sugar
3 Tbsp. flour
1 Tbsp. mustard
1 Tbsp. celery seed
½ tsp. turmeric

Directions

Combine corn, onions, cabbage and vinegar. Bring to a boil and simmer for 30 minutes. Add salt and sugar. Blend together flour, mustard, celery seed and turmeric. Wet, then thin, with vinegar. Add to vegetables. Cook for 15 minutes. Seal in sterilized jars.

Makes 3 to 4 quarts.

—Mrs. Fred Smith

Mom's Strawberry Jam

Ingredients

4 cups strawberries
1 Tbsp. vinegar
3 cups white sugar

Directions

Wash and hull the strawberries. Add vinegar and bring to a boil, cover and boil for 1 minute. Add sugar and boil 20 minutes uncovered, stirring occasionally.

Pour into a large bowl and let stand overnight. Pour into sterilized jars, cover with melted paraffin wax, cool and put lids on.

Makes about 1 quart.

—Joan Bridgeman Hoepner

Four Berry Jam

Ingredients

3 cups raspberries
1 cup strawberries
2 cups blueberries
2 cups Saskatoon berries
4 cups honey
2 pkgs. powdered pectin

Directions

In a large pot, bring the berries and the honey to a rolling boil and simmer for about 15 minutes. Add the 2 packages of pectin, bring back to a rolling boil and boil for 2 minutes.

Pour into hot sterilized jars and seal.

Makes 6 pints.

—*Cary Elizabeth Marshall*

Black Currant Jam

Ingredients

4 cups black currants
2 cups boiling water
6 cups granulated sugar
Butter

Directions

Wash and drain the currants. Add boiling water, bring to a boil and cook for 8 minutes.

Meanwhile, warm sugar slowly in a large pan in the oven. Add to currants, mix thoroughly and bring to a boil, stirring occasionally. Boil hard for 4 minutes. Remove from heat and add small piece of butter. Skim jam and pour into sterilized jars. Seal with melted paraffin wax.

Makes 8 jelly glasses.

—*Kathy Turner*

Red Plum Jam

Ingredients

2 lbs. red plums
1 cup water
6 cups sugar
1 Tbsp. butter

Directions

Pit and cut up the plums. Cook, covered with water, until soft. Remove from heat, mash, and add sugar, stirring until it is completely dissolved. Cook over medium heat stirring to prevent sticking.

Boil the mixture until candy thermometer registers 220°F. Remove from heat, skim the froth and stir in the butter.
Place in jars and cap.

Makes 9 jelly jars.

—*Mary Dzielak*

Blackberry & Apple Jam

Ingredients

3 lbs. green apples
2 cups water
2½ lbs. blackberries
9 cups sugar
½ cup lemon juice
1 Tbsp. butter

Directions

Peel, core and slice the apples. Place in a pot with water and cook until soft — about 10 to 15 minutes. Remove from heat and mash. Add the blackberries, mix thoroughly, then add the sugar and lemon juice and stir until the sugar is completely dissolved. Boil the mixture until the candy thermometer registers 220°F.

Remove from heat and skim the froth off the top of the jam with a large metal spoon. Stir in the butter. Pour into hot, sterilized jars and cap immediately.

Makes 10 jelly jars.

—*Mary Dzielak*

Yellow Tomato Marmalade

Ingredients

3¼ cups peeled & chopped yellow tomatoes
Rind of 1 large lemon, grated
¼ cup lemon juice
6 cups sugar
1 bottle Certo

Directions

Cook tomatoes, covered, for 10 minutes without any water. Add lemon rind, lemon juice and sugar. Bring to a boil over moderate heat, stirring constantly, and boil hard for 1 minute. Turn off heat. Add Certo and stir vigorously for 5 minutes. Bottle in sterile jars.

Makes 1½ pints.

—Mary Reid

Wild Rose Jelly

Ingredients

2 cups apple juice
3 cups tightly-packed fresh wild rose petals
3 cups white sugar
½ bottle Certo

Directions

Heat apple juice to the boiling point. Place washed and drained rose petals in large saucepan and pour apple juice over them. Bring to a boil and boil for 20 minutes. Strain juice into another large saucepan. Add sugar, stir, bring to a boil and stir in Certo. Boil for 1 minute. Pour into sterile jelly glasses and seal with wax.

Makes 6 jelly glasses.

—Shirley Morrish

Paradise Jelly

Ingredients

6 cups washed & cubed quince
6 cups quartered crabapples
3 cups cranberries
Granulated sugar
Rose geranium leaves

Directions

Boil quince in just enough water to cover. When it begins to soften, add apples and then cranberries. When all are soft, place in a jelly bag and drain into a bowl. Add a scant cup of sugar to each cup of fruit juice. Boil for about 20 minutes or until mixture gels when dropped onto a plate.

Pour into glasses, put a rose geranium leaf in each glass, and seal with paraffin.

Makes 6 pints.

—Cary Elizabeth Marshall

Peachstone Jelly

Ingredients

Skins, peach stones & overripe peaches
1¼ cups strained lemon juice
7¼ cups sugar
1 bottle Certo

Directions

Place peaches, stones and skins in a large pot and barely cover with water. Bring to a boil and simmer, covered, for 10 minutes. Place in a strainer and squeeze out juice to make 3½ cups.

Add the lemon juice and sugar and mix well. Place over high heat and bring to a boil, stirring constantly. Stir in Certo, bring to a full rolling boil and boil hard for 1 minute, stirring constantly.

Remove from heat, skim off foam and pour into jars. Cover with hot paraffin.

Makes 5 to 6 pints.

—Ruth Anne Laverty

Blueberry Jam

Ingredients

2 cups blueberries
1 cup sugar

Directions

In a 2-quart saucepan, combine blueberries and 3 Tbsp. water. Bring to a boil and cook, uncovered, for 10 minutes. Add sugar and boil, uncovered, to jam stage — about 10 minutes. Carefully pour the jam into jars.

Makes 1½ cups.

—Glenna Keating

Apricot Jam Amandine

Ingredients

1 lb. dried apricots
6 cups water
⅓ cup lemon juice
8 cups sugar
1 Tbsp. butter
2 oz. slivered almonds

Directions

Cut up the apricots and soak in water overnight. Cook gently, covered, until tender — about 20 minutes. Remove from heat, mash and stir in lemon juice and sugar until completely dissolved.

Return to heat and boil until it reaches 220°F. Remove from heat, skim the froth, and stir in the butter and almonds. Fill and cap jars.

Makes 9 jelly jars.

—Mary Dzielak

Raspberry or Blackberry Jam

Ingredients

6 cups berries
6 cups sugar

Directions

Place berries in flat-bottomed pan and mash with potato masher as they heat. Bring to a full boil and boil for 2 minutes. Add sugar and boil for 1 minute.

Remove from heat and beat with electric mixer for 4 minutes. Pour jam into hot, clean jars and pour hot wax over to seal.

Makes about 3 pints.

—Beth Hopkins

Rowanberry Jelly

Rowanberry is known as Mountain Ash in central Canada. The berries should be gathered after frost and should taste tart, but not so bitter that your mouth puckers.

Ingredients

4 qts. ripe rowanberries
1 qt. water
8 cups sugar
1 pkg. pectin

Directions

Simmer the berries in water until soft. Mash, then strain the juice through a cloth. Bring juice to a boil and add sugar. Add pectin when sugar is dissolved and boil for 1 or 2 minutes or until it tests done. Seal with ¼ inch paraffin wax.

Makes 2 pints.

—Cary Elizabeth Marshall

Elderberry Jelly

Ingredients

3 cups elderberry juice
½ cup lemon juice
7½ cups sugar
1 bottle Certo

Directions

Boil juices and sugar, then add the Certo. Bring to a full rolling boil and cook for 1 minute. Remove from the stove, stir and skim off the foam. Pour into jars and seal.

Makes 4 to 6 jelly glasses.

—Joanne Ramsy

Peach Chutney

Ingredients

6 cups peeled, chopped peaches
4 cups peeled, chopped apples
2 cups raisins
4 cups brown sugar
1½ cups cider or malt vinegar
2 tsp. cinnamon
1 tsp. cloves
1 tsp. allspice
2 tsp. salt
⅛ tsp. black pepper

Directions

Combine all ingredients and cook slowly, stirring frequently, until thick — about 1 hour. Pour into hot sterilized jars and seal.

Makes 4 to 5 pints.

—Carolyn Hills

Tomato Chutney

Ingredients

4 lbs. tomatoes
1 lb. chopped apples
3 onions, finely chopped
2 cups vinegar
2 Tbsp. salt
½ tsp. allspice
2 cloves garlic
2 cups honey
1 cup raisins
1 tsp. cinnamon
1 Tbsp. dry mustard
1 tsp. cayenne
1 tsp. cloves

Directions

Chop tomatoes and add remaining ingredients. Cook until thick and clear, stirring occasionally. Seal in hot sterilized jars.

Makes 5 pints.

—Lisa Brownstone

Apple Jelly

Ingredients

4 lbs. green apples
½ cup lemon juice
3 cups water
Sugar

Directions

Wash and cut up apples without peeling or coring. Add lemon juice and water and boil until tender.

Remove from heat, mash and strain through jelly bag. Measure the juice and add 1 cup sugar for each cup of juice. Boil until juice reaches 220°F, remove from heat and skim the froth. Place in jars and cap.

—Mary Dzielak

Mint Jelly

Ingredients

1 cup packed fresh mint leaves
½ cup vinegar
1¼ cups water
1½ lbs. sugar

Directions

Wash the mint, chop finely and bring to a boil with water and vinegar. Remove from heat and let stand for a few minutes. Add sugar and bring back to a boil. Boil for 20 minutes or until jelled.
Place in jar.

—C. Majewski

Pineapple Jelly

Ingredients

1 qt. pineapple juice
1 qt. tart apple juice
6 cups sugar

Directions

Bring combined juices to a boil, stir in sugar and boil rapidly until syrup sheets. Pour into sterile jars and seal.

Makes 4 to 6 pints.

—Janice Touesnard

Tomato Butter

Ingredients

6-qt. basket ripe tomatoes
1 Tbsp. salt
4 cups white sugar
2 cups white vinegar
2 Tbsp. mixed pickling spice, tied in a bag

Directions

Peel and cut up tomatoes. Sprinkle with salt and let stand overnight. In the morning, pour off the juice.

Add remaining ingredients to tomatoes, place in a large heavy pot and simmer until thick — about 2 hours.

Bottle in sterile jars.

Makes 4 to 6 quarts.

—Alice Wires

Lemon Butter

This preserve is delicious spread on toast for everyday use, or on Christmas pudding for a special treat.

Ingredients

8 eggs, well beaten
4 cups sugar
1 cup butter
¼ cup grated lemon rind
1 cup lemon juice

Directions

Combine eggs and sugar in a double boiler. Add butter, lemon rind and lemon juice. Cook over gently boiling water, stirring frequently, until it thickens. Bottle and cool.

Makes eight 8-ounce jelly glasses.

—Kathy Turner

Banana Chutney

Ingredients

2 onions, finely chopped
1 lb. very ripe bananas, mashed
1 lb. pitted dates
1 cup cider vinegar
¾ cup brown sugar
½ cup molasses
4 cloves garlic, crushed
1-inch slice fresh ginger, crushed
1 Tbsp. cinnamon
½ Tbsp. nutmeg
½ Tbsp. ground cloves
½ Tbsp. ground cardamom
½ Tbsp. ground coriander
1 tsp. fenugreek
1 tsp. cumin
1 tsp. turmeric

Directions

Combine onions, bananas, dates, vinegar, sugar and molasses in a heavy saucepan. Crush all the spices, mix together and stir into banana-date mixture.

Heat quickly to a boil and stir, while boiling, for 5 minutes. Reduce heat and simmer for 20 minutes. Let cool and pour into jars. Seal.

Makes 1 quart.

—Ingrid Birker

Colonel Gray's Chutney

Chutneys, which originated in India as accompaniments to curried dishes, are now as varied as the different cultures that have adopted them. Spicy, flavorful and exotic, they add a piquant touch to chicken, pork, lamb and curries.

Ingredients

1 qt. vinegar
4 lbs. demerara sugar
5 lbs. Granny Smith apples
4 oz. ginger root
2 cloves garlic
1 oz. red chilies in muslin bag
1 tsp. cayenne pepper
2 tsp. salt
½ lb. seedless raisins

Directions

Heat vinegar and sugar until sugar is dissolved. Peel and slice apples. Scrape and grate ginger. Peel and crush garlic.

Combine all ingredients in a heavy saucepan. Cook until thick and dark, removing chilies after 5 minutes. Place in jars and seal.

Makes 2 to 3 quarts.

—Eileen Deeley

Brandied Cherries

Ingredients

2 lbs. sweet cherries
2 cups sugar
2 cups water
Brandy

Directions

Place unpitted cherries in a large bowl and cover with ice cold water. Let them stand for 30 to 40 minutes. Drain.

Dissolve sugar in 2 cups water, stirring all the time, and bring to a full boil. Boil rapidly for 5 minutes. Add the cherries and bring once more to a rolling boil. Remove from heat, wait until the boiling stops and repeat operation twice more, stirring gently with a wooden spoon.

Fill sterilized jars three-quarters full with fruit and syrup, place covers loosely on jars and let stand until cool, then fill each jar with brandy. Stir with a silver or wooden spoon. Seal. Turn jars upside down overnight, then store in a cool, dark place right side up, for at least 3 months before using.

Makes 4 pints.

—Kathleen Fitzgerald

Winnifred's Apple Butter

Ingredients

10 lbs. apples, sliced
5 cups water
4 cups sugar
1 cup corn syrup
2 tsp. cinnamon
1 tsp. allspice

Directions

Place apple slices in Dutch oven and add water. Boil and cook down for 1 hour. Sieve or put through a blender and add sugar and syrup. Return to heat and cook down until desired thickness is reached — 2 to 3 hours. Add spices and pack into jars.

Makes about 4 quarts.

—Debbie Winder

Rhubarb Marmalade

Ingredients

6 large oranges
6 cups finely chopped rhubarb
1 cup water
9 cups sugar

Directions

Peel and section 4 oranges. Chop pulp into small pieces, discarding rinds. Wash the other 2 oranges and cut up coarsely. Put through fine blade of food chopper.

Combine rhubarb, orange pieces and ground orange in a kettle. Add water, cover, and bring to a boil. Uncover, add sugar and stir until sugar is dissolved. Boil hard, uncovered, until mixture thickens — 20 to 30 minutes.

Skim and ladle into sterilized jars. Top with thin layer of paraffin.

Makes about ten 8-oz. jars.

—Joanne Kellog

Peach Marmalade

Ingredients

1 orange
2 lemons
1 cup water
2 lbs. ripe peaches
5 cups sugar
½ bottle liquid pectin

Directions

Grind orange and 1 lemon in blender with water. Put into a small pot and add juice from the other lemon. Boil, covered, for 20 minutes.

Peel, pit and chop peaches finely. Put in large pot with citrus mixture and sugar. Boil hard for 2 minutes. Add pectin and boil until jelly thermometer reaches 221°F. Remove from heat and stir and skim foam for about 10 minutes. Pour into sterile jars and seal.

Makes 2 pints.

—Judy Wuest

Scotch Orange Marmalade

Ingredients

6 navel oranges
10 cups water
10 cups sugar
1 cup lemon juice
1 Tbsp. butter
½ cup Scotch whiskey

Directions

Shred the oranges, discarding the tough center fibre. Put them in a pan with the water and soak overnight. The next day, cook, covered, until tender.

Let cool, then stir in the sugar and lemon juice until dissolved. Boil until mixture reaches 220°F. Remove from heat, skim the froth and stir in the butter and whiskey. Pour into jars and seal.

Makes 12 jelly glasses.

—Mary Dzielak

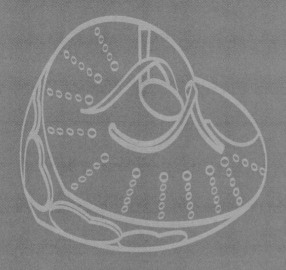

Desserts

Jersey Cream Pudding

A light and fluffy pudding, this is delicious served with most fresh fruits.

Ingredients

2–3 eggs, separated
3 cups milk
⅓ cup sugar
¼ tsp. salt
2 heaping Tbsp. flour
¼ cup cream
1 tsp. vanilla
Nutmeg

Directions

Beat egg whites until stiff and set aside. Scald together the milk, sugar and salt in a double boiler. Mix together flour and cream to form a thin batter. Add egg yolks and stir until smooth. Slowly add hot milk to yolk mixture and stir until smooth. Return to heat, over hot water, and continue cooking and stirring until thick, at least 5 to 10 minutes. Add vanilla, fold in egg whites, pour into a bowl and top with nutmeg.

Serves 4 to 6.

—B. Caldwell

Chocolate Pudding

Ingredients

1 cup flour
2 tsp. baking powder
½ tsp. salt
¾ cup sugar
6 Tbsp. cocoa
½ cup milk
4 Tbsp. melted butter
½ tsp. vanilla
1 cup brown sugar
1¾ cups hot water

Directions

Combine flour, baking powder, salt, sugar, 2 Tbsp. cocoa, milk, butter and vanilla. Spread in greased 8-inch square pan and sprinkle with brown sugar combined with remaining cocoa. Pour hot water over this. Do not stir. Bake at 350°F for 40 to 45 minutes.

—Rae Anne Huth

Fruit Bread Pudding

Ingredients

6 slices bread
1 banana, sliced
½ cup raisins
¼ cup walnuts
1 apple, cored & diced
1 cup brown sugar
⅔ cup water
½ tsp. cinnamon

Directions

Toast bread at 325°F for 15 minutes. Cut into cubes and combine with fruit and nuts.

Mix sugar, water and cinnamon together and add to fruit mixture. Toss to coat evenly. Let stand 5 minutes and stir again. Turn into a greased 8-inch square casserole dish.

Bake uncovered at 325°For 30 to 35 minutes.

—Helen Potts

Orange Cake Pudding

Lemon juice and rind can be substituted for orange in this dessert for an equally delicious pudding.

Ingredients

¼ cup flour
1 cup sugar
¼ tsp. salt
1 Tbsp. grated orange rind
½ cup orange juice
2 eggs, separated
¾ cup milk

Directions

Sift flour, sugar and salt together. Stir in orange rind and juice, egg yolks and milk. Blend well.

Beat egg whites until stiff but not dry. Pour orange mixture over egg whites and fold gently to blend.

Pour into a greased 1-quart baking dish. Set in a pan of hot water. Bake at 350°F for 50 minutes or until a knife inserted into the cake comes out clean.

—Johanna Vanderheyden

Baba au Rhum

Ingredients

1 tsp. sugar
1 envelope dry yeast
½ cup lukewarm water
¼ cup soft butter
2 cups granulated sugar
3 eggs
¼ tsp. salt
½ tsp. vanilla
½ tsp. grated lemon rind
2–3 cups flour
4 Tbsp. chopped red & green glazed cherries
2 Tbsp. chopped light raisins
½ cup corn syrup
2½ cups apricot nectar
Grated rind of 1 orange
1½ cups light rum

Directions

Dissolve 1 tsp. sugar and yeast in water. Let stand until foamy — 10 minutes. Beat together butter, ½ cup sugar and eggs until fluffy. Add salt, vanilla, lemon rind and ½ cup flour. Beat in yeast mixture and enough flour to make a drop-type batter. Add cherries and raisins.

Half-fill 30 small greased muffin tins. Let stand until batter fills tins. Bake at 375°F for 8 to 10 minutes, until golden. Remove from tins when cool.

To make rum sauce, combine in a heavy saucepan the remaining 1½ cups sugar, corn syrup, apricot nectar and orange rind. Bring to a boil and simmer until sugar dissolves — 5 minutes. Remove from heat and stir in rum. Cool.

One hour before serving, place the baba cakes in wide-mouthed jars or deep mixing bowls. Pour the sauce over them slowly, allowing it to soak in. Serve topped with whipped cream or lemon sauce.

Makes 30 baba cakes.

—Shirley Hill

Maple Mousse Glacée

Ingredients

4 eggs, separated
1 cup pure maple syrup
½ tsp. vanilla
1½ cups whipping cream

Directions

Beat egg yolks thoroughly and add maple syrup. Beat well to blend. In a heavy saucepan cook over very low heat, stirring constantly, until the consistency of a soft custard sauce is reached. Remove from heat, add vanilla and cool thoroughly.

Whip cream and fold in. Beat egg whites until stiff but not dry and fold in. Pour into parfait glasses and freeze until very firm. Let stand a few minutes at room temperature before serving. Garnish with whipped cream and toasted almonds.

Serves 6.

—Julienne Tardif

Raspberry Sherbet

Ingredients

½ cup sugar
1 cup water
1 tsp. gelatin
2 Tbsp. water
¾ cup corn syrup
1 pint raspberries, crushed
¼ cup lemon juice
¼ cup orange juice
2 egg whites

Directions

Simmer sugar and 1 cup water for 5 minutes. Soften gelatin in 2 Tbsp. water, then dissolve in hot sugar and water. Add corn syrup and cool.

Stir berries and juices into cooled syrup and freeze until firm. Beat until light and fluffy. Beat egg whites, and fold into berry mixture. Spoon into individual serving dishes and freeze.

Serves 8.

—Elizabeth Vigneault

Gooseberry Fool

This dessert can be made equally successfully with almost any fruit.

Ingredients

1 lb. ripe gooseberries
3 Tbsp. water
½ cup sugar
1 cup whipping cream

Directions

Top and tail gooseberries. Combine with water and sugar and stew until tender. Press through sieve and chill the purée. Beat cream until stiff. Carefully fold in gooseberry purée. Serve in individual dishes with more whipped cream.

Serves 4.

—Sheila Bear

Syllabub

This old English dish is a frothy chilled dessert which separates into two layers.

Ingredients

2 egg whites
½ cup sugar
Juice of ½ lemon
1 cup whipping cream
½ cup white wine

Directions

Whip egg whites until stiff, then carefully fold in sugar and lemon juice. Whip cream until peaks form and fold this into the egg whites along with the wine. Pour into individual glasses and chill for 2 hours before serving.

Serves 4.

—Sheila Bear

Raspberry Bombe

Many berry juices other than raspberry can be used in this recipe.

Ingredients

2 envelopes plain gelatin
3 cups raspberry juice
½ pint whipping cream

Directions

Soften gelatin in small amount of cold water. Add ¼ cup boiling water to dissolve. Add gelatin mixture to berry juice. Cool until syrupy, then whip until frothy.

Whip cream until stiff. Add one quarter of juice-gelatin mixture to whipped cream and stir, then add remaining juice.

Pour into a mold or individual serving dishes and refrigerate until set. Serve topped with whipped cream and fresh raspberries.

Serves 4.

—Signe Nickerson

Chocolate Cheesecake

Ingredients

3 eggs, separated
8 oz. cream cheese, mashed
1 cup sour cream
½ cup sugar
1½ Tbsp. flour
½ tsp. vanilla
1 Tbsp. lemon juice
1 cup chocolate chips

Directions

Beat egg yolks and add to cream cheese. Add sour cream, sugar, flour, vanilla and lemon juice. Mix well.

Beat egg whites until stiff peaks form, and gently but thoroughly fold into batter.

Melt chocolate chips in saucepan over low heat. Swirl through batter. Pour into a lightly greased 10-inch springform pan.

Bake at 300°F for 1 hour, turn off heat and leave cake in oven for 1 more hour. Cool cheesecake, then refrigerate until serving time.

Serves 10 to 12.

—Melissa Eder

Streusel Squares

Ingredients

½ cup butter
1 cup granulated sugar
2 eggs
1 tsp. vanilla
1 cup sour cream or buttermilk
2 cups flour
¼ tsp. salt
1 tsp. baking powder
1 tsp. baking soda
⅓ cup brown sugar
1 tsp. cinnamon
¼ cup chopped walnuts

Directions

Cream together butter and granulated sugar. Mix in eggs, one at a time. Add vanilla to sour cream or buttermilk. Sift together flour, salt, baking powder and baking soda. Add dry ingredients to butter mixture gradually, alternating with cream. Combine lightly.

Place half this mixture in 9" x 13" pan. Combine remaining ingredients and sprinkle half over the batter. Spread with remaining batter and top with sugar mixture.

Bake at 350°F for 30 minutes. Cool in pan.

—Nel vanGeest

Mincemeat Squares

Ingredients

1½ cups brown sugar
2 eggs
2 Tbsp. molasses
1 Tbsp. butter
1 tsp. vanilla
2 cups flour
½ tsp. salt
½ tsp. baking soda
1 tsp. cinnamon
1 tsp. cloves
3 Tbsp. hot water
½ cup chopped walnuts
¼ cup raisins
1½ cups mincemeat
1½ cups icing sugar
3 Tbsp. hot milk
½ tsp. vanilla
½ tsp. almond extract

Directions

Mix thoroughly brown sugar, eggs, molasses, butter and 1 tsp. vanilla. Add flour, salt, baking soda, cinnamon, cloves, hot water, walnuts, raisins and mincemeat and mix well.

Spread smoothly in 2 well-greased 9" x 13" pans. Bake at 400°F for 12 to 15 minutes.

Combine remaining ingredients and spread over squares while they are still warm.

—Dawn Livingstone

Kiffle

These filled crescents have a rich, sour cream dough.

Ingredients

1 envelope dry yeast
1 Tbsp. water
2 cups flour
½ cup butter
2 eggs, separated
½ cup sour cream
Icing sugar
1 cup finely chopped walnuts
½ cup sugar
1 tsp. vanilla

Directions

Dissolve yeast in water and let stand for 10 minutes.

Cut butter into flour until crumbly. Combine egg yolks and sour cream and add dissolved yeast. Pour over flour and butter. Mix in and knead for 5 minutes. Form into a ball, place in a greased bowl, cover with wax paper and then a tea towel. Chill for 1 hour.

Divide dough into 3 equal parts. Sprinkle icing sugar onto board, roll each part into a 10-inch circle and cut into 8 wedges.

Combine walnuts, sugar, stiffly beaten egg whites and vanilla. Place some of this filling on each piece of dough and roll up from the wide end in.

Place well apart on greased cookie sheets and bake at 375°F for 25 minutes or until golden brown.

Makes 24.

—Mrs. Ed Stephens

Apple-Oat Squares

Ingredients

⅓ cup butter
½ cup brown sugar
1 cup flour
½ tsp. baking soda
½ tsp. salt
1 cup rolled oats
2½ cups peeled, sliced tart apples
2 Tbsp. butter
¼–⅓ cup sugar

Directions

Cream butter and mix sugar in gradually. Sift flour, add baking soda and salt, and combine with creamed mixture until crumbly. Stir in rolled oats. Spread half the mixture into a greased 8-inch square cake pan. Cover with sliced apples. Dot with butter and sprinkle with sugar (and cinnamon if desired). Spread remainder of crumb mixture on top.

Bake at 350°F for 40 to 45 minutes.

—Johanna Vanderheyden

Baklava

Ingredients

¾ lb. butter, cut into ¼-inch pieces
½ cup vegetable oil
40 sheets filo pastry
4 cups walnuts, crushed
¾ cup honey
1 Tbsp. lemon juice

Directions

Melt butter over low heat, removing foam as it rises to the surface. Remove from heat, let rest 2 to 3 minutes and spoon off clear butter. Discard milky solids.

Stir oil into butter and coat 9" x 13" baking dish with 1 Tbsp. of mixture, using a pastry brush. Lay a sheet of pastry in baking dish, brush with butter, lay down another sheet and brush with butter. Sprinkle with 3 Tbsp. of walnuts. Repeat this pattern to make 19 layers. Top with 2 remaining sheets of filo and brush with remaining butter.

Score top of pastry with diagonal lines ½-inch deep, 2 inches apart, to form diamond shapes.

Bake at 350°F for 30 minutes, reduce heat to 300° and bake 15 minutes longer, or until top is golden brown.

Remove from oven. Combine honey and lemon juice and pour slowly over baklava. Slice when cool.

—*Carol Gasken*

Rhubarb Squares

This recipe originated with the author's grandmother, who owned a bakery in Toronto in the 1940s. It has been adapted to make use of whole grains and natural sweeteners.

Ingredients

3 cups chopped rhubarb
¾ cup water
Honey
3 Tbsp. cornstarch
1 cup whole wheat flour
1 cup rolled oats
½ tsp. baking powder
¼ tsp. salt
¼ tsp. nutmeg
½ tsp. cinnamon
2 Tbsp. demerara sugar
½ cup melted butter

Directions

Cook rhubarb in ½ cup water, with honey to taste. Mix cornstarch in ¼ cup water and add to stewed rhubarb. Cook, stirring, until thickened, and set aside.

Mix remaining ingredients together. Put half the oat mixture on the bottom of an 8-inch square baking dish. Pat down and fill with rhubarb. Sprinkle remaining oat mixture on top.

Bake 35 minutes at 350°F. Allow to cool for 30 minutes before cutting into squares.

—*Sandra James-Mitchell*

Scotch Apple pudding

Ingredients

2 cups sliced apples
½ cup granulated sugar
¼ tsp. cinnamon
1 egg
½ cup milk
¼ tsp. salt
½ cup brown sugar
½ cup rolled oats
½ cup flour
2 tsp. baking powder
½ tsp. vanilla
⅓ cup butter

Directions

Arrange apples in bottom of buttered baking dish. Sprinkle with sugar and cinnamon.

Mix remaining ingredients and pour over apples. Bake at 350°F for 1 hour or until apples are tender.

—Barb Curtis

Peach Crumble

Ingredients

6 medium-sized peaches, peeled, pitted & thinly sliced
½ cup brown sugar, firmly packed
Dash mace
1 cup flour
½ tsp. salt
4 Tbsp. butter

Directions

Toss peach slices with ¼ cup of the brown sugar and the mace in a buttered 6-cup baking dish.

Mix flour, remaining sugar and salt in a bowl. Cut in butter. Spread over the peaches and pat down lightly. Bake at 350°F for 45 minutes or until golden. Serve warm with cream.

—Erika Johnston

Apple Brown Betty

Ingredients

1½ cups brown sugar
1¼ cups flour
⅔ cup butter
2 cups thinly sliced apples, pared & cored
Cream or milk

Directions

Rub flour, sugar and butter together to form a corn meal texture. Press half of mixture into bottom of a 10-inch square pan. Spread apples evenly on top. Cover with rest of flour mixture and pat flat with hand or fork.

Bake 15 to 20 minutes at 350°F until lightly browned and apples are tender. Serve warm with milk or cream.

—Deborah Exner

Blueberry Crisp

Ingredients

4 cups blueberries
2 Tbsp. tapioca
⅓ cup sugar
1 Tbsp. lemon juice
½ tsp. lemon peel
⅔ cup brown sugar
¾ cup rolled oats
½ cup flour
½ tsp. cinnamon
⅛ tsp. salt
6 Tbsp. butter

Directions

Combine blueberries, tapioca, sugar, lemon juice and lemon peel and mix well. Pour into greased 9-inch square baking pan.

Mix together remaining ingredients and place on top of berries.

Bake at 375°F for 40 minutes.

—Ken Parejko

Blueberry Buckle

Ingredients

¼ cup butter
¼ cup honey
1 egg
Salt
1 cup flour
1 tsp. baking soda
⅓ cup buttermilk or yogurt
2 cups blueberries
¼ cup butter
2 Tbsp. honey
⅓ cup flour
½ tsp. cinnamon

Directions

Cream together ¼ cup butter, ¼ cup honey, egg and salt. Add 1 cup flour, baking soda, buttermilk or yogurt and mix well. Spread in a greased 8-inch square cake pan. Cover with blueberries.

Combine remaining ingredients and spread over blueberries.

Bake at 350°F for 40 minutes.

—Water Street Co-op

Fresh Apple Fritters

Ingredients

⅝ cup flour
½ tsp. baking powder
½ tsp. salt
1 egg, separated
3 Tbsp. milk
1 cup chopped apples
Oil for deep frying
Powdered sugar

Directions

Combine flour, baking powder and salt and mix well. Beat egg yolk and milk together and stir into dry ingredients. Add apples. Beat egg white until stiff and fold into batter.

Drop by spoonfuls into oil heated to 350°F. Fry until golden brown, drain well and roll in powdered sugar. Serve with maple syrup or honey.

Serves 4 to 6.

—Janis Huisman

Strawberry Shortcake

This shortcake has a muffin-like texture and a rough exterior—all the better to trap the whipped cream and strawberries.

Ingredients

½ tsp. salt
3 cups flour
1 Tbsp. baking powder
4 Tbsp. granulated sugar
1 cup soft shortening
1 egg, slightly beaten with enough milk to make 1 cup of liquid
½ tsp. vanilla
1 qt. strawberries, cleaned & hulled
2 cups whipping cream, whipped

Directions

Sift together salt, flour, baking powder and sugar. Cut in shortening with pastry blender. When well blended, add egg-milk mixture and vanilla. Mix only until flour is moistened. Spoon into a greased 8-inch square pan, leaving dough in clumps. Bake at 350°F for 30 to 40 minutes. Cool. To serve, cut cake into 9 pieces, split each piece open and top with whipped cream and strawberries.

Serves 9.

Pastry

Ingredients

5¼ cups flour
1 Tbsp. salt
1 Tbsp. sugar
1 lb. shortening
1 large egg

Directions

Sift dry ingredients into a large bowl. Cut in the shortening.

Beat egg and add water to make 1 cup. Pour slowly into flour mixture, stopping to mix with a fork. Add only enough liquid to make pastry form a ball.

Turn out onto a floured board and knead until mixture is smooth. Divide into 4 portions, wrap well and refrigerate or freeze.

Makes enough pastry for 4 double-crust pies.

—Carolyn Hills

Sautéed Bananas

Ingredients

½ cup softened butter
½ cup firmly packed brown sugar
½ tsp. cinnamon
½ tsp. nutmeg
¼ tsp. cloves
Salt
4–6 bananas

Directions

Combine all ingredients except bananas and mix well.

Peel and slice the bananas in half lengthwise. To cook each banana, melt 2 Tbsp. butter-sugar mixture and sauté banana over high heat.

Serve with vanilla ice cream.

Serves 4 to 6.

—Jill den Hertog

Apple Pan Cake

Ingredients

2 Tbsp. butter
2 apples, quartered & thinly sliced
¼ cup firmly packed brown sugar
¼ tsp. cinnamon
3 eggs
½ cup milk
½ cup flour
¼ tsp. salt
1 Tbsp. brown sugar

Directions

Melt butter in a 9-inch round cake pan. Add apples and coat with butter. Sprinkle with ¼ cup brown sugar and cinnamon. Place in 400°F oven while preparing batter.

Mix eggs, milk, flour and salt together. Pour over the apples, sprinkle with 1 Tbsp. brown sugar, dot with butter and bake 15 to 20 minutes.

Serves 2.

—Lisa Fainstein

Fresh Raspberry Pie

Ingredients

Pastry for 9-inch
double-crust pie
4 cups raspberries
⅔ cup sugar
2 Tbsp. quick-cooking tapioca
1 Tbsp. lemon juice
2 Tbsp. butter

Directions

Toss berries lightly with sugar and tapioca. Line a pie dish with pastry and fill with berries. Sprinkle with lemon juice and dot with butter.

Cover with top crust. Slash crust. Bake at 425°F for 20 minutes, then reduce heat to 350° and bake until filling has thickened and pastry is golden, about 40 minutes. Cool before cutting.

—Joan Airey

Raspberry Sour Cream Pie

Ingredients

Pastry for 9-inch pie shell
2 eggs
1⅓ cups sour cream
1 tsp. vanilla
1 cup sugar
⅓ cup flour
Salt
3 cups fresh raspberries
½ cup loosely packed brown
  sugar
½ cup flour
½ cup chopped walnuts or
  pecans
¼ cup chilled butter

Directions

Line pie plate with pastry.

Beat eggs and whisk in sour cream and vanilla. Mix sugar, flour and salt and add to egg mixture. Gently stir in raspberries. Pour into pie shell and bake at 400°F for 30 to 35 minutes or until center is almost set.

Mix brown sugar, flour and nuts. Cut in butter until mixture is crumbly. Sprinkle over pie and return to oven for another 10 to 15 minutes.

—Carol Parry

Raspberry Flan

This recipe is fast and easy to make and there is no pastry to roll. It makes a wonderful dessert in the winter with frozen berries.

Ingredients

1 cup flour
Salt
2 Tbsp. sugar
½ cup butter
1 Tbsp. vinegar
1 cup sugar
2 Tbsp. flour
3 cups raspberries

Directions

Combine 1 cup flour, salt and 2 Tbsp. sugar. Add butter and vinegar and mix well with hands. Press gently into 9-inch pie plate.

Mix together gently 1 cup sugar, 2 Tbsp. flour and 2 cups raspberries. Place in pie plate. Bake at 400°F for 50 to 60 minutes. Sprinkle with remaining berries after removing from oven.

—Donna Gordon

Fresh Strawberry Pie

Ingredients

Baked 8-inch pie shell
1 qt. strawberries, cleaned & hulled
1 cup sugar
⅓ cup cornstarch
1 Tbsp. lemon juice
Whipped cream to garnish

Directions

Mix strawberries with sugar and let sit overnight. In morning, drain off juice and add water to make 1¾ cups of liquid.

Blend cornstarch to a paste with ¼ cup liquid in double boiler. Add remaining liquid and cook over direct heat, stirring constantly, until sauce boils and is clear. Place in double boiler, cover and cook another 15 minutes. Remove from heat, add lemon juice and fold in berries.

Cool to lukewarm, then pour into pie shell. Garnish with whipped cream.

—Cindy McMillan

Blueberry Chantilly Pie

Ingredients

Baked 9-inch pie shell
4 cups blueberries
½ cup honey
½ cup water
2 Tbsp. cornstarch
1 Tbsp. butter
2 Tbsp. Cointreau or Grand Marnier
1 cup whipping cream
2 Tbsp. honey
¼ tsp. almond extract
½ cup sliced almonds

Directions

Blend together 1 cup blueberries, honey and water. Add cornstarch and cook until thick. Stir in butter and Cointreau or Grand Marnier. Cool.

Fold in remaining 3 cups of blueberries and pour into baked pie shell.

Whip cream with honey and almond extract. Spoon on top of pie and sprinkle with almonds.

—David Slabotsky

Crabapple Pie

Ingredients

Pastry for 9-inch double-crust pie
4 cups sliced crabapples
¾ cup sugar
1 tsp. cinnamon
1 tsp. nutmeg
1 Tbsp. butter

Directions

Line pie plate with pastry and fill with sliced crabapples. Combine sugar and spices and sprinkle over the crabapples. Dot with butter and top with pastry. Crimp edges and slash top.

Bake at 425°F for 15 minutes, reduce heat to 350° and bake 45 minutes longer.

—Sandra Lloyd

Sour Cream Peach Pie

Ingredients

Pastry for 9-inch pie shell
1 Tbsp. flour
¾ cup sour cream
½ cup granulated sugar
⅓ cup flour
¼ tsp. almond extract
4 cups peeled, sliced peaches
¼ cup brown sugar

Directions

Sprinkle pie crust with 1 Tbsp. flour.

Combine sour cream, sugar, ⅓ cup flour and almond extract and stir until smooth. In pie shell, alternate layers of peaches with cream mixture, ending with cream.

Bake at 425°F for 20 minutes, reduce heat to 350° and bake another 35 minutes. Sprinkle with brown sugar and broil until golden.

Cool before serving.

—Shirley Thomlinson

Apple Pie

Ingredients

Pastry for 9-inch double-crust pie
8 cups pared, cored & thinly sliced cooking apples
⅓ cup firmly packed brown sugar
⅓ cup granulated sugar
1 Tbsp. cornstarch or 2 Tbsp. flour
1 tsp. cinnamon
¼ tsp. nutmeg
¼ tsp. salt
2 Tbsp. butter
Water or milk
Sugar to sprinkle on top

Directions

Place sliced apples in a large bowl. Mix sugars, cornstarch or flour, cinnamon, nutmeg and salt in a small bowl and sprinkle over the apples. Let stand for 10 minutes, until a little juice forms.

Line pie plate with pastry and pile apple mixture into it. Dot with butter and top with pastry. Seal.

Brush top of pastry with a little milk or water and sprinkle lightly with sugar. Slash top.

Bake at 375°F for 40 to 50 minutes or until juice bubbles through slashes and apples are tender.

—Marva Blackmore

Rhubarb Strawberry Crumb Pie

Ingredients

Pastry for 9-inch pie shell
3 cups chopped rhubarb
2 cups strawberries, sliced
1½ cups sugar
⅓ cup flour
1 cup sour cream
½ cup flour
½ cup brown sugar
¼ cup soft butter

Directions

Arrange rhubarb and strawberries in unbaked pie shell. Mix sugar and ⅓ cup flour with sour cream and pour evenly over fruit.

Combine ½ cup flour, brown sugar and butter until crumbly and sprinkle over top.

Bake at 450°F for 15 minutes, reduce heat to 350° and bake another 30 minutes, until fruit is tender.

Chill before serving.

—Margaret Silverthorn

Pecan Pie

Ingredients

9-inch pie shell, baked for 5 minutes
½ cup granulated sugar
3 Tbsp. butter
1 cup corn syrup
3 eggs
1 cup pecan halves
1 tsp. vanilla

Directions

Boil together sugar, butter and corn syrup for 2 minutes. Beat eggs and mix with pecans. Pour sugar mixture over eggs and nuts. Add vanilla. Pour mixture into partially baked pie shell and bake at 350°F for 35 to 40 minutes.

—Shirley Hill

Frozen Yogurt Pie

Ingredients

¾ cup ground walnuts
½ cup flour
2 Tbsp. oil
1 cup tofu
¾ cup plain yogurt
¼ cup powdered milk
½ cup honey
Almond extract

Directions

Combine walnuts, flour and oil. Press into 9-inch pie plate. Bake at 450°F for 10 to 15 minutes, being careful not to burn. Cool.

Thoroughly drain the tofu and combine with yogurt. Stir with a whisk until smooth. Add milk powder 1 Tbsp. at a time. Add honey and almond extract to taste. Mix well.

Pour into pie crust and freeze overnight. Allow to stand at room temperature for 15 minutes before serving.

—Janet Flewelling

French Silk Pie

Ingredients

Graham cracker crust for
    9-inch pie
2 oz. unsweetened chocolate
2 Tbsp. brandy
2 Tbsp. instant coffee
1 cup butter
1 cup sugar
2 eggs
½ cup ground almonds
½ cup ground hazelnuts

Directions

Line pie plate with graham cracker crust; refrigerate.

In double boiler, melt chocolate, then stir in brandy and coffee. Cream butter and sugar together. Beat in eggs one at a time. Stir in chocolate mixture and nuts. Pour filling into shell and chill. Serve cold.

—Michael Bruce-Lockhart

Pumpkin Pie

Ingredients

Pastry for 9-inch pie shell
2 eggs, lightly beaten
2¾ cups cooked mashed pumpkin
¾ cup brown sugar
½ tsp. salt
1 tsp. cinnamon
½ tsp. ginger
¼ tsp. cloves
1⅔ cups light cream
Whipped cream to garnish

Directions

Combine all ingredients except pastry in order given. Pour into pie shell. Bake at 350°F for 45 minutes or until knife inserted in filling comes out clean. Cool. Top with whipped cream.

—Shirley Morrish

Custard Pie

Ingredients

Pastry for 9-inch pie shell
1¾ cups milk
3 eggs
⅓ cup honey
½ tsp. salt
⅛ tsp. nutmeg
½ tsp. vanilla

Directions

Heat milk until lukewarm. Beat eggs, then add honey, salt, nutmeg, vanilla and milk. Blend thoroughly and pour into pie shell.

Bake at 450°F for 10 minutes. Reduce heat to 325° and bake until custard is set 30 to 40 minutes.

—Winona Heasman

Butter Tarts

Ingredients

Pastry for 14–16 tart shells
1½ cups brown sugar
2 eggs
1–2 tsp. butter, softened
1 tsp. vanilla
1 tsp. vinegar
½ cup raisins
4 Tbsp. milk
½ cup chopped walnuts

Directions

Combine all ingredients except pastry and mix until just blended.

Line tart shells with pastry and fill two-thirds full with mixture. Bake at 350°F for 15 minutes, until filling is firm.

Makes 14 to 16 tarts.

—Mary McEwen

Rhubarb Custard Pie

Ingredients

Pastry for double-crust 9-inch pie
2 eggs
1 cup granulated sugar
1 Tbsp. melted butter
2 Tbsp. flour
2½ cups rhubarb

Directions

Beat together eggs, sugar, flour and butter. Mix in rhubarb and pour into pie shell. Top with upper crust. Bake at 400°F for 15 minutes, reduce heat to 350° and cook for another 15 minutes.

—Sharron Jansen

Walnut Cranberry Pie

Tangy, tart and attractive, this pie, with its garnish of orange slices and whole berries, will be a festive addition to the Christmas menu.

Ingredients

Pastry for 9-inch pie shell
3½ cups fresh cranberries
½ cup seedless raisins
1½ cups sugar
2 Tbsp. flour
¼ cup corn syrup
1 tsp. grated orange rind
¼ tsp. salt
1 Tbsp. soft butter
¾ cup walnuts, coarsely chopped
Orange slices & whole cranberries to garnish

Directions

Grind cranberries and raisins together. Add sugar, flour, corn syrup, orange rind, salt and butter and mix well. Stir in nuts and turn into pie shell.

Bake at 375°F for 40 to 45 minutes. Cool.

Garnish with orange slices and whole cranberries and serve with ice cream.

—Nina Kenzie

Pumpkin Cheesecake

Ingredients

1½ cups zwieback crumbs
3 Tbsp. sugar
3 Tbsp. melted butter
16 oz. cream cheese, softened
1 cup light cream
1 cup cooked pumpkin
¾ cup sugar
4 eggs, separated
3 Tbsp. flour
1 tsp. vanilla
1 tsp. ground cinnamon
½ tsp. ground ginger
½ tsp. ground nutmeg
¼ tsp. salt
1 cup sour cream
2 Tbsp. sugar
½ tsp. vanilla

Directions

Combine crumbs, 3 Tbsp. sugar and melted butter. Press into bottom and 2 inches up the sides of a 9-inch spring pan. Bake for 5 minutes at 325°F.

Combine cream cheese, cream, pumpkin, ¾ cup sugar, egg yolks, flour, vanilla, spices and salt. Fold in stiffly beaten egg whites and turn into crust. Bake at 325°F for 1 hour.

Combine sour cream, 2 Tbsp. sugar and vanilla. Spread over cheesecake and return to oven for 5 more minutes. Chill before serving.

—Elizabeth Clayton

Lemon Meringue Pie

Lemon meringue pie is a particularly fascinating dessert as it can turn out wretchedly — gelatinous and oversweet (as it is served in most restaurants) — or, if made properly, can be a creamy ambrosia of lemony custard, delicate crust and fluffy meringue. This recipe will produce the gourmet result. It takes more time than opening a package of lemon filling, but the result is incomparable.

Ingredients

Baked 9-inch pie shell
1 cup sugar
6 Tbsp. cornstarch
¼ tsp. salt
2 cups milk
3 eggs, separated
3 Tbsp. butter
⅓ cup lemon juice
1 Tbsp. grated lemon rind
¼ tsp. cream of tartar
3 Tbsp. sugar
½ tsp. vanilla

Directions

Combine the sugar, cornstarch and salt in the top of a double boiler. Slowly add the milk, stirring constantly. Cook and stir these ingredients over hot water until the mixture thickens — about 15 minutes. Cover the pan and allow to cook 10 minutes longer. Stir occasionally. Remove from heat. Beat the egg yolks in a separate bowl and add about ½ cup of the thickened milk. Then stir this mixture back into the double boiler. Cook and stir over boiling water for 5 to 6 minutes. Remove from heat and stir in butter, lemon juice and lemon rind. Cool this custard, stirring gently every 10 minutes or so. When cool, pour into pie shell.

For the meringue, beat egg whites with cream of tartar until they are stiff but not dry. Beat in sugar, ½ tsp. at a time, followed by vanilla. Heap onto pie and spread with spatula so that meringue goes all the way out to the crust, around the whole pie. Use a light back-and-forth motion of the spatula to make decorative waves in the meringue. Bake at 350°F for 12 to 15 minutes until the meringue is delicately browned on top.

Serves 6.

—Alice O'Connell

Frozen Blueberry Ripple Cheesecake

Ingredients

1 cup sugar
⅓ cup water
⅛ tsp. cream of tartar
3 egg whites
16 oz. cream cheese
½ cup sour cream
2 tsp. vanilla
1 Tbsp. grated lemon rind
½–1 cup blueberry preserves or blueberry jam
Whipped cream
Blueberries

Directions

Combine sugar, water and cream of tartar in a small saucepan and bring to a boil. Boil rapidly until syrup registers 236°F on a candy thermometer — 5 to 9 minutes.

Meanwhile in large bowl of electric mixer, beat egg whites until stiff. Pour hot syrup in a thin stream over egg whites while beating constantly. Continue beating until very stiff peaks form and mixture cools — 10 to 15 minutes.

Beat cream cheese, sour cream, vanilla and rind until light and fluffy. Gently fold meringue into cheese mixture until well blended.

Spoon one-quarter of blended mixture into a decorative serving dish or bowl and drizzle blueberry preserves over this. Continue to layer in this manner, then run knife through completed layering to give a swirl effect. Freeze overnight or until firm. Decorate with whipped cream and berries and serve.

Serves 12.

—Joann Alho

Chocolate Amaretto Cheesecake

Already a rich dessert, this cheesecake is made even more delicious by the addition of chocolate and amaretto. As cheesecakes are egg-based, it is very important to cook at a low temperature and to store in the refrigerator.

Crust Ingredients

1¼ cups chocolate wafer crumbs or 1 cup graham
    wafer crumbs & ¼ cup cocoa
2 Tbsp. sugar
¼ cup melted butter

Filling Ingredients

16 oz. cream cheese
½ cup sugar
2 large eggs
6 oz. semisweet chocolate, melted & cooled
½ tsp. almond extract
1 tsp. vanilla
⅓ cup amaretto
⅔ cup sour cream

Topping Ingredients

2 oz. semisweet chocolate
1 tsp. shortening

Directions

Combine crumbs, sugar and melted butter and press into bottom and halfway up sides of greased 8-inch springform pan. Chill while making filling.

Beat cream cheese until smooth. Beat in sugar gradually. Beat in eggs one at a time at low speed. Add cooled chocolate, flavorings, amaretto and sour cream. Beat at low speed until thoroughly blended then pour into prepared pan.

Bake at 300°F for 1 hour. Turn off heat and leave cake in oven for 1 hour longer. Cool in pan at room temperature, then chill for at least 24 hours in refrigerator.

For topping, melt chocolate with shortening and spread over top of cake.

Serves 8.

—Vanessa Lewington

Chocolate Mousse Torte

This dessert is so rich that it will easily serve 12 chocolate-loving people.

Ingredients
Butter
Fine bread crumbs
6 oz. unsweetened chocolate
2 oz. semisweet chocolate
1 Tbsp. dry instant coffee
¼ cup boiling water
8 eggs, separated
⅔ cup sugar
1 tsp. vanilla
⅛ tsp. salt
1 cup whipping cream, whipped

Directions
Butter a 9-inch pie plate and dust with bread crumbs. Place chocolate in top of double boiler over hot water. Dissolve coffee in boiling water and stir into chocolate. Cover and melt over low heat, stirring occasionally. Cool slightly.

Beat egg yolks for 5 minutes or until pale and thickened. Gradually add sugar, beating on high for another 5 minutes. Add vanilla and chocolate mixture. Beat slowly until smooth.

Add salt to egg whites and whip until whites hold shape but are not stiff. Fold half the egg whites into chocolate mixture in three additions, then fold chocolate into remaining whites. Remove 3½ cups of mousse, cover and refrigerate.

Line pie plate with remaining mousse and bake at 350°F for 25 minutes. Turn oven off, but leave torte there for 5 more minutes. Remove and cool completely. Place chilled mousse in baked shell and refrigerate for at least 2 to 3 hours. Top with whipped cream and serve.

Serves 12.

—*Brenda Kennedy*

Bakewell Tart

Ingredients
Pastry for 9-inch pie shell
2 Tbsp. jam
⅓ cup butter
½ cup sugar
½ cup rice flour
¼ cup ground almonds
1 egg, beaten
Almond extract
Blanched almonds

Directions
Line pie plate with pastry and spread with jam. Cream butter and sugar. Add rice flour and ground almonds alternately with beaten egg. Add a few drops of almond extract.

Spread mixture over jam and decorate with a lattice of pastry strips and blanched almonds. Bake at 375°F for 40 to 45 minutes.

—*Sue Davies*

Raspberry Blueberry Pie

Ingredients
Pastry for double 9-inch pie shell
1½ cups raspberries
2 cups blueberries
⅔ cup sugar
2 Tbsp. instant tapioca
½ tsp. grated lemon rind
2 Tbsp. lemon juice
2 Tbsp. butter

Directions
Lightly toss together berries, sugar, tapioca, lemon rind and lemon juice. Place in pastry-lined pie shell and dot with butter. Cover with top crust, flute edges and cut vents. Bake at 425°F for 15 minutes, reduce heat to 350° and bake for 30 more minutes.

—*Valerie Gillis*

Grasshopper Pie

Crust Ingredients
1¼ cups finely crushed chocolate wafers
¼ cup sugar
3 Tbsp. melted butter

Filling Ingredients
1½ tsp. gelatin
6 Tbsp. cold water
¼ cup sugar
1 egg yolk, slightly beaten
⅓ cup crème de menthe
¼ cup white crème de cacao
1 cup whipping cream

Topping Ingredients
1 cup whipping cream
2 Tbsp. sugar
1 square semisweet chocolate, shaved

Directions

Combine crust ingredients and press into bottom and sides of well-buttered 9-inch pie plate. Bake at 450°F for 2 to 3 minutes and cool.

To make filling, sprinkle gelatin over cold water in small saucepan. Place over low heat and stir until dissolved. Combine sugar and egg yolk in a bowl and add gelatin and liqueurs. Chill until the consistency of unbeaten egg whites. Whip cream and fold into gelatin mix. Pour into crust and chill for 3 to 4 hours.

For topping, whip cream and sugar. Spoon onto pie and top with shaved chocolate.

—Kirsten McDougall

Gerri's Banana Cream Pie

Ingredients
Pastry for 10-inch pie shell
¾ cup sugar
¼ cup cornstarch
½ tsp. salt
1 Tbsp. gelatin
4 egg yolks
3 cups milk
2 Tbsp. butter
1 tsp. vanilla
1 cup whipping cream
4 medium bananas, thinly sliced
Lemon juice

Directions

Line pie plate with pastry and bake at 325°F for 20 minutes, or until done. Combine sugar, cornstarch, salt and gelatin. Beat in egg yolks and milk until very smooth. Cook mixture over low heat until thickened — 15 minutes — stirring constantly. Stir in butter and vanilla. Cover and chill.

Whip cream. Reserving some banana for garnish, fold cream and bananas into custard and spoon into pie crust. Chill.

Dip remaining banana slices into lemon juice and garnish top of pie.

—Eila Koivu

Orange Chiffon Pie

Ingredients

Pastry for 9-inch pie shell
3 Tbsp. flour
⅓ cup sugar
Salt
3 eggs, separated
2 Tbsp. lemon juice
1 cup orange juice
½ tsp. vanilla
1 Tbsp. butter
3 Tbsp. cream
Sesame seeds

Directions

Line pie plate with pastry and bake at 325°F for 20 minutes, or until golden. In top of double boiler, combine flour, sugar, salt, egg yolks, lemon juice and orange juice. Cook, stirring, over boiling water until very thick. Remove from heat and stir in vanilla, butter and cream. Cover pan and set in cold water. Beat egg whites until stiff and fold into orange mixture. Pour into pie shell and garnish with sesame seeds. Bake at 400°F for 10 minutes. Cool before serving.

—Lisa Calzonetti

Danish Rice Dish

This dish is traditionally served as part of a Danish Christmas dinner.

Ingredients

¾ cup brown rice
4 cups milk
2 tsp. vanilla
2 tsp. almond extract
1½ Tbsp. sugar
1 cup whipping cream
1 cup ground almonds
2 cups raspberries

Directions

Cook rice in milk over low heat until tender — this will take a long time. Cool. Add vanilla, almond extract and sugar. Blend well. Whip cream and fold into mixture along with almonds. Refrigerate.

When ready to serve, warm raspberries and serve on top of pudding.

Serves 8.

—G.L. Jackson

Rich Ricotta Custard

Ingredients

1 cup ricotta cheese
3 egg yolks
1 cup milk
⅓ cup sugar
1 Tbsp. rum
Grating of orange rind

Directions

Beat together cheese, egg yolks, milk and sugar. Add rum and orange rind to flavor. Bake at 325°F until set — about 45 minutes. Serves 4 to 6.

—Elizabeth Templeman

Mandarin Mousse

Ingredients

2 10-oz. cans mandarin orange sections,
  well drained
2 Tbsp. lemon juice
2 Tbsp. orange liqueur
1 tsp. vanilla
¼ cup cold water
1 envelope gelatin
½ cup sugar
2 cups whipping cream

Directions

Purée mandarins until smooth. Turn into large
bowl and add the lemon juice, liqueur and
vanilla. Pour water into measuring cup and add
gelatin to soften. Turn into saucepan and heat,
stirring constantly, over medium heat until
mixture becomes almost clear — approximately 2
minutes. Add sugar and stir until dissolved.

Stir into fruit mixture and cool to room temperature. Whip cream until it will hold soft peaks.
Stir in quarter of mixture, then fold in remaining
cream. Turn into dessert dishes and chill until set,
approximately 2 hours.

Serves 6.

—Judy Black

Lemon Snow Pudding with Custard Sauce

Pudding Ingredients

4 Tbsp. cornstarch
1 cup sugar
Salt
½ cup cold water
1¾ cups hot water
4 Tbsp. lemon juice
2 tsp. grated lemon peel
2 egg whites

Sauce Ingredients

2 egg yolks
1 tsp. cornstarch
2 Tbsp. sugar
Salt
¾ cup milk

Directions

Mix cornstarch, sugar and salt in saucepan. Add
cold water, mix until smooth and then add hot
water. Stir over medium heat until thickened.

Remove from heat and add lemon juice and
peel. Fold into stiffly beaten egg whites and chill.

To make custard sauce, combine all ingredients and heat slowly, until mixture coats spoon.
Chill. Serve over pudding.

Serves 6 to 8.

—Patricia E. Wilson

Pavlova and Yogurt Chantilly

Ingredients

2 egg whites
1 tsp. white wine vinegar
3 Tbsp. hot water
1 cup sugar
1 tsp. cornstarch
1 tsp. vanilla
⅔ cup whipping cream
⅔ cup unflavored yogurt
2 Tbsp. confectioners' sugar
2 kiwi fruit, peeled and sliced

Directions

Combine egg whites, vinegar, water, sugar, cornstarch and ½ tsp. vanilla in large bowl and beat until mixture holds a firm peak. Mark an 8-inch circle on a piece of foil on a cookie sheet. Heap the meringue onto the foil and spread it evenly within the circle. Bake at 250°F for 1½ hours. When cool, transfer to a serving plate.

Whip the cream until stiff. Fold in yogurt, sugar and remaining ½ tsp. vanilla. Chill well. Just before serving, pile the whipped cream mixture onto the meringue and top with sliced fruit.

Serves 6 to 8.

—Sylvia Petz

Kiwi Sherbet

Invented at Christmastime, when kiwi are very cheap, this is a light, fruity dessert, the perfect end to a heavy meal.

Ingredients

1 envelope gelatin
½ cup cold water
½ cup boiling water
Juice of 1 lemon
1 cup milk
1 cup sugar
7 kiwi fruit
¼ cup white rum

Directions

Soften gelatin in cold water. After 20 minutes, add boiling water and whisk to dissolve. Add lemon juice, milk and sugar. Mash 3 peeled kiwi and add to mixture. Add about ¼ cup white rum and place sherbet in freezer in a shallow pan or metal bowl.

Rewhisk when it forms crystals — at least twice. Do not let it freeze hard — keep breaking up the crystals. Allow about 4 hours for freezing. Just before serving, slice 1 kiwi into each of 4 individual serving dishes, placing slices in bottom and up sides. Add sherbet and top with a kiwi slice.

Serves 4.

—Randi Kennedy

Hot Fudge Cake

Ingredients

1 cup flour
2 tsp. baking powder
¼ tsp. salt
¾ cup sugar
5 Tbsp. cocoa
½ cup milk
2 Tbsp. melted butter
1 cup brown sugar
2 cups boiling water

Directions

Sift together flour, baking powder, salt, sugar and 1 Tbsp. cocoa. Stir in the milk and melted butter. Place in an ungreased, square cake pan. Combine the brown sugar and 4 Tbsp. cocoa. Spread over the mixture in the pan. Pour the boiling water over the whole mixture just before putting it into the oven. Do not stir.

Bake at 350°F for 45 to 55 minutes.

Serves 4 to 6.

—*Catherine Gardner*

Rhubarb Apple Compote

This rhubarb-apple sauce is delicious served with warm custard for dessert, or served over pancakes for Sunday brunch.

Ingredients

5 rhubarb stalks, chopped
½ cup water
5 apples, diced
½ tsp. cinnamon
⅛ tsp. coriander
¼ cup honey

Directions

Cook rhubarb in water for 10 minutes. Add diced apples and spices. Cook for 20 more minutes, then add honey.

Serves 6.

—*Louise Carmel*

Honey Cake

Ingredients

3 eggs
1 cup sugar
¾ cup oil
½ cup honey
¼ cup maple syrup
3 cups flour
2 tsp. baking powder
1 tsp. cinnamon
1 cup warm coffee or tea
1 tsp. baking soda
1 tsp. vanilla

Directions

Combine eggs and sugar on high speed of mix-master. Add oil, honey and maple syrup on low speed. Sift together flour, baking powder and cinnamon. Combine coffee or tea and baking soda and let cool. Add to creamed mixture alternately with dry ingredients. Add vanilla.

Bake in greased tube pan lined with wax paper at 350°F for 1¼ hours. Let cool for at least 1 hour before removing from pan.

Serves 10 to 12.

—*Kathryn MacDonald*

Baked Pears

Main Ingredients

4 pears
½ cup sugar
1 cup water
Grated peel of ½ lemon
Ginger

Sauce Ingredients

½ cup sugar
¼ cup Grand Marnier
½ cup whipping cream
2 egg yolks

Directions

Cut pears in half and core. Combine sugar, water, lemon peel and ginger and heat to dissolve sugar. Pour over pears and bake at 350°F for 20 minutes. Drain and cool.

Prepare cream sauce by combining all ingredients and whipping until stiff peaks form. Spoon over pears.

Serves 4.

—Jill Harvey-Sellwood

Blueberry Cobbler

Ingredients

3 cups blueberries, fresh or frozen
½ cup water
½ cup sugar
1 tsp. lemon juice
½ tsp. cinnamon
1½ cups flour
2 Tbsp. butter
2 tsp. baking powder
¼ tsp. salt
2 Tbsp. sugar
⅓–½ cup milk

Directions

Wash blueberries and mix with the water, sugar and lemon juice in bottom of 8-inch pan. Sprinkle with cinnamon.

Stir together flour, butter, baking powder, salt and sugar with a fork until mixture is consistency of corn meal. Stir in milk. Roll dough on floured board, cut into serving-sized squares to fit pan and place over berries. Sprinkle with a little sugar and brush with some melted butter.

Bake uncovered at 400°F for 25 minutes.

Serves 6.

—Janet Ueberschlag

Fruit Fritters

Ingredients

2 eggs, separated
½ cup milk
1 cup flour
½ tsp. salt
2 tsp. sugar
2 Tbsp. melted butter
Oil
2 bananas, sliced
2 apples, peeled, cored & quartered
2 pears, peeled, cored & quartered
2 peaches, peeled, pitted & quartered
Sugar
Custard

Directions

Beat egg yolks until light, then add milk. Sift together flour, salt and sugar and add to milk-egg mixture. Add butter. Beat egg whites until stiff and fold into batter.

Heat oil. Dip fruit in batter and fry in hot oil a few at a time. Cook until golden brown. Remove and drain on paper towels. Roll in sugar, then keep warm while making remaining fritters. Serve with custard if desired.

Serves 4.

—Patricia E. Wilson

Maple Cheesecake

Truly a cheesecake for maple-syrup lovers, this one is rich, creamy and smooth.

Crust Ingredients

1¾ cups graham wafer crumbs
¼ cup butter, melted
3 Tbsp. brown sugar

Filling Ingredients

½ cup flour
¼ tsp. baking soda
¼ tsp. salt
3 eggs
¾ cup sugar
8 oz. cream cheese
1¼ cups heavy cream
1 cup maple syrup
1 tsp. vanilla

Topping Ingredients

1 cup heavy cream
½ cup maple syrup
pecans for garnish

Directions

For crust: Mix together crust ingredients and press into springform pan. Bake at 350°F for 10 minutes.

For filling: Sift together flour, baking soda and salt. Beat eggs thoroughly. Add sugar and blend well. Cream the cream cheese until fluffy. Add cream slowly and beat until smooth. Blend in 1 cup maple syrup, egg mixture and flour mixture. Add vanilla and mix well.

Pour filling into crust. Bake at 350°F for 1½ hours, or until center has set. Turn off oven and let sit for 15 minutes. Chill.

Just before serving, whip cream and ½ cup maple syrup together and spread over cheesecake. Garnish with pecans.

—Jane Durward

Honey Cheesecake

Crust Ingredients
1½ cups graham cracker crumbs
½ cup butter, melted
2 Tbsp. sugar

Filling Ingredients
16 oz. cream cheese
⅓ cup honey
2 tsp. cinnamon
2 eggs
2 heaping Tbsp. sour cream
1 tsp. vanilla

Topping Ingredients
½ pint plus 2 Tbsp. sour cream
1 tsp. vanilla
2 Tbsp. honey
juice of ⅓ lemon

Sauce Ingredients
1½ cups sliced strawberries
½ cup brandy

Directions
Combine crust ingredients and press into large springform pan. Bake at 350°F for 10 minutes, then cool for 5 minutes.

Mix all filling ingredients together and spoon into cooled crust. Bake at 325°F for 30 minutes. Turn heat off and leave pie in oven for 10 more minutes.

Combine topping ingredients and pour over filling. Bake for 8 minutes at 400°F. or until set. Combine berries and brandy, and spoon over cake.

—Lisa Reith

Rhubarb Cream Pie

Developed by the contributor's Pennsylvanian mother-in-law for farmhands during haying, this rhubarb pie is for cinnamon lovers.

Ingredients
pastry for 9-inch pie shell
2 lbs. rhubarb, cut into ½" pieces
1½ cups brown sugar
3 Tbsp. quick-cooking tapioca
2 eggs
¼ cup heavy cream
2 Tbsp. cinnamon
2 Tbsp. butter

Directions
Line pie plate with pastry. Combine rhubarb, sugar, tapioca, eggs, cream and cinnamon. Toss gently to coat rhubarb. Place in pastry and dot with butter. Bake at 425°F for 10 minutes, reduce heat to 350° and bake for another 20 to 30 minutes.

—Patricia P. Marzke

Maple Custard

Ingredients
½ cup maple syrup
3 eggs, beaten
2 cups milk
salt
mace

Directions
Add syrup to eggs and beat well. Beat in milk and salt. Spoon into 4 custard cups and sprinkle with mace. Place cups in pan with 1 inch water. Bake at 350°F for 40 minutes.

Serves 4.

—Mrs. L.M. Cyre

Lemon Custard Pudding

Ingredients

¾ cup sugar
1 Tbsp. butter
2 eggs, separated
2 Tbsp. flour
1 cup milk
juice of 1 lemon

Directions

Cream sugar and butter together. Beat egg yolks and add to sugar-butter mixture. Mix in flour, milk and lemon juice. Beat egg whites until stiff and fold into batter. Pour into small, buttered oven-proof dish. Place dish in pan containing ½ inch water. Bake at 325°F for about 50 minutes.

Serves 2 to 3.

—Ruth Henly

Berries in Lemon Mousse

Ingredients

4 cups blueberries, raspberries or strawberries
1 cup sugar
5 eggs, separated
juice of 2 large lemons
1 cup heavy cream, whipped
2 Tbsp. grated lemon rind

Directions

Wash berries, remove stems and drain well. Pour into glass serving bowl and sprinkle with ¼ cup sugar. In top of double boiler, beat egg yolks with remaining ¾ cup sugar until light yellow in color. Add lemon juice and continue to cook over simmering water, whisking constantly, until mixture is thick enough to heavily coat a spoon. Remove from heat and allow to cool. Beat egg whites until stiff but not dry. Fold gently into cooled lemon mixture. Fold in whipped cream and lemon rind. Be sure everything is well incorporated and the mousse is very smooth. Chill well. Immediately before serving, cover berries with mousse.

Serves 4 to 6.

—Holly Andrews

Blueberry Crisp

Ingredients

4 cups blueberries, fresh or frozen
¾ cup sugar
1 tsp. nutmeg
⅓ cup butter
⅓ cup brown sugar
6 Tbsp. flour
¾ cup oatmeal
1 tsp. cinnamon

Directions

Place berries in greased 9-inch casserole dish. Mix sugar and nutmeg and pour over berries. Cream butter and brown sugar. Add flour, oatmeal and cinnamon. Crumble over berries. Bake at 350°F for 30 minutes. Good warm or cold, topped with ice cream or yogurt.

Serves 4 to 5.

—Valerie L. Arnason

Poppy Seed Fruit Salad Dressing

Ingredients

3 Tbsp. onion juice
1 cup honey
1 Tbsp. dry mustard
2 tsp. salt
⅔ cup cider vinegar
2 cups oil
3 Tbsp. poppy seeds

Directions

Make onion juice by grinding a large onion in a blender or food processor, then scraping pulp into a strainer over a bowl. Press pulp with a spoon to remove juice. Set aside.

Mix honey, mustard, salt and vinegar in blender on slow speed. Add onion juice and continue blending. Add oil to blender a few drops at a time, still on slow speed, then in a thin stream, until dressing is thick. At the very last, add poppy seeds, blending just to incorporate. Store in refrigerator. Serve on fruit such as melons, green grapes, pineapple, pears or as a dressing for fruit salad.

—Kristine Marie Halls Reid

Crème Brûlée

Serve this very rich pudding with fresh fruit for a tasty and colorful dessert.

Ingredients

4 egg yolks
1 Tbsp. castor sugar
2 cups heavy cream
1 vanilla bean, split
handful unblanched almonds
sugar

Directions

Mix egg yolks and castor sugar well. Place cream and vanilla bean in top of double boiler. Cover and bring to scalding point, remove vanilla bean and pour cream onto egg yolks, whisking well. Return to pan and cook until thickened, stirring constantly. Do not allow to boil. Pour into serving bowl and let stand overnight.

Prepare praline: Place almonds in heavy saucepan. Heat until nuts begin spitting. Add sugar to cover nuts and bottom of pan. Cook without stirring over medium heat until sugar has turned dark caramel in color. Pour onto well-oiled plate and cool. When cold, pound in mortar and pestle until praline is in small pieces. Two hours before serving, place pralines on pudding.

Serves 6.

—Crissie Hunt

Best Vanilla Ice Cream

Topped with rhubarb sauce, this ice cream makes a very special early-summer treat. Simply cook sliced rhubarb until tender, then add sugar and cinnamon to taste. The use of buttermilk makes this recipe very unusual — the result is less rich and the taste is lovely.

Ingredients

1½ cups sugar
1 Tbsp. flour
¼ tsp. salt
4–5 eggs, beaten
3 cups milk
2 cups cold buttermilk
3 cups heavy cream
3 tsp. vanilla

Directions

Combine sugar, flour and salt, then add to beaten eggs. Heat milk to scalding and slowly add egg mixture. Cook over low heat, stirring constantly, until thick enough to coat a spoon. Set pot in ice water and stir until cooled to room temperature.

Add buttermilk, cream and vanilla, then churn in ice-cream maker, following instructions on machine.

Makes approximately 1 gallon.

—Susan Hodges & Tim Denny

Lemon Ice Cream

This recipe will last for months in the freezer—but is not likely to if ice-cream lovers know where it is.

Ingredients

2 lemons
3 eggs, separated
¾ cup sugar
1 cup heavy cream

Directions

Squeeze juice from lemons to make 5 Tbsp. Finely grate peel from 1 lemon. Place egg whites in large bowl and beat until stiff peaks form. Gradually add ¼ cup sugar, continuing to beat. Sprinkle with lemon peel. Place yolks in another bowl and whisk with remaining ½ cup sugar and lemon juice. Fold into egg whites until just blended.

In another bowl, whip cream until soft peaks form. Fold into egg mixture, gently but thoroughly. Place in freezer container and freeze for several hours.

Serves 6 to 8.

—Laurabel Miller

Ruth's Pecan Ice Cream

"I developed this recipe when I was a teenager, somehow managing to convince my mother that just one more test was needed to make sure I had it right! One day I ran out of ice for the ice-cream machine in the midst of the procedure, which would have been disastrous except that, just then, it began to hail. I was able to finish cranking using hailstones instead of ice, and the ice cream turned out just fine." Make vanilla sugar by placing a vanilla bean in a jar of white sugar and letting it sit for several weeks.

Ingredients

4 cups milk
2 cups heavy cream
1 small vanilla bean
2 egg yolks
4 eggs
2 cups vanilla sugar
1 Tbsp. cornstarch
½ tsp. salt
¼ cup sugar
¼ lb. pecans

Directions

Scald milk and cream with vanilla bean. Discard bean (or rinse well and keep for re-use).

Blend together yolks, eggs, vanilla sugar, cornstarch and salt. Cook in top of double boiler, stirring constantly. When warm, slowly stir in milk-cream mixture. Continue heating until thick enough to coat the back of a spoon. Chill.

Place sugar and pecans in heavy skillet and cook over low heat until sugar has melted and is light brown. Cool, then crush.

When custard is very cold, freeze in ice-cream machine, following manufacturer's instructions. Mix in pecans when done.

Makes approximately 3 quarts.

—Ruth Ellis Haworth

Index